Preface and Acknowledgements

This directory is an outgrowth of the final conference of the UN Decade for women (1976-1985) that was held in Nairobi, Kenya in July 1985. The *Forward Looking Strategies* document approved by all delegates stressed the importance of quality reproductive health care for women and outlined a series of recommendations for actions to be taken by governments.

As a follow-up to these recommendations, The Population Institute conducted a worldwide survey of women's organizations to learn the extent of their involvement with population issues in general and reproductive health care programs in particular. The information that we received is included in this Directory. We hope that it will be a useful and enjoyable tool in expanding contacts and building solidarity among women's organizations throughout the world.

Although we surveyed over 2,000 organizations in three languages, we recognize that some organizations are missing. We ask that any organizations not included send us information about their activities. If enough organizations write, The Population Institute will gladly issue a supplement at a future date.

We thank all of you who took the time to respond to the survey questionnaire, and we are deeply grateful to the United Nations Fund for Population Activities whose support has made the publication and dissemination of this Directory possible.

Lalita Harvyasi-Curtis, Director of the Population Institute's Community Leaders Network, served as Editor and Coordinator of the Directory. She, along with the Institute's staff members and interns who assisted in the compilation, writing and editing of the information contained herein, have my special thanks and gratitude. The individuals listed on the following page are noted for their fine work.

Werner Fornos
President
The Population Institute
Washington, D.C.

I

Acknowledgements

The Population Institute Staff:
Lalita Harvyasi-Curtis, Editor,
Project Coordinator

Research and Analysis:
Linda Casey
Anne Driscoll
Eileen Hanlon
Linda Malcolm
Elizabeth Nickerson
Gerda Newbold
Phyllis Solomon
Gena Waddle

Network Assistants:
Barbra L. Bragg
Aracely M. Panameno
Colette Taddy

Translators and Proofing:
Marten Bassett
Connie Clark
Jeanne Duvall
Maureen Frances
Sharmila Ghosh
Sally LuKash
Tammy Marable
Kathy Meek
Edith Raphael
Alex Singer
Herb Stone
Nick Taylor
Deborah Wheeler

Editing:
Shirley Smith-Anderson
Hal Burdet
David D. Meyer

Consultants:
Sally Yudelman, Writer
Joni Seeger, Editing

Foreign National Reviewers:
Modupeola Abisoye, Nigeria
Hamelmal Aklilu, Ethiopia
Esperanza Uribe de Alaniz,
Mexico
V.A. Anozie, Nigeria
Naheed Awan, Pakistan
Susan A. Ayina, Nigeria
Anwara Begum, Bangladesh
Joyce T. Daicun, Nigeria
Yasmin Dastur, Pakistan
Agnes Gichuru, Kenya
Jaya Gupta, India
Sofinas Haryono, Indonesia
Amudalat Doyin Ijauja, Nigeria
Jane Amavi Kwawu, Kenya
Cecilia Manyame, Zimbabwe
Grace Mbote, Kenya
Saeeda Najmunnessa, Bangladesh
Fazilatun Nesha, Bangladesh
Edah S. Ngaira, Kenya
Veronica Nwosu, Nigeria
O.M. Obayemi, Nigeria
Penina Apiyo Ochola, Kenya
Constance Onuoha, Nigeria
Olukemi O. Oshin, Nigeria
Kadra Awaleh Osman, East Africa
Nkechi B. Osondu, Nigeria
Aracely M. Panameno, El
Salvador
Azeliya Ranjitrar, Nepal
Dorcas Nomathemba Senda,
Zimbabwe
Jiraporn Thinrungroj, Thailand
Dorcas Olalompe Tonade, Nigeria
Kande K. Tshibanda, East Africa
I.N. Ugwuh, Nigeria
Mina Williams, Gambia

The Nairobi Challenge

Global Directory of Women's Organizations
Implementing Population Strategy

Printed in the United States of America
by Corporate Press, Washington, D.C.

Library of Congress Catalog Card Number: 87-062578
ISBN 0-9619165-3-2 $9.95.

THE POPULATION INSTITUTE
110 MARYLAND AVE., N.E.
WASHINGTON, DC 20002
202/544-3300

THE NAIROBI FORWARD-LOOKING STRATEGIES FOR THE ADVANCEMENT OF WOMEN

To obtain a copy of the *FORWARD LOOKING STRATEGIES* write to:

United Nations   Cost: $30.00
Sales Section
Room DC2-853
New York, New York 10017
U.S.A.

To facilitate delivery request the "Report of the World Conference to Review and Appraise the Achievements of the United Nations Decade for Women," document No. E.85 IV. 10.

For a copy of this directory, THE NAIROBI CHALLENGE, write:

The Population Institute   Cost: $9.95
Women's Project
110 Maryland Avenue, NE
Washington, D.C. 20002

To obtain a copy of *Inventory of Population Projects in Developing Countries Around the World 1985/86* write:

Cecile Cuffley   Cost: $30.00
UNFPA
220 East 42nd
New York, New York 10017

HOW TO USE THIS DIRECTORY

The overlapping nature of "women's" organizations and "population" organizations made it necessary to survey both in the quest to measure the level of worldwide implementation of population strategies. The Women's Organization in Population category includes those women's organizations which are exclusively or in part implementing population strategies.

The Population Organization category is included because their principal purpose automatically creates a vehicle for the implementation of population strategy. This category also includes Health and Development Organizations. The level of awareness of the Forward-Looking Strategies among these organizations is reflected in their responses. Only those organizations that returned the survey were included. Please note that organizations that are part of a multilateral organization (for example, I.P.P.F.) who returned the survey are listed in their region, as well as the appendix. This category is by no means a comprehensive guide to worldwide population programs. Information on how to obtain a worldwide inventory of population projects is contained in the front of this directory.

The Women's Organization Category includes all respondents who, while dedicated to improving the status of women, are not implementing specific population strategies. Many are implementing other Forward-Looking Strategies, or are interested in implementing population strategies in the future.

The Appendix includes multilateral organizations, as well as those organizations who have program offices too numerous to list in the regional format. Although they are all population or development organizations, each has indicated full awareness of the Forward-Looking Strategies.

The Index is intended to provide a convenient reference list of the organizations listed in this directory. It does not include subject matter or pertinent individuals.

Organizations may be found in the alphabetical order of the country in which they are located and within their regional category?

Finally, the poetry and pictures are included for reader enjoyment. The poetry has all been written by women of the regions in which they appear. Likewise, the pictures are all of women of the region in which they appear.

World Bank 9985

TABLE OF CONTENTS

Introduction

Perhaps the most significant outcome of the United Nations Decade for Women (1976-1985) has been the wide range of political and economic actions undertaken by women on their own behalf. Women throughout the world have joined together in formal organizations and grassroots movements. In the process they have gained self-confidence, skills, the ability to carry out economic projects and the capacity to organize and press for change. In spite of the diversity of cultures in which they live and the different contexts in which they operate, women increasingly have come to share a common belief that "equality, peace and development by and for the poor and oppressed are inextricably inter-linked with equality, peace and development by and for poor women."[1]

The Decade is witness to women's efforts to bring the right of all human beings to live in dignity to the forefront of human consciousness, to their struggles for more equal access to resources and to their questioning of policies and practices that often have been detrimental to them. In this on-going struggle women have had to challenge "the full social, economic and psychological weight of gender oppression (and often class, national and ethnic oppression as well)."[2] In spite of women's efforts, however, and the fact that over one third of all families in the Third World are headed by women, increased resource allocation for women has been minimal, and in many countries, the political will to implement legal and other changes beneficial to women has been weak or sorely lacking. The *Forward Looking Strategies* document accepted by all delegates to the Nairobi conference in July 1985 thus stands as a challenge to society in general and to governments in particular to integrate women into the political and economic lives of their countries by the year 2000.

Most participants in both the official conference and the non-governmental forum at Nairobi recognized that women's ability to control their own fertility is a basic need and a basic right, if women are to achieve equal status. As the official conference document pointed out, "the ability of women to control their fertility forms an important basis for the enjoyment of other rights."[3] *Forward Looking Strategies* also urged governments to make information and medically approved and appropriate methods of family planning available, and to approve policies to encourage delay in the commencement of child bearing, raise the age of marriage in countries where it is low and provide sex education to adolescent girls and boys. The document further recommended that incentive programs should neither coerce nor discriminate against non-participants.

Women have been increasingly outspoken about their need for quality reproductive health care that includes not only access to safe contraception, but also infertility counseling, treatment for sexually transmitted diseases and other gynecological problems and infant/child health services. Women in the Third World in particular are well aware that poor women are more likely to marry young, have pregnancies at dangerously close intervals and be overworked and undernourished with few opportunities for education or training that might offer alternatives to childbearing. "These women," a former foundation official has written,

". . . will spend most of their lives from ages 15 to 45 pregnant or lactating, recovering from the effects of birth or clandestinely induced abortions or tolerating contraceptive side effects or the discomforts and consequences of sexually transmitted diseases. Many thousands more will have to cope with the personal and social trauma of infertility."[4]

This preoccupation is timely, both from the point of view of women concerned about the relationship between women's health and women's poverty and from the point of view of those concerned about the increase in global population. Efforts to alleviate the former are closely linked to efforts to alleviate the pressures and problems caused by the latter.

There are now over five billion people on earth; by the year 2000 that number is projected to increase to over six billion.[5] Growth is occurring, however, at very different rates in different parts of the world. Between 1950 and 1985, for example, the industrialized world grew from 0.8 billion to 1.2 billion; during the same period the population of the Third World increased from 1.7 billion to 3.7 billion.[6] Slow growth regions include Western and Eastern Europe, the Soviet Union, North America (Canada and the United States), Australia and New Zealand and East Asia.[7] Rapid growth regions include Southeast Asia, the South Pacific, Latin America and the Caribbean, the Indian sub-continent, the Middle East and Africa. In the case of Africa, birth rates are collectively the world's highest, and unlike rates in other developing areas, show no signs of falling. Current death rates in Africa are also among the world's highest and life expectancy at birth is low.

Thus as the end of the century approaches, the world is rapidly

". . . dividing into countries where population growth is slow or non-existent and where living conditions are improving and those where population growth is rapid and living conditions are deteriorating or in danger of doing so."[8]

In many countries experiencing rapid population growth the "carrying capacity" of the ecological system is already severely strained. When the demands of people exceed the sustainable yields of forests, pastures and croplands, the resource base is seriously threatened. Food production declines and rural to urban migration increases, threatening to overwhelm the ability of cities to provide services and generate employment, in turn causing incomes to fall. This cycle has already begun in countries suffering from a combination of severe ecological damage and an economic slowdown brought about by rising external debt. Highly skewed income distribution and increasing numbers of unemployed youth further complicate the problem, raising the potential for political conflict and violence. An additional 800 million new jobs will have to be created by the turn of the century just to keep unemployment levels where they are now.

X

Factors that lead to a decline in fertility include: the delivery of family planning services and the availability of safe contraceptives; decreases in children's contribution to the family labor force and income; less need for children as insurance against old age and accidents; increase in the marriage age of women; raising rural incomes and women's participation in wage employment.[10] There must also be changes in attitudes within cultures where the parents' manhood and womanhood are linked to their having a large number of children. Finally, while economic development *and* family planning programs may be able to promote fertility decline independently of one another, the impact is greater and more rapid when the two occur together.

Non-governmental organizations, including women's organizations, private physicians and commercial suppliers, provide about one quarter of family planning services worldwide.[11] In several countries and regions they have been instrumental in launching the first family planning programs. Women's organizations play a particularly important role because they offer women at all levels of a society the opportunity to organize around issues that are of primary importance to them—such as quality reproductive health care. In addition, these organizations raise women's awareness of both practical and strategic gender issues, train them as managers and future leaders, and provide access to resources.

There are many different kinds of women's organizations, each with its own special history. Traditional service organizations such as national women's organizations have existed for years in most countries. These organizations have provided important education, health/nutrition and maternal/child care services to women. Such organizations usually have access to resources and policymakers, are well organized, and have large and often diverse memberships and systematic methods for transferring skills and building leadership. Researchers rightly point out that:

> "These institutions can function as effective pressure groups, lobbying for the rights and needs of poor women; they can act as linkage between poor women and policymakers at the national level."[12]

Other types of women's organizations include arms of political parties or governments; worker- or peasant-based movements or federations; the poverty- and equity-oriented organizations that flowered during the Decade as a result of support from international donor agencies; local grassroots and feminist groups (many of which have organized around health issues), and research organizations involved in action—or policy—research and women studies associations. Finally, there are informal women's movements that have mobilized around issues of peace, nuclear energy, violence against women, sex tourism, sexual exploitation and racism.

Whatever their initial *raison d'etre*, most women's organizations have dealt with the issues and problems surrounding the provision of quality reproductive health care to women. Traditional women's organizations have provided direct services. Women's arms of political parties and governments have pressured and lobbied for access to resources such as better health care and changes in laws. Workers' movements have confronted the exploitation of women in the workplace and their need for health services and daycare facilities in plants and factories. Peasant women's federations have trained their members as community health workers and demonstrated on behalf of agrarian reforms that would provide women with access to land on which to grow food for their families. Many poverty- and equity-oriented organizations have health and family planning components within their programs or refer women to appropriate services.

As women's organizations, governments and international agencies move to implement the recommendations of *Forward Looking Strategies*, women's organizations in particular need to strengthen existing networks, expand their constituencies and forge alliances with one another. Because women share a commonality of interests across class lines, they can form coalitions to take collective action. Alliances with male-run organizations and with committed men sympathetic to women's issues will also be important. Women alone cannot achieve the objectives set forth in *Forward Looking Strategies*. Thus, the challenge of achieving "equality, development and peace" calls upon women's organizations to enhance their lobbying and communications skills in order to influence and pressure policymakers in governments and in international donor agencies who control resources. Strategies, however, will vary from country to country depending on government policies toward women, the political climate and the economic situation.

In undertaking these efforts, access to information will play an important role. Women need to know what organizations and activists are doing, not only in their own countries, but in other countries as well. They need to share strategies, information and experiences across national borders. The purpose of this Directory is to assist in that effort by providing information about organizations and networks that will strengthen the already existing "undercurrent of confidence and cooperation among women that is new to the world and has great promise."[13]

UN Photo A. Fisher/JMcG

UN Photo Doranne Jacobson

NOTES

1. Sen, Gita With Grown, Caren. *Development, Crises and Alternative Visions: Third World Women's Perspectives*. Development Alternatives with Women for a New Era (DAWN). Media-Rejaksjonen, Norway. 1985. p.14.
2. Sen, Gita with Grown, Caren. Ibid., p. 15.
3. *Forward-Looking Strategies*, paragraph 156.
4. Germain, Adrienne. "Toward a Programmatic Definition of Reproductive Health Care for Poor Women in the Third World." International Women's Health Coalition, New York City, New York. 1986. p. 1.
5. Population Reference Bureau. *World Population: Toward the Next Century*. Washington, D.C. 1985. p. 2.
6. World Resources Institute and International Institute for Environment and Development. *World Resources 1986: An Assessment of the Resource Base that Supports the Global Economy*. Basic Books, Inc., New York City, New York. 1986. p.10.
7. Principally China and Japan although as the Population Reference Bureau recently reported: "If Beijing continues to ease up on its population policy, it will shatter current assumptions about a continuing slowdown in the global population growth rate . . . China's sheer size dominates the entire demographic picture." *Washington Post*, Washington, D.C. 4/14/87.
8. Brown, Lester. *State of the World 1987: a World Watch Report on Progress Toward a Sustainable Society*. W.W. Norton & Co., New York City, New York. 1987. p. 21.
9. World Resources Institute and International Institute for Environment and Development. Ibid., p. 15.
10. World Resources Institute and International Institute for Environment and Development. Ibid., p. 16.
11. World Resources Institute and International Institute for Environment and Development. Ibid., p. 23.
12. Buvinic, Mayra. *Projects for Women in the Third World: Explaining Their Misbehavior*. International Center for Research on Women, Washington, D.C. 1984. p. 17.
13. Sivard, Ruth. *Women: a World Survey*. World Priorities, Washington, D.C. 1985. p. 5.

UN Photo 154321: Gayle Jann

Round Table Discussion Highlights UN Observance of International Women's Day

UN Photo 161,354/milton grant

NOTES

POPULATION RELATED FORWARD-LOOKING STRATEGIES
TAKEN FROM
THE NAIROBI FORWARD-LOOKING STRATEGIES FOR THE ADVANCEMENT OF WOMEN

(As adopted by the World Conference to review and appraise the Achievements of the United Nations Decade for Women: equality, development and peace, Nairobi, Kenya, 15–26 July 1985).

The following are the relevant paragraphs under the section entitled Current Trends and Perspectives to the Year 2000 in the Forward-Looking Strategies:

PARAGRAPH 28: During the period from 1986 to the year 2000, changes in the natural environment will be critical for women. One area of change is that of the role of women as intermediaries between the natural environment and society with respect to agro-ecosystems, as well as the provisions of safe water and fuel supplies and the closely associated questions of sanitation. The problem will continue to be greatest where water resources are limited—in arid and semi-arid areas and in areas experiencing demographic pressure. In a general manner an improvement in the situation of women could bring about a reduction in mortality and morbidity as well as better regulation of fertility and hence of population growth, which would be beneficial for the environment and ultimately, for women, children and men.

PARAGRAPH 29: The issues of fertility rates and population growth should be treated in a context that permits women to exercise effectively their rights in matters pertaining to population concerns, including the basic right to control their own fertility which forms an important basis for the enjoyment of other rights, as stated in the report of the International Population Conference held at Mexico City in 1984.

Part IV—Areas of Special Concern, Paragraph 287 raises the concern that the increase in the number of young women looking for employment will lead to exploitation in the workplace. This coupled with low nutritional levels and unwanted pregnancies, will seriously threaten the health of young women.

PARAGRAPH 156: The ability of women to control their fertility forms an important basis for the enjoyment of other rights. As recognized in the World Population Plan of Action and reaffirmed at the International Conference on Population, 1984, all couples and individuals have the basic human right to decide freely and responsibly the number and spacing of their children; maternal and child health and family planning components of primary health care should be strengthened; and family planning information should be produced and services created.

PARAGRAPH 157: Governments should make available, as a matter of urgency, information, education and the means to assist women to make decisions about their desired number of children. To ensure a voluntary and free choice, family planning information, education and means should include all medically approved and appropriate methods of family planning. Education for responsible parenthood and family life education should be widely available and should be directed towards both men and women.

PARAGRAPH 158: Recognizing that pregnancy occurring in adolescent girls, whether married or unmarried, has adverse effects on morbidity and mortality of both mother and child, governments are urged to develop policies to encourage delay in the commencement of childbearing. Governments should make efforts to raise the age of entry into marriage in countries in which this age is still quite low. Attention should be given to ensuring that adolescents, both girls and boys, receive adequate information and education.

PARAGRAPH 159: All government should ensure that fertility control methods conform to adequate standards of quality, efficiency and safety. This should also apply to organizations responsible for distributing and administering these methods. Programs of incentives and disincentives should be neither coercive nor discriminatory and should be consistent with internationally recognized human rights, as well as with changing individual and cultural values.

Asia &
the Pacific

Asia and the Pacific

In 1986 the total population of Asia and the Pacific was 2.7 billion; this figure represents 56 percent of the world's population and includes six of the world's ten most populous countries. China and India make up two thirds of Asia's people, and Indonesia, Japan, Pakistan and Bangladesh all have populations exceeding 100 million. And the population is young; 40 percent is under 15 years of age.

Agricultural production has increased and imports count for less than ten percent of regional food consumption. Primary school education is available to most children, and health care, sanitation and nutrition have improved. Life expectancy in Japan, Australia and New Zealand is the same as in North America (75 years), and in Southeast Asia, life expectancy has risen to 66 years.

There are, however, enormous differences between countries. In South Asia—India, Pakistan and Bangladesh—fertility remains high and the combined population of the three countries will increase by an estimated 440 million between 1985-2000. Growth rates in the countries of the South Pacific are also high, 3.7 percent in the Solomon Islands, for example. Among the countries of East and Southeast Asia, on the other hand, South Korea, China, Singapore, Thailand, Malayasia and Indonesia, birthrates have declined since the 1960's. Australia, New Zealand and Japan are similar to North America and Western Europe in that growth rates are low and populations are aging.

Migration between countries in Asia is severely restricted, but there has been significant emigration from the South Pacific (Tonga and the Cook Islands) to New Zealand and the United States. Large numbers of temporary migrants have gone from Thailand, the Philippines, South Korea, India and Pakistan to the Middle East, and others have moved permanently from South Korea, the countries of Indochina and the Philippines to the United States. Political conditions have resulted in large numbers of refugees, particularly from Vietnam, Cambodia, Laos and Afghanistan who have placed strains on receiving countries such as Thailand and Pakistan.

Despite the considerable economic growth that has taken place, most of the countries of Asia and the Pacific remain poor. Seventy-five percent of the population lives in low-income countries, primarily in China, India, Bangladesh, Nepal and Pakistan. These countries are characterized by large rural population and vast numbers of unskilled and illiterate workers. Life expectancy is 52 years and infant mortality rates are high. The labor force is projected to grow from 298 million in 1980 to 464 million by the year 2000. As in Africa, it is agriculture that will have to absorb much of this surplus labor.

At the same time, deforestation is a problem in many countries, especially in India and Nepal because of the demand for firewood. Timber, especially exotic hardwood is also a valuable export. The disappearance of forests is leading to loss of plant and animal life, erosion and a decline in agricultural production. Some countries—Japan, North and South Korea, China, Australia and New Zealand—have reforestation programs.

The level of urbanization varies as well, from 80 percent of Japan's population living in cities to only 24 percent of India's and six percent of Nepal's. By the year 2000, Asia will have 11 megacities with populations of more than 10 million. As in other parts of the Third World, urban growth has caused environmental problems and strained the ability of governments to provide water and sewage facilities, housing and to generate employment. South Korea, the Philippines and Thailand, in particular, have experienced primary growth in their capital cities.

Family planning is widely accepted throughout the region and seen as playing a critical role in economic and social progress. India and China, the world's most populous countries, have put considerable money and efforts into family planning programs. India's family planning program was launched in 1952, the first in the Third World, but has had its ups and downs. The emergency sterilization drive of the 1970s produced a considerable backlash. The current focus is to link family planning and development activities, train 200,000 "village guides" to provide information and emphasize family spacing, delayed marriage and conventional contraceptives. In spite of renewed efforts, fertility is still over five births per woman and the population is projected to double by the year 2025.

China's early family planning program stressed late marriage, long birth intervals and two children. In 1979, the drive for one-child-per-couple was launched. Incentives such as free medical care, school tuitions, direct monthly cash payments, housing, and pensions or a guaranteed standard of living for parents in old age are offered. But China's population prospects are largely determined by the fertility behavior of the 80 percent of the Chinese who live in rural areas where there is a strong male preference, a need for children to support their parents in old age, and where the one-child policy is most likely to be ignored. The current goal of 1.2 billion by the year 2000 is likely to be exceeded by 150 million.

A third country that has a strong family planning program is Indonesia, whose government initiated its efforts in Java and Bali in 1969 and in ten outer islands in 1974. Although fertility has declined, the current population growth rate of two percent per year poses challenges to achieving the national goal of a 50 percent reducton in fertility by the year 2000.

The status of women is closely linked to high fertility rates. Despite gains in education, health services and access to family planning, women in the poorer countries are still likely to be illiterate, malnourished, receive fewer health services and marry early. In countries such as Australia and New Zealand, the status of women is similar to that of North America; women have access to resources and participate in the wage labor force but still carry the primary responsibility for household chores and child-care. Although opportunities have increased for women in Japan, Taiwan and South Korea, these countries are still patriarchal societies and social and economic equality lies in the future.

Women's organizations of many kinds have flourished in Asia, in part as a result of the UN Decade for Women. Women in India, Bangladesh, Sri Lanka, the Philippines, Thailand and Indonesia have established research institutions to provide credit and technical assistance to women's economic projects and to press for changes in legal systems. Women in Australia and New Zealand have played key roles in organizing the anti-nuclear movement in the Pacific. The growing number of competent and effective women's organizations is bound to have an increasing impact on women's status in Asia and the Pacific as the century draws to a close.

4

What a Little Girl had on her Mind

What a little girl had on her mind was:
Why do the shoulders of other men's wives
give off so strong a smell like magnolia;
or like gardenias?
What is it,
that faint veil of mist,
over the shoulders of other men's wives?
She wanted to have one,
that wonderful thing
even the prettiest virgin cannot have.

The little girl grew up.
She became a wife and then a mother.
One day she suddenly realized;
the tenderness
that gathers over the shoulders of wives,
is only fatigue
from loving others day after day.

Ibaragi Noriko

United Nations Photo: R. Witlin

Gay colors flow
down streets that swirl
with dressed up girls
as winter comes on.

I listen to the pulse of a life
different from mine
in my womb,
and with it I can hear my own lonely heart.

DAILY WAGES

In a corner of blue sky
The mill of night whistles,
A white thick smoke
Pours from the moon-chimney.

In dream's many furnaces
Labourer love
Is stoking all the fires

I earn our meeting
Holding you for a while,
My day's wages.

Goto Miyoko

Amrita Pritam

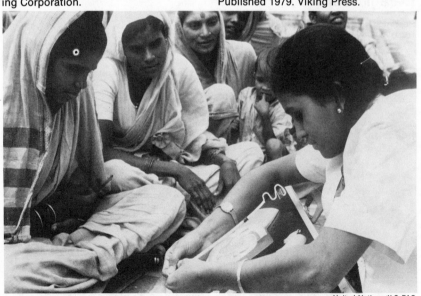

United Nations/ILO PAS

Te Kaha

oh well tonight or some other night
you or someone else will put
the usual proposition and I
will warm and waver and decline

there are nappies snapping
at the soggy breeze
white is the baby's
Invercargill flesh
he bites Makwini's brown breast

the conger eel has been undressed
and the shark is a white knife
wanting a woman this time

you will or will not know my want
blunt as a boulder
sleek as a butterfish

but I am a boat afloat
and I see many a fin

I could rock you in the sun
I could be babied and reborn
but I age, I rage
at other men
laughing and lying at their wives
and trying the tips of their knives

Rachel McAlpine

Reprinted from *Fifteen Contemporary New Zealand Poets*. Reprinted with the kind permission of Pilgrim South Press.

Woman to Child

You who are darkness warmed my
    flesh
where out of darkness rose the seed.
Then all a world I made in me;
all the world you hear and see
hung upon my dreaming blood.

There moved the multitudinous
    stars,
and coloured birds and fishes
    moved.
There swam the sliding continents.
All time lay rolled in me, and
    sense,
and love that knew not its beloved.

O node and focus of the world;
I hold you deep within that well
you shall escape and not escape-
that mirrors still your sleeping
    shape;
that nurtures still your crescent cell.

Judith Wright

Reprinted from Judith Wright, *Selected Poems, Five Senses* with kind permission of Angus & Robertson Publishers.

My Mother

Rebellion was in her character.
Sullenly beautiful. of ariki
Descent, childbearing utterly wrecked her,
So that she died young in Tahiti
Where she was buried. (There's a snapshot
Of her flower-strewn grave, with my sister
Morose with grief beside it.) I forgot
To cry being puzzled, but later missed her.

Sleepless tonight in hospital I search
My memory, but I can find no trace
Of that rebellion, yet like a damp torch
It smouldered in her, lighting up her face
With unearthly beauty. What was its name
If not tuberculosis of the womb?

Alistair Campbell

Reprinted with permission of The Pegasus Press.

UN Photo 152005/John Isaac

Women's Organizations in Population

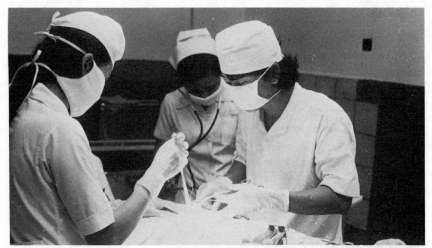

The Population Institute

UN Photo R. Witlin

9

Council for the Single Mother and Her Child

AUSTRALIA

ADDRESS:

GPO Box 1399M, Melbourne 3001, Victoria, Australia

EXECUTIVE OFFICER:	BRANCH OFFICES:

TELEPHONE NUMBER:	TELEX NUMBER:
03/634 755	

APPROX. STAFF SIZE:	VOLUNTEER STAFF:	YEAR ESTABLISHED:
3-4		1969

NUMBER OF INDIVIDUAL MEMBERS:

900

FUNDING: Federal and state governments.

PRINCIPAL PURPOSE: To work to protect the rights of single parent families to have adequate income support, both within and outside the workforce. To further the right of single women to have and raise children with dignity, pride and self-esteem.

MAIN ACTIVITIES: Provision of information and referral service, legal counseling, community education and information and help with the Department of Social Security and Ministry of Health.

POPULATION CONCERNS: None indicated.

SPECIFIC POPULATION ACTIVITIES: Counseling.

FORWARD-LOOKING STRATEGIES IMPLEMENTATIONS: Pregnancy counseling, providing information, advertising and promoting the rights of women.

OBSTACLES TO THE IMPLEMENTATION OF THE FORWARD-LOOKING STRATEGIES: None indicated.

NOTES:

Endeavour Forum, Incorporating
Women Who Want To Be Women AUSTRALIA

ADDRESS:

18 Cavell Crt., Beaumaris, Vic.3193, Australia

EXECUTIVE OFFICER:			BRANCH OFFICES:
Mrs. Babette Francis			

TELEPHONE NUMBER:	TELEX NUMBER:
(03) 20 5218	

APPROX. STAFF SIZE:	VOLUNTEER STAFF:	YEAR ESTABLISHED:
		1979

NUMBER OF INDIVIDUAL MEMBERS:

2,000

FUNDING: Membership subscriptions and fundraising activities.

PRINCIPAL PURPOSE:

MAIN ACTIVITIES: Publishing a newsletter, organizing seminars, disseminating information, lobbying and providing pregnancy support.

POPULATION CONCERNS: Concerned about the possibility that contraceptive programs in developing countries may involve coercion and exploit women.

SPECIFIC POPULATION ACTIVITIES: Education, contraceptive research, counselling, advocacy, pregnancy support, delivery of services and natural family planning.

FORWARD-LOOKING STRATEGIES IMPLEMENTATIONS: Involved in promoting pro-family and pro-life Strategies.

OBSTACLES TO THE IMPLEMENTATION OF FORWARD-LOOKING STRATEGIES: The dissemination of misleading information. The lack of emphasis on the value of freedom and the free enterprise system. A devotion to socialism which has caused famine in Africa and shortages in Europe.

NOTES:

New South Wales
Women Justices's Association

AUSTRALIA

ADDRESS:

7 The Crescent, The Entrance 2261, NSW Australia

EXECUTIVE OFFICER:			BRANCH OFFICES:
Elizabeth Hunt, NSW State President			

TELEPHONE NUMBER:	TELEX NUMBER:
043 321113	

APPROX. STAFF SIZE:	VOLUNTEER STAFF:	YEAR ESTABLISHED:
5	5	1923

NUMBER OF INDIVIDUAL MEMBERS:

200 + 4 affiliated chapters

FUNDING: Subscriptions.

PRINCIPAL PURPOSE: To become involved in the problems of women and children and to improve their legal status.

MAIN ACTIVITIES: Investigation and lobbying.

POPULATION CONCERNS: Concerned with population issues that are related to the rights of women and children.

SPECIFIC POPULATION ACTIVITIES: Advocacy, pill, IUD, diaphragm, foam, Norplant, Depo-Provera, natural family planning.

FORWARD-LOOKING STRATEGIES IMPLEMENTATIONS: None.

OBSTACLES TO THE IMPLEMENTATION OF FORWARD-LOOKING STRATEGIES: Although family planning is legal in NSW Australia, ignorance still seems to be a problem..

NOTES:

Soroptimist International
of Canberra

AUSTRALIA

ADDRESS:

P.O. Box 30 Campbell, ACT 2601, Australia

EXECUTIVE OFFICER:			BRANCH OFFICES:
Elizabeth Brown, President			

TELEPHONE NUMBER:	TELEX NUMBER:	

APPROX. STAFF SIZE:	VOLUNTEER STAFF:	YEAR ESTABLISHED:
		1955

NUMBER OF INDIVIDUAL MEMBERS:

35

FUNDING: Voluntary contributions

PRINCIPAL PURPOSE: To carry out the objectives of Soroptimist International

MAIN ACTIVITIES: Lobbying the government for community causes; fundraising for local, national and international causes; assisting with projects aimed at raising the status of women; maintaining links with other Soroptimist clubs, and broadening the knowledge of members.

POPULATION CONCERNS: Family planning as a human right.

SPECIFIC POPULATION ACTIVITIES: Education and advocacy.

FORWARD-LOOKING STRATEGIES IMPLEMENTATIONS: Contributing to training, education and economic improvement of women in developing countries.

OBSTACLES TO THE IMPLEMENTATION OF FORWARD-LOOKING STRATEGIES: None directly.

NOTES:

United Nations Association of Australia
Status of Women Committee **AUSTRALIA**

ADDRESS:

155 Pirie Street, Adelaide, South Australia 5092

EXECUTIVE OFFICER:

Beverly Hall, President

BRANCH OFFICES:

TELEPHONE NUMBER:

223-1960

TELEX NUMBER:

APPROX. STAFF SIZE:	VOLUNTEER STAFF:	YEAR ESTABLISHED:
Unspecified No.	Unspecified No.	1975

NUMBER OF INDIVIDUAL MEMBERS:

35 Chapters

FUNDING: Membership fees and state government grants.

PRINCIPAL PURPOSE: To serve as a link between all women's organizations in the state and with similar organizations in Australia and internationally. Originally established for the Decade for Women but will exist through the year 2000.

MAIN ACTIVITIES: Highlighting the needs of women in Australia and in developing countries. Organizing seminars, conferences, exhibitions and lectures.

POPULATION CONCERNS: Concerned about family planning in Australia and developing countries, the issue of abortion and the balance between resources and population.

SPECIFIC POPULATION ACTIVITIES: Education and advocacy.

FORWARD-LOOKING STRATEGIES IMPLEMENTATIONS: Implementing the Strategies in a general way through main activities.

OBSTACLES TO THE IMPLEMENTATION OF FORWARD-LOOKING STRATEGIES: None

NOTES:

Women's Agricultural Bureau of South Australia

AUSTRALIA

ADDRESS:

Box 1671 G.P.O., Adelaide 5001, South Australia

EXECUTIVE OFFICER:

Mrs. Diana Penniment

BRANCH OFFICES:

TELEPHONE NUMBER:

082271090

TELEX NUMBER:

APPROX. STAFF SIZE:	VOLUNTEER STAFF:	YEAR ESTABLISHED:
3	10	1917

NUMBER OF INDIVIDUAL MEMBERS:

1600

FUNDING: Subscription fees.

PRINCIPAL PURPOSE: To provide services for women interested in rural and agricultural matters.

MAIN ACTIVITIES: Monthly meetings, workshops, regional and state conferences.

POPULATION CONCERNS: Promotion of education at the state level.

SPECIFIC POPULATION ACTIVITIES: Education, contraceptive research, counselling, and natural family planning services.

FORWARD-LOOKING STRATEGIES IMPLEMENTATIONS:

OBSTACLES TO THE IMPLEMENTATION OF FORWARD-LOOKING STRATEGIES: Funding.

NOTES:

Women's Electoral Lobby-Australia

AUSTRALIA

ADDRESS:

3 Lobelia Street, O'Connor, ACT 2601 Australia

EXECUTIVE OFFICER:

Lynn Lee, National Coordinator

BRANCH OFFICES:

TELEPHONE NUMBER:

062-476679

TELEX NUMBER:

APPROX. STAFF SIZE:	VOLUNTEER STAFF:	YEAR ESTABLISHED:
2		1972

NUMBER OF INDIVIDUAL MEMBERS:

5000 in 7 Chapters

FUNDING: Government subsidy and funds from affiliates

PRINCIPAL PURPOSE: To lobby the government on issues of concern to women; to bring about changes in the bureaucracy that have positive results for women in legislation, procedures, and attitudes.

MAIN ACTIVITIES: Lobby of the government, business sector, educational organizations, and the media. Articulation of women's concerns and action on local and national levels. Production of newsletter.

POPULATION CONCERNS: Extension of family planning services so that they are available to all women throughout the country; abortion and reproductive rights; and the effects of new technology on women.

SPECIFIC POPULATION ACTIVITIES: Education and advocacy.

FORWARD-LOOKING STRATEGIES IMPLEMENTATIONS: Voice the concerns of women and protect rights for women to control their own bodies.

OBSTACLES TO THE IMPLEMENTATION OF FORWARD-LOOKING STRATEGIES:

NOTES:

Women's Health Care House

AUSTRALIA

ADDRESS:

92 Thomas Street, West Perth, West Australia 6005

EXECUTIVE OFFICER:

Elizabeth Stroud, Administrator

BRANCH OFFICES:

TELEPHONE NUMBER:

09-321-2383

TELEX NUMBER:

APPROX. STAFF SIZE:

10*

VOLUNTEER STAFF:

YEAR ESTABLISHED:

1976

NUMBER OF INDIVIDUAL MEMBERS:

15

FUNDING: Health Department of West Australia.

PRINCIPAL PURPOSE: To assist women to make informed decisions, to promote women's overall self-esteem, independence, responsibility for her own body and to respond to other needs expressed by women.

MAIN ACTIVITIES: Medical services, including preventive health care, cancer screening and gynecological services. Health information, education and referral services.

POPULATION CONCERNS: Fertility control through provision of information on all forms of birth control.

SPECIFIC POPULATION ACTIVITIES: Education, advocacy, contraceptive research and delivery of services including sterilization, the Pill, IUD, diaphragm, foam and natural family planning.

FORWARD-LOOKING STRATEGIES IMPLEMENTATIONS: Provision of non-judgmental information on all aspects of women's health.

OBSTACLES TO IMPLEMENTATION OF FORWARD-LOOKING STRATEGIES: Lack of funds.

NOTES: *Six are women doctors

Women's Service Guilds
of West Australia

AUSTRALIA

ADDRESS:

53 Hamersley Street, North Beach 6020, West Australia

EXECUTIVE OFFICER:	**BRANCH OFFICES:**
Miss D.M. Boyle, State President	

TELEPHONE NUMBER:	**TELEX NUMBER:**	
447-8651		

APPROX. STAFF SIZE:	**VOLUNTEER STAFF:**	**YEAR ESTABLISHED:**
3		1905

NUMBER OF INDIVIDUAL MEMBERS:

100 in 3 chapters

FUNDING: Funded by members.

PRINCIPAL PURPOSE: To support the standpoint of women in movements of protest, defense and uplift of humanity. Equal citizenship rights for women and men. To educate women on moral, social and economic questions. To form a link with women throughout the world.

MAIN ACTIVITIES: Pressure on state and Federal governments for community betterment through legislation. Environmental protection, and all issues concerning women and children.

POPULATION CONCERNS: W.S. Guilds have worked to make family planning, abortion, health education and clinics freely available to women.

SPECIFIC POPULATION ACTIVITIES: Education and advocacy.

FORWARD-LOOKING STRATEGIES IMPLEMENTATIONS: Are aware of the strategies but did not indicate that they were implementing them.

OBSTACLES TO THE IMPLEMENTATION OF THE FORWARD-LOOKING STRATEGIES: Males predominate in the corridors of power.

NOTES:

*Business Address: Suite 2-2nd Floor, Wesley Centre, Corner Hay and Williams Streets, Perth 6000, West Australia, tele: 321-3096

ORGANIZATION:	
Bangladesh Mahila Samity	**BANGLADESH**

ADDRESS:
New Baily Road, Dhaka, Bangladesh

EXECUTIVE OFFICER: Dr. Neelima Ibrahim	**BRANCH OFFICES:**

TELEPHONE NUMBER: 401741	**TELEX NUMBER:**	

APPROX. STAFF SIZE: 24	**VOLUNTEER STAFF:** 30	**YEAR ESTABLISHED:** 1948

NUMBER OF INDIVIDUAL MEMBERS:
1000

FUNDING: Organizational sources of income, government and donations from different local and foreign donor agencies.

PRINCIPAL PURPOSE: Welfare and development of women and children.

MAIN ACTIVITIES: Running income generating institutions, eg. secretarial and typing school, sewing, knitting and embroidery training classes; Institute for dropouts, running shops, etc.

POPULATION CONCERNS: Women's and children's welfare and mother and child care centers to limit fertility.

SPECIFIC POPULATION ACTIVITIES: Education, counselling, advocacy, legal counselling, sterilization, pill, foam, Norplant, Depo-provera, and natural family planning.

FORWARD-LOOKING STRATEGIES IMPLEMENTATIONS: Presentation to the government, the demands of women for implementation of the World Plan of Action.

OBSTACLES TO THE IMPLEMENTATION OF FORWARD-LOOKING STRATEGIES: Social, religious, and financial obstacles.

NOTES:

Concerned Women of Bangladesh

BANGLADESH

ADDRESS:

108 Kakrail, Dhaka 2 Bangladesh

EXECUTIVE OFFICER:			BRANCH OFFICES:
TELEPHONE NUMBER: 401064	**TELEX NUMBER:** 642762		
APPROX. STAFF SIZE: 100	**VOLUNTEER STAFF:**	**YEAR ESTABLISHED:** 1976	
NUMBER OF INDIVIDUAL MEMBERS: 50			

FUNDING: Asia Foundation, Ford Foundation and others.

PRINCIPAL PURPOSE: Household deliverys of Family Planning Services to under served Bengali women.

MAIN ACTIVITIES: Door to door services

POPULATION CONCERNS: Women's access to quality Family Planning Services

SPECIFIC POPULATION ACTIVITIES: Delivery of Family Planning services through referral education.

FORWARD-LOOKING STRATEGIES IMPLEMENTATIONS: Yes, through every day activities.

OBSTACLES TO THE IMPLEMENTATION OF THE FORWARD-LOOKING STRATEGIES: None

NOTES:

All India Women's Conference

INDIA

ADDRESS:

6 Bhagwandas Road, New Delhi-1, India

EXECUTIVE OFFICER:

Mrs. Asoka Gupta

BRANCH OFFICES:

TELEPHONE NUMBER:

381439

TELEX NUMBER:

APPROX. STAFF SIZE:

15

VOLUNTEER STAFF:

YEAR ESTABLISHED:

1926

NUMBER OF INDIVIDUAL MEMBERS:

FUNDING: AIWC resources and government grants for special programs.

PRINCIPAL PURPOSE: Social justice to all.

MAIN ACTIVITIES: Social legislation, education of women, health, family planning, and legal advice to women.

POPULATION CONCERNS: Education.

SPECIFIC POPULATION ACTIVITIES: Education, counselling, advocacy, and sterilization.

FORWARD-LOOKING STRATEGIES IMPLEMENTATIONS: Aware of strategies.

OBSTACLES TO THE IMPLEMENTATION OF FORWARD-LOOKING STRATEGIES: Non-availability of executive positions.

NOTES:

Centre for Women's Development Studies

INDIA

ADDRESS:

B-43, Panchsheel Enclave, New Delhi India-110017

EXECUTIVE OFFICER:	BRANCH OFFICES:
Dr. Vina Mazumdar, Director	

TELEPHONE NUMBER:	TELEX NUMBER:
6438428	31 - 62395 NKSG IN

APPROX. STAFF SIZE:	VOLUNTEER STAFF:	YEAR ESTABLISHED:
45		1980

NUMBER OF INDIVIDUAL MEMBERS:

48 and 2 affiliated chapters

FUNDING: Donations, grants and funding for projects by affiliated organizations.

PRINCIPAL PURPOSE: To strive for the realization of women's equality and development in all spheres of life. To promote, develop and disseminate information on the evolution of women's roles in society and trends in social, economic and political organizations which hinder their development and status.

MAIN ACTIVITIES: Research in such topics as: women and rural transformation; families; sex-role distribution; socialization practices; cultural values; traditional laws; the dynamics of change; the role of women in popular social movements; the inner world of women's consciousness; women, law and crime; women in the political process; women's access to land and other productive resources, etc.

POPULATION CONCERNS: New developments in the field of biotechnology and misuse of scientific knowledge and technology.

SPECIFIC POPULATION ACTIVITIES: Education and demographic research.

FORWARD-LOOKING STRATEGIES IMPLEMENTATIONS: The Centre is focusing research in areas related to: the equality of women and men; the role of women in political, social and cultural development; employment opportunities for women, etc.

OBSTACLES TO THE IMPLEMENTATION OF FORWARD-LOOKING STRATEGIES: Lack of statistical data. Traditional views of women and the home, especially in rural areas. Devaluation of domestic work. The inferior status of women. Political opposition to efforts to stop discrimination against women. Traditional opposition to changes in social attitudes.

NOTES:

Joint-Women's Programme (JWP)   INDIA

ADDRESS:

JWP, 14-Jangpura-B, Mathura Road, New Delhi, India 110014

EXECUTIVE OFFICER:			BRANCH OFFICES:
Ms. Jyotsna Chatterji			

TELEPHONE NUMBER:		TELEX NUMBER:	
619821		IRIS-IN61416	

APPROX. STAFF SIZE:	VOLUNTEER STAFF:	YEAR ESTABLISHED:	
35		1977	

NUMBER OF INDIVIDUAL MEMBERS:	
44	

FUNDING: William Carey Study and Research Centre. Central Social Welfare State Councils for Child Welfare and other organizations.

PRINCIPAL PURPOSE: The aim is to bring consciousness of legal and socio-economic rights of women, so that women will strive for equality in society.

MAIN ACTIVITIES: Support of and cooperation with women's groups, training courses, for community workers, leadership programmes, tailoring centers, meetings, conferences, and workshops to promote dialogue and action on pertinent issues concerning the status of women.

POPULATION CONCERNS: Family planning, nutrition, child care, and adult education on health issues.

SPECIFIC POPULATION ACTIVITIES: Education, demographic research, counselling, advocacy, referral of family planning cases to primary health care centers.

FORWARD-LOOKING STRATEGIES IMPLEMENTATIONS: Implementing strategies related to equality and development in areas of health, education, water, communication, housing, community development, environment, justice, peace and social services.

OBSTACLES TO THE IMPLEMENTATION OF FORWARD-LOOKING STRATEGIES:

NOTES:

Programme for Women's Development
Indian Social Institute

INDIA

ADDRESS:

10 Lodi Road Institutional Area, New Dehli-110003, India

EXECUTIVE OFFICER:

Dr. W. Fernandes, Director

BRANCH OFFICES:

TELEPHONE NUMBER:

622372

TELEX NUMBER:

APPROX. STAFF SIZE:	VOLUNTEER STAFF:	YEAR ESTABLISHED:
50	0	1951

NUMBER OF INDIVIDUAL MEMBERS:

n/a

FUNDING: 50% from self-generated funding and 50% from external sources.

PRINCIPAL PURPOSE: To help empower marginalized groups in rural areas through a process of awareness building and organization.

MAIN ACTIVITIES: Action research, training of grassroots workers, promotion of campaigning and consultation on issues relevant to marginalized groups.

POPULATION CONCERNS: Education concerning community health programs, focus on women's role in society.

SPECIFIC POPULATION ACTIVITIES: Education, Advocacy, Natural Family Planning, Demographic Research.

FORWARD-LOOKING STRATEGIES IMPLEMENTATIONS: Continued work on building awareness of women's health issues. Focus on population issues. Participation in campaigns.

OBSTACLES TO THE IMPLEMENTATIONOF FORWARD-LOOKING STRATEGIES: None

NOTES:

Project Five-O Calcutta

INDIA

ADDRESS:

8A Palm Place, Calcutta, 700019, India

EXECUTIVE OFFICER:

Mrs. Aroti Dutt, President

BRANCH OFFICES:

TELEPHONE NUMBER:	TELEX NUMBER:
46-2152	

APPROX. STAFF SIZE:	VOLUNTEER STAFF:	YEAR ESTABLISHED:
7	10	1982

NUMBER OF INDIVIDUAL MEMBERS:

FUNDING: Funding from various sources: Self-financing projects; UNESCO; Lutheran World Service; American Federation of University Women; Soroptimist Club of San Clemente, California.

PRINCIPAL PURPOSE: Promotion of health, nutrition and productivity of citizens, with emphasis on women and children.

MAIN ACTIVITIES: Training in weaving, tailoring and sewing; promotion of nutrition, especially for children; travelling library; balwadi (pre-primary class for children); construction of latrines and other community improvement projects; tree planting; educational seminars; future program planned for family planning (additional space and funds are necessary for this program).

POPULATION CONCERNS: Concerned with the needs and situations of village and poor urban women and children. Concentration on education, demographic research, contraceptive research, counselling and Natural Family Planning

SPECIFIC POPULATION ACTIVITIES: Education, demographic research, contraceptive research, counselling, natural family planning.

FORWARD-LOOKING STRATEGIES IMPLEMENTATIONS: Implementing paragraphs 28 and 29, which deal with the role of women as intermediaries between the environment and society and women's right to control their own fertility.

OBSTACLES TO THE IMPLEMENTATION OF FORWARD-LOOKING STRATEGIES: Financial stringency makes implementation difficult.

NOTES:

Research Centre for Women's Studies

INDIA

ADDRESS:

S.N.D.T. Women's University Research Centre for Women's Studies
Vithaldas Vidyavihar, Santa Cruz (West), Bombay-400 049, India

EXECUTIVE OFFICER:

Dr. Maithreyi Krishna Raj

BRANCH OFFICES:

TELEPHONE NUMBER:

6128462, Ext. 18

TELEX NUMBER:

APPROX. STAFF SIZE:	VOLUNTEER STAFF:	YEAR ESTABLISHED:
10	0	1979

NUMBER OF INDIVIDUAL MEMBERS:

FUNDING: S.N.D.T. Women's University, University Grants Commission, State Government, and some funding agencies for specific projects (national and international).

PRINCIPAL PURPOSE: To identify issues and problems of women and to undertake studies pertaining to women's role and status in society; to collect information and build documentation and reference material on women; to assist in the preparation and teaching of women's studies; to link with individuals and institutions here and abroad; to encourage and support programs for the improvement of women.

MAIN ACTIVITIES: Research is the principal activity of the Centre. The Centre has trained many women in research methodology and in feminist perspectives and preparation of teaching material. Seminars and workshops are regular features. A documentation center makes research reports, seminar and conference papers and various types of data and materials for research available to scholars.

POPULATION CONCERNS: Concerned with promotion of women's reproductive rights and health as they relate to women's status in society.

SPECIFIC POPULATION ACTIVITIES: Demographic research.

FORWARD-LOOKING STRATEGIES IMPLEMENTATIONS: Not implementing specific strategies, but strongly believe that women should have the right to control their own fertility. Maternal and child health must be strengthened and should form the main component of primary health care.

OBSTACLES TO THE IMPLEMENTATION OF FORWARD-LOOKING STRATEGIES: Not answered.

NOTES:

Self Employed Women's Association (SEWA)

INDIA

ADDRESS:

SEWA Reception Centre, Opp. Victoria Garden, Ahmedabad-380 001, India

EXECUTIVE OFFICER:			BRANCH OFFICES:
Ela R. Bhatt, General Secretary			

TELEPHONE NUMBER:	TELEX NUMBER:
390577	

APPROX. STAFF SIZE:	VOLUNTEER STAFF:	YEAR ESTABLISHED:
	100	1972

NUMBER OF INDIVIDUAL MEMBERS:

22,000

FUNDING: Membership fees, sales generated through cooperatives, government projects and assistance from international organizations.

PRINCIPAL PURPOSE: To help self employed women organize, become more visible, and earn fair wages.

MAIN ACTIVITIES: Promoting unionization, providing training to upgrade skills, creating banking and credit facilities, cooperativising women within trade groups and advocating social security benefits.

POPULATION CONCERNS: Making contraceptive information available to women, organizing to protest unsafe and discriminatory programs and policies and promoting reproductive freedom.

SPECIFIC POPULATION ACTIVITIES: Education, advocacy and delivery of services: pill, IUD, condom and natural family planning.

FORWARD-LOOKING STRATEGIES IMPLEMENTATIONS: Organization of women into trade unions and cooperatives, demanding statutory commission for self employed workers.

OBSTACLES TO THE IMPLEMENTATION OF FORWARD-LOOKING STRATEGIES: Fighting fixed concepts of 'worker', 'union' and 'viable'. Fighting contract system and vested interests.

NOTES:

University Women's Association, PUNE

INDIA

ADDRESS:

Working Women's Hostel, 270 E. Bhambhurda, Pune 411016, India

EXECUTIVE OFFICER:			BRANCH OFFICES:
Dr. Usha Bambawale, President			

TELEPHONE NUMBER:		TELEX NUMBER:
59694		

APPROX. STAFF SIZE:	VOLUNTEER STAFF:	YEAR ESTABLISHED:
9	20	1955

NUMBER OF INDIVIDUAL MEMBERS:
150

FUNDING: Self-funding, charity drives, donations, membership fees.

PRINCIPAL PURPOSE: Advancement of women.

MAIN ACTIVITIES: Working Women's Hostel (82 residents), pre-primary school, creche, Musiquest, Progress Eves, House Journal, continuous education programs/lectures, marital counselling, scholarships, legal aid centre.

POPULATION CONCERNS: Collaboration with the Family Planning Association of India, reflecting the University Women's Association's interest in advancement of women and attention to women's right to control their fertility.

SPECIFIC POPULATION ACTIVITIES: None reported.

FORWARD-LOOKING STRATEGIES IMPLEMENTATIONS: Not implementing strategies.

OBSTACLES TO THE IMPLEMENTATION OF FORWARD-LOOKING STRATEGIES: Too many agencies working in this field.

NOTES:

ORGANIZATION:	
Women's Indian Association	**INDIA**

ADDRESS:	
43, Greenways Road, Madras 600 028, SOUTH INDIA	

EXECUTIVE OFFICER:	BRANCH OFFICES:
Smt. Sarojini Varadappan, President	

TELEPHONE NUMBER:	TELEX NUMBER:
416607	

APPROX. STAFF SIZE:	VOLUNTEER STAFF:	YEAR ESTABLISHED:
46	70, approximately	1917

NUMBER OF INDIVIDUAL MEMBERS:
6,500

FUNDING: Government grant and contributions by organization members and constituent branches

PRINCIPAL PURPOSE: To advance the status of women in society to promote equality, self-development and ensure a better future for India.

MAIN ACTIVITIES: Running working women's hostels; old age homes; creches; balwadis*; nursery schools; printing press; primary, secondary, higher secondary and training schools; tailoring units; garment making; special classes for Hindi; music; dance and secretarial courses and many socioeconomic units; public cooperation camps to explain family planning methods.

POPULATION CONCERNS: Concerned with motivating couples to use family planning methods, and family welfare.

SPECIFIC POPULATION ACTIVITIES: Education, contraceptive research, counselling, delivery of services, sterilization, Pill, IUD, and Natural Family Planning

FORWARD-LOOKING STRATEGIES IMPLEMENTATIONS: Implementing strategies put forth in paragraphs 157, 158 and 159 that governments should take an active role in encouraging voluntary family planning, information dissemination and ensuring adequate quality of services.

OBSTACLES TO THE IMPLEMENTATION OF FORWARD-LOOKING STRATEGIES: None.

NOTES: *(Pre-primary classes for children)

The Women's Voluntary Service of Tamil Nadu

INDIA

ADDRESS:

No. 19 East Spur Tank Road, Chetput, Madras 600 031, South India, India

EXECUTIVE OFFICER:

Tmt. Sarojini Varadappan, Assistant Director

BRANCH OFFICES:

TELEPHONE NUMBER:	TELEX NUMBER:
664025	

APPROX. STAFF SIZE:	VOLUNTEER STAFF:	YEAR ESTABLISHED:
326	14	1972

NUMBER OF INDIVIDUAL MEMBERS:

80

FUNDING: Government grants and local contributions.

PRINCIPAL PURPOSE: Dedicated to the uplifting of down-trodden women, children and the handicapped for their overall development.

MAIN ACTIVITIES: Adult literacy for women, aid to disabled persons, ambulance service, canteen, community welfare activities, creche centers for children, dairy unit for women, garment unit for physically handicapped women, hospital welfare services, hostel for working women, scholarship to college students, vocational training for women.

POPULATION CONCERNS: Concerned with welfare of families in the city slums, rural and coastal areas, including the availability of family planning services.

SPECIFIC POPULATION ACTIVITIES: Education, counselling, organized family welfare orientation training camps for 16,720 women, and distribution of family planning materials and appropriate education.

FORWARD-LOOKING STRATEGIES IMPLEMENTATIONS: Implementation occurring through one-day training camps in the slum areas and in rural and coastal areas for women's education and responsible parenthood. Also organizing health camps for women and children, distributing family planning materials and film shows.

OBSTACLES TO THE IMPLEMENTATION OF FORWARD-LOOKING STRATEGIES: The campaign for implementation needs to be organized in a sustained manner. The community must be persuaded repeatedly on the issues. Absence of proper transport, lack of publicity materials and illiteracy within the population hinder implementation.

NOTES:

Working Women's Forum (India)　　**INDIA**

ADDRESS:

55 Bhimasena Garden Road, Mylapore, Madras-600 004., Tamil Nadu, India

EXECUTIVE OFFICER:			BRANCH OFFICES:
Ms. Jaya Arunachalam, President			

TELEPHONE NUMBER:		TELEX NUMBER:	
74553			

APPROX. STAFF SIZE:	VOLUNTEER STAFF:	YEAR ESTABLISHED:
3	400	1978

NUMBER OF INDIVIDUAL MEMBERS:

55,570

FUNDING: Membership, national government and bilateral agencies.

PRINCIPAL PURPOSE: To provide organizational support to women workers on trade lines in order to improve their living/working conditions. To make the organizational structure to be grassroot in nature in order to reach large numbers of women workers. To promote women's status to address caste, class and gender oppressions of women.

MAIN ACTIVITIES: Program strategies addressing the needs of women workers in area of credit, employment, health, nutrition and family planning.

POPULATION CONCERNS: Concerned with the productive versus the reproductive roles of women.

SPECIFIC POPULATION ACTIVITIES: Education, counselling, Delivery of services: sterlization, Pill, and I.U.D.

FORWARD-LOOKING STRATEGIES IMPLEMENTATIONS: Making effort to encourage family planning so women can strengthen economic roles. Organizing women to counter exploitative trade practices.

OBSTACLES TO THE IMPLEMENTATION OF FORWARD-LOOKING STRATEGIES: Scattered distribution of productive assets, local power hierarchies, elite domination, conflicts among the poor are the main obstacles impeding progress.

NOTES:

International Feminists of Japan

JAPAN

ADDRESS:

c/o Agora, Shinjuku 1-9-6, Shinjuku-ku Tokyo 160, Japan

EXECUTIVE OFFICER:	BRANCH OFFICES:
Coordinators: Marga Clegg, and Angela Coutts	

TELEPHONE NUMBER:	TELEX NUMBER:
354-9014 (Japanese only)	

APPROX. STAFF SIZE:	VOLUNTEER STAFF:	YEAR ESTABLISHED:
		1979

NUMBER OF INDIVIDUAL MEMBERS:

72

FUNDING: Memberships and donations.

PRINCIPAL PURPOSE: To support and foster communication among English-speaking women in Japan. To pursue educational and social activities and reduce isolation.

MAIN ACTIVITIES: Organizing educational meetings and publishing a monthly networking newsletter for members.

POPULATION CONCERNS: Reproductive rights, new reproductive technologies, etc.

SPECIFIC POPULATION ACTIVITIES: Education.

FORWARD-LOOKING STRATEGIES IMPLEMENTATIONS: None.

OBSTACLES TO THE IMPLEMENTATION OF FORWARD-LOOKING STRATEGIES: None.

NOTES:

National Women's Education Centre   JAPAN

ADDRESS:

728 Sugaya, Ranzan-machi, Hiki-gun, Saitama-ken, 355-02, Japan

EXECUTIVE OFFICER:			BRANCH OFFICES:
Ms. Atsuka Shikuma			

TELEPHONE NUMBER:		TELEX NUMBER:	
0493(62)6711			

APPROX. STAFF SIZE:	VOLUNTEER STAFF:	YEAR ESTABLISHED:
43	65	1977

NUMBER OF INDIVIDUAL MEMBERS:

FUNDING: State financed.

PRINCIPAL PURPOSE: To promote women's education.

MAIN ACTIVITIES: Practical training of leaders in women's education. To conduct specialized research in the field of women's education and family education.

POPULATION CONCERNS: Education from the women's studies point of view.

SPECIFIC POPULATION ACTIVITIES: Education.

FORWARD-LOOKING STRATEGIES IMPLEMENTATIONS: The purpose and the activities of our organization contribute to the implementation of the FLS.

OBSTACLES TO THE IMPLEMENTATION OF FORWARD-LOOKING STRATEGIES: None indicated.

NOTES:

Korean Women's Development Institute **KOREA**

ADDRESS:

C.P.O. Box 2267, Seoul, Korea

EXECUTIVE OFFICER:	BRANCH OFFICES:
Ms. Hyung-Deok Kim, President	

TELEPHONE NUMBER:	TELEX NUMBER:
784-9108	K 23230

APPROX. STAFF SIZE:	VOLUNTEER STAFF:	YEAR ESTABLISHED:
164		1983

NUMBER OF INDIVIDUAL MEMBERS:

FUNDING: Fully subsidized by the Korean government.

PRINCIPAL PURPOSE: To make a comprehensive study of women's issues and to reflect its findings in government policies. The major task is to integrate women into the national development process.

MAIN ACTIVITIES: Undertake research and survey projects on women's issues, to provide education and training for cultivating women's potential, to foster and support NGO's activities and to sponsor the women's resource bank and welfare programmes for underpriviliged women and to manage information and publication.

POPULATION CONCERNS: Improvement of women's health and their quality of life. Several research studies on population concerns including; "Study of unwed mothers (1984)," "Consultation for the development of research proposals on women's health ('83-'84)," "Survey on the health condition of rural women ('86-'87)" and "Development of educational program for prevention of unwed mothers ('86-'87)."

SPECIFIC POPULATION ACTIVITIES: Education, Demographic research, Counselling, Advocacy.

FORWARD-LOOKING STRATEGIES IMPLEMENTATIONS:

OBSTACLES TO THE IMPLEMENTATION OF FORWARD-LOOKING STRATEGIES:

NOTES:

Sarawak Federation of Women's Institutes

MALAYSIA

ADDRESS:

SFWI Centre, P.O. Box 366, 98007 MIRI, Sarawak Malaysia

EXECUTIVE OFFICER:			BRANCH OFFICES:
Administrative Secretary			

TELEPHONE NUMBER:	TELEX NUMBER:
08536235	

APPROX. STAFF SIZE:	VOLUNTEER STAFF:	YEAR ESTABLISHED:
12	12	1962

NUMBER OF INDIVIDUAL MEMBERS:

12,000

FUNDING: Government grant and membership dues.

PRINCIPAL PURPOSE: To improve the living standard of women and their families, especially in rural areas, in their social and economic roles.

MAIN ACTIVITIES: Providing facilities to women to obtain knowledge in basic health & nutrition education, child care, family planning, etc.

POPULATION CONCERNS: Due to the vast majority of membership living in rural areas, and the fact that most are illiterate, our focus is on the education aspects of population.

SPECIFIC POPULATION ACTIVITIES: Education, Contraceptive research, Counselling, Pill, IUD, Natural Family Planning.

FORWARD-LOOKING STRATEGIES IMPLEMENTATIONS: The National and State Government are begining to implement some of the Forward-Looking Strategies, and our organization is ready to participate in the program when it is started.

OBSTACLES TO THE IMPLEMENTATION OF FORWARD-LOOKING STRATEGIES: At the state levels, communication could be one of the obstacles apart from funds.

NOTES:

Association of Anglican Women

NEW ZEALAND

ADDRESS:

℅ Mrs. J. E. Woodall, Whitehall RD4, Cambridge 2351, New Zealand

EXECUTIVE OFFICER:			BRANCH OFFICES:
Mrs. J. E. Woodall, President			

TELEPHONE NUMBER:	TELEX NUMBER:	
27-6635		

APPROX. STAFF SIZE:	VOLUNTEER STAFF:	YEAR ESTABLISHED:
	12,000	1969

NUMBER OF INDIVIDUAL MEMBERS:

FUNDING: Membership subscription.

PRINCIPAL PURPOSE: Fellowship; to promote and safeguard Christian Family life; to unite in prayer; to participate in the mission of the Anglican church.

MAIN ACTIVITIES: Leadership training; outreach; support of missionaries in New Zealand and overseas; evangelism; education on family life; Bible study; support of local church.

POPULATION CONCERNS:

SPECIFIC POPULATION ACTIVITIES: Education & counselling.

FORWARD-LOOKING STRATEGIES IMPLEMENTATIONS: Encouragement of members to submit their viewpoint to parlimentary select committees on issues of particular concern to women, children, and/or family.

OBSTACLES TO THE IMPLEMENTATION OF FORWARD-LOOKING STRATEGIES: Male domination of roles and resistance from women of more senior years.

NOTES:

Broadsheet Magazine Collective

NEW ZEALAND

ADDRESS:

L 85 Karangahape Rd., Auckland I, NEW ZEALAND

EXECUTIVE OFFICER:

Athina Tsoulis, Bus. Manager

BRANCH OFFICES:

TELEPHONE NUMBER:	TELEX NUMBER:
794-751	

APPROX. STAFF SIZE:	VOLUNTEER STAFF:	YEAR ESTABLISHED:
5	5	1972

NUMBER OF INDIVIDUAL MEMBERS:

FUNDING: From magazine sales and subscriptions.

PRINCIPAL PURPOSE: To analyze and comment on the situation of women in Adtedroa/New Zealand; to provide a forum for feminism.

MAIN ACTIVITIES: Publishing a 45pg. magazine ten times a year.

POPULATION CONCERNS: Reports on research; make available information; and give publicity to feminist analysis of population concerns.

SPECIFIC POPULATION ACTIVITIES: Education.

FORWARD-LOOKING STRATEGIES IMPLEMENTATIONS: Through publishing a feminist magazine which also provides 5 jobs for women.

OBSTACLES TO THE IMPLEMENTATION OF FORWARD-LOOKING STRATEGIES: Lack of resources.

NOTES:

ORGANIZATION:

Collective of Independent Women's Refuges

NEW ZEALAND

ADDRESS:

P.O. Box 6386, Te Aro, Wellington, New Zealand

EXECUTIVE OFFICER:			BRANCH OFFICES:
Rosemary Ash, National Coordinator			

TELEPHONE NUMBER:	TELEX NUMBER:	
856768		

APPROX. STAFF SIZE:	VOLUNTEER STAFF:	YEAR ESTABLISHED:
7	1	1974

NUMBER OF INDIVIDUAL MEMBERS:

1350

FUNDING: Subsidies from the Department of Social Welfare for wages and operating costs. Local fundraising and donations.

PRINCIPAL PURPOSE: To provide support and safe homes for battered women in New Zealand.

MAIN ACTIVITIES: Operation of refuges and education of the public on the prevention of violence towards women and children.

POPULATION CONCERNS: Support of women's rights to choose family size.

SPECIFIC POPULATION ACTIVITIES: Education, advocacy and health.

FORWARD-LOOKING STRATEGIES IMPLEMENTATIONS: Education of the community on women's rights to choose, support of women to gain access to health resources.

OBSTACLES TO THE IMPLEMENTATION OF FORWARD-LOOKING STRATEGIES: Antagonism from right wing religious groups.

NOTES:

*Business Address: Reid House-2nd Floor, Corner Vivien and Cuba Streets, Te Aro, Wellington, New Zealand

Maori Women's Welfare League, Inc.

NEW ZEALAND

ADDRESS:

P.O. Box 12072, Wellington, New Zealand

EXECUTIVE OFFICER:			BRANCH OFFICES:
Georgia Kirby, National President			

TELEPHONE NUMBER:		TELEX NUMBER:
736451		TATAU TATAU

APPROX. STAFF SIZE:	VOLUNTEER STAFF:	YEAR ESTABLISHED:
1	20	1951

NUMBER OF INDIVIDUAL MEMBERS:

4000 in 4 organizations

FUNDING: Through members and the government's Department of Maori Affairs.

PRINCIPAL PURPOSE: To enable members to play an effective part in the cultural, social and economic development of the Maori and people of New Zealand.

MAIN ACTIVITIES: Fellowship and humanitarian action on issues of culture, health, education, social justice, economics and employment.

POPULATION CONCERNS: All issues that affect women and children.

SPECIFIC POPULATION ACTIVITIES: Demographic and contraceptive research, education, advocacy, counselling and the delivery of services, including the Pill, IUD, diaphragm, foam, Norplant, Depo-Provera and natural family planning.

FORWARD-LOOKING STRATEGIES IMPLEMENTATIONS: Indigenous rights, self determination, health, education and economics for all New Zealanders by the year 2000.

OBSTACLES TO THE IMPLEMENTATION OF FORWARD-LOOKING STRATEGIES: Attitudes, overstretching of individual members and the lack of funds.

NOTES:

---

*Business Address: 24 Burnell Avenue, Thorndon, Wellington-1, New Zealand

New Zealand Federation of University Women

NEW ZEALAND

ADDRESS:

P.O. Box 1713, Palinentor North, New Zealand

EXECUTIVE OFFICER:			BRANCH OFFICES:
Mary Davis, President			

TELEPHONE NUMBER:		TELEX NUMBER:	
64-063-83-513			

APPROX. STAFF SIZE:	VOLUNTEER STAFF:	YEAR ESTABLISHED:	
9	2000	1921	

NUMBER OF INDIVIDUAL MEMBERS:

FUNDING: Members subscriptions, Investments

PRINCIPAL PURPOSE: Advancement of women through education, particularly tertiary education.

MAIN ACTIVITIES: Providing scholarships for women, encouraging girls & women to become educators, public affairs generally, and lobbying.

POPULATION CONCERNS: A general interest in the right and ability of women to control their own fertility.

SPECIFIC POPULATION ACTIVITIES: None.

FORWARD-LOOKING STRATEGIES IMPLEMENTATIONS: Only by monitoring government action in population & fertility education.

OBSTACLES TO THE IMPLEMENTATION OF FORWARD-LOOKING STRATEGIES: None.

NOTES:

New Zealand Women's Electoral Lobby

NEW ZEALAND

ADDRESS:

P.O. Box 11285, Wellington, New Zealand

EXECUTIVE OFFICER:			BRANCH OFFICES:
National Coordinator			

TELEPHONE NUMBER:		TELEX NUMBER:	
(04)769301			

APPROX. STAFF SIZE:	VOLUNTEER STAFF:	YEAR ESTABLISHED:	
3	3	1975	

NUMBER OF INDIVIDUAL MEMBERS:	
500	

FUNDING: Through donations and subscriptions.

PRINCIPAL PURPOSE: To achieve equality for women. To encourage women to use the political system and be active in public life. To ensure that people who work towards equality for women are elected and appointed to public office.

MAIN ACTIVITIES: Monitoring legislation; making submissions to the government; conducting education seminars on lobbying and skills training; encouraging affirmative action programs and networking with other women's organizations.

POPULATION CONCERNS: Fertility control is essential for women's equality. Free contraceptive advice, safe legal abortions and choices in sterilization options should be available. Endorsement of the Family Planning Association.

SPECIFIC POPULATION ACTIVITIES: Education and advocacy.

FORWARD-LOOKING STRATEGIES IMPLEMENTATIONS: Teaching women to be leaders and encouraging them into positions of authority. Particular emphasis this year is to enable women to be elected to local and rural governments.

OBSTACLES TO THE IMPLEMENTATION OF FORWARD-LOOKING STRATEGIES: Agreement in principle within the white, middle-class, male hierarchy that governs New Zealand, but little action.

NOTES:

Women's Health Committee   **NEW ZEALAND**

ADDRESS:

Board of Health, P.O. Box 5148, Wellington, New Zealand

EXECUTIVE OFFICER:			BRANCH OFFICES:
Dr. Judith Johnston, Chairperson			

TELEPHONE NUMBER:		TELEX NUMBER:
727-627		

APPROX. STAFF SIZE:	VOLUNTEER STAFF:	YEAR ESTABLISHED:
15		1985

NUMBER OF INDIVIDUAL MEMBERS:

FUNDING: Annual government grant.

PRINCIPAL PURPOSE: Advisory committee to the Ministry of Health to advise on the whole range of women's health matters.

MAIN ACITIVITIES: Advising the Ministry of Health.

POPULATION CONCERNS: In a general sense the Committee is concerned with consumer issues, such as the availability of services and appropriate education.

SPECIFIC POPULATION ACTIVITIES: Education and advocacy.

FORWARD-LOOKING STRATEGIES IMPLEMENTATIONS: Are aware of the Strategies but are not implementing them.

OBSTACLES TO THE IMPLEMENTATION OF FORWARD-LOOKING STRATEGIES: None indicated.

NOTES:

Women's National Abortion Action Campaign

NEW ZEALAND

ADDRESS:

P.O. Box 2669, Wellington, Aotearoa, New Zealand

EXECUTIVE OFFICER:			BRANCH OFFICES:
Di Cleary, Treasurer			

TELEPHONE NUMBER:		TELEX NUMBER:	

APPROX. STAFF SIZE:	VOLUNTEER STAFF:	YEAR ESTABLISHED:
	12	1972

NUMBER OF INDIVIDUAL MEMBERS:

200 in 6 chapters

FUNDING: Donations and newsletter subscriptions.

PRINCIPAL PURPOSE: To repeal present abortion laws making abortion freely available, safe and paid for by the state.

MAIN ACTIVITIES: Lobbying the government, media activities such as pickets and rallies, leaflet publication and distribution on sex education and abortion.

POPULATION CONCERNS: That contraception is freely available to all women and men and that this be advertised in all languages to reach all people.

SPECIFIC POPULATION ACTIVITIES: Education and advocacy.

FORWARD-LOOKING STRATEGIES IMPLEMENTATIONS: Revolved around reproductive rights, to unite women in New Zealand, Maori and Pacific Island area believing that contraception be made free and available to all men and women.

OBSTACLES TO THE IMPLEMENTATION OF FORWARD-LOOKING STRATEGIES: Resistance from the mainstream media. We have always been struggling against restrictive laws and moral paranoia concerning sex education and contraception. Lack of resources makes it difficult to cross language barriers.

NOTES:

Women's Studies Association (N.Z.) Inc.

NEW ZEALAND

ADDRESS:

P.O. Box 5067, Auckland I, NEW ZEALAND

EXECUTIVE OFFICER:		BRANCH OFFICES:

TELEPHONE NUMBER:	TELEX NUMBER:
892-510	

APPROX. STAFF SIZE:	VOLUNTEER STAFF:	YEAR ESTABLISHED:
	26	1974

NUMBER OF INDIVIDUAL MEMBERS:

420

FUNDING: From membership subscriptions.

PRINCIPAL PURPOSE: To effect radical social change through the medium of women's studies.

MAIN ACTIVITIES: Producing: quarterly newsletter, biannual journal, annual collected conference papers. Organizing annual conferences, supporting women involved in research/documentation on women; supporting women setting up women's study courses; and tutoring in women studies.

POPULATION CONCERNS: The Association regards population concerns as a basic area of women's studies.

SPECIFIC POPULATION ACTIVITIES: Education.

FORWARD-LOOKING STRATEGIES IMPLEMENTATIONS: The Association regards its existence and its publications as part of the implementations of the Forward Looking Strategies.

OBSTACLES TO THE IMPLEMENTATION OF FORWARD-LOOKING STRATEGIES: Lack of resources.

NOTES:

The Asian Women's Institute

PAKISTAN

ADDRESS:

c/oAssociation of Kinnaird College for Women, Lahore, Pakistan

EXECUTIVE OFFICER:			BRANCH OFFICES:
Mrs. Santosh Singha, Coordinator			

TELEPHONE NUMBER:		TELEX NUMBER:
418128		

APPROX. STAFF SIZE:	VOLUNTEER STAFF:	YEAR ESTABLISHED:
4 to 5	varies	1975

NUMBER OF INDIVIDUAL MEMBERS:

universities

FUNDING: Donor agencies, individual gifts and other sources.

PRINCIPAL PURPOSE: Not answered.

MAIN ACTIVITIES: Educational seminars and conferences held triannually in a region in Asia in which participants include universities and colleges and others from various women's institutions; career counselling and guidance; continuing education; peace education; panelists and speakers; discussion groups on various issues concerning women.

POPULATION CONCERNS: Concerned with education on issues of population, family and health, as they relate to the status of women.

SPECIFIC POPULATION ACTIVITIES: Education, counselling, advocacy.

FORWARD-LOOKING STRATEGIES IMPLEMENTATIONS: Educational programs, organized on campuses, deal with population, family and health issues.

OBSTACLES TO THE IMPLEMENTATION OF FORWARD-LOOKING STRATEGIES: Traditional values and culture and attitudes of conservative groups are resistant to change.

NOTES:

Center for Women's Resources   PHILIPPINES

ADDRESS:

2nd Floor Marsantos Bldg., 43 Roces Ave., Quezon City, Philippines

EXECUTIVE OFFICER:			BRANCH OFFICES:
Carolyn Medel-Anonuevo			

TELEPHONE NUMBER:	TELEX NUMBER:	
992755		

APPROX. STAFF SIZE:	VOLUNTEER STAFF:	YEAR ESTABLISHED:
8	2	1981

NUMBER OF INDIVIDUAL MEMBERS:

24

FUNDING: Project to project basis by local and international agencies, and women's organizations.

PRINCIPAL PURPOSE: Provide venue for discussing women's issues. Provide education and training services for women on the *Woman Question* and skills such as speaking, organizing, training, communicating, finance management, etc.

MAIN ACTIVITIES: Education and training; research; library services; supporting organizing work; supporting campaigns for women.

POPULATION CONCERNS:

SPECIFIC POPULATION ACTIVITIES: Education, contraceptive research, advocacy.

FORWARD-LOOKING STRATEGIES IMPLEMENTATIONS: Not yet.

OBSTACLES TO THE IMPLEMENTATION OF FORWARD-LOOKING STRATEGIES: None.

NOTES:

Civic Assembly of Women of the Philippines

PHILIPPINES

ADDRESS:

CAWP PW University, Taft avenue, Manila, Philippines

EXECUTIVE OFFICER:			BRANCH OFFICES:
Dr. Trinidad A. Gomez, President			

TELEPHONE NUMBER:	TELEX NUMBER:	
58-82-01		

APPROX. STAFF SIZE:	VOLUNTEER STAFF:	YEAR ESTABLISHED:
4		1946

NUMBER OF INDIVIDUAL MEMBERS:

30,000,000

FUNDING: By annual fees of individual members and by affiliation fees from organizations.

PRINCIPAL PURPOSE: To have a central body that would coordinate programs of affiliate organizations that help promote the well being of people.

MAIN ACTIVITIES: Activities focus on health and nutrition, education and research, community development, livelihood programs, etc.

POPULATION CONCERNS: Concerned with population issues as they relate to community health issues.

SPECIFIC POPULATION ACTIVITIES: Education, counselling, delivery of services and natural family planning.

FORWARD LOOKING-STRATEGIES IMPLEMENTATIONS: Nearly all Forward-Looking Stratgies are already being implemented in the Philippines.

OBSTACLES TO THE IMPLEMENTATION OF FORWARD-LOOKING STRATEGIES: Lack of political commitment and personal indifference to the issues.

NOTES:

ORGANIZATION:	
GABRIELA	**PHILIPPINES**

ADDRESS:

#41 Timog Avenue, Quezon City, Philippines 2800

EXECUTIVE OFFICER:	BRANCH OFFICES:
Sr. Mary John Mananzan, Chairperson	

TELEPHONE NUMBER:	TELEX NUMBER:	
91-51-46		

APPROX. STAFF SIZE:	VOLUNTEER STAFF:	YEAR ESTABLISHED:
5	5	1984

NUMBER OF INDIVIDUAL MEMBERS:

28,000

FUNDING: Membership dues, donations and grants.

PRINCIPAL PURPOSE: To equip each woman with the consciousness, motivation and skills to take active and leading roles in social change and development. To gain public support for the cause of women's emancipation with special emphasis on the plight of grassroots women. To facilitate the active participation of women in the quest for a democratic and sovereign society.

MAIN ACTIVITIES: Education/protest campaigns on various women's issues and national concerns; development programs for grassroots women along the lines of consciousness-raising; alternative health care and support services for working mothers.

POPULATION CONCERNS: Interested in subjects such as: reproductive freedom for women, maternal and child health care, breastfeeding, parenting and family planning, primary health care and AIDS.

SPECIFIC POPULATION ACTIVITIES: Education, contraceptive research, counselling and advocacy.

FORWARD-LOOKING STRATEGIES IMPLEMENTATIONS: GABRIELA actively lobbies for legislation that guarantees equality for women; promotes non-sexist, liberal and accessible education; protests sexual discrimination in the workplace and advocates social services and support systems for women.

OBSTACLES TO THE IMPLEMENTATION OF FORWARD-LOOKING STRATEGIES: None.

NOTES:

Katipunan Ng Bagong Pilipina
Association of the New Filipina PHILIPPINES

ADDRESS:

25 S. Pascual Street, Malabon, Metro Manila, Philippines

EXECUTIVE OFFICER:			BRANCH OFFICES:
Filomena D. Tolentino, President			

TELEPHONE NUMBER:		TELEX NUMBER:	
221595			

APPROX. STAFF SIZE:	VOLUNTEER STAFF:	YEAR ESTABLISHED:
21	21	1975

NUMBER OF INDIVIDUAL MEMBERS:

20,000

FUNDING: Through membership, donations and projects (launched by the organization and projects funded by different agencies).

PRINCIPAL PURPOSE: Consciousness raising of women on a grassroots level, and mobilizing them in support of issues which have a bearing on their lives. Projects include cooperatives, health and day-care centers, mutual help associations and income generating activities.

POPULATION CONCERNS: Family planning and maternal and child care.

SPECIFIC POPULATION ACTIVITIES: Education.

FORWARD-LOOKING STRATEGIES IMPLEMENTATIONS: A committee named Forward Looking Women (FLOW) was formed. This committee will take charge of the implementation of the Forward Looking Strategies.

OBSTACLES TO THE IMPLEMENTATION OF FORWARD-LOOKING STRATEGIES: Inadequate funds for the production of materials to be used in the dissemination of the Forward-Looking Strategies.

NOTES:

Pilipina, Inc.

PHILIPPINES

ADDRESS:

12 Pasaje de la Paz Street, Project 4, Quezon City, Philippines

EXECUTIVE OFFICER:			BRANCH OFFICES:
Ms. Teresita Quintos-Deles, Program Coordinator			

TELEPHONE NUMBER:	TELEX NUMBER:	
775341		

APPROX. STAFF SIZE:	VOLUNTEER STAFF:	YEAR ESTABLISHED:
3	12	1981

NUMBER OF INDIVIDUAL MEMBERS:

300

FUNDING: Donations and program funding agencies are the principal sources of funding.

PRINCIPAL PURPOSE: Promotion of women's health.

MAIN ACTIVITIES: Education, organizing activities and research are the main activities.

POPULATION CONCERNS: Concerned with women's health and reproductive issues relationship with health issues.

SPECIFIC POPULATION ACTIVITIES: Education, demographic research, and advocacy are the primary population activities.

FORWARD-LOOKING STRATEGIES IMPLEMENTATIONS: Education of women and a peace campaign are implementations of the Strategies.

OBSTACLES TO IMPLEMENTATION OF FORWARD-LOOKING STRATEGIES: Financial support and concerned, motivated individuals are lacking.

NOTES:

Women's Rights Movement of The Philippines

PHILIPPINES

ADDRESS:

90 Hemady, Quezon City, Philippines

EXECUTIVE OFFICER:			BRANCH OFFICES:
Mrs. Josefina Albarraein			

TELEPHONE NUMBER:		TELEX NUMBER:	
70-46-30			

APPROX. STAFF SIZE:	VOLUNTEER STAFF:	YEAR ESTABLISHED:	
2		1957	

NUMBER OF INDIVIDUAL MEMBERS:

108

FUNDING: Membership dues.

PRINCIPAL PURPOSE: To pronounce, protect and promote women's rights.

MAIN ACTIVITIES: Inform, educate, and adjust public opinion on the rights of women.

POPULATION CONCERNS: Health values.

SPECIFIC POPULATION ACTIVITIES: Education, demographic research, counselling and natural family planning.

FORWARD LOOKING-STRATEGIES IMPLEMENTATIONS: The Women's Rights Movement is implementing the FLS, although no specific strategies have been emphasized.

OBSTACLES TO THE IMPLEMENTATION OF FORWARD-LOOKING STRATEGIES: Finaincial limitations.

NOTES:

ORGANIZATION:	
Solomon Islands National Council of Women	**SOLOMON ISLANDS**

ADDRESS:

P.O. Box 494, Moniara, Solomon Islands

EXECUTIVE OFFICER:	BRANCH OFFICES:
Afu Billy Sade, General Secretary	

TELEPHONE NUMBER:	TELEX NUMBER:
23166	

APPROX. STAFF SIZE:	VOLUNTEER STAFF:	YEAR ESTABLISHED:
2		1981

NUMBER OF INDIVIDUAL MEMBERS:

Members in 5 provinces

FUNDING: Grants from local government and overseas.

PRINCIPAL PURPOSE: Information network and lobby of the government on women's issues.

MAIN ACTIVITIES: Coordination of information and activities, and lobby of the government.

POPULATION CONCERNS: None indicated.

SPECIFIC POPULATION ACTIVITIES: Education and advocacy.

FORWARD-LOOKING STRATEGIES IMPLEMENTATIONS: Are aware of the Strategies but are not implementing them directly.

OBSTACLES TO THE IMPLEMENTATION OF FORWARD-LOOKING STRATEGIES: Interpreting them so as to be understood by local people.

NOTES:

ADDRESS:

Girl Guide Headquarters, 10 Sir Arcus Fernando Mawatha, Colombo 7, Sri-Lanka

EXECUTIVE OFFICER:	BRANCH OFFICES:
Mrs. Veneth Gamage, Chief Commissioner	

TELEPHONE NUMBER:	TELEX NUMBER:
595720	

APPROX. STAFF SIZE:	VOLUNT_ER STAFF:	YEAR ESTABLISHED:
5	932	1917

NUMBER OF INDIVIDUAL MEMBERS:

15,328

FUNDING: Very little from the government-Education Dept. Girl Guides of U.K. & Sweden. Fundraising by the association.

PRINCIPAL PURPOSE: To provide leadership training. Service to the community. To foster international friendship and understanding. Service to the community.

MAIN ACTIVITIES: Leadership training through badge work/test work. Community development or service, eg. primary health care, population awareness, conservation, health & sanitation, water, income generating activities.

POPULATION CONCERNS: Population awareness programmes.

SPECIFIC POPULATION ACTIVITIES: Education, advocacy, demographic research, contraceptive research, and counselling.

FORWARD-LOOKING STRATEGIES IMPLEMENTATIONS: Providing safe drinking water, and sanitation programme, and health and family planning education.

OBSTACLES TO THE IMPLEMENTATION OF FORWARD-LOOKING STRATEGIES: Need for coordination of work between NGO's, and also between NGOs and government departments.

NOTES:

The National Council
of Women of Thailand

THAILAND

ADDRESS:

Manangkasila Mansion, Lanluang Road, Bangkok 10300, Thailand

EXECUTIVE OFFICER:

Dr. Soodsarkorn Tuchinda, President

BRANCH OFFICES:

TELEPHONE NUMBER:	TELEX NUMBER:
281-0081	

APPROX. STAFF SIZE:	VOLUNTEER STAFF:	YEAR ESTABLISHED:
20	200	1956

NUMBER OF INDIVIDUAL MEMBERS:

500,000

FUNDING: Partial support by Thai government, self-fundraising, and some projects supported by international agencies such as CIDA, CCF, and UNICEF.

PRINCIPAL PURPOSE: To serve as a center to collect views and ideas and to perform the work of the National Council of Women and other women's organizations in Thailand.

MAIN ACTIVITIES: Study and exchange of information and ideas among women's associations and organizations in Thailand and abroad in order to promote welfare, livelihood and mutual understanding among the people of the world, especially women.

POPULATION CONCERNS: Involved with women and youth; concerned with education and delivery of family planning methods.

SPECIFIC POPULATION ACTIVITIES: Education, delivery of services, Natural Family Planning.

FORWARD-LOOKING STRATEGIES IMPLEMENTATIONS: Engaged in a project to train rural women to pursue income generating activities.

OBSTACLES TO THE IMPLEMENTATION OF FORWARD-LOOKING STRATEGIES: Lack of administrative personnel to carry out the project continuously.

NOTES:

Population Organizations

Bangladesh Asso. for Voluntary Sterilization

Bangladesh Asso. for Voluntary Sterilization

Family Planning Association
A.C.T. Inc.

AUSTRALIA

ADDRESS:	
Health Promotion Centre, Childers Street, Canberra City, ACT Australia 2600	

EXECUTIVE OFFICER:	BRANCH OFFICES:
Sandra MacKenzie, Executive Officer	

TELEPHONE NUMBER:	TELEX NUMBER:
473077	

APPROX. STAFF SIZE:	VOLUNTEER STAFF:	YEAR ESTABLISHED:
60	10 members	1972

NUMBER OF INDIVIDUAL MEMBERS:
30

FUNDING: Federal and state grants.

PRINCIPAL PURPOSE: To promote services and resources to advance the health and welfare of people in relation to contraception, breast/cervical cancer, sexually transmitted diseases and other matters related to fertility regulation and sexuality.

MAIN ACTIVITIES: Family planning services, education and training programs, individual counselling, promotion and campaigns for social legislation reforms relevant to the objects of the Association, and cooperation with other groups with similar interests.

POPULATION CONCERNS: No specific population policies.

SPECIFIC POPULATION ACTIVITIES: Education, counselling, training and the delivery of services including; vasectomies, the pill, IUD, diaphragm, foam, Depo-Provera and natural family planning.

FORWARD-LOOKING STRATEGIES IMPLEMENTATIONS: Did not indicate that they were aware of the Strategies.

OBSTACLES TO THE IMPLEMENTATION OF FORWARD-LOOKING STRATEGIES: None.

NOTES:

Family Planning Association of New South Wales

AUSTRALIA

ADDRESS:

161 Boadway, NSW, 2007, Australia

EXECUTIVE OFFICER:			BRANCH OFFICES:
Ms. Margaret McDonald			

TELEPHONE NUMBER:		TELEX NUMBER:	

APPROX. STAFF SIZE:	VOLUNTEER STAFF:	YEAR ESTABLISHED:	
250-300		1916	

NUMBER OF INDIVIDUAL MEMBERS:			
27 clinics & 11 association members			

FUNDING: Government grants, income from education programs and sales of contraceptives, books and *Healthright* (the Associaton's journal).

PRINCIPAL PURPOSE: To provide information and services related to: contraception, sexuality, fertility, minor gynecological problems and other women's health matters. Clients include married and single people, teenagers, older people and people with disabilities.

MAIN ACTIVITIES: Providing clinical and educational services.

POPULATION CONCERNS: Concerned about family planning and women's health.

SPECIFIC POPULATION ACTIVITIES: Involved in: education, counselling, advocacy, sterilization, pill, IUD, diaphragm, foam, natural family planning, pregnancy testing and counselling, pap smears, breast examination, vasectomies, menopause counselling, training of medical personnel, sex education, community education in birth control, sexual health, sexuality and personal development, professional training, consultation in program design, assertiveness training, book sales, pamphlets, audiovisual resources, Healthright Journal and a library.

FORWARD-LOOKING STRATEGIES IMPLEMENTATIONS: Not implementing.

OBSTACLES TO THE IMPLEMENTATION OF FORWARD-LOOKING STRATEGIES: None.

NOTES:

Family Planning Association of N.T., Inc.

AUSTRALIA

ADDRESS:

P.O. Box 3158, Darwin 5794, Australia

EXECUTIVE OFFICER:

Deborah C. Gough, Executive Officer

BRANCH OFFICES:

PO Box 1107, Alice Springs 5750 AUSTRALIA

TELEPHONE NUMBER:

81-5335

TELEX NUMBER:

APPROX. STAFF SIZE:	VOLUNTEER STAFF:	YEAR ESTABLISHED:
5	20	1973

NUMBER OF INDIVIDUAL MEMBERS:

60

FUNDING: Commonwealth and N.T. government funded.

PRINCIPAL PURPOSE: To provide confidential and up-to-date information and advice on all aspects of family planning including broader ranging sexuality issues.

MAIN ACTIVITIES: Provision of family planning clinics and education.

POPULATION CONCERNS: Adequate community education and free access to fertility control.

SPECIFIC POPULATION ACTIVITIES: Education, counselling and the delivery of services including the pill, IUD, diaphragm, foam, Depo-Provera, condoms, caps and natural family planning.

FORWARD-LOOKING STRATEGIES IMPLEMENTATIONS: Were not aware of the Strategies.

OBSTACLES TO THE IMPLEMENTATION OF FORWARD-LOOKING STRATEGIES: None.

NOTES:

---

*Business Address: 133 Mitchell Street, Darwin AUSTRALIA

The Family Planning Association of Victoria

AUSTRALIA

ADDRESS:

P.O. Box 274, Richmond, Victoria 3121, Australia

EXECUTIVE OFFICER:

Yvonne Dunstan, Executive Officer

BRANCH OFFICES:

TELEPHONE NUMBER:

(03)429-1177

TELEX NUMBER:

APPROX. STAFF SIZE:	VOLUNTEER STAFF:	YEAR ESTABLISHED:
100		1969

NUMBER OF INDIVIDUAL MEMBERS:

200

FUNDING: Commonwealth and state government grants.

PRINCIPAL PURPOSE: To promote responsible parenthood, a healthy family life and marital happiness, the birth and upbringing of healthy children, to relieve poverty and to prevent ill-health in the field of family life.

MAIN ACTIVITIES: Family planning clinics with services including sexuality, pregnancy and menopause counselling. Training and education including professional courses, community education, school programs, film rentals and book sales.

POPULATION CONCERNS: To ensure every child is a wanted child.

SPECIFIC POPULATION ACTIVITIES: Education, counselling, advocacy, contraceptive research and delivery of services including the pill, IUD, diaphragm, foam, Depo-Provera and natural family planning.

FORWARD-LOOKING STRATEGIES IMPLEMENTATIONS: Providing family planning clinics and family planning information through education and training.

OBSTACLES TO THE IMPLEMENTATION OF FORWARD-LOOKING STRATEGIES: Insufficient funding for training and education.

NOTES:

*Business Address: 270 Church Street, Richmond, Victoria 3121

Bangladesh Institute of Development Studies

BANGLADESH

ADDRESS:

E-17, Agargaon, Sher-e-Bangla-nagar, Dhaka-7, G.P.O. Box No. 3854, Bangladesh

EXECUTIVE OFFICER:		BRANCH OFFICES:
Prof. Rehman Sobhan, Director General		

TELEPHONE NUMBER:	TELEX NUMBER:	

APPROX. STAFF SIZE:	VOLUNTEER STAFF:	YEAR ESTABLISHED:
136	0	1957

NUMBER OF INDIVIDUAL MEMBERS:

FUNDING: Government grants and donations are principal funding sources.

PRINCIPAL PURPOSE: To promote research and training to facilitate development.

MAIN ACTIVITIES: Promote study, research and dissemination of knowledge on development economics, demography and other social sciences relating to planning for national development and social welfare. Collect information, conduct investigations and undertake research projects for implementing plans and policies. Provide training facilities on economics, demography and other social sciences and provide information and offer advice on modern research techniques and methodology in economics, demography and advice on modern research techniques and methodology in economics, demography and social sciences.

POPULATION CONCERNS: Two divisions focus on population issues: Population, and Human Resource Development.

SPECIFIC POPULATION ACTIVITIES: Education, counselling, demographic research.

FORWARD-LOOKING STRATEGIES IMPLEMENTATIONS: None.

OBSTACLES TO THE IMPLEMENTATION OF FORWARD-LOOKING STRATEGIES: None.

NOTES:

Bangladesh Rural Advancement Committee

BANGLADESH

ADDRESS:

66, Mohakhali, Commercial Area, Dhaka-12, Bangladesh

EXECUTIVE OFFICER:	BRANCH OFFICES:
Fazle Hasan Abed, Executive Director	

TELEPHONE NUMBER:	TELEX NUMBER:
600106-7	642940 ADAB BJ

APPROX. STAFF SIZE:	VOLUNTEER STAFF:	YEAR ESTABLISHED:
2510	0	1972

NUMBER OF INDIVIDUAL MEMBERS:

FUNDING: Donations by international funds and United Nations organizations.

PRINCIPAL PURPOSE: Advancement and development of the rural poor

MAIN ACTIVITIES: General rural development programs, education programs, child survival programs, training and research programs.

POPULATION CONCERNS: Concerned with advancement of landless and disadvantaged people in rural areas.

SPECIFIC POPULATION ACTIVITIES: Education and child survival programs.

FORWARD-LOOKING STRATEGIES IMPLEMENTATIONS: Not implementing strategies.

OBSTACLES TO THE IMPLEMENTATION OF FORWARD-LOOKING STRATEGIES:

NOTES:

Sabah Family Planning Association

EAST MALAYSIA

ADDRESS:

P.O. Box 11361, 88815, Kota Kinabalu, Sabah, East Malaysia

EXECUTIVE OFFICER:	BRANCH OFFICES:
Mr. Henry H. P. Chai	

TELEPHONE NUMBER:	TELEX NUMBER:
55202	

APPROX. STAFF SIZE:	VOLUNTEER STAFF:	YEAR ESTABLISHED:
40	5	1967

NUMBER OF INDIVIDUAL MEMBERS:

350

FUNDING: Receive most free contraceptive donations from IPPF, sell the contraceptives and generate income, other service income are PAP Smear and pregnancy test fees.

PRINCIPAL PURPOSE: Disseminate healthy reliable Family Planning information.

MAIN ACTIVITIES: Provide scientific and conventional methods of FP services, community based, family life education, population education series, youth & women development programmes, advocating child-spacing and encourage production of health clinics.

POPULATION CONCERNS: Population education for youth particularly school youths.

SPECIFIC POPULATION ACTIVITIES: Education, demographic research, contraceptive research, counselling, advocacy, and delivery of services which include: Sterilization, Pill, IUD, Diaphragm, Foam, Norplant, Depo-provera, and Natural Family Planning.

FORWARD LOOKING-STRATEGIES IMPLEMENTATIONS:

OBSTACLES TO THE IMPLEMENTATION OF FORWARD-LOOKING STRATEGIES:

NOTES:

Asian Youth and Population Coalition

INDIA

ADDRESS:

F-13 South Extension, Part-one, New Delhi-49, India

EXECUTIVE OFFICER:	BRANCH OFFICES:
Ravi Narayan	

TELEPHONE NUMBER:	TELEX NUMBER:
11-624776	

APPROX. STAFF SIZE:	VOLUNTEER STAFF:	YEAR ESTABLISHED:
4	5	1974

NUMBER OF INDIVIDUAL MEMBERS:

350 in 6 chapters

FUNDING: Contributions and membership dues.

PRINCIPAL PURPOSE: To educate youth on population-related matters. To coordinate youth-related activities in Asia. To provide channel of communication between youth NGOs and funding agencies. To provide information on latest population-related items.

MAIN ACTIVITIES: Organizing seminars, workshops and training courses. Issuing newsletter. Coordinating regional youth efforts.

POPULATION CONCERNS: Overpopulation; size of young population; adolescent fertility; urbanization; young women and girls are the main concerns.

SPECIFIC POPULATION ACTIVITIES: Education, counselling, advocacy, natural family planning.

FORWARD-LOOKING STRATEGIES IMPLEMENTATIONS: Unspecified.

OBSTACLES TO THE IMPLEMENATION OF FORWARD-LOOKING STRATEGIES: Lack of funding. Verbal commitments seldom translate into action.

NOTES:

Family Planning Association of India   INDIA

ADDRESS:

Bangalore Branch, Sai Krupa 65 Raulway Parallel Rd, Kumarapark West, Bangalore 560 020 India

EXECUTIVE OFFICER:		BRANCH OFFICES:
Mr. K. R. Sreenath, Organizing Secretary		

TELEPHONE NUMBER:	TELEX NUMBER:
365647	

APPROX. STAFF SIZE:	VOLUNTEER STAFF:	YEAR ESTABLISHED:
85	Many volunteers	

NUMBER OF INDIVIDUAL MEMBERS:

70 in 44 branches

FUNDING: International Planned Parenthood Federation.

PRINCIPAL PURPOSE: Family Welfare and Mother and Childhealth. Education, motivation, and service in family welfare and women's development programmes.

MAIN ACTIVITIES: Disseminating correct information regarding welfare & MCH to eligible couples. Motivation of couples to accept family planning.

POPULATION CONCERNS: Education, Counselling, Advocacy, Delivery of Services including; Sterilization, Pill, IUD, Foam, and condoms.

SPECIFIC POPULATION ACTIVITIES: Aware of the strategies, but were only implementing them in the course of activities. Limited resources and financial constraints.

FORWARD-LOOKING STRATEGIES IMPLEMENTATIONS:

OBSTACLES TO THE IMPLEMENTATION OF FORWARD-LOOKING STRATEGIES:

NOTES:

The Gandhigram Institute of
Rural Health & Family Welfare Trust

INDIA

ADDRESS:

P.O. Ambathurai R.S., Anna District, Tamilnadu, India-624 309

EXECUTIVE OFFICER:			BRANCH OFFICES:
Dr. G. Raman, MBBS, DTM&H, DPH			

TELEPHONE NUMBER:		TELEX NUMBER:
346, Chinnalapatti		

APPROX. STAFF SIZE:	VOLUNTEER STAFF:	YEAR ESTABLISHED:
200	0	1959

NUMBER OF INDIVIDUAL MEMBERS:

200

FUNDING: National, government and international agencies.

PRINCIPAL PURPOSE: To promote national and state health and family welfare programs through research, training and services.

MAIN ACTIVITIES: Research in population and health issues (field-based). Training of various cadres of health and family welfare personnel. Services: family welfare, maternity and child health, running of 5 mini health centers and 18 creches.

POPULATION CONCERNS: Containing population growth rate, promoting the small family norm, enhancing the health of mothers, children and rural people.

SPECIFIC POPULATION ACTIVITIES: Education, counselling, advocacy, demographic research, contraceptive research, delivery of services: sterilization, pill, foam, IUD, diaphragm.

FORWARD-LOOKING STRATEGIES IMPLEMENTATIONS: Involved in promoting and strengthening the government's family welfare and maternal and child health programs. Also create an awareness about national priorities and the status of women and provide information, education and assistance to men and women in making decisions about their desired number of children.

OBSTACLES TO THE IMPLEMENTATION OF FORWARD-LOOKING STRATEGIES: Lack of constant financial support and, consequently, lack of manpower support, tend to limit our area of operation.

NOTES:

The Institute of Cultural Affairs

INDIA

ADDRESS:

13 Sankli Street, 2nd Floor, Byculla, Bombay-400008, India

EXECUTIVE OFFICER:			BRANCH OFFICES:
Executive Officer rotates			

TELEPHONE NUMBER:		TELEX NUMBER:	
(91-22) 39-77-51		(953) 115849 Attn: ICA	

APPROX. STAFF SIZE:	VOLUNTEER STAFF:	YEAR ESTABLISHED:
75	9	1971

NUMBER OF INDIVIDUAL MEMBERS:

75 in 4 chapters

FUNDING: Funding from individuals, corporations and agencies.

PRINCIPAL PURPOSE: To release the human potential for planetary development.

MAIN ACTIVITIES: Training, research and demonstration are primary activities. Through the Human Resource Development Centre, conducting programs that catalyze individual development, organizational effectiveness, development interchange and new age exploration.

POPULATION CONCERNS: Concerned with processs by which women, especially those in rural areas, come to realize that they have reproductive options.

SPECIFIC POPULATION ACTIVITIES: Women's advancement programs.

FORWARD-LOOKING STRATEGIES IMPLEMENTATIONS: Implementing strategies indirectly, by focusing on individual development.

OBSTACLES TO THE IMPLEMENTATION OF FORWARD-LOOKING STRATEGIES: Difficulties with process of translation of essentially "macro" concepts to a "micro" operation.

NOTES:

International Institute for Population Sciences

INDIA

ADDRESS:

Deonar, Bombay-400088, India

EXECUTIVE OFFICER:

Dr. K. Srinivasan, Director

BRANCH OFFICES:

TELEPHONE NUMBER:	TELEX NUMBER:
5511347	

APPROX. STAFF SIZE:	VOLUNTEER STAFF:	YEAR ESTABLISHED:
125	0	1956

NUMBER OF INDIVIDUAL MEMBERS:

FUNDING: Funding by government of India.

PRINCIPAL PURPOSE: Organization focuses on teaching and research in population sciences.

MAIN ACTIVITIES: Teaching-certificate, diploma and Masters in Philosophy in Population Sciences. Research-P.H.D. and other research science projects. Publications.

POPULATION CONCERNS: Concerned with all aspects of populations.

SPECIFIC POPULATION ACTIVITIES: Education and demographic research.

FORWARD-LOOKING STRATEGIES IMPLEMENTATIONS: None.

OBSTACLES TO THE IMPLEMENTATION OF FORWARD-LOOKING STRATEGIES: None.

NOTES:

ORGANIZATION:

Institute of Social Studies Trust

INDIA

ADDRESS:

S.M.M. Theatre Crafts Museum 5, Deen Dayal Upadhyay Marg, New Delhi-2, India

EXECUTIVE OFFICER:		BRANCH OFFICES:
Mrs. Devaki Jain		ISST, Tharanga, 10th Cross, Raj mahal Vilas Ext., Bangalore-80, India, tel: 360315

TELEPHONE NUMBER:	TELEX NUMBER:	
3312972, 3312861		

APPROX. STAFF SIZE:	VOLUNTEER STAFF:	YEAR ESTABLISHED:

NUMBER OF INDIVIDUAL MEMBERS:

FUNDING: Funding through Ministry of Human Resource Development, Ministry of Labour, Ministry of Education and from international organizations.

PRINCIPAL PURPOSE: To provide research and information input into development studies, especially development aimed at elimination of poverty. In 1975, International Women's Year, ISST added to its focus issues related to the unequal roles, rights and responsibilities of men and women, especially in the context of the development process.

MAIN ACTIVITIES: Data collection, research and analysis, as an intermediary organization which influences policy-making and planning bodies; as a social action and service organization; as a documentation and information storage, retrieval and dissemination centre.

POPULATION CONCERNS: Investigation into the practice of amniocentesis and female infanticide.

SPECIFIC POPULATION ACTIVITIES: Research.

FORWARD-LOOKING STRATEGIES IMPLEMENTATIONS: Indirect implementation through dissemination of information, and consciousness-raising.

OBSTACLES TO THE IMPLEMENATION OF FORWARD-LOOKING STRATEGIES: None.

NOTES:

Karnataka Welfare Society

INDIA

ADDRESS:

P.B. No. 28, Vasavi Dharmashala Road, Chikballapur-562101, Karnataka, India

EXECUTIVE OFFICER:	BRANCH OFFICES:
C.K.M. Dastagir, Executive Director	

TELEPHONE NUMBER:	TELEX NUMBER:
286	

APPROX. STAFF SIZE:	VOLUNTEER STAFF:	YEAR ESTABLISHED:
30	5	1976

NUMBER OF INDIVIDUAL MEMBERS:

400

FUNDING: Project-related grants from donor agencies and government of India.

PRINCIPAL PURPOSE: Development of weaker sections in rural and urban areas.

MAIN ACTIVITIES: Health and family welfare. Dairy, community agriculture development. Dryland development. Social forestry.

POPULATION CONCERNS: Creating awareness about family welfare, health, nutrition.

SPECIFIC POPULATION ACTIVITIES: Education, advocacy, counselling, delivery of services.

FORWARD-LOOKING STRATEGIES IMPLEMENTATIONS: Implementing strategies put forth in paragraph 29.

OBSTACLES TO THE IMPLEMENTATION OF FORWARD-LOOKING STRATEGIES: None.

NOTES:

New Delhi Branch of Family Planning Association of India

INDIA

ADDRESS:

HQ Famliy Planning Association of India, Bajaj Bhavan, Nariman Point, Bombay-400021, India

EXECUTIVE OFFICER:

Brig. K.N. Sharma, (Ret.) Executive Secretary

TELEPHONE NUMBER:

2029080

TELEX NUMBER:

APPROX. STAFF SIZE:

150

VOLUNTEER STAFF:

8

YEAR ESTABLISHED:

1963

NUMBER OF INDIVIDUAL MEMBERS:

161

BRANCH OFFICES:

New Delhi Branch of Family Planning Association of India, No. 10 Sector-IV, R.K. Puram, New Delhi-110022, India, tel: 672359

FUNDING: Partly by FPIA-Bombay, partly by Ministry of Health and Family Welfare.

PRINCIPAL PURPOSE: Promote adoption of family planning practives through education and information. Provide supportive clinical services to acceptors of family planning methods of their choice and on voluntary basis. Provide medical termination of pregnancy as a health measure. Impart "population education" and "family life education." Undertake activites for raising status of women.

MAIN ACTIVITIES: Information and education of specified population about family planning programs. Providing population education to the younger generation. Conduct educational programs on family life as well as impart sex education wherever possible. Provide maternal and child health care. Provide clinical services in the field of famly planning. Carry out medical termination of pregnancy as a health measure. Undertake activities directed towards raising status of women.

POPULATION CONCERNS: Rapidly growing population; high level of illiteracy; high infant mortality rate; low level of nutrition.

SPECIFIC POPULATION ACTIVITIES: Education, advocacy, income-generating activities to raise status of women, counselling, delivery of services: pill, IUD, diaphragm, medical termination of pregnancy.

FORWARD-LOOKING STRATEGIES IMPLEMENTATIONS: Conduct programs to disseminate knowledge, impart education to promote family planning practices. Provide supportive clinical services, like sterilization, IUD inserton, and supply contraceptives of acceptors' choice and on a voluntary basis. Carry out developmental/income-generating activities to raise social status of women.

OBSTACLES TO THE IMPLEMENTATION OF FORWARD-LOOKING STRATEGIES: Illiteracy and tradition have created a bound society.

NOTES:

Association of Southeast Asian Nations
Population Coordination Unit INDONESIA

ADDRESS:

J1, M.T. Haryono 9-11, P.O. Box 186 JKT, Jakarta 10002, Indonesia

EXECUTIVE OFFICER:		BRANCH OFFICES:
Benjamin D. DeLeon, Executive Director		

TELEPHONE NUMBER:	TELEX NUMBER:
8195-251	48181 BKKBN IA

APPROX. STAFF SIZE:	VOLUNTEER STAFF:	YEAR ESTABLISHED:
4	0	1980

NUMBER OF INDIVIDUAL MEMBERS:

FUNDING: Funding from Australian government and UNFPA.

PRINCIPAL PURPOSE: To coordinate and monitor the implementation of the ASEAN Population Progam.

MAIN ACTIVITIES: To serve the ASEAN countries (Brunei, Darussalam, Indonesia, Malaysia, Philippines, Singapore, Thailand) in developing and implementing cooperative projects in the field of population.

POPULATION CONCERNS: Projects on the contribution of women to population and development; integration of population and development; ASEAN training for population and development; population mobility and urbanization; population information network; morbidity and mortality differential and aging.

SPECIFIC POPULATION ACTIVITIES: Education, demographic research, promotion of women's welfare.

FORWARD-LOOKING STRATEGIES IMPLEMENTATIONS: Enhancing the welfare of women through income-generating opportunities and promotion of population education and health.

OBSTACLES TO THE IMPLEMENATION OF FORWARD-LOOKING STRATEGIES: None.

NOTES:

Department of Community Nutrition & Family Resources

INDONESIA

ADDRESS:

Dept. GMSK Facultas Institut Pertanian Bogor, J1, Raya Pajararan, Bojor 16143, Indonesia

EXECUTIVE OFFICER:

Dr. Hidayat Syarief

BRANCH OFFICES:

TELEPHONE NUMBER:

(0251) 23081 ext. 248

TELEX NUMBER:

APPROX. STAFF SIZE:	VOLUNTEER STAFF:	YEAR ESTABLISHED:
30	6	1963

NUMBER OF INDIVIDUAL MEMBERS:

FUNDING:

PRINCIPAL PURPOSE: Education and training to prepare students in the field of community in the field of community nutrition and family resources with major concern for improvement of welfare of the people; research; extension of public services.

MAIN ACTIVITIES: Training, research, and public services.

POPULATION CONCERNS: Integration of nutrition and family planning.

SPECIFIC POPULATION ACTIVITIES: Education, demographic research, counselling, delivery of services.

FORWARD LOOKING-STRATEGIES IMPLEMENTATIONS: Extension activities; training students through courses, family resource management.

OBSTACLES TO THE IMPLEMENTATION OF FORWARD-LOOKING STRATEGIES: Budget restraints.

NOTES:

International for Family Health

INDONESIA

ADDRESS:

J1. Pasirkaliki 186, Bandung, Indonesia

EXECUTIVE OFFICER:			BRANCH OFFICES:
Executive Secretary			

TELEPHONE NUMBER:		TELEX NUMBER:	
(22) 52902			

APPROX. STAFF SIZE:	VOLUNTEER STAFF:	YEAR ESTABLISHED:	
8	0	1977	

NUMBER OF INDIVIDUAL MEMBERS:

7 affiliated chapters

FUNDING: Major donor agencies.

PRINCIPAL PURPOSE: Not specified.

MAIN ACTIVITIES: Research and training.

POPULATION CONCERNS: Women's and children's health.

SPECIFIC POPULATION ACTIVITIES: Education, contraceptive research, delivery of services: Norplant, sterilization.

FORWARD-LOOKING STRATEGIES IMPLEMENTATIONS: None.

OBSTACLES TO THE IMPLEMENATION OF FORWARD-LOOKING STRATEGIES: None.

NOTES:

Asian-Pacific Youth Forum

JAPAN

ADDRESS:

6-12 Izumi 3-chome, Suginami-ku, Tokyo 168, Japan

EXECUTIVE OFFICER:

Tadahiko Okumura, Chairman

BRANCH OFFICES:

TELEPHONE NUMBER:	TELEX NUMBER:
322-5164	c/o J29397 OISCA

APPROX. STAFF SIZE:	VOLUNTEER STAFF:	YEAR ESTABLISHED:
	unspecified no.	1979

NUMBER OF INDIVIDUAL MEMBERS:

17 affiliated chapters

FUNDING:

PRINCIPAL PURPOSE: Coordination of youth organizatons' activities in Asia and the Pacific countries in the field of development.

MAIN ACTIVITIES:

POPULATION CONCERNS:

SPECIFIC POPULATION ACTIVITIES:

FORWARD-LOOKING STRATEGIES IMPLEMENTATIONS: None.

OBSTABLES TO THE IMPLEMENATION OF FORWARD-LOOKING STRATEGIES: None.

NOTES:

Japanese Organization for International Cooperation in Family Planning (JOICFP) **JAPAN**

ADDRESS:

JOICEP, Hoken Kaikan Bekkan, Sixth Floor, 1-1 Sadohara-cho, Tokoyo, 162, Japan

EXECUTIVE OFFICER:			BRANCH OFFICES:
Chojiro Kunii			

TELEPHONE NUMBER:	TELEX NUMBER:	
(03) 268-5875		

APPROX. STAFF SIZE:	VOLUNTEER STAFF:	YEAR ESTABLISHED:
24 secretariat level		1968

NUMBER OF INDIVIDUAL MEMBERS:

FUNDING:

PRINCIPAL PURPOSE: JOICFP is a non-governmental organization which provides cooperation and assistance to family planning and maternal child health programmes in developing countries and seeks to motivate the Japanese public on global population issues.

MAIN ACTIVITIES: JOICFP focal activity is the Integrated Family Planning, Nutrition and Parasite Control Programmes (IP), in addition, JOICFP offers educational aids such as maternal and child health handbooks, flip charts, slides, video tapes, and the monthly magazine "World and Population."

POPULATION CONCERNS: Family Planning conferences, workshops, and the monthly magazine "World and Population."

SPECIFIC POPULATION ACTIVITIES: Education and advocacy.

FORWARD-LOOKING STRATEGIES IMPLEMENTATIONS: Implementation in a general way.

OBSTACLES TO THE IMPLEMENTATION OF FORWARD-LOOKING STRATEGIES: None.

NOTES:

The International Cultural Society

JAPAN

ADDRESS:

%Bon Muse, Asahi Bldg. B1, 1-1 Hakata-eki-mae, Z chōme, Hakata-ku, Fukuoka City, 812 Japan

EXECUTIVE OFFICER:			BRANCH OFFICES:
Nobuko Yamaguchi, President			

TELEPHONE NUMBER:	TELEX NUMBER:
092-441-1821	

APPROX. STAFF SIZE:	VOLUNTEER STAFF:	YEAR ESTABLISHED:
0	5	1978

NUMBER OF INDIVIDUAL MEMBERS:

37

FUNDING: Annual membership fee, subscription for meeting, and interest from publishing are principal funding sources.

PRINCIPAL PURPOSE: Lifelong education for women; study (especially foreign languages) of the members; teaching students not only languages, but also history and culture of their society.

MAIN ACTIVITIES: Monthly board meetings, regular meetings with invited guest speakers, travel abroad with prolonged stay in foreign countries; publishing summaries of speeches and textbooks. Concerned with women's and adults' roles in society and family planning.

POPULATION CONCERNS:

SPECIFIC POPULATION ACTIVITIES: Education, natural family planning

FORWARD-LOOKING STRATEGIES IMPLEMENTATIONS: Chief Executive lectures extensively for many organizations.

OBSTACLES TO THE IMPLEMENTATION OF FORWARD-LOOKING STRATEGIES: Difficulties with fundraising and stereotypical thought patterns in Japan inhibit implementation.

NOTES:

Federation of Family Planning Associations, Malaysia

MALAYSIA

ADDRESS:

81A, Jalan SS 15/5A, Subang Jaya, 47500 PETALING JAYA

EXECUTIVE OFFICER:			BRANCH OFFICES:
Mrs. Cheng Yin Mooi, Executive Director,			

TELEPHONE NUMBER:	TELEX NUMBER:
7339409/7336290	

APPROX. STAFF SIZE:	VOLUNTEER STAFF:	YEAR ESTABLISHED:
187	2162	1958

NUMBER OF INDIVIDUAL MEMBERS:

3423

FUNDING: International Planned Parenthood Federation; Malaysian Government Grant; Private Donations.

PRINCIPAL PURPOSE: To advocate the utilization of family planning programmes and services for the achievement of strong, healthy and developed family units. To complement the government's efforts in social development, preventative health and family planning programes. To recruit women to provide consumer platform for designing future services.

MAIN ACTIVITIES: Family life education programmes; Women's development projects to promote health; and resource develoment projects to generate income.

POPULATION CONCERNS: To promote family planning in the country.

SPECIFIC POPULATION ACTIVITIES: Support services; (pap smear, breast and cervix examination, infertility test, gynecological treatment, male involvement program etc.)

FORWARD-LOOKING STRATEGIES IMPLEMENTATIONS: Implementing special women's development project which focuses on health education,decision making, and reproductive health needs. Clinics provide family planning services ranging from cancer screening to health counselling for women.

OBSTACLES TO THE IMPLEMENTATION OF FORWARD-LOOKING STRATEGIES: Government is aware of the importance of the role of women in nation building. A Prime Minister's Secretariat for women has been established. However, some politicians misinterpreted the new population policy and advocated that women stay home to have more children. This has created a confused environment towards family planning.

NOTES:

International Council on Management of Population Programs **MALAYSIA**

ADDRESS:

158 Jalan Dahlia, Taman Uda Jaya, 68000 Ampang, Kuala Lumpur, Malaysia

EXECUTIVE OFFICER:	BRANCH OFFICES:
Dr. M.A. Sattar, Executive Director	

TELEPHONE NUMBER:	TELEX NUMBER:
4573234	MA 33685

APPROX. STAFF SIZE:	VOLUNTEER STAFF:	YEAR ESTABLISHED:
12	0	1973

NUMBER OF INDIVIDUAL MEMBERS:

57

FUNDING: Numerous sources such as CIDA, SIDA, IDRC, CFTC, UNFPA, Hewlett Foundation, Ford Foundation, OPEC Fund, etc.

PRINCIPAL PURPOSE: The improvement of management of population programs, worldwide.

MAIN ACTIVITIES: Training workshops on population program management at regional and international levels. International conference of members who are heads of national population programs or directors of management institutes concerned with social sector management. Publications (books, reports, newsletter) on population program. Management projects and research on various aspects of population program management, on a world-wide basis.

POPULATION CONCERNS: Concerned with improved management of population programs. In that area, many aspects of development are covered as population programs become more and more integrated with development.

SPECIFIC POPULATION ACTIVITIES: Women's programs, program management, women in development, community participation, information dissemination, training and consultation.

FORWARD-LOOKING STRATEGIES IMPLEMENTATIONS: Involved in a project entitled Leadership and Management for Women. This project is presently in seven countries of Asia and has plans to expand to Africa and Latin America. Research activities have started in Latin America.

OBSTACLES TO THE IMPLEMENTATION OF FORWARD-LOOKING STRATEGIES: No serious obstacles. There is a new awareness among both international agencies and within the developing world about the importance of skills training and management development for women both within government programs and NGOs. From a modest start in 1973, the project has expanded considerably. In all training programs, women are given preference.

NOTES:

Sarawak Family Planning Association

MALAYSIA

ADDRESS:

P.O. Box 788, 93716 Kuching, Sarawak, Malaysia

EXECUTIVE OFFICER:

Dr. C.K. Lam, Executive Secretary

BRANCH OFFICES:

TELEPHONE NUMBER:	TELEX NUMBER:
426982	

APPROX. STAFF SIZE:	VOLUNTEER STAFF:	YEAR ESTABLISHED:
42	100+	1964

NUMBER OF INDIVIDUAL MEMBERS:

19,500 in 17 affiliated chapters

FUNDING: Commodity grant from IPPF. A small annual cash grant from government. Financial self-reliance.

PRINCIPAL PURPOSE: To disseminate knowledge of family planning and facilities for scientific contraception so that married couples may space or limit their families and thus promote thier happiness in married life and mitigate the evils of ill-health and overcrowding.

MAIN ACTIVITIES: Clinical planning services, including Pap smear, pregnancy test, etc. Information and educational family planning services. Infertility consultation. Day care, nursey service.

POPULATION CONCERNS: Concerned with making family planning services available to members of the reproductive age group.

SPECIFIC POPULATION ACTIVITIES: Education, counselling, day care nursery, delivery of services: pill, IUD, diaphragm, foam, Depo-Provera and condom.

FORWARD-LOOKING STRATEGIES IMPLEMENTATIONS: Implementing those adopted by IPPF.

OBSTACLES TO THE IMPLEMENTATION OF FORWARD-LOOKING STRATEGIES: None.

NOTES:

*Business Address: Jalan Jawa 93400 Kuching, Sarawak, Malaysia

New Zealand Family Planning Association, Inc.

NEW ZEALAND

ADDRESS:

P.O. Box 68-200, Newton, Auckland, New Zealand

EXECUTIVE OFFICER:

Gillian Burrell, Executive Secretary

BRANCH OFFICES:

TELEPHONE NUMBER:

31-834

TELEX NUMBER:

FAM PLAN

APPROX. STAFF SIZE:

VOLUNTEER STAFF:

occasional

YEAR ESTABLISHED:

1936

NUMBER OF INDIVIDUAL MEMBERS:

900

FUNDING: Government grants for staff salaries, and client fees.

PRINCIPAL PURPOSE: To advocate and promote facilities for scientific contraception. To provide facilities where any person can receive advice on contraception, infertility and sexuality. To provide education, for all age groups, on contraception, human relationships and the implications of population growth.

MAIN ACTIVITIES: Clinic services and education programs.

POPULATION CONCERNS: None.

SPECIFIC POPULATION ACTIVITIES: Education, advocacy, demographic and contraceptive research and delivery of services including the Pill, IUD, diaphragm, foam, Norplant, Depo-Provera, natural family planning, condoms and male sterilization.

FORWARD-LOOKING STRATEGIES IMPLEMENTATIONS: Education of women and men in all aspects of sexuality.

OBSTACLES TO THE IMPLEMENTATION OF FORWARD-LOOKING STRATEGIES: Lack of funds for educational projects.

NOTES: Originally started by a group of women who lobbied the government to set up birth control clinics, it became a member of IPPF in 1959.

---

*Business Address: 3 France Street, Newton, Auckland, New Zealand

Family Planning Association of Pakistan

PAKISTAN

ADDRESS:

3-A, Temple Road, Lahore, Pakistan

EXECUTIVE OFFICER:

Begum Surayya Jabeen, Director General

BRANCH OFFICES:

TELEPHONE NUMBER:	TELEX NUMBER:
306183, 212999	44877 PEARL PK

APPROX. STAFF SIZE:	VOLUNTEER STAFF:	YEAR ESTABLISHED:
443	0	1953

NUMBER OF INDIVIDUAL MEMBERS:

3500 in 137 chapters

FUNDING: Government of Pakistan, international agencies and local fundraising.

PRINCIPAL PURPOSE: Promotion of family planning to achieve a balance between Pakistan's population and resources.

MAIN ACTIVITIES: Mother and child health, family planning, emphasis on women and youth development in rural areas. Training, community development, functional research, evaluation and communications.

POPULATION CONCERNS: Improving quality of life, health, education, income. Lowering of fertility, mortality and morbity rates. Improvement in status of women, child welfare and community development.

SPECIFIC POPULATION ACTIVITIES: Education, demographic research, contraceptive research, counselling, advocacy, social surveys, delivery of services: sterilization, pill, IUD, diaphragm, foam, Norplant, Depo-Provera, condom and Norigest.

FORWARD-LOOKING STRATEGIES IMPLEMENTATIONS: Attended conference and implementing unspecified strategies.

OBSTACLES TO THE IMPLEMENTATION OF FORWARD-LOOKING STRATEGIES: Difficult to get skilled manpower and resources, especially transportation to go to distant areas.

NOTES:

Maternity and Child Welfare Association

PAKISTAN

ADDRESS:

30 F Gulburg II, Lahore, PAKISTAN

EXECUTIVE OFFICER:

Dr. A.K. Awan, President

BRANCH OFFICES:

TELEPHONE NUMBER:	TELEX NUMBER:
882146	NWFP/MCWAP-Sind

APPROX. STAFF SIZE:	VOLUNTEER STAFF:	YEAR ESTABLISHED:
20	31	1961

NUMBER OF INDIVIDUAL MEMBERS:

574

FUNDING: Voluntary fundraising.

PRINCIPAL PURPOSE: Promoting maternal and child health, fertility health.

MAIN ACTIVITIES: Developing MCH Centers for providing MCH services, and practical research.

POPULATION CONCERNS: Family Planning and Child Spacing.

SPECIFIC POPULATION ACTIVITIES: Education, counselling, sterilization, Pill, IUD, Diaphram and Depo-provera

FORWARD-LOOKING STRATEGIES IMPLEMENTATIONS:

OBSTACLES TO THE IMPLEMENTATION OF FORWARD-LOOKING STRATEGIES:

NOTES:

Asian Development Bank   **PHILIPPINES**

ADDRESS:

P.O. Box 789, Manila, Philippines 2800

EXECUTIVE OFFICER:			BRANCH OFFICES:
Masao Fujioka, President			

TELEPHONE NUMBER:		TELEX NUMBER:
831-72-11		23103

APPROX. STAFF SIZE:	VOLUNTEER STAFF:	YEAR ESTABLISHED:
1600	0	1966

NUMBER OF INDIVIDUAL MEMBERS:

N/A

FUNDING: The financial resources of the Bank consist of ordinary capital resources, comprising subscribed capital, reserves and funds raised through borrowings; and Special Funds, comprising contributions made by member countries and amounts previously set aside from the paid-in capital.

PRINCIPAL PURPOSE: To promote economic and social progress in the Bank's developing member countries in the Asia Pacific region.

MAIN ACTIVITIES: To make loans and equity investments for the economic and social advancement of developing member countries; to provide technical assistance for the preparation and execution of development projects and programs and advisory services; to promote investment of public and private capital for development purposes; and to respond to requests for assistance in coordinating development policies and plans of member countries.

POPULATION CONCERNS: The Bank, wherever possible, includes population components in its health projects and in other projects where feasible. Free standing population projects may also be considered.

SPECIFIC POPULATION ACTIVITIES: Education, counselling, delivery of services (all appropriate family planning methods are considered).

FORWARD-LOOKING STRATEGIES IMPLEMENTATIONS: Implementing strategies as part of ongoing health and population work and as part of our new Women and Development Strategy.

OBSTACLES TO THE IMPLEMENTATION OF FORWARD-LOOKING STRATEGIES: No particular obstacles have yet been identified.

NOTES:

Asian Nongovernmental Organization Coalition for Agrarian Reform **PHILIPPINES**

ADDRESS:

P.O. Box 870, M.C.P.O. Makati, Philippines

EXECUTIVE OFFICER:

Edgardo T. Valenzuela, Executive Secretary

BRANCH OFFICES:

TELEPHONE NUMBER:	TELEX NUMBER:
816-30-33	23312 RHP-PH*

APPROX. STAFF SIZE:	VOLUNTEER STAFF:	YEAR ESTABLISHED:
6	0	1979

NUMBER OF INDIVIDUAL MEMBERS:

23 chapters

FUNDING: Foreign grants, membership dues, consultancy.

PRINCIPAL PURPOSE: To promote NGO involvement in rural development and to initiate selected programs which assist in strengthening capabilities of NGOs in the Asian region. ANGOC programs are related to the outcome of the World Conference on Agrarian Reform and Rural Development.

MAIN ACTIVITIES: Promotion of GOVT./NGO/Donor cooperation in rural development, capability building of NGOs, study tours, workshops, conferences, development publications.

POPULATION CONCERNS: Programs relating to the effect of population on rural poor, e.g. landless workers.

SPECIFIC POPULATION ACTIVITIES: Advocacy.

FORWARD-LOOKING STRATEGIES IMPLEMENTATIONS: ANGOC is appraising its action-research program focused on women in rural development.

OBSTACLES TO THE IMPLEMENTATION OF FORWARD-LOOKING STRATEGIES: Unknown, program is still in planning stages.

NOTES: *TELEX must read: ANGOCARRD MANILA

---

*Business Address: 47 Matrinco Building 2178, Pasong Tamo Street Makati, Metro Manila 3117, Philippines

Dr. J. Fabella Mem. Hospital Comprehensive Family Planning Center . PHILIPPINES

ADDRESS:

Lope de Vega St., Sta. Cruz, Manila, Philippines

EXECUTIVE OFFICER:

Dr. Ruben A. Apelo, Project Driector

BRANCH OFFICES:

TELEPHONE NUMBER:

711-76-86

TELEX NUMBER:

APPROX. STAFF SIZE:

50

VOLUNTEER STAFF:

YEAR ESTABLISHED:

1970

NUMBER OF INDIVIDUAL MEMBERS:

FUNDING: 72% of the core staff is funded by JFMH and POPCOM supports the remaining 28%.

PRINCIPAL PURPOSE: To support the National Population Program goals of reducing population growth rate and promoting family welfare.

MAIN ACTIVITIES: Clinic services, IEC activities, home visits of defaulters by fieldworkers, family planning counselling, staff training, medical training and human reproduction research and counselling,

POPULATION CONCERNS:

SPECIFIC POPULATION ACTIVITIES: Contraceptive research, counselling, training, and delivery of services which include: Sterilization, Pill, IUD, Norplant and Depo-provera.

FORWARD LOOKING-STRATEGIES IMPLEMENTATIONS:

OBSTACLES TO THE IMPLEMENTATION OF FORWARD-LOOKING STRATEGIES:

NOTES:

Family Planning Organization of the Philippines

PHILIPPINES

ADDRESS:

No. 50 Doña Hemady Street, New Manila, Quezon City, Philippines

EXECUTIVE OFFICER:

Atty. Ramon A. Tagle, Jr., Executive Director

BRANCH OFFICES:

TELEPHONE NUMBER:

721-7101, 721-4067, 721-7302

TELEX NUMBER:

APPROX. STAFF SIZE:	VOLUNTEER STAFF:	YEAR ESTABLISHED:
162	0	1969

NUMBER OF INDIVIDUAL MEMBERS:

500+ in 24 chapters

FUNDING:

PRINCIPAL PURPOSE: Five major purposes: 1. complement and supplement national effort in service delivery; 2. complement and supplement population education programs for youth; 3. strengthen women's development programs in rural and urban depressed communities; 4. upgrade staff and volunteer capabilities; 5. re-adopt pioneering/advocacy role to promote and improve acceptance of family planning program among media, policymakers, religious and community leaders.

MAIN ACTIVITIES: Clinic services: family planning and other related clinic services. Training, intensive information and media campaign including mass media, community activities, interpersonal communication, evaluation and research.

POPULATION CONCERNS: To adhere to a non-coercive approach which respects religious beliefs in family planning practice. To provide all family planning methods that will cater to specific choice of clientele. To increase participation of women in national development efforts. To inculcate population values and norms among pre-schoolers and promote awareness on adolescent fertility care/management.

SPECIFIC POPULATION ACTIVITIES: Education, contraceptive research, counselling, advocacy, delivery of services: sterilization, pill, IUD, diaphragm, foam, Depo-Provera, natural family planning. Training, evaluation.

FORWARD-LOOKING STRATEGIES IMPLEMENTATIONS: Women in development training program. Women in development through income-generating projects. Development and family life education for the youth.

OBSTACLES TO THE IMPLEMENTATION OF FORWARD-LOOKING STRATEGIES: Dwindling support funds, lukewarm cooperation of community leaders, peace and order situation, politics.

NOTES:

Makati Family Planning and Population Center

PHILIPPINES

ADDRESS:

Ground Floor Makati Municipal Building/J.P. Rizal, Makati, Metro Manila, Philippines

EXECUTIVE OFFICER:

Iva C. Anastacio, M.D., M.P.H., Chief of Family Planning Dept.

BRANCH OFFICES:

TELEPHONE NUMBER:

854458

TELEX NUMBER:

APPROX. STAFF SIZE:	VOLUNTEER STAFF:	YEAR ESTABLISHED:
22	5	1972

NUMBER OF INDIVIDUAL MEMBERS:

96 in 24 chapters

FUNDING: Makati Municipality funding and a budget of 50,000 pesos a year go to salaries.

PRINCIPAL PURPOSE: To implement a comprehensive family planning and population program through IEC, training and clinical services which are aimed to reduce fertility and ultimately to improve the quality of life of the family and the society.

MAIN ACTIVITIES: IEC, training, clinical services (contraceptives, tubal ligation and vasectomy), cancer detection.

POPULATION CONCERNS: Availability of family planning methods.

SPECIFIC POPULATION ACTIVITIES: Education, demographic research, counselling, advocacy, pre-marital counselling, delivery of services: sterilization, pill, IUD (copper T), diaphragm, foam, Depo-Provera, natural family planning.

FORWARD-LOOKING STRATEGIES IMPLEMENTATIONS: Counsel women troubled by unwanted pregnancies by doing menstrual regulation (up to 8 weeks delayed menstruation only). Motivation to use family planning methods and sterilization. Nutrition lectures.

OBSTACLES TO THE IMPLEMENTATION OF FORWARD-LOOKING STRATEGIES: Misconceptions, particularly of husbands and influence of religion, (Catholicism) in the Philippines.

NOTES:

FUNDING: Funding by both local and foreign funding institutions, e.g. Philippine government, AID, UNFPA, WHO.

PRINCIPAL PURPOSE: To provide management and technical services and increase the involvement of the private sector in efforts to bring about timely and effective solutions to the Philippine population problem.

MAIN ACTIVITIES: Research and research utilization, project research and development training, communication, audio-visual production and publications. The Foundation provides services in these areas not only to population agencies but to other local and foreign development agencies.

POPULATION CONCERNS: Adolescent fertility management, community resource development, health and family planning, women in development, commercial marketing of contraceptives, curriculum integration of population for program professionals, made-specific approaches in family planning.

SPECIFIC POPULATION ACTIVITIES: Education, counselling, contraceptive research, advocacy, evaluation of programs.

FORWARD-LOOKING STRATEGIES IMPLEMENTATIONS: Implementing strategies which seek to eliminate obstacles to equality of women created by stereotypes, perceptions and attitudes through formal and informal education and training. Also implementing strategies that seek to involve women in the mainstream of development through projects that develop their managerial/organizational/ planning abilities and help them engage in economic activities.

OBSTACLES TO THE IMPLEMENTATION OF FORWARD-LOOKING STRATEGIES: Difficulty in dealing with stereotypes, perceptions and attitudes which discriminate against women.

NOTES:

---

*Business Address: South Superhighway off Villamor Interchange, Makati, Metro Manila, Philippines

Singapore Planned Parenthood Association

SINGAPORE

ADDRESS:

11 Penang Lane #05-02, Singapore Council of Social Service, Singapore 0923

EXECUTIVE OFFICER:

Mrs. Amy Tan, Executive Director

BRANCH OFFICES:

TELEPHONE NUMBER:	TELEX NUMBER:
3385155	

APPROX. STAFF SIZE:	VOLUNTEER STAFF:	YEAR ESTABLISHED:
7	1	1949

NUMBER OF INDIVIDUAL MEMBERS:

84

FUNDING: By the International Planned Parenthood Federation and local resources.

PRINCIPAL PURPOSE: The Association promotes the concept of family life and parenthood education through informational and educational programmes aimed at improving the quality of life with emphasis on the special needs of adolescents and young people.

MAIN ACTIVITIES: To provide information and education services in family life education and counselling.

POPULATION CONCERNS:

SPECIFIC POPULATION ACTIVITIES: Education, Counselling

FORWARD-LOOKING STRATEGIES IMPLEMENTATIONS: Aware of the strategies, and are implementing them in daily course of activities.

OBSTACLES TO THE IMPLEMENTATION OF FORWARD-LOOKING STRATEGIES: Not applicable.

NOTES:

Department of Labor

SRI-LANKA

ADDRESS:

Workers Education Division, Colombo 5, Sri-Lanka

EXECUTIVE OFFICER:		BRANCH OFFICES:
Commissioner of Labor		

TELEPHONE NUMBER:	TELEX NUMBER:
586313	

APPROX. STAFF SIZE:	VOLUNTEER STAFF:	YEAR ESTABLISHED:
2500		1964

NUMBER OF INDIVIDUAL MEMBERS:

FUNDING: By the State and UNFPA for special projects.

PRINCIPAL PURPOSE: Educating the work force on labor matters, on family welfare to enable them to improve their quality of life.

MAIN ACTIVITIES: Education.

POPULATION CONCERNS: To maintain moderate population.

SPECIFIC POPULATION ACTIVITIES: Education, demographic research, counselling and advocacy.

FORWARD-LOOKING STRATEGIES IMPLEMENTATIONS: Leadership training of women.

OBSTACLES TO THE IMPLEMENTATION OF FORWARD-LOOKING STRATEGIES:

NOTES:

Family Planning Association of Sri Lanka

SRI LANKA

ADDRESS:

37/27 Bullers Lane, P.O. Box 365, Colombo 7, Sri Lanka

EXECUTIVE OFFICER:			BRANCH OFFICES:
Daya Abeywickrema, Executive Director			

TELEPHONE NUMBER:	TELEX NUMBER:	
584157	22238 TRUST CE	

APPROX. STAFF SIZE:	VOLUNTEER STAFF:	YEAR ESTABLISHED:
130	75 mngmnt, 40,000+	1953

NUMBER OF INDIVIDUAL MEMBERS:

450 in field

FUNDING: IPPF, Family Health International, and Programme for International Training in Health, North Carolina.

PRINCIPAL PURPOSE: To educate the people of Sri Lanka on the need for family planning to establish better living standards and improved health.

MAIN ACTIVITIES: Field level inter-personal educational programs using 40,000 volunteers who are mainly women. Distribute contraceptives through a contraceptive retail marketing program. Conduct a Clinical Training and Services Centre, population education program for youth, research on contraceptives and general family planning work.

POPULATION CONCERNS: Concerned with need for family planning to achieve better living standards and improved health.

SPECIFIC POPULATION ACTIVITIES: Education, counselling, contraceptive research, advocacy, demographic research, delivery of services: sterilization, pill, IUD, diaphragm, foam, Norplant, Depo-Provera, natural family planning.

FORWARD-LOOKING STRATEGIES IMPLEMENTATIONS: Implementing whenever possible. For example, int the area of nutrition, mother-child care, environmental educational programs for women.

OBSTACLES TO THE IMPLEMENTATION OF FORWARD-LOOKING STRATEGIES: Shortage of funds.

NOTES:

Sarvodaya Shramadana Sangamaya

SRI LANKA

ADDRESS:

98 Rawatawatte Road, Moratuwa, Sri Lanka

EXECUTIVE OFFICER:			BRANCH OFFICES:
Dr. A.T. Ariyaratne, President			

TELEPHONE NUMBER:	TELEX NUMBER:	
507159		

APPROX. STAFF SIZE:	VOLUNTEER STAFF:	YEAR ESTABLISHED:
250	3000 field workers	1958

NUMBER OF INDIVIDUAL MEMBERS:

1465 members in 28 chapters

FUNDING: Membership fees, local contributions, international funding.

PRINCIPAL PURPOSE: To bring about self-reliance among people, especially in the rural area, through self-development and integrated activities involving maximum citizens' participation and to create a "no poverty society."

MAIN ACTIVITIES: Village development activities such as day care for children, health and sanitation, agricultural programs, leadership training, women's development, small scale industries, educational programming for youth, religious and cultural activities, all geared towards improving the quality of life.

POPULATION CONCERNS: Educating mothers and young women in matters relating to child and family welfare.

SPECIFIC POPULATION ACTIVITIES: Education, arranging for counselling at village and district levels, delivery of services: natural family planning. Creating awareness among women of available facilities and assisting them in obtaining them.

FORWARD-LOOKING STRATEGIES IMPLEMENTATIONS: Emphasizing village level decision-making and policy planning, integrating women into every aspect of society, women's rights, building awareness, legal literacy, raising women's consciousness.

OBSTACLES TO THE IMPLEMENTATION OF FORWARD-LOOKING STRATEGIES: Getting the participation and understanding of men, necessary in the process of implementation of the Forward-Looking Strategies.

NOTES:

The Planned Parenthood of Thailand THAILAND

ADDRESS:

8 Soi Dai-Dee, Vibhavadi-Rangsit Rd, Ladyao, Bangken, Bangkok 10900, Thailand

EXECUTIVE OFFICER:			BRANCH OFFICES:
Dr. Aree Somboonsuk, Pres. & Dr. Charoong, Pasuwan, Ex. Dir.			

TELEPHONE NUMBER:	TELEX NUMBER:	
579-0084-6	Cable Code: Patthai, Bankok	

APPROX. STAFF SIZE:	VOLUNTEER STAFF:	YEAR ESTABLISHED:
89	3	1970

NUMBER OF INDIVIDUAL MEMBERS:

1,300

FUNDING: The Royal Thai Government and The International Planned Parenthood Federation (IPPF).

PRINCIPAL PURPOSE: To provide extensive family planning and family life information to the general public through IEC, clinical, training, and counselling services, and to promote population development.

MAIN ACTIVITIES: Community-Based Delivery of contraceptives; Information, Education, & Communication; Clinical Services; Family Life Education Promotion through training, lecturing and counselling; Integrated quality of life improvement; resource development.

POPULATION CONCERNS: Family Planning and Quality of Life Improvement.

SPECIFIC POPULATION ACTIVITIES: Education, Counselling Advocacy, Delivery of Services including; Sterilization, Pill, IUD, Norplant, Depo-provera, and Natural Family Planning.

FORWARD-LOOKING STRATEGIES IMPLEMENTATIONS: Alleviate the under status of women by educating them about their reproductive right, which is basic to human rights, and enhancing career development, and the setting up of community funds for better home economic management and other forms of well-being for women.

OBSTACLES TO THE IMPLEMENTATION OF FORWARD-LOOKING STRATEGIES: Some women are still ignorant and indifferent towards having equal status & the same basic rights as men. Community participation in career development and the setting up of community funds has to be encouraged more. A complete cycle of comprehensive rural development needs to be further introduced.

NOTES:

Population & Community Development Association

THAILAND

ADDRESS:

8 Sukhumvit 12, Bangkok 10110, Thailand

EXECUTIVE OFFICER:	BRANCH OFFICES:
Mechai Viravaidya, Secretary General	

TELEPHONE NUMBER:	TELEX NUMBER:
2510402-3	82603 PDA TH

APPROX. STAFF SIZE:	VOLUNTEER STAFF:	YEAR ESTABLISHED:
618	12000	1977

NUMBER OF INDIVIDUAL MEMBERS:

FUNDING: Some PDA programs are self-supporting; others funded by international NGOs, international governmental organizations, official foreign donor agencies and the Royal Thai government.

PRINCIPAL PURPOSE: To foster development throughout the country in the areas of primary health care, parasite control, sanitation, appropriate technology, refugee assistance, water supply, agricultural marketing, and family planning.

MAIN ACTIVITIES: Family planning and primary health care programs focus on urban and rural mobile sterilization clinics, vasectomy festivals, health services to school children, family planning counselling to adults. Appropriate technology and rural development includes sanitation and water resource development, integrated farming and animal husbandry, marketing, local income-generating and small scale industries development. Research and dissemination. Emergency relief and social welfare.

POPULATION CONCERNS: The Association recognizes that only through a reduction of the population growth rate can development activities be successful. Most of PDA's concerns are directly related to population concerns.

SPECIFIC POPULATION ACTIVITIES: Education, counselling, delivery of services: sterilization, pill, IUD, diaphragm, foam, Norplant, Depo-Provera.

FORWARD-LOOKING STRATEGIES IMPLEMENTATIONS: To ensure a voluntary and free choice, family planning information, education and services including all appropriate methods of family planning are made available on a nationwide basis.

OBSTACLES TO THE IMPLEMENTATION OF FORWARD-LOOKING STRATEGIES: No specific obstacles, but PDA's activities must be consistent with the principles of community-based fertility-led development, and with the broad development goals of the Royal Thai governemnt.

NOTES:

UN Economic & Social Commission for Asia and the Pacific-Population Division **THAILAND**

ADDRESS:

United Nations Economic & Social Commission for Asia and the Pacific, Rajdamern Nok Ave., Bankok 10200, Thailand

EXECUTIVE OFFICER:	BRANCH OFFICES:
Mr. Nibhon Debavalya, Chief,, Population Division, ESCAP	

TELEPHONE NUMBER:	TELEX NUMBER:
282-9161	82392 ESCAPT

APPROX. STAFF SIZE:	VOLUNTEER STAFF:	YEAR ESTABLISHED:
45		1969

NUMBER OF INDIVIDUAL MEMBERS:

47 member and associate member governments

FUNDING: Projects mainly through UNFPA; some posts by the regular budget of the United Nations.

PRINCIPAL PURPOSE: To educate about overpopulation and study trends in the region.

MAIN ACTIVITIES: Publications & Studies.

POPULATION CONCERNS: The monitoring of overpopulation and recommendations for the region.

SPECIFIC POPULATION ACTIVITIES: Education, Demographic research.

FORWARD-LOOKING STRATEGIES IMPLEMENTATIONS: Paragraphs 57, 77, 119, 156, 208, 310, 314, 315, 323, 331-334, 352, 359, 369, and 372.

OBSTACLES TO THE IMPLEMENTATION OF FORWARD-LOOKING STRATEGIES: With regard to paragraph 315, it currently is not possible to hire female staff owing to a hiring freeze.

NOTES:

National Primary Health Care Advisory Committee

TUVALU

ADDRESS:

Ministry of Social Services, P.O. Box 36, Vaiaku, Funafuti, Tuvalu

EXECUTIVE OFFICER:			BRANCH OFFICES:

TELEPHONE NUMBER:		TELEX NUMBER:	
751			

APPROX. STAFF SIZE:	VOLUNTEER STAFF:	YEAR ESTABLISHED:
20	8 island leaders	1982

NUMBER OF INDIVIDUAL MEMBERS:
80 in 10 chapters

FUNDING: Overseas aid, mostly from World Health Organization.

PRINCIPAL PURPOSE: To initiate, advise and support national primary health care plans.

MAIN ACTIVITIES: To see that primary health care plans are implemented and that family planning is made a priority.

POPULATION CONCERNS: Overpopulation in Tuvalu and rise in trends such as rates of unwed mothers and rates of discontinued use of contraception.

SPECIFIC POPULATION ACTIVITIES: Education, counselling, family planning campaigns and delivery of services including sterilization, the pill, IUD, Depo-Provera, natural family planning and condoms.

FORWARD-LOOKING STRATEGIES IMPLEMENTATIONS: Were not aware of the Strategies.

OBSTACLES TO THE IMPLEMENTATION OF FORWARD-LOOKING STRATEGIES: None.

NOTES:

Women's Organizations

Boston Globe Photo

Union of Australian Women **AUSTRALIA**

ADDRESS:

Box 24, Trades Hall, 4 Woulburn Street, Sydney NSW 2000, Australia

EXECUTIVE OFFICER:		BRANCH OFFICES:
Audrey McDonald, National Secretary		

TELEPHONE NUMBER:	TELEX NUMBER:
264-2880	

APPROX. STAFF SIZE:	VOLUNTEER STAFF:	YEAR ESTABLISHED:
		1950

NUMBER OF INDIVIDUAL MEMBERS:

1000

FUNDING: Membership dues, donations, fundraising, government grants

PRINCIPAL PURPOSE: Improve the status of women in the workplace.

MAIN ACTIVITIES: Women's lobby group, Deputations, Pickets, etc.

POPULATION CONCERNS:

SPECIFIC POPULATION ACTIVITIES:

FORWARD-LOOKING STRATEGIES IMPLEMENTATIONS: Assisting government in taking up FLS issues in its' National Agenda for Woman's Policy directives to improve the status of women.

OBSTACLES TO THE IMPLEMENTATION OF FORWARD-LOOKING STRATEGIES: None indicated

NOTES:

Women's Action Alliance Australia

AUSTRALIA

ADDRESS:

493 Riversdale Road, Camberwell, Victoria, Australia 3124

EXECUTIVE OFFICER:

Pauline Smit, Natl' President

BRANCH OFFICES:

TELEPHONE NUMBER:

(03) 882-8809

TELEX NUMBER:

APPROX. STAFF SIZE:	VOLUNTEER STAFF:	YEAR ESTABLISHED:
No paid staff	varies	1975

NUMBER OF INDIVIDUAL MEMBERS:

8 chapter-all states

FUNDING: Membership Subscriptions, donations, and fundraising.

PRINCIPAL PURPOSE: To raise the status of women in the Australian community and to strengthen the family as the basis of Australian society.

MAIN ACTIVITIES: Lobby politicians, public education, women's development, training courses, and telephone and referral services.

POPULATION CONCERNS: None indicated.

SPECIFIC POPULATION ACTIVITIES: Recognition of women's unpaid work.

FORWARD-LOOKING STRATEGIES IMPLEMENTATIONS: None indicated.

OBSTACLES TO THE IMPLEMENTATION OF FORWARD-LOOKING STRATEGIES:

NOTES:

Kali for Women

INDIA

ADDRESS:

N-84 Panchshila Park, New Delhi-110017, India

EXECUTIVE OFFICER:

Ms. Ritu Menon & Ms. Urvashi Butalia, Executive Trustees

BRANCH OFFICES:

TELEPHONE NUMBER:	TELEX NUMBER:
6436597	

APPROX. STAFF SIZE:	VOLUNTEER STAFF:	YEAR ESTABLISHED:
4		1984

NUMBER OF INDIVIDUAL MEMBERS:

FUNDING: Occasional grants, revenue generated by the sale of our books, and providing editorial consultancy.

PRINCIPAL PURPOSE: To publish academic and creative work by women writers, mostly from the Third World.

MAIN ACTIVITIES: Produce reasonably priced material in the social services, humanities, general non-fiction, and fiction.

POPULATION CONCERNS: Not Applicable.

SPECIFIC POPULATION ACTIVITIES: None indicated.

FORWARD-LOOKING STRATEGIES IMPLEMENTATIONS: None indicated.

OBSTACLES TO THE IMPLEMENTATION OF FORWARD-LOOKING STRATEGIES:

NOTES:

ORGANIZATION:

Kasturba Mahila Utthan Mandal Kumaun

INDIA

ADDRESS:

Lakshmi Ashram, P.O. Kausani, District Almora, Uttar Pradesh 263639, India

EXECUTIVE OFFICER:

Miss Radha Bhatt, Secretary

BRANCH OFFICES:

TELEPHONE NUMBER:

Kausani 23

TELEX NUMBER:

APPROX. STAFF SIZE:	VOLUNTEER STAFF:	YEAR ESTABLISHED:
20		1946

NUMBER OF INDIVIDUAL MEMBERS:

FUNDING: Funded through government grants and individual private donations.

PRINCIPAL PURPOSE: Focus is on educational and social work for social and economic advancement of women of Kumaun.

MAIN ACTIVITIES: Schooling on Gandhian ideals of basic education; training center for spinning and weaving; village center activities (oil press, flour mill, library); pre-school balwadi program; Dhauladevi Block (Almora); environmental work, especially for reforestation and against ill managed mining; income generation program.

POPULATION CONCERNS: No direct population concerns.

SPECIFIC POPULATION ACTIVITIES: None

FORWARD-LOOKING STRATEGIES IMPLEMENTATIONS: Not implementing strategies.

OBSTACLES TO THE IMPLEMENTATION OF FORWARD-LOOKING STRATEGIES: N/A

NOTES:

Japanese Association of University Women

JAPAN

ADDRESS:

Toyama Mansions 2411, OG 7-7-18 Shinjuku, Shinjuku, Tokyo, 160, Japan

EXECUTIVE OFFICER:			BRANCH OFFICES:
Ms. Sumiko Ito, President			

TELEPHONE NUMBER:	TELEX NUMBER:	
(03)202-0572		

APPROX. STAFF SIZE:	VOLUNTEER STAFF:	YEAR ESTABLISHED:

NUMBER OF INDIVIDUAL MEMBERS:

FUNDING:

PRINCIPAL PURPOSE:

MAIN ACTIVITIES:

POPULATION CONCERNS:

SPECIFIC POPULATION ACTIVITIES:

FORWARD-LOOKING STRATEGIES IMPLEMENTATIONS:

OBSTACLES TO THE IMPLEMENTATION OF FORWARD-LOOKING STRATEGIES:

NOTES:

The above information was not provided.

Pan Pacific and South-East Asia Women's Association of Japan **JAPAN**

ADDRESS:

2-20-2 Higashi Nakano, Nakanoku, Tokyo 164, Japan

EXECUTIVE OFFICER:			BRANCH OFFICES:
Rinko Yamazaki			

TELEPHONE NUMBER:	TELEX NUMBER:
03-361-1490	

APPROX. STAFF SIZE:	VOLUNTEER STAFF:	YEAR ESTABLISHED:
11	40	1928

NUMBER OF INDIVIDUAL MEMBERS:

FUNDING: Membership fees and donations.

PRINCIPAL PURPOSE: Broadening and deepening mutual understanding and friendship between countries and areas in Pacific and South-East Asia. Cooperation for the improvement of social contributions and thereby contributing towards establishing a truly peaceful World.

MAIN ACTIVITIES: Seminars, community study meetings, English conversation class, and publications.

POPULATION CONCERNS: Rapidly aging population in Japan.

SPECIFIC POPULATION ACTIVITIES:

FORWARD-LOOKING STRATEGIES IMPLEMENTATIONS: Aware

OBSTACLES TO THE IMPLEMENTATION OF FORWARD-LOOKING STRATEGIES: Yes

NOTES:

The National Collective of Rape Crisis & Related Groups of Aoteasoa, Inc. NEW ZEALAND

ADDRESS:

P.O. Box 6181, Te Aro, Wellington, New Zealand

EXECUTIVE OFFICER:		BRANCH OFFICES:

TELEPHONE NUMBER:	TELEX NUMBER:
856768	

APPROX. STAFF SIZE:	VOLUNTEER STAFF:	YEAR ESTABLISHED:
3 National workers	24 local workers	1985

NUMBER OF INDIVIDUAL MEMBERS:

33

FUNDING: Government funds, donations, grants, pledges.

PRINCIPAL PURPOSE: To be a strongly political body, providing a public profile for the issue of rape, and working towards the elimination of violence against women and children.

MAIN ACTIVITIES: Counselling, Support, Education, Prevention, and Advocacy.

POPULATION CONCERNS: Concerns with high population areas, and also outreach and work in rural, lower population areas.

SPECIFIC POPULATION ACTIVITIES:

FORWARD-LOOKING STRATEGIES IMPLEMENTATIONS: Not aware of the strategies

OBSTACLES TO THE IMPLEMENTATION OF FORWARD-LOOKING STRATEGIES:

NOTES:

Pan-Pacific & Southeast Asia Women's Association- New Zealand Branch NEW ZEALAND

ADDRESS:

Ms. E. Grant, Natl' Secretary, 51 B Patapu Street, Wanganui, New Zealand

EXECUTIVE OFFICER:			BRANCH OFFICES:
Miss P.M. Payne, Natl' President			

TELEPHONE NUMBER:	TELEX NUMBER:	
064-36-354		

APPROX. STAFF SIZE:	VOLUNTEER STAFF:	YEAR ESTABLISHED:
	3	1928

NUMBER OF INDIVIDUAL MEMBERS:

120

FUNDING: Membership.

PRINCIPAL PURPOSE: To arouse and foster interest among New Zealand women in strengthening the bonds of peace by promoting better understanding and friendship with women of other pacific and southeast Asian countries.

MAIN ACTIVITIES: Sponsoring Pacific islands nurses to attend seminars, and occasionally supplying medical equipment through a medical trust fund. Sponsoring speakers; donating to numerous relief appeals and offering hospitality to overseas students.

POPULATION CONCERNS: No direct involvement

SPECIFIC POPULATION ACTIVITIES: Education

FORWARD-LOOKING STRATEGIES IMPLEMENTATIONS: The Association is aware of the strategies, but has not yet begun implementation.

OBSTACLES TO THE IMPLEMENTATION OF FORWARD-LOOKING STRATEGIES: Sexual discrimination, cultural taboos, rural domination of caste in administrative processes.

NOTES:

Metro Manila Council of
Women Balikatan Movement, Inc. PHILIPPINES

ADDRESS:

82-A Midland 11, Washington, Greenhills West, San Juan, Metro Manila, Philippines

EXECUTIVE OFFICER:	BRANCH OFFICES:
Leonarda N. Camacho, Chairperson	

TELEPHONE NUMBER:	TELEX NUMBER:
785725	

APPROX. STAFF SIZE:	VOLUNTEER STAFF:	YEAR ESTABLISHED:
8	70	1980

NUMBER OF INDIVIDUAL MEMBERS:

17,000

FUNDING: Funded donations of friends, members and foreign friends.

PRINCIPAL PURPOSE: To enhance the socio-economic-legal status of its members through regular seminars on varied subjects; study tours of places of interest and relevance; cultural events and livelihood projects.

MAIN ACTIVITIES: Thrice-a-week seminars, monthly meetings, monthly study tours of places of interest and relevance, demonstrations on the use of herbal plants and preparation of selected recipes, and annual cultural events.

POPULATION CONCERNS: Breastfeeding.

SPECIFIC POPULATION ACTIVITIES: Education.

FORWARD-LOOKING STRATEGIES IMPLEMENTATIONS: Main activities are already implementations of the strategies.

OBSTACLES TO THE IMPLEMENTATION OF FORWARD-LOOKING STRATEGIES: None.

NOTES:

Africa:
North Africa & the Middle East

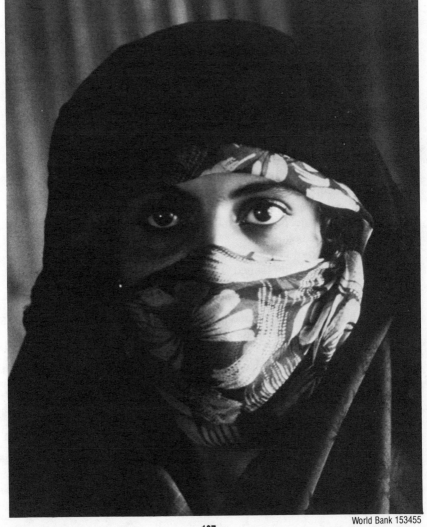

World Bank 153455

The Middle East and North Africa

High fertility rates—the result of early marriage, the low status of women and cultural and religious attitudes—characterize the demographic pattern of the Middle East and North Africa. Women bear an average of six children, in contrast to two children per woman in the industrialized countries. In 1986 the population of the region was 286 million, and the United Nations projects the population to grow to 466 million by the year 2000, a 40 percent increase in 14 years. As in other parts of the Third World, it is a young population; 40 percent are under 15 years of age.

The Middle East and North Africa include rich oil-producing countries such as Saudi Arabia and Kuwait, poor countries such as Afghanistan and North and South Yemen, and middle-income countries such as Israel, Lebanon and Cyprus. With the exception of Israel and Cyprus, the Muslim faith is the dominant religion and agriculture is the way of life for the majority. There are also large numbers of migrant workers from countries outside the region (India, Pakistan, Thailand and the Philippines) as well as from countries within the region (Jordan, Lebanon, Syria, North and South Yemen, Egypt) into the United Arab Emirates and Saudi Arabia. Concern about the political and cultural impact of workers from outside the region has led recently to immigration controls.

Israel however, has had an "open door" immigration policy for all Jews since independence in 1948. Initially the population growth rate was high, primarily due to the high fertility of the Oriental Jews and the Arab minority. In 1948, 85 percent of the Jewish population was of European origin; by 1981, the balance had shifted to 52 percent of Afro-Asian origin. What kind of a society Israel becomes in the future will be determined to a great extent by its ethnic balance.

The rapid growth of cities throughout the region has been, for the most part, uncontrolled and unplanned. This urban explosion has severely taxed the ability of governments to provide housing, schools, hospitals, roads, sanitation and other public utilities. It has also contributed to the deterioration of the environment. Food production has fallen and many Middle Eastern countries now import more than half of their food supply. Increasing agricultural production is constrained not only by the lack of modern agricultural techniques, but also by serious water shortages and soil erosion caused by overgrazing.

The resolution of smoldering political conflicts is another challenge for the region. The establishment of Israel as a Jewish homeland in 1948 has been a continuing source of conflict, primarily due to the displacement of the Palestinian population. More than two million Palestinians, original refugees and their descendants, are registered with the United Nations Relief and Works Agency for Palestinian Refugees. In addition, more than one million Afghans have crossed into Pakistan since the Russian invasion in 1979, and the Iran-Iraq war has caused 250,000 deaths and another

700,000 casualties since 1980. Finally, the civil war in Lebanon shows no signs of abating.

Despite increases in literacy and improved living standard since World War II, fertility has not declined. It appears that, unlike Western Europe, economic development alone will not reduce fertility among Muslims. Life expectancy varies greatly, with a high of 70 years in Israel, Cyprus and Kuwait and close to it in the United Arab Emirates, Saudi Arabia, Bahrain, Jordan and Lebanon. On the low end of the scale are North and South Yemen (48 years), the three North African countries (57 years) and Afghanistan (37 years).

Attitudes toward family planning vary also. Concerned about the impact of rapid population growth on social and economic development, Egypt and Tunisia have family planning programs, and Morocco provides information through its public health service and a non-governmental organization. Other countries are trying to improve health services for women and life in rural areas to stem the tide of migration to the cities. Political, cultural and religious obstacles, however, continue to block the implementation of family planning programs.

One of the biggest obstacles is the low status of women, particularly in the more traditional societies. Women's legal rights and levels of participation are severely restricted in many countries. As a result, more than 50 percent of women throughout the region are illiterate and their participation in the labor force is low. Women's life is marriage and child bearing with great stress placed on having male children. High fertility and consecutive pregnancies are linked to high death and sickness rates among children and their mothers.

The status of women in Israel is similar to that of women in Western Europe, and the status of women in Cyprus, Lebanon, Jordan, Turkey and the three North African countries is changing for the better. Women's organizations in these countries have been instrumental in bringing about the changes that have taken place.

United Nations/K. Muldoon/ARA

The future is for tomorrow
The future is soon

Beyond the walls closed like clenched fists
Through the bars encircling the sun
Our thoughts are vertical and our hopes
The future coiled in the heart climbs towards the sky
Like upraised arms in a sign of farewell
Arms upright, rooted in the light
In a sign of an appeal to love
To return to my life
I press you against my breast my sister
And I say to you await tomorrow
Builder of liberty and tenderness
For we know

The future is soon
The future is for tomorrow.

Anna Greki
Translator:
Mildred P. Mortimer

Reprinted from Mildred P. Mortimer, "Algerian Poetry of French Expression," Volume 6, *African Literature Today*, E. D. Jones, editor, published by Holmes & Meier Publishers, New York, 1973. Reprinted with permission of the publisher and editor.

World Bank Photo by Tomas Sennett

Women's Organizations in Population

UN Photo 153,468/John Isaac

Israel Women's Network

ISRAEL

ADDRESS:

P.O.B. 3171, Jerusalem, 91037, Israel

EXECUTIVE OFFICER:

Alice Shalvi, Chairperson

BRANCH OFFICES:

TELEPHONE NUMBER:	TELEX NUMBER:
02-528057	

APPROX. STAFF SIZE:	VOLUNTEER STAFF:	YEAR ESTABLISHED:
1	Depends on activities	1982

NUMBER OF INDIVIDUAL MEMBERS:

600

FUNDING: Donations.

PRINCIPAL PURPOSE: To lobby and educate against discrimination of women in Israel.

MAIN ACTIVITIES: Education and lobbying.

POPULATION CONCERNS: Currently lobbying for the ability of women to obtain legal abortions in Jerusalem.

SPECIFIC POPULATION ACTIVITIES: Education and advocacy.

FORWARD-LOOKING STRATEGIES IMPLEMENTATIONS: Aware of the strategies, but not currently implementing them.

OBSTACLES TO THE IMPLEMENTATION OF FORWARD-LOOKING STRATEGIES:

NOTES:

NA'AMAT Movement of Working Women & Volunteers

ISRAEL

ADDRESS:

93 Arlozorov Street, 62098 Tel Aviv, Israel

EXECUTIVE OFFICER:

Masha Lubelsky, President

BRANCH OFFICES:

TELEPHONE NUMBER:

(03) 262362

TELEX NUMBER:

APPROX. STAFF SIZE:	VOLUNTEER STAFF:	YEAR ESTABLISHED:
4,500	100's	1921

NUMBER OF INDIVIDUAL MEMBERS:

750,000

FUNDING: Histadrut subsidy, Government subsidy, contributions of Na'amat Organizations in 12 countries.

PRINCIPAL PURPOSE: Well-being and advancement of women and children.

MAIN ACTIVITIES: Day Care, vocational training, political training for women, etc.

POPULATION CONCERNS: In some of the branches there are seminars and study days on the subject of family planning.

SPECIFIC POPULATION ACTIVITIES: Education.

FORWARD-LOOKING STRATEGIES IMPLEMENTATIONS:

OBSTACLES TO THE IMPLEMENTATION OF FORWARD-LOOKING STRATEGIES:

NOTES:

The Union of Women's Work Committees

ISRAEL

ADDRESS:

Jerusalem-Beitthanina, P.O. Box 20576, ISRAEL

EXECUTIVE OFFICER:			BRANCH OFFICES:
Zahira Kamal, Chief Exec.			

TELEPHONE NUMBER:	TELEX NUMBER:
283937	

APPROX. STAFF SIZE:	VOLUNTEER STAFF:	YEAR ESTABLISHED:
19	12	1978

NUMBER OF INDIVIDUAL MEMBERS:

53,500

FUNDING: Several European donor organizations.

PRINCIPAL PURPOSE: To organize the large mass of women in rural and urban areas to develop their abilities and improve their economic, social cultural standards, and to strengthen their role in the general national struggle of our people. To improve vocational training opportunities to women and provide the means which can help by being a productive member in society. To improve the educational social and political level; to coordinate with worker's unions to defend women workers' rights. To improve the health situation of women and family.

MAIN ACTIVITIES: Vocational centers, collective projects, literacy centers, nurseries and kindergarten, to provide health guidance to all women specially mothers.

POPULATION CONCERNS:

SPECIFIC POPULATION ACTIVITIES: Education, counselling and Natural Family Planning.

FORWARD-LOOKING STRATEGIES IMPLEMENTATIONS:

OBSTACLES TO THE IMPLEMENTATION OF FORWARD-LOOKING STRATEGIES:

NOTES:

WIZO

ISRAEL

ADDRESS:

WIZO, David Hamelech, 38, Tel-Aviv Israel

EXECUTIVE OFFICER:

Mrs. Raya Yaglom

BRANCH OFFICES:

TELEPHONE NUMBER:	TELEX NUMBER:
03-257321	wiz 98151

APPROX. STAFF SIZE:	VOLUNTEER STAFF:	YEAR ESTABLISHED:
		1920

NUMBER OF INDIVIDUAL MEMBERS:

FUNDING: Note indicated.

PRINCIPAL PURPOSE: Social welfare, women's advancement, children's education.

MAIN ACTIVITIES: Children's education from 0-17 and advancement of all women in all the aspects.

POPULATION CONCERNS:

SPECIFIC POPULATION ACTIVITIES: Education, counselling and natural family planning.

FORWARD-LOOKING STRATEGIES IMPLEMENTATIONS: Working to affect legislation.

OBSTACLES TO THE IMPLEMENTATION OF FORWARD-LOOKING STRATEGIES:

NOTES:

Village Welfare Society

LEBANON

ADDRESS:

Box 576 Beirut, Lebanon

EXECUTIVE OFFICER:

Mrs. Fuad Najjar

BRANCH OFFICES:

TELEPHONE NUMBER:	TELEX NUMBER:
34-32-84	20669 LE

APPROX. STAFF SIZE:	VOLUNTEER STAFF:	YEAR ESTABLISHED:
5	15	1951

NUMBER OF INDIVIDUAL MEMBERS:

50

FUNDING: UNESCO gift coupons, donations and subscriptions.

PRINCIPAL PURPOSE: To help women migrating from villages to cities develop working skills.

MAIN ACTIVITIES: Improving literacy and maintaining five dispensaries and women's youth clubs.

POPULATION CONCERNS: Educating villagers on family planning so they may act as informed couples.

SPECIFIC POPULATION ACTIVITIES: Education, demographic research, counselling and natural family planning.

FORWARD-LOOKING STRATEGIES IMPLEMENTATIONS: None.

OBSTACLES TO THE IMPLEMENTATION OF FORWARD-LOOKING STRATEGIES: Financial constraints and security problems due to the war in Lebanon.

NOTES:

International Alliance of Women

MALTA

ADDRESS:

P.O. Box 355, Valletta, Malta

EXECUTIVE OFFICER:

Mrs. Olive, President

BRANCH OFFICES:

TELEPHONE NUMBER:	TELEX NUMBER:
824098	

APPROX. STAFF SIZE:	VOLUNTEER STAFF:	YEAR ESTABLISHED:
4		1904

NUMBER OF INDIVIDUAL MEMBERS:

850

FUNDING: Membership fees and donations.

PRINCIPAL PURPOSE: To promote equality of men and women in liberties, status and opportunities. To encourage women to accept responsibilities and to use their rights so that women's status will be respected.

MAIN ACTIVITIES: Advocacy liaison between affiliated organizations of the alliance and the United Nations and its special agencies.

POPULATION CONCERNS: Those population issues related to the status of women and family life.

SPECIFIC POPULATION ACTIVITIES: Education (seminars, workshops and related projects).

FORWARD LOOKING-STRATEGIES IMPLEMENTATIONS: These five commissions are working in the FLS: Civil and Political, Economic, Education International understanding, and Social.

OBSTACLES TO THE IMPLEMENTATION OF FORWARD-LOOKING STRATEGIES: Lack of funds.

NOTES:

Union Nationale des
Femmes Marocaines

MOROCCO

ADDRESS:

3 rue El Afghani, Rabat, Morocco

EXECUTIVE OFFICER:

Princess Lalla Fatima Zohra, President

BRANCH OFFICES:

TELEPHONE NUMBER:	TELEX NUMBER:
27937	

APPROX. STAFF SIZE:	VOLUNTEER STAFF:	YEAR ESTABLISHED:
2500	0	1969

NUMBER OF INDIVIDUAL MEMBERS:

53000

FUNDING: Moroccan government and UNFPA.

PRINCIPAL PURPOSE: To help women in all sectors.

MAIN ACTIVITIES: Creating women's artisan and agricultural cooperatives, fighting illiteracy, protecting infancy.

POPULATION CONCERNS: Helping poor, deprived, rural women in above activities.

SPECIFIC POPULATION ACTIVITIES: Education, demographic and contraceptive research, counselling and advocacy, delivery of services: pill, natural family planning.

FORWARD LOOKING-STRATEGIES IMPLEMENTATIONS: Aware, but not currently implementing.

OBSTACLES TO THE IMPLEMENTATION OF FORWARD-LOOKING STRATEGIES: None.

NOTES:

Association Turque des Femmes des Carrieres Juridiques

TURKEY

ADDRESS:

Abdulhak Hamit caddesi, No. 8/3, Taksim, Turkey

EXECUTIVE OFFICER:

Hikmet Gungor, President

BRANCH OFFICES:

TELEPHONE NUMBER:	TELEX NUMBER:
1501243	

APPROX. STAFF SIZE:	VOLUNTEER STAFF:	YEAR ESTABLISHED:
		1968

NUMBER OF INDIVIDUAL MEMBERS:

140

FUNDING: Membership fees.

PRINCIPAL PURPOSE: To perform studies on women's rights.

MAIN ACTIVITIES: Sponsoring conferences, panel discussions and seminars.

POPULATION CONCERNS: Concerned with those population issues related to women's rights.

SPECIFIC POPULATION ACTIVITIES: Counselling and advocacy.

FORWARD-LOOKING STRATEGIES IMPLEMENTATIONS: None.

OBSTACLES TO THE IMPLEMENTATION OF FORWARD-LOOKING STRATEGIES: None.

NOTES:

National Council of Turkish Women

TURKEY

ADDRESS:

Akay Cad. No. 15-2, Bakanliklar - Ankara, Turkey

EXECUTIVE OFFICER:			BRANCH OFFICES:
Enise Arat, President			

TELEPHONE NUMBER:		TELEX NUMBER:
172604		

APPROX. STAFF SIZE:	VOLUNTEER STAFF:	YEAR ESTABLISHED:
	52	1959

NUMBER OF INDIVIDUAL MEMBERS:

200 and 14 affiliated chapters

FUNDING: Member fees, donations and income from social activities.

PRINCIPAL PURPOSE: To ensure solidarity in the material and moral development of Turkish women.

MAIN ACTIVITIES: The National Council of Turkish Women is affiliated with the International Council of Women and pursues activities related to ICW resolutions. Examples are: initiating education programs for women, especially in rural areas and sponsoring seminars and publishing material on topics such as changing technology and its effect on women.

POPULATION CONCERNS: Concerned with many population issues and how they relate to Turkish women.

SPECIFIC POPULATION ACTIVITIES: Education, demographic research, counselling, scientific conferences.

FORWARD-LOOKING STRATEGIES IMPLEMENTATIONS: Sponsor educational conferences on the Forward-Looking Strategies in rural areas.

OBSTACLES TO THE IMPLEMENTATION OF FORWARD-LOOKING STRATEGIES: Tradition and cultural attitudes toward women.

NOTES:

Population, Development & Health Organizations

UN Photo 152,237/John Isaac

UN Photo 153,537/John Isaac

Cyprus Family Planning Association

CYPRUS

ADDRESS:

25 Bouboulinas Street, Nicosia, Cyprus

EXECUTIVE OFFICER:

Niki Pastalides, Executive Director

BRANCH OFFICES:

TELEPHONE NUMBER:	TELEX NUMBER:
452791	

APPROX. STAFF SIZE:	VOLUNTEER STAFF:	YEAR ESTABLISHED:
5	30	1971

NUMBER OF INDIVIDUAL MEMBERS:

150

FUNDING: International Planned Parenthood Federation and local funds.

PRINCIPAL PURPOSE: To educate for responsible parenthood and family life and to provide family planning clinical services.

MAIN ACTIVITIES: Conducting campaigns on family planning and sex education and providing clinical services, marriage guidance counselling services and youth advisory services.

POPULATION CONCERNS: The association has submitted to the government suggestions for the implementation of a population policy.

SPECIFIC POPULATION ACTIVITIES: Education, advocacy, counselling, and making available the pill, IUD, diaphragm and natural family planning.

FORWARD LOOKING-STRATEGIES IMPLEMENTATIONS: The association is working on implementation, although no specific strategies have been targeted.

OBSTACLES TO THE IMPLEMENTATION OF FORWARD-LOOKING STRATEGIES: Opposition from religious and pro-natalist groups as well as individuals.

NOTES:

Central Agency for Public Mobilization and Statistics, Population Studies and Research Centre   EGYPT

ADDRESS:

PSRC, Nasr City, Cairo, Egypt

EXECUTIVE OFFICER:			BRANCH OFFICES:
Mr. Ahmed El Baz, Chief of Central Administration			

TELEPHONE NUMBER:	TELEX NUMBER:	
604393	92395, CAPMAS, U.N.	

APPROX. STAFF SIZE:	VOLUNTEER STAFF:	YEAR ESTABLISHED:
127		1971

NUMBER OF INDIVIDUAL MEMBERS:

127 and five affiliated chapters

FUNDING: Government funding.

PRINCIPAL PURPOSE: To study and analyse population statistics and censuses, to conduct specialized population field surveys, and to sponsor training sessions in demography.

MAIN ACTIVITIES: Perform demographic studies and projections on topics such as: fertility, mortality, migration, nuptiality, employment, etc. The findings are published semi-annually.

POPULATION CONCERNS: Population studies and demographic analysis.

SPECIFIC POPULATION ACTIVITIES: Demographic research.

FORWARD-LOOKING STRATEGIES IMPLEMENTATIONS: None.

OBSTACLES TO THE IMPLEMENTATION OF FORWARD-LOOKING STRATEGIES: None.

NOTES:

Egyptian Nurses Syndicate

EGYPT

ADDRESS:

5 Sarai Street, Hanial, Cairo, Egypt

EXECUTIVE OFFICER:

BRANCH OFFICES:

TELEPHONE NUMBER:

987627

TELEX NUMBER:

APPROX. STAFF SIZE:	VOLUNTEER STAFF:	YEAR ESTABLISHED:
12	6	1952

NUMBER OF INDIVIDUAL MEMBERS:

37,000

FUNDING: Membership fees, donations and the support of Ministry of Health and Ministry of Social Affairs.

PRINCIPAL PURPOSE: Counselling; nursing by-laws; services to members; seminars and workshops.

MAIN ACTIVITIES: To provide counselling and services to members. To act as an ad-hoc committee for Ministry of Health (Nursing department).

POPULATION CONCERNS: Family Planning, child survival, population welfare and nurses welfare.

SPECIFIC POPULATION ACTIVITIES: Education, counselling and advocacy.

FORWARD LOOKING STRATEGIES IMPLEMENTATIONS: Health education, conferences and meetings for family planning protection of nurses rights.

OBSTACLES TO THE IMPLEMENTATION OF FORWARD-LOOKING STRATEGIES: Misunderstanding from governing bodies.

NOTES:

Hoda Shaarawi

EGYPT

ADDRESS:
1057 Corniche El, Nile, Cairo, Egypt

EXECUTIVE OFFICER:			BRANCH OFFICES:
Fawkiya Wahbi, Chairman of the Board			

TELEPHONE NUMBER:		TELEX NUMBER:	
847682			

APPROX. STAFF SIZE:	VOLUNTEER STAFF:	YEAR ESTABLISHED:
15	some	1923

NUMBER OF INDIVIDUAL MEMBERS:
700 in 50 chapters

FUNDING: Did not indicate.

PRINCIPAL PURPOSE: To help the Egyptian family.

MAIN ACTIVITIES: Family planning centers, child care centers, library, literacy classes, and vocational training including sewing and production classes.

POPULATION CONCERNS: None indicated.

SPECIFIC POPULATION ACTIVITIES: Family planning services.

FORWARD-LOOKING STRATEGIES IMPLEMENTATIONS: Did not indicate awareness of the Strategies.

OBSTACLES TO THE IMPLEMENTATION OF FORWARD-LOOKING STRATEGIES: None.

NOTES:

Social Research Center of the American University of Cairo

EGYPT

ADDRESS:

113 Sharia Kasr, El Aini, Cairo, Egypt

EXECUTIVE OFFICER:	BRANCH OFFICES:
Dr. Laila El Hamamsy, Director	

TELEPHONE NUMBER:	TELEX NUMBER:
355-6701, ext. 6962, 355-6681	92224 AUCCAIUN

APPROX. STAFF SIZE:	VOLUNTEER STAFF:	YEAR ESTABLISHED:
40		1953

NUMBER OF INDIVIDUAL MEMBERS:

FUNDING: Grants from different institutions.

PRINCIPAL PURPOSE: To conduct and encourage social science research in Egypt, to train students and workers in research methods and techniques, and assist scholars and organizations engaged in social science research in the area.

MAIN ACTIVITIES: Research, seminars and conferences.

POPULATION CONCERNS: Demographic research and family planning.

SPECIFIC POPULATION ACTIVITIES: Demographic and contraceptive research, counselling, and delivery of services including the pill, IUD, diaphragm and natural family planning.

FORWARD-LOOKING STRATEGIES IMPLEMENTATIONS: Are aware of the Strategies but are not implementing them.

OBSTACLES TO THE IMPLEMENTATION OF FORWARD-LOOKING STRATEGIES: None.

NOTES:

ORGANIZATION:

Israel Family Planning Association

ISRAEL

ADDRESS:

P.O. Box 11595, Tel Aviv, Israel

EXECUTIVE OFFICER:

Ruth Landau

BRANCH OFFICES:

14 Sport Street
Haifa, ISRAEL

TELEPHONE NUMBER:

03-281228

TELEX NUMBER:

7 McDonald Street
Natanya, ISRAEL

APPROX. STAFF SIZE:	VOLUNTEER STAFF:	YEAR ESTABLISHED:
8	100	1966

NUMBER OF INDIVIDUAL MEMBERS:

350

FUNDING: IPPF cash grant and income from activities.

PRINCIPAL PURPOSE: Promoting family planning, family life and sex education.

MAIN ACTIVITIES: Training professionals in family planning, family life and sex education, individual counselling for adolescents and providing written material on these subjects.

POPULATION CONCERNS: IFPA promotes voluntary and free choice on issues of family planning, based on adequate information.

SPECIFIC POPULATION ACTIVITIES: Education, counselling, advocacy.

FORWARD LOOKING-STRATEGIES IMPLEMENTATIONS: Promoting the ideas of free choice accompanied by adequate information and education.

OBSTACLES TO THE IMPLEMENTATION OF FORWARD-LOOKING STRATEGIES: Financial obstacles.

NOTES:

Jordan Family Planning and Protection Association

ISRAEL

ADDRESS:

P.O. Box 19999 Jerusalem, via Israel

EXECUTIVE OFFICER:	BRANCH OFFICES:
Judge Hasan Abu Maizar	

TELEPHONE NUMBER:	TELEX NUMBER:
283636	

APPROX. STAFF SIZE:	VOLUNTEER STAFF:	YEAR ESTABLISHED:
32	13	1964

NUMBER OF INDIVIDUAL MEMBERS:

160

FUNDING: Grants from IPPF, membership subscriptions and income from contraceptive sales and clinical fees.

PRINCIPAL PURPOSE: To protect the health of mothers and children through family planning education and provision of services.

MAIN ACTIVITIES: Providing information and education on family planning and sex education, providing contraceptive services and performing studies on related subjects.

POPULATION CONCERNS: Medico-social development.

SPECIFIC POPULATION ACTIVITIES: Education, counselling, advocacy and delivery of services: pill, IUD, foam, natural family planning.

FORWARD-LOOKING STRATEGIES IMPLEMENTATIONS: Advocating the basic right of women to control their own fertility.

OBSTACLES TO THE IMPLEMENTATION OF FORWARD-LOOKING STRATEGIES: Family planning is not a national priority.

NOTES:

Arab Centre for Information Studies on Population, Development and Reconstruction   SYRIA

ADDRESS:

Cornich Tijara, Damascus, Syria

EXECUTIVE OFFICER:

Zoubeir Seif El Islam, General Secretary

BRANCH OFFICES:

TELEPHONE NUMBER:

425-303

TELEX NUMBER:

APPROX. STAFF SIZE:

6

VOLUNTEER STAFF:

YEAR ESTABLISHED:

1975

NUMBER OF INDIVIDUAL MEMBERS:

FUNDING: Membership fees, local contributions, international funding.

PRINCIPAL PURPOSE: To bring about self-reliance among people, especially in the rural area, through self-development and integrated activities involving maximum citizens' participation and to create a "no poverty society."

MAIN ACTIVITIES: Village development activities such as day care for children, health and sanitation, agricultural programs, leadership training, women's development, small scale industries, educational programming for youth, religious and cultural activities, all geared towards improving the quality of life.

POPULATION CONCERNS: Educating mothers and young women in matters relating to child and family welfare.

SPECIFIC POPULATION ACTIVITIES: Education, arranging for counselling at village and district levels, delivery of services: natural family planning. Creating awareness among women of available facilities and assisting them in obtaining them.

FORWARD-LOOKING STRATEGIES IMPLEMENTATIONS: Emphasizing village level decision making and policy planning, integrating women into every aspect of society, women's rights, building awareness, legal literacy, raising women's consciousness.

OBSTACLES TO THE IMPLEMENTATION OF FORWARD-LOOKING STRATEGIES: Getting the participation and understanding of men, necessary in the process of implementation of the Forward-Looking Strategies.

NOTES:

Centre Arabe des Etudes*
d'Info. sur la Pop., Dev. et Construction   SYRIA

ADDRESS:

B.P. 11542 Damascus Syria

EXECUTIVE OFFICER:	BRANCH OFFICES:
Zoubeir Seif El Islam, Sec. Gen.	

TELEPHONE NUMBER:	TELEX NUMBER:
425303	

APPROX. STAFF SIZE:	VOLUNTEER STAFF:	YEAR ESTABLISHED:
5	26	1974

NUMBER OF INDIVIDUAL MEMBERS:

FUNDING: Membership dues, contributions from various Arab governments.

PRINCIPAL PURPOSE: To develop Arab mass media to help in population and development advocacy.

MAIN ACTIVITIES: The orientation of young journalists toward problems of demographics and development.

POPULATION CONCERNS: Regulation of births and family planning.

SPECIFIC POPULATION ACTIVITIES: Education and demographic research.

FORWARD LOOKING-STRATEGIES IMPLEMENTATIONS:

OBSTACLES TO THE IMPLEMENTATION OF FORWARD-LOOKING STRATEGIES:

NOTES: *Arab Center for the Study of Information Concerning Population, Development and Construction

The Family Planning Association of Turkey

TURKEY

ADDRESS:

Ataç Sokak 73/3, Ankara Turkey

EXECUTIVE OFFICER: Semra Koral			BRANCH OFFICES:
TELEPHONE NUMBER: 318355/311878	**TELEX NUMBER:**		
APPROX. STAFF SIZE:	**VOLUNTEER STAFF:**	**YEAR ESTABLISHED:** 1963	
NUMBER OF INDIVIDUAL MEMBERS:			

FUNDING: IPPF and local support from government (the Ministry of Health) and, UNFPA

PRINCIPAL PURPOSE: To play an advocatory role to promote awareness and to develop a greater sense of involvement and acceptance of family planning among men, women, and influential groups; and to support governments efforts in family planning.

MAIN ACTIVITIES: Projects addressing different target groups in the community such as family planning, education for industrial workers, for religious leaders, family planning clinic and pathology laboratories, and family planning for military officers.

POPULATION CONCERNS: To promote the use and acceptance of family planning methods in Turkey.

SPECIFIC POPULATION ACTIVITIES: Education, counselling, and delivery of services.

FORWARD-LOOKING STRATEGIES IMPLEMENTATIONS:

OBSTACLES TO THE IMPLEMENTATION OF FORWARD-LOOKING STRATEGIES:

NOTES:

Women's Organizations

/World Bank Yosef Hadar

UN 54,679

National Union of Western
Saharan Women

ALGERIA

ADDRESS:

B.P. No 10 Almouradia, Alger, Algeria

EXECUTIVE OFFICER:

Mme. Guesmoula Ebbi, Secretary General

BRANCH OFFICES:

TELEPHONE NUMBER:	TELEX NUMBER:
60-10-50	66-258

APPROX. STAFF SIZE:	VOLUNTEER STAFF:	YEAR ESTABLISHED:
53		1974

NUMBER OF INDIVIDUAL MEMBERS:

45

FUNDING: Contributions and support from other organizations.

PRINCIPAL PURPOSE: To organize women for the struggle for political and social emancipation and the liberation of the homeland.

MAIN ACTIVITIES: Raising awareness and organizing several kinds of activities related to health education, lobbying, agricultural production, industry, etc.

POPULATION CONCERNS: Concerned about maternal and child health and child development.

SPECIFIC POPULATION ACTIVITIES: None.

FORWARD-LOOKING STRATEGIES IMPLEMENTATIONS: None.

OBSTACLES TO THE IMPLEMENTATION OF FORWARD-LOOKING STRATEGIES: None.

NOTES:

Arab Women's Solidarity Association

EGYPT

ADDRESS:

25 Murad Street, Giza, Egypt

EXECUTIVE OFFICER:

Dr. Nawal el Saadawi, President

BRANCH OFFICES:

TELEPHONE NUMBER:

738 350

TELEX NUMBER:

723 976

APPROX. STAFF SIZE:	VOLUNTEER STAFF:	YEAR ESTABLISHED:
5	15	1982

NUMBER OF INDIVIDUAL MEMBERS:

115 in 9 chapters

FUNDING: Did not indicate.

PRINCIPAL PURPOSE: To promote the development of the social, economic and cultural status of Arab women and strengthen the ties between them.

MAIN ACTIVITIES: Programs towards raising the consciousness of Arab women and abolishing illiteracy, ecouragement of young women in various areas, field studies and research on women in urban and rural areas, conferences on women in Arab society and publications of materials on Arab women.

POPULATION CONCERNS: None indicated.

SPECIFIC POPULATION ACTIVITIES: None indicated.

FORWARD-LOOKING STRATEGIES IMPLEMENTATIONS: Promotion of Arab women in many areas and in several countries.

OBSTACLES TO THE IMPLEMENTATION OF FORWARD-LOOKING STRATEGIES: None indicated.

NOTES:

Association des Femmes d'Egypt*

EGYPT

ADDRESS:

18 Rue Abou Bakr, El-Seidik Heliopolis, Cairo, Egypt

EXECUTIVE OFFICER:			BRANCH OFFICES:
Biadate Maher, Director			

TELEPHONE NUMBER:		TELEX NUMBER:	
244-0871			

APPROX. STAFF SIZE:	VOLUNTEER STAFF:	YEAR ESTABLISHED:
55	11	1946

NUMBER OF INDIVIDUAL MEMBERS:

300

FUNDING: State grants and donations.

PRINCIPAL PURPOSE: Serve the Egyptian family and aid those in need of help.

MAIN ACTIVITIES: Child care centers, literacy classes, construction of a home for the aged, and workshops for young girls.

POPULATION CONCERNS: Child care, material aide, charity and education.

SPECIFIC POPULATION ACTIVITIES: Education and natural family planning.

FORWARD LOOKING-STRATEGIES IMPLEMENTATIONS: Service to the young and the aged.

OBSTACLES TO THE IMPLEMENTATION OF FORWARD-LOOKING STRATEGIES: Lack of funds.

NOTES: *Association of Egyptian Women

Maadi Women's Guild

EGYPT

ADDRESS:

Maadi, Community Church, P.O. Box 218, Maadi, Cairo, EGYPT

EXECUTIVE OFFICER:			BRANCH OFFICES:
Sandy Steele, President			

TELEPHONE NUMBER:		TELEX NUMBER:	
351-2755			

APPROX. STAFF SIZE:	VOLUNTEER STAFF:	YEAR ESTABLISHED:
24		1946

NUMBER OF INDIVIDUAL MEMBERS:

180

FUNDING: Self-supporting.

PRINCIPAL PURPOSE: To raise funds for charitable organizations requesting assistance from our benevolence committee.

MAIN ACTIVITIES: Christmas bazaar, publication of phone book and cookbook, Bible study, biweekly newsletter and benevolence.

POPULATION CONCERNS:

SPECIFIC POPULATION ACTIVITIES:

FORWARD-LOOKING STRATEGIES IMPLEMENTATIONS:

OBSTACLES TO THE IMPLEMENTATION OF FORWARD-LOOKING STRATEGIES:

NOTES:

Africa: Subsaharan Africa

World Bank Photo/Kay Chernush

137

Sub-Saharan Africa

The 46 predominantly agricultural countries of Sub-Saharan Africa have a combined population of 434 million. The annual growth rate is 3.1 percent and rising. According to the United Nations, the total fertility rate of the region is 6.9 children per woman; the average of eight births per woman in Kenya is among the world's highest. Projections suggest that more than one billion people may be added to Africa's population between 1980 and 2025. As in other parts of the Third World, the population is young — 45 percent is under the age of fifteen in all countries save Gabon and South Africa.

Current prospects for sustained economic and social progress are not good. From near self-sufficiency in food production in 1970, per capita agricultural production has fallen drastically, and coupled with severe drought, has resulted in widespread famine in 19 countries that has taken many thousands of lives. Government policies (which are now changing) have not helped. The price of imported food has been kept artificially low to favor urban dwellers and has thus depressed the demand for local food crops, 60-80 percent of which are grown by women. In many countries the "carrying capacity" of the ecological systems is sorely strained. Forests are disappearing and overgrazing has led to the erosion and degradation of arable and pasture lands. Political violence and war, resulting in hundreds of thousands of refugees, has put additional strains on receiving countries. Finally, most African governments are staggering under heavy external debt burdens.

Sub-Saharan Africa is characterized by substantial migration, both within countries and across borders. This has brought rapid urbanization and the development of "primate" cities where the majority of urban populations lives. In 1960 only seven cities had populations of more than 500,000; by 1980 that number had increased to 35, nine of them in Nigeria alone. Migration across borders in search of work, particularly to South Africa, the Ivory Coast and Nigeria (which expelled two million workers when oil prices fell in 1983) is heavy. Other migrations have been involuntary; as with the refugees from war, political strife and drought. According to the United Nations, 700,000 refugees have fled from Ethiopia into Somalia, and another 700,000 into the Sudan from Uganda, Zaire, Chad and again, Ethiopia. Violence in Southern Africa, in South Africa, Angola and Mozambique, has produced additional refugees.

The rapid growth of cities has strained government abilities to provide housing, transportation, public utilities and other services such as health care and education, and to generate employment. Underemployment and unemployment are high and there is a large informal sector in urban areas. In the years ahead, however, it is the rural areas that will have to absorb surplus labor. At the same time, according to the Food and Agricultural Organization of the United Nations, populations in 14 countries are too large for the cultivable land available. Some experts believe that production can increase only by putting more land under production in the 11 countries of Central Africa that have unused or under-used land. Increases in agricultural production will be difficult to implement because of traditional practices, erosion, deforestation and desertification, land distribution inequities, and the fact that agricultural extension services in many countries do not provide credit and technical assistance to women farmers.

African governments have made heroic efforts to educate their populations. Two thirds of African countries devote at least 16 percent of their annual budgets to education, in contrast to five to seven percent for health. However, due to the eradication of smallpox, better control of malaria and yellow fever and food relief for famine victims, death rates have slowly declined. But infant and child mortality rates are high, 100 per 1,000 live births in all but nine countries. The major causes of death are infectious diseases, diarrhea and subsequent dehydration, intestinal parasites and malnutrition. Life expectancy is low, ranging from 43 years in Burkina Faso, Gambia, Mali, Niger and Angola to 56 years in Zimbabwe.

Despite the progress achieved by many governments, rapid population growth is working against their best efforts to feed, educate and care for their people; generate employment; provide services to growing cities and protect the land base. Few governments, however, have population policies. They perceive the pressure to reduce their population growth as coming from aid donors in the industrialized countries. Like the structuralist in Latin America, they believe the world economic order is unjust and at the root of their poverty, and they think that social and economic development will lower birth rates. In addition, family planning is a touchy political issue because of religious and tribal rivalries. By mid-1984, nevertheless, five countries (Botswana, Ghana, Kenya, Rwanda and Uganda) had adopted population policies aimed at reducing their populations, and some 26 countries were providing government family planning services. About 20 of the 46 countries have private services provided by national family planning associations affiliated with International Planned Parenthood Federation. The rationale for family planning in most countries however, is to improve the health of mothers and children, not necessarily to curb population growth. This is one reason why child spacing programs have been readily accepted. Child spacing has been practiced for a long time because of taboos against closely spaced births. Further, coverage is limited, especially in rural areas where many contraceptive technologies are not appropriate. In general, though, the trend is toward more open discussion of policies and programs.

Despite the fact that women grow 60 to 80 percent of the food crops, their role in most countries is restricted. Women have limited legal rights, less access to schooling and less access to resources in general. Illiteracy among women is high. In 1980 only five percent of all adult women (in contrast to 18 percent of adult men) were literate in Burkina Faso. The percentage of adult women ever enrolled in primary school ranges from a low of nine percent in Ethiopia to a high of 48 percent in Kenya.

In most parts of the world women who work outside the home have fewer children. Although urban women in Africa are beginning to participate in the formal labor force, fertility rates have not yet been affected. The urban fertility rate of 6.1 in Nigeria is nearly the same as the rural rate. Because most African women are peasant farmers with low incomes, they often welcome children to help them with the hard labor. The unmet need for contraception, therefore, is lower than in other parts of the Third World. Not only do women have children because they want them, but also because male honor is linked to the fathering of many children. There are also political reasons; for example, large numbers of children guarantee the future of the tribe. Many demographers believe that it will be the daughters of the present generation who will want smaller families.

Women in West Africa in particular have a long history of informal associations and collective action. Today there are a number of women's organizatons in Ghana, Nigeria, Sierra Leone, Senegal and the Ivory Coast, for example. There is an African women's research organization and a growing number of women academics investigating women's issues at universities throughout the continent. Women's organizations that provide credit, organize and assist women's economic projects, press governments for increased services and lobby for changes in legal structure are also beginning to flower in both East and West Africa. These organizations, and others that will surely come into existence, will play an increasingly important role in a rapidly changing Africa in the years to come.

World Bank Photo/Ray Witlin, 1976

Waiting for Mother

There are many people returning from the market
The mother of the child has a god of her own to protect her.
She will come home for us, a-running
And carrying what she bought.
What will she bring from the market?
She will trade salt, and from the profit
She will buy some meat.
When she returns, she will drop it on the floor.
She will say: "Let me have my baby!"
And she will kiss you
And she will carry you
And she will give you her breast.

Reprinted from Charlotte and Wolf Leslau, *African Poems and Love Songs*, published by Peter Pauper Press, White Plains, New York, 1970. Reprinted with permission of the publisher.

World Bank Photo/Kay Chernush

Women's Organizations in Population

Bethlehem Training Centre   # ETHIOPIA

ADDRESS:

P.O. Box 6558, Addis Abeba, Ethiopia

EXECUTIVE OFFICER:			**BRANCH OFFICES:**
Sr. Mary T. Ryan, Administrator			

TELEPHONE NUMBER:		**TELEX NUMBER:**	
184197			

APPROX. STAFF SIZE:	**VOLUNTEER STAFF:**	**YEAR ESTABLISHED:**	
18	4	1976	

NUMBER OF INDIVIDUAL MEMBERS:

FUNDING: Development funds from overseas, sale of products made by women and girls.

PRINCIPAL PURPOSE: Social and personal development of young women from the lowest economic bracket through training in income-generating activities.

MAIN ACTIVITIES: Training in employable skills, social development of young women, pre-school and day-care programme for their children.

POPULATION CONCERNS: Education of young women in self-respect, and information about family planning.

SPECIFIC POPULATION ACTIVITIES: Education, counselling, advocacy and natural family planning services.

FORWARD-LOOKING STRATEGIES IMPLEMENTATIONS: Ensuring that pregnant and lactating women have medical care and extra nutrition.

OBSTACLES TO THE IMPLEMENTATION OF FORWARD-LOOKING STRATEGIES: Lack of knowledge and cultural attitudes of poor women.

NOTES:

Women's Bureau

GAMBIA

ADDRESS:

No. 1 Marina Parade, %President's Office, State House, Banjul, Gambia, W. Africa

EXECUTIVE OFFICER:

S.K. Singhateh, Executive Secretary

BRANCH OFFICES:

TELEPHONE NUMBER:	TELEX NUMBER:
27327, 28730	

APPROX. STAFF SIZE:	VOLUNTEER STAFF:	YEAR ESTABLISHED:
21	2	1980

NUMBER OF INDIVIDUAL MEMBERS:

FUNDING: Through the Gambia government and through donor agencies such as UNIFEM, Africare, Canadian Mission Administered Funds, GTZ, OEFI, and others.

PRINCIPAL PURPOSE: To advise government on all matters affecting the welfare of women; to initiate projects and programmes that would improve the status of women in collaboration with other institutions; to integrate women into the socio-economic development of the Gambia as equal partners and beneficiaries.

MAIN ACTIVITIES: Institute income generating projects; provide labor-saving equipment; organize training workshops; carry out research on the status of women; maintain a women in development library and provide loans for business women.

POPULATION CONCERNS: We encourage family planning in order to restrict child-bearing to the most appropriate times in a woman's life, thus avoiding dangerous early or late pregnancies and reducing interference with her educational and career opportunities, and by keeping family size at a manageable level; to reduce women's domestic burdens while at the same time ensuring that each child receives the financial, health and educational support required.

SPECIFIC POPULATION ACTIVITIES: Education and advocacy.

FORWARD LOOKING STRATEGIES IMPLEMENTATIONS: As the government machinery charged with monitoring and improving the status of women, the Women's Bureau sits on various government committees, including the law reform commission, to see that women's needs are represented and to erase inequalities that have existed in the past. Through workshops, The Women's Bureau tries to eliminate detrimental stereotypes and attitudes towards women. Through its projects, the bureau strives to increase the income-earning capacity of women and introduces labor-saving devices to reduce time spent on tedious and strenuous household chores. The bureau also carries out research in order to effectively evaluate the status of women.

OBSTACLES TO THE IMPLEMENTATION OF FORWARD-LOOKING STRATEGIES: Lack of adequate resources and manpower to carry out activities.

NOTES:

Revolutionary Ethiopia Women's Association (REWA)

ETHIOPIA

ADDRESS:

The Central Council of REWA, P.O. Box 31246, Addis Ababa, ETHIOPIA

EXECUTIVE OFFICER:			BRANCH OFFICES:
Assegedech Bezuneh, Chairperson			

TELEPHONE NUMBER:		TELEX NUMBER:	
125000			

APPROX. STAFF SIZE:	VOLUNTEER STAFF:	YEAR ESTABLISHED:	
39		1980	

NUMBER OF INDIVIDUAL MEMBERS:

5.1 million

FUNDING: Through membership fees and income generating activities.

PRINCIPAL PURPOSE: To make every effort to ensure that the necessary conditions are created for women to exercise their rights and discharge their responsibilities, as mothers, workers and citizens. To prepare women to participate in socialist construction alongside their fellow men and thereby liberate themselves from ecnomic dependence and backward cultural practices.

MAIN ACTIVITIES: Ensure that women are afforded the opportunity to be productive citizens as well as to discharge their responsibilities as mothers and to this end appropriate conditions are created for them; in cooperation with others make every effort to establish and expand kindergartens; make every effort to eradicate customs and practices which deny women of their human rights; participate in the world democratic movement of women and cooperate with women's association which struggle for peace, equality, freedom, democracy, social progress, the rights of women and the welfare of children, etc.

POPULATION CONCERNS: REWA collaborates very closely with the Ministry of Public Health in MCH programmes and the like.

SPECIFIC POPULATION ACTIVITIES: Education, Delivery of Services, and Natural Family Planning.

FORWARD-LOOKING STRATEGIES IMPLEMENTATIONS: In collaboration with the Ministry of Public Health works towards expansion of health services to expectant mothers; training of traditional birth attendants; vaccination and innoculation to mothers and children; eradication of backward practices such as early marriage; dissemination of information about child and family care.

OBSTACLES TO THE IMPLEMENTATION OF FORWARD-LOOKING STRATEGIES: Skilled manpower.

NOTES:

National Council on Women and Development

GHANA

ADDRESS:

P.O. Box M. 53, Accra GHANA

EXECUTIVE OFFICER:

Gertrude Zakaria-Ali, Exec. Secretary

BRANCH OFFICES:

TELEPHONE NUMBER:	TELEX NUMBER:
229119	

APPROX. STAFF SIZE:	VOLUNTEER STAFF:	YEAR ESTABLISHED:
214		1975

NUMBER OF INDIVIDUAL MEMBERS:

FUNDING: By government.

PRINCIPAL PURPOSE: To raise the consciousness of Ghanaian women so that they may attain their full potential and contribute to the development of their nation. To raise the standard of living on a broad national basis by bringing the unskilled into the productive sector of the economy, the majority of whom are women.

MAIN ACTIVITIES: Research, counselling, and public education.

POPULATION CONCERNS: Women and their right to fertility, education on population issues and socio-economic development of women.

SPECIFIC POPULATION ACTIVITIES: Education, demographic research, contraceptive research, counselling and advocacy.

FORWARD-LOOKING STRATEGIES IMPLEMENTATIONS: Education, health, employment, legal issues and political participation.

OBSTACLES TO THE IMPLEMENTATION OF FORWARD-LOOKING STRATEGIES: Financial, transportation and finding qualified personnel.

NOTES:

Young Women's Christian Association (YWCA)

GHANA

ADDRESS:

P.O. Box 1504, ACCRA, GHANA

EXECUTIVE OFFICER:

Mrs. Kate Parkes, Nat. Gen. Secretary

BRANCH OFFICES:

TELEPHONE NUMBER:

228677

TELEX NUMBER:

APPROX. STAFF SIZE:

32

VOLUNTEER STAFF:

YEAR ESTABLISHED:

1952

NUMBER OF INDIVIDUAL MEMBERS:

200+ and 15 Chapters

FUNDING: Through grants, donations, individual contributions, members and branch allocations, and fund raising activities.

PRINCIPAL PURPOSE: To bring together women and girls of different christian traditions into a world wide fellowship. To help develop their skills and talents to enable them to lead more useful lives and to contribute towards the development of the society in which they live. Non christians are welcome to participate in activities of their choice.

MAIN ACTIVITIES: Non formal and informal educational programmes; service programmes to benefit women and families such as day care centre; income generating projects including farming, educational institutions; and social and recreational activities.

POPULATION CONCERNS: Early pregnancies and abortion.

SPECIFIC POPULATION ACTIVITIES: Education and counselling.

FORWARD-LOOKING STRATEGIES IMPLEMENTATIONS: Women and health related educational programmes.

OBSTACLES TO THE IMPLEMENTATION OF FORWARD-LOOKING STRATEGIES:

NOTES:

ORGANIZATION:	
Kenya Medical Women's Association	**KENYA**

ADDRESS:

P.O. Box 49877, Nairobi, Kenya

EXECUTIVE OFFICER:	BRANCH OFFICES:
Dr. A.U. Onyango-Akena, Chairperson	

TELEPHONE NUMBER:	TELEX NUMBER:
21744 NRB	

APPROX. STAFF SIZE:	VOLUNTEER STAFF:	YEAR ESTABLISHED:
11	11	1983

NUMBER OF INDIVIDUAL MEMBERS:

250

FUNDING: Membership fees, financial assistance, drugs provided by pharmaceutical companies.

PRINCIPAL PURPOSE: To provide a means of communication between Medical Women, and opportunities for them to meet and confer, especially on problems relating to maternal and child health.

MAIN ACTIVITIES: Voluntary services to improve maternal and child health, annual scientific seminars.

POPULATION CONCERNS: Maternal Health.

SPECIFIC POPULATION ACTIVITIES: Counselling, advocacy and sterilization.

FORWARD-LOOKING STRATEGIES IMPLEMENTATIONS: Wider spread of family planning facilities.

OBSTACLES TO THE IMPLEMENTATION OF FORWARD-LOOKING STRATEGIES: None indicated.

NOTES:

ORGANIZATION:

Kenya Women Finance Trust, Inc. KENYA

ADDRESS:

P.O. Box 55919, Nairobi, Kenya

EXECUTIVE OFFICER:			BRANCH OFFICES:
E.M. Okelo, Chairman Br. of Directors			

TELEPHONE NUMBER:		TELEX NUMBER:	
25595/20853			

APPROX. STAFF SIZE:	VOLUNTEER STAFF:	YEAR ESTABLISHED:
20	3	1981

NUMBER OF INDIVIDUAL MEMBERS:

200

FUNDING: Donations, membership fees, and community fund drives.

PRINCIPAL PURPOSE: Business skills training and credit facilities for small scale business women and women's groups; To increase women's involvement in the Kenyan economy.

MAIN ACTIVITIES: Providing business training and credit facilities.

POPULATION CONCERNS: Concerned with population issues that affect the economic status of women and their families.

SPECIFIC POPULATION ACTIVITIES: Education, demographic research and advocacy.

FORWARD-LOOKING STRATEGIES IMPLEMENTATIONS: Facilitating economic development and increasing literacy with business skills training.

OBSTACLES TO THE IMPLEMENTATION OF FORWARD-LOOKING STRATEGIES: Not enough funds to handle all the requests for assistance.

NOTES:

Maendeleo ya Wanawake Organization

KENYA

ADDRESS:

P.O. Box 44412, Nairobi, Kenya

EXECUTIVE OFFICER:

Mrs. Jennifer J. Mukolwe, Prm. Mngr.

BRANCH OFFICES:

TELEPHONE NUMBER:

220956

TELEX NUMBER:

APPROX. STAFF SIZE:	VOLUNTEER STAFF:	YEAR ESTABLISHED:
100	500	1952

NUMBER OF INDIVIDUAL MEMBERS:

6

FUNDING: Donors.

PRINCIPAL PURPOSE: To uplift the standard of living of women and their families through various activities and projects.

MAIN ACTIVITIES: Education and training of women leaders; promotion of income generating activities; promotion of food production, preparation, and preservation; promotion and dissemination of family planning information; and promotion of resource saving and planting of trees.

POPULATION CONCERNS: Welfare of women and families.

SPECIFIC POPULATION ACTIVITIES: Education, advocacy, counselling, and delivery of services including the pill, foam, Norplant and Depo-Provera.

FORWARD-LOOKING STRATEGIES IMPLEMENTATIONS: Family planning and raising the standard of living for women.

OBSTACLES TO THE IMPLEMENTATION OF FORWARD-LOOKING STRATEGIES: None.

NOTES:

Nairobi Business and Professional Women Club

KENYA

ADDRESS:

P.O. Box 45597, Nairobi, Kenya

EXECUTIVE OFFICER:

Mrs. Beth Mugo

BRANCH OFFICES:

TELEPHONE NUMBER:

TELEX NUMBER:

APPROX. STAFF SIZE:

1

VOLUNTEER STAFF:

YEAR ESTABLISHED:

1950

NUMBER OF INDIVIDUAL MEMBERS:

500

FUNDING: Self help fundraising.

PRINCIPAL PURPOSE: To improve the standard of life for women and children.

MAIN ACTIVITIES: Business seminars for women, educational seminars for women and girls, Mabati (home building) groups, water for health projects and tree planting projects.

POPULATION CONCERNS: Child spacing, control over the number of children in families and health of all members of families.

SPECIFIC POPULATION ACTIVITIES: Education, counselling, contraceptive research, and natural family planning.

FORWARD-LOOKING STRATEGIES IMPLEMENTATIONS: None.

OBSTACLES TO THE IMPLEMENTATION OF FORWARD-LOOKING STRATEGIES: Aware of the Strategies, but there is a lack of funds for implementation.

NOTES:

Rural Development
Co-operative Society, LTD

KENYA

ADDRESS:

P.O. Box 54229, Nairobi, Kenya

EXECUTIVE OFFICER:

Ms. Lina Tungo Chesaro, Exec. Chairwoman

BRANCH OFFICES:

TELEPHONE NUMBER:	TELEX NUMBER:
332428	

APPROX. STAFF SIZE:	VOLUNTEER STAFF:	YEAR ESTABLISHED:
5		1972

NUMBER OF INDIVIDUAL MEMBERS:

over 10,000

FUNDING: Through members contributions, government grants, and support from donor agencies.

PRINCIPAL PURPOSE: To promote the welfare of rural women in Kenya through promotion of women's activities.

MAIN ACTIVITIES: Production and marketing of handicrafts, communication, and supporting women's group efforts.

POPULATION CONCERNS: To reduce population by increasing women's income so that they do not continue striving to have many children for old age security. Instead if they have income and developed homes, they will see no need for many children.

SPECIFIC POPULATION ACTIVITIES: Education, demographic research, counselling, and economic promotion and counselling.

FORWARD-LOOKING STRATEGIES IMPLEMENTATIONS: The Chairwoman of the organization is on the Kenya Task Force Committee for the FLS.

OBSTACLES TO THE IMPLEMENTATION OF FORWARD-LOOKING STRATEGIES: Funds to cover time spent on meetings and production of various reports that have already been produced: Report on the Nairobi 1985 Conference and NGO Forum, etc.

NOTES:

Zonta Club of Nairobi Milimani

KENYA

ADDRESS:

P.O. Box 43874, Nairobi, Kenya

EXECUTIVE OFFICER:

Grace Githu, Chairperson

BRANCH OFFICES:

TELEPHONE NUMBER:

TELEX NUMBER:

APPROX. STAFF SIZE:	VOLUNTEER STAFF:	YEAR ESTABLISHED:
Unknown	0	1984

NUMBER OF INDIVIDUAL MEMBERS:

25

FUNDING: Unknown.

PRINCIPAL PURPOSE: Membership of women executives united to improve the legal, political, economic, and professional status of women.

MAIN ACTIVITIES: Provide maternal assistance to homes for the destitute, administer scholarships for girls and aid international projects.

POPULATION CONCERNS: Concerned about the high population growth rate in Kenya.

SPECIFIC POPULATION ACTIVITIES: Education, advocacy and counselling.

FORWARD-LOOKING STRATEGIES IMPLEMENTATIONS: None.

OBSTACLES TO THE IMPLEMENTATION OF FORWARD-LOOKING STRATEGIES: None.

NOTES:

Union Nationale des Organ. Feminines*
Catholiques a Madagascar **MADAGASCAR**

ADDRESS:

CNPC derriere la Poste, Antanimena, Atananarivo, Madagascar

EXECUTIVE OFFICER:

Elizabeth Razafiearinelina, President

BRANCH OFFICES:

TELEPHONE NUMBER:

TELEX NUMBER:

APPROX. STAFF SIZE:	VOLUNTEER STAFF:	YEAR ESTABLISHED:
5	5	1968

NUMBER OF INDIVIDUAL MEMBERS:

32

FUNDING: Not indicated.

PRINCIPAL PURPOSE: Promote Catholic women in both the ecclesiastoc and humanistic communities so that they may better fill their roles.

MAIN ACTIVITIES: Coordination of activities of each member organization, information on all pastoral activities and overseeing the completion of work in these areas.

POPULATION CONCERNS: Each member organization tries, in their region of parish to aide needy families.

SPECIFIC POPULATION ACTIVITIES: Education and natural family planning.

FORWARD LOOKING-STRATEGIES IMPLEMENTATIONS: Were not aware of the strategies.

OBSTACLES TO THE IMPLEMENTATION OF FORWARD-LOOKING STRATEGIES:

NOTES: *National Union of Catholic Women's Organizations.

Women's Islamic Movement

MAURITIUS

ADDRESS:

P.O. Box 1015, Port Louis, Mauritius

EXECUTIVE OFFICER:			BRANCH OFFICES:
Rosenby Ramtoola			

TELEPHONE NUMBER:		TELEX NUMBER:	
081634		4750 Shahada IW	

APPROX. STAFF SIZE:	VOLUNTEER STAFF:	YEAR ESTABLISHED:
2	10	1973

NUMBER OF INDIVIDUAL MEMBERS:

50 in 5 chapters

FUNDING: Contributions from members.

PRINCIPAL PURPOSE: To spread the message of Islam.

MAIN ACTIVITIES: Maintain a library and book shop, distribute magazines, and sponsor lectures, a youth camp and sewing and writing classes.

POPULATION CONCERNS: Counselling of young married couples.

SPECIFIC POPULATION ACTIVITIES: Natural family planning.

FORWARD-LOOKING STRATEGIES IMPLEMENTATIONS: Were not aware of the strategies.

OBSTACLES TO THE IMPLEMENTATION OF FORWARD-LOOKING STRATEGIES: None.

NOTES:

National Council of Women's Societies, Nigeria

NIGERIA

ADDRESS:

NCWS House, Plot PC 14, Off Idowu Taylor Street, Victoria Island, P.O. Box 3063, Lagos, Nigeria

EXECUTIVE OFFICER:		BRANCH OFFICES:
Mrs. Hilda Adefarasin, President		

TELEPHONE NUMBER:	TELEX NUMBER:	
612091		

APPROX. STAFF SIZE:	VOLUNTEER STAFF:	YEAR ESTABLISHED:	
10		1958	

NUMBER OF INDIVIDUAL MEMBERS:	
22 Chapters	

FUNDING: Fundraising grants, annual dues and donations.

PRINCIPAL PURPOSE: To bring into being a federation of non-political women's organizations; to assist women in towns and villages in their important role as home-makers and nations-builders; and to create an awareness of good citizenship.

MAIN ACTIVITIES: Increasing awareness in women; adult education; family planning; child welfare programs; exchange visits with women of other countries; initiating improvements in social services; and collaborating with the government to foster the welfare of women.

POPULATION CONCERNS: Overpopulation and child spacing.

SPECIFIC POPULATION ACTIVITIES: Education, counselling, advocacy and the delivery of services including sterilization, pill, IUD, Depo-Provera and natural family planning.

FORWARD-LOOKING STRATEGIES IMPLEMENTATIONS: Family Planning and dissemination of information to the public.

OBSTACLES TO THE IMPLEMENTATION OF FORWARD-LOOKING STRATEGIES: Ignorance, superstition, taboos, cultural and other traditional practices.

NOTES:

Young Women's Christian Association (Y.W.C.A.)

NIGERIA

ADDRESS:

8–Moloney Street, P.O. Box 449, Lagos, Nigeria

EXECUTIVE OFFICER:	BRANCH OFFICES:
National President/National General Secretary	

TELEPHONE NUMBER:	TELEX NUMBER:
01-630950	

APPROX. STAFF SIZE:	VOLUNTEER STAFF:	YEAR ESTABLISHED:
15	8	1906

NUMBER OF INDIVIDUAL MEMBERS:

12,800 and 50 affiliated chapters

FUNDING: Receive a grant from the government, and raise funds locally.

PRINCIPAL PURPOSE: To Unite members in groups for fellowship, service and activities; to awaken in them a sense of social responsibility which will result in the best of their community; to foster understanding and appreciation of the beliefs and customs of other nationalities and races.

MAIN ACTIVITIES: Providing educational, social and welfare services to women in general and creating awareness of important national issues.

POPULATION CONCERNS: Education, family life, (planning to curb population explosion) job opportunity for the unemployed and primary health care.

SPECIFIC POPULATION ACTIVITIES: Education, counselling, delivery of services which include: Pill, IUD, and Natural Family Planning.

FORWARD-LOOKING STRATEGIES IMPLEMENTATIONS: Greater awareness created; government's involvement in Family Life Education; more concern for women and development at governmental level; ban on withdrawal of girls from schools for marriage.

OBSTACLES TO THE IMPLEMENTATION OF FORWARD-LOOKING STRATEGIES: Religious.

NOTES:

Association of African Women for Research and Development

SENEGAL

ADDRESS:

B.P. 3304, Dakar, SENEGAL

EXECUTIVE OFFICER:

Ms. Zenebeworke Tadesse, Exec. Secretary

BRANCH OFFICES:

TELEPHONE NUMBER:	TELEX NUMBER:
23 02 11	3339 CODES SG

APPROX. STAFF SIZE:	VOLUNTEER STAFF:	YEAR ESTABLISHED:
3		1977

NUMBER OF INDIVIDUAL MEMBERS:

400

FUNDING: Grants in aid from bilateral and multilateral organizations promoting development cooperation.

PRINCIPAL PURPOSE: Promotion and coordination of research by African women on role of women and development and activities geared to social transformation.

MAIN ACTIVITIES: Coordination of research and dissemination of research findings; organization of workshops and conferences responding to AAWRD objectives; publication programme and building of resource-base; contribution to networking among women's organizations and among African NGOs; organization of training programmes for members.

POPULATION CONCERNS: Research Working Group on "Women, Population Policy, Fertility and Family Planning"—a spin-off from earlier Working Group on Women and Reproduction in Africa—is under constitution.

SPECIFIC POPULATION ACTIVITIES: Education and demographic research.

FORWARD-LOOKING STRATEGIES IMPLEMENTATIONS: All the main activities of the organization are being implemented with the FLS.

OBSTACLES TO THE IMPLEMENTATION OF FORWARD-LOOKING STRATEGIES: Have not yet surveyed members for a proper evaluation.

NOTES:

Association Senegalaise*
pour le Bien-Etre Familiale

SENEGAL

ADDRESS:

B.P. 6084, Dakar, Senegal

EXECUTIVE OFFICER:	BRANCH OFFICES:
Amadou Gueye, Executive Secretary	

TELEPHONE NUMBER:	TELEX NUMBER:	
22 7608		

APPROX. STAFF SIZE:	VOLUNTEER STAFF:	YEAR ESTABLISHED:
29	30	1975

NUMBER OF INDIVIDUAL MEMBERS:

50

FUNDING: Internationnaly funded.

PRINCIPAL PURPOSE: Family planning, family life education and women's development.

MAIN ACTIVITIES: Family planning clinics and services, motivation campaigns, information, education and communication, and women's projects.

POPULATION CONCERNS: None indicated.

SPECIFIC POPULATION ACTIVITIES: Education, counseling, and delivery of services including sterilization, the pill, IUD, diaphragm and Neo-sampoon.

FORWARD-LOOKING STRATEGIES IMPLEMENTATIONS: Did not indicate awareness of the Strategies.

OBSTACLES TO THE IMPLEMENTATION OF FORWARD-LOOKING STRATEGIES: None.

NOTES: *Senegalaise Association for Family Well-Being

*Business Address: Route du Front de Terre, Dakar, Senegal

Seychelles Women's Council   SEYCHELLES

ADDRESS:

P.O. Box 91, Victoria, Mahe, Seychelles

EXECUTIVE OFFICER:	BRANCH OFFICES:
Mrs. Rita Sinon	

TELEPHONE NUMBER:	TELEX NUMBER:
24030	2226 SPF SZ

APPROX. STAFF SIZE:	VOLUNTEER STAFF:	YEAR ESTABLISHED:
3	121	1970

NUMBER OF INDIVIDUAL MEMBERS:

2000

FUNDING: Seychelles Government, projects submitted to member states, party annual allocation, UNDP, Development fund.

PRINCIPAL PURPOSE: To unite women so that they can be aware to participate in the political, social, cultural and economic affairs of the country. To educate women of their rights and duties for their participation in natural development. To preserve the rights and liberties of women.

MAIN ACTIVITIES: Examining and evaluating the contribution of women in the economic, social and cultural fields.

POPULATION CONCERNS: To be aware of the statistics on the population issue through the Ministry of Health and the statistics division and advise on education programme.

SPECIFIC POPULATION ACTIVITIES: Education; work in close collaboration with health education unit of The Ministry of Health, other services indicated are provided by the Ministry in all districts. UNFPA has projects with Ministry.

FORWARD-LOOKING STRATEGIES IMPLEMENTATIONS: Pressing for convention on elimination of discrimination against women to be ratified, Central Committee of party has approved; necessary legislation is being amended in attorney general's office to be endorsed by assembly.

OBSTACLES TO THE IMPLEMENTATION OF FORWARD-LOOKING STRATEGIES: Difficulties in obtaining funds for projects for the benefit of women.

NOTES:

Women's Education Department   SOMALIA

ADDRESS:

Ministry of Education, P.O. Box 421, Mogadishu, Somalia

EXECUTIVE OFFICER:

Ms. Hawa Aden Mohamed, Director

BRANCH OFFICES:

TELEPHONE NUMBER:	TELEX NUMBER:
22104	

APPROX. STAFF SIZE:	VOLUNTEER STAFF:	YEAR ESTABLISHED:
736	3	1974

NUMBER OF INDIVIDUAL MEMBERS:

4000

FUNDING: Government, UNICEF, UNESCO, USAID, and UNHCR.

PRINCIPAL PURPOSE: To formulate non-formal education programs for women and children; coordination of policies for the education of women; negotiation of funding of women's education within government budgets.

MAIN ACTIVITIES: The training of specialists and field workers; planning, preparation and production of educational materials; and supervision, monitoring and evaluation of women's educational programs.

POPULATION CONCERNS: High child/mother mortality; high number of births per woman; closely spaced pregnancies. Need of health improvement and knowledge of women.

SPECIFIC POPULATION ACTIVITIES: Education and advocacy.

FORWARD-LOOKING STRATEGIES IMPLEMENTATIONS: To ensure that family planning information is widely available.

OBSTACLES TO THE IMPLEMENTATION OF FORWARD-LOOKING STRATEGIES: Lack of clear policies concerning child spacing. Lack of resources, such as manpower, educational materials and research.

NOTES:

ADDRESS:

P.O. Box 35915, 0102 Menlo Park, Pretoria, South Africa

EXECUTIVE OFFICER:	BRANCH OFFICES:
Joan S. Whitmore, President	

TELEPHONE NUMBER:	TELEX NUMBER:
(012) 363-0951	

APPROX. STAFF SIZE:	VOLUNTEER STAFF:	YEAR ESTABLISHED:
	8	1923

NUMBER OF INDIVIDUAL MEMBERS:

500

FUNDING: Dues, fundraising, subscriptions.

PRINCIPAL PURPOSE: To improve educational and career opportunities for women. To improve conditions of service for women and to promote women's participation in the betterment of the community.

MAIN ACTIVITIES: Supporting tertiary education for women as well as sponsoring training seminars and development projects.

POPULATION CONCERNS: Those issues related to the education, employment and self-development of women.

SPECIFIC POPULATION ACTIVITIES: Education, advocacy and delivery of services.

FORWARD-LOOKING STRATEGIES IMPLEMENTATIONS: General implementation.

OBSTACLES TO THE IMPLEMENTATION OF FORWARD-LOOKING STRATEGIES: The apathy and disinterest of many women.

NOTES:

Wanawake Wakatoliki Tanzania **TANZANIA**

ADDRESS:

P.O. Box 9361, Dar-es-Salaam, Tanzania

EXECUTIVE OFFICER:			BRANCH OFFICES:
Betty Mwaluli, President			

TELEPHONE NUMBER:		TELEX NUMBER:
(051) 30071		

APPROX. STAFF SIZE:	VOLUNTEER STAFF:	YEAR ESTABLISHED:
6	6	1972

NUMBER OF INDIVIDUAL MEMBERS:

600,000

FUNDING: Self help fundraising and grants from donor agencies and friends.

PRINCIPAL PURPOSE: To change the situation of women in society and in the church.

MAIN ACTIVITIES: Projects concerning women and the church, social and economic development of women, family life and health, labour and employment, and income generating activities.

POPULATION CONCERNS: Reduction of infant mortality; family planning, family life and health.

SPECIFIC POPULATION ACTIVITIES: Education and demographic research.

FORWARD-LOOKING STRATEGIES IMPLEMENTATIONS: Seminars to educate women on education, health, socio-economic problems, and peace.

OBSTACLES TO THE IMPLEMENTATION OF FORWARD-LOOKING STRATEGIES: Lack of resources.

NOTES:

Association of Women's Clubs of Zimbabwe

ZIMBABWE

ADDRESS:

P.O. Box UA339, Harare, Zimbabwe

EXECUTIVE OFFICER:			BRANCH OFFICES:
Betty Mtero			P.O. Box 174 Bulawayo
TELEPHONE NUMBER:		**TELEX NUMBER:**	
726910			P.O. Box 811 Gweru
APPROX. STAFF SIZE:	**VOLUNTEER STAFF:**	**YEAR ESTABLISHED:**	
17	3	1950	Box M56 Masvingo
NUMBER OF INDIVIDUAL MEMBERS:			
23,000			

FUNDING: Membership fees, fundraising and donations.

PRINCIPAL PURPOSE: To provide a platform whereby rural women meet to exchange information, ideas and skills. Raising the standard of living through income generating activities identified by women in the communities.

MAIN ACTIVITIES: Leadership training, project identification, planning and evaluation, income generating projects, pre-school education, and other projects such as reforestation, promotion of nutrition and family planning education.

POPULATION CONCERNS: Working to include family planning education with other rural concerns and home craft skills.

SPECIFIC POPULATION ACTIVITIES: Education and advocacy.

FORWARD-LOOKING STRATEGIES IMPLEMENTATIONS: Establishment of income generating projects and educating and training. Encouraging women to be confident and speak for themselves.

OBSTACLES TO THE IMPLEMENTATION OF FORWARD-LOOKING STRATEGIES: Financial constraints.

NOTES:

*Business Address: No. 64 Selous Avenue, Harare, Zimbabwe

National Federation of Women's Institutes of Zimbabwe

ZIMBABWE

ADDRESS:

P.O. Box 8263 Causeway, Harare Zimbabwe

EXECUTIVE OFFICER:

Mrs. G. M. Flanagan, National President

BRANCH OFFICES:

TELEPHONE NUMBER:	TELEX NUMBER:

APPROX. STAFF SIZE:	VOLUNTEER STAFF:	YEAR ESTABLISHED:
6	4	1925

NUMBER OF INDIVIDUAL MEMBERS:

700

FUNDING: Subscriptions from members and donations.

PRINCIPAL PURPOSE: To enable women to take an effective part in the life and development of the country, to improve and develop the conditions of our national and community lives.

MAIN ACTIVITIES: Standing committees on agriculture and home economics, health and welfare, and creative arts. Publication of magazines.

POPULATION CONCERNS: Support of child spacing program as every woman has the right to limit her family and information should be made available to women to this end.

SPECIFIC POPULATION ACTIVITIES: Education and advocacy.

FORWARD-LOOKING STRATEGIES IMPLEMENTATIONS: Ensuring that family planning information is made available.

OBSTACLES TO THE IMPLEMENTATION OF FORWARD-LOOKING STRATEGIES: None.

NOTES:

Population, Development & Health Organizations

UN Photo B. Wolff

National Committee of Benin for Family Promotion

BENIN

ADDRESS:

Carre No. 857, Aidjedo, Cotonou-4, Benin

EXECUTIVE OFFICER:			BRANCH OFFICES:

Mrs. Aurore d'Almeida, Administrator

TELEPHONE NUMBER:	TELEX NUMBER:
32-00-49	5111-5112

APPROX. STAFF SIZE:	VOLUNTEER STAFF:	YEAR ESTABLISHED:
48		1972

NUMBER OF INDIVIDUAL MEMBERS:

2550

FUNDING: IPPF, membership dues, gifts, government grants and support from NGOs.

PRINCIPAL PURPOSE: To contribute to the well-being of the family and society through education and by providing family planning services.

MAIN ACTIVITIES: Increasing awareness through conference-debates, films, seminars and workshops, training in family planning, contraceptive research and provision of clinical services.

POPULATION CONCERNS: Achieving a balance between demographic growth, natural resources and economic development.

SPECIFIC POPULATION ACTIVITIES: Education, contraceptive research, counselling, and delivery of services: pill, IUD, diaphragm, spermicides and condoms.

FORWARD-LOOKING STRATEGIES IMPLEMENTATIONS: None.

OBSTACLES TO THE IMPLEMENTATION OF FORWARD-LOOKING STRATEGIES: None.

NOTES:

Institut de Formation et de*
Recherche Demographiques (IFORD) Cameroon

ADDRESS:

B.P. 1556, Yaounde, Cameroon

EXECUTIVE OFFICER:

Mpembele Sala-Dia Kanda, Director

BRANCH OFFICES:

TELEPHONE NUMBER:	TELEX NUMBER:
22.24.71	

APPROX. STAFF SIZE:	VOLUNTEER STAFF:	YEAR ESTABLISHED:
24		1972

NUMBER OF INDIVIDUAL MEMBERS:

25 Countries

FUNDING: From member nations and UNFPA.

PRINCIPAL PURPOSE: To train demographers for francophone African countries, to promote demographic research in Africa and provide consultation services to member nations.

MAIN ACTIVITIES: Training demographers, organizing seminars and colloquiums on population problems, organizing national training courses for mid level administrators in statistics and demographics and organizing advanced training for demographers.

POPULATION CONCERNS: Migration, fertility, mortality, spatial distribution, population and development.

SPECIFIC POPULATION ACTIVITIES: Education and demographic research.

FORWARD LOOKING-STRATEGIES IMPLEMENTATIONS:

OBSTACLES TO THE IMPLEMENTATION OF FORWARD-LOOKING STRATEGIES:

NOTES: *Institute for Education and Demographic Research

Central Kenya Field of
Seventh Day Adventists Church

KENYA

ADDRESS:

P.O. Box 41352, Nairob, Kenya

EXECUTIVE OFFICER:

Elijah Ernest Njagi, Executive Director

BRANCH OFFICES:

TELEPHONE NUMBER:	TELEX NUMBER:
520201"-2"	

APPROX. STAFF SIZE:	VOLUNTEER STAFF:	YEAR ESTABLISHED:
50		1953

NUMBER OF INDIVIDUAL MEMBERS:

14,000

FUNDING:

PRINCIPAL PURPOSE: To preach the gospel of Jesus Christ as understood by the Seventh-Day Adventists.

MAIN ACTIVITIES: To establish churches, erect and run church, schools, medical and health institutions, and to publish christian literature.

POPULATION CONCERNS: Educating members not to have more children than they can manage and provide for their needs and education.

SPECIFIC POPULATION ACTIVITIES: Educating and counselling.

FORWARD LOOKING-STRATEGIES IMPLEMENTATIONS: Educating church memebers.

OBSTACLES TO THE IMPLEMENTATION OF FORWARD-LOOKING STRATEGIES:

NOTES:

Diocese of Maseno South

KENYA

ADDRESS:

P.O. Box 380, Kisumu, Kenya

EXECUTIVE OFFICER:

Emmanuel Madote, Director

BRANCH OFFICES:

TELEPHONE NUMBER:

3316

TELEX NUMBER:

APPROX. STAFF SIZE:

120

VOLUNTEER STAFF:

YEAR ESTABLISHED:

NUMBER OF INDIVIDUAL MEMBERS:

1975

FUNDING: From different funding agencies.

PRINCIPAL PURPOSE: Total development for people.

MAIN ACTIVITIES: Programs in health, appropriate technology, water development, and women's activities.

POPULATION CONCERNS: Family planning is included in the health program.

SPECIFIC POPULATION ACTIVITIES: Education, counselling, and the delivery of services including the pill, foam and condoms.

FORWARD-LOOKING STRATEGIES IMPLEMENTATIONS: Are aware of the Strategies but are not implementing them.

OBSTACLES TO THE IMPLEMENTATION OF FORWARD-LOOKING STRATEGIES: The Health program is not mobile enough to reach rural areas. More funds and staff are needed.

NOTES:

Kenya Obstetrical and Gynecological Society

KENYA

ADDRESS:

P.O. Box 30588, Nairobi, Kenya

EXECUTIVE OFFICER:

Mr. S.W. Musila Frcog

BRANCH OFFICES:

TELEPHONE NUMBER:

TELEX NUMBER:

APPROX. STAFF SIZE:

VOLUNTEER STAFF:

YEAR ESTABLISHED:

1974

NUMBER OF INDIVIDUAL MEMBERS:

250

FUNDING: Membership fees.

PRINCIPAL PURPOSE: To bring together gynecologists and contribute to research and services for women in Kenya. To uphold the ethical practice of obstetrics and gynecology, to organize continuing education programs and to advise institutions and the public on matters related to health of women.

MAIN ACTIVITIES: To organize scientific meetings, to publish the Journal of Obstetrics and Gynecology of Eastern and Central Africa, and to advise on reproductive health issues.

POPULATION CONCERNS: The safety aspects of population growth and family planning.

SPECIFIC POPULATION ACTIVITIES: Education and consultancy.

FORWARD LOOKING-STRATEGIES IMPLEMENTATIONS: Continuing education programs.

OBSTACLES TO THE IMPLEMENTATION OF FORWARD-LOOKING STRATEGIES: Financial

NOTES:

<table>
<tr><td colspan="3">

ORGANIZATION:

The Salvation Army

</td><td>

KENYA

</td></tr>
</table>

ORGANIZATION:		
The Salvation Army		**KENYA**

ADDRESS:

P.O. Box 40575, Nairobi, Kenya

EXECUTIVE OFFICER:	BRANCH OFFICES:
Colonel Angoya, Territorial Commander	

TELEPHONE NUMBER:	TELEX NUMBER:
27541-2-9	

APPROX. STAFF SIZE:	VOLUNTEER STAFF:	YEAR ESTABLISHED:
4	15	1923

NUMBER OF INDIVIDUAL MEMBERS:

47,000

FUNDING: Local and overseas giving.

PRINCIPAL PURPOSE: Christian evangelical and social welfare.

MAIN ACTIVITIES: Evangelical, pastural, social, educational and work with the handicapped.

POPULATION CONCERNS:

SPECIFIC POPULATION ACTIVITIES: Education and counselling.

FORWARD LOOKING-STRATEGIES IMPLEMENTATIONS: Are aware of the strategies but did not indicate implementation.

OBSTACLES TO THE IMPLEMENTATION OF FORWARD-LOOKING STRATEGIES:

NOTES:

Nurses and Midwives Council of Malawi

MALAWI

ADDRESS:

P.O. Box 30361, Lilongwe 3, Malawi

EXECUTIVE OFFICER:

Stella Sagawa, Registrar

BRANCH OFFICES:

TELEPHONE NUMBER:

730461

TELEX NUMBER:

APPROX. STAFF SIZE:	VOLUNTEER STAFF:	YEAR ESTABLISHED:
15	0	1966

NUMBER OF INDIVIDUAL MEMBERS:

5,000

FUNDING: Government grants and licensing and examination fees.

PRINCIPAL PURPOSE: The Council serves as a legislative body for nursing and midwifery.

MAIN ACTIVITIES: Providing guidelines for the education of nurses and midwives and prescribing conditions for monitoring that education.

POPULATION CONCERNS: Concerned with population issues that are related to health and childbirth.

SPECIFIC POPULATION ACTIVITIES: Education.

FORWARD-LOOKING STRATEGIES IMPLEMENTATIONS: Were not aware of the strategies.

OBSTACLES TO THE IMPLEMENTATION OF FORWARD-LOOKING STRATEGIES: None

NOTES:

Institut du Sahel/USED*

MALI

ADDRESS:

B.P. 1530, Bamako, Mali

EXECUTIVE OFFICER:			BRANCH OFFICES:
Papa Syr Diagne, Coordinator			

TELEPHONE NUMBER:		TELEX NUMBER:	
22-21-48 and 22-21-78		432/INSAH	

APPROX. STAFF SIZE:	VOLUNTEER STAFF:	YEAR ESTABLISHED:
17		1977

NUMBER OF INDIVIDUAL MEMBERS:

FUNDING: USED is funded by USAID, UNFPA and UNDP.

PRINCIPAL PURPOSE: Explore, analyze, write and publish studies in the area of population and development.

MAIN ACTIVITIES: Studies on demography, infant mortality in the Sahel, relation between health and development, migration, sanitation and socio-economic planning for the Sahel religion.

POPULATION CONCERNS:

SPECIFIC POPULATION ACTIVITIES: Education, demographic and contraceptive research.

FORWARD LOOKING-STRATEGIES IMPLEMENTATIONS: Were not aware of the strategies.

OBSTACLES TO THE IMPLEMENTATION OF FORWARD-LOOKING STRATEGIES:

NOTES: *Institute of Sahel

Action Familiale*

MAURITIUS

ADDRESS:

Royal Road, Rose Hill, Mauritius

EXECUTIVE OFFICER:			BRANCH OFFICES:
Pierre Rivet, Chairman			

TELEPHONE NUMBER:		TELEX NUMBER:	
4-3512		4349 Moritiur IW	

APPROX. STAFF SIZE:	VOLUNTEER STAFF:	YEAR ESTABLISHED:	
13, 132 part-time	31	1963	

NUMBER OF INDIVIDUAL MEMBERS:

300

FUNDING: Government grants, public donations, and international funding agencies.

PRINCIPAL PURPOSE: To promote the welfare and happiness of families, to foster ideas of harmonious married life and responsible parenthood, and to support all methods of regulating childbirth.

MAIN ACTIVITIES: National natural family planning programs, information and education through the media, nurses's training, marriage counseling, men's information and education program, and Human Life education for youth.

POPULATION CONCERNS: Responsible parenthood and family welfare.

SPECIFIC POPULATION ACTIVITIES: Education, demographic research, counseling, and natural family planning.

FORWARD-LOOKING STRATEGIES IMPLEMENTATIONS: Promotion of family planning and breastfeeding and education towards family harmony through relationships based on human dignity, equality and rights.

OBSTACLES TO THE IMPLEMENTATION OF FORWARD-LOOKING STRATEGIES: Financial constraints.

NOTES: *Family Action

Mauritius Family Planning Association

MAURITIUS

ADDRESS:

30 Sir Seewoosagur Ramgoolan St., Port Louis, Mauritius

EXECUTIVE OFFICER:

Mrs. Geeta Oodit, Executive Director

BRANCH OFFICES:

TELEPHONE NUMBER:		TELEX NUMBER:
08-2784 08-4184		4664 IW

APPROX. STAFF SIZE:	VOLUNTEER STAFF:	YEAR ESTABLISHED:
35	2	1957

NUMBER OF INDIVIDUAL MEMBERS:

1000

FUNDING: IPPF and the government of Mauritius.

PRINCIPAL PURPOSE: To play a pioneering role in family planning and to provide family planning services.

MAIN ACTIVITIES: Seminars and training on material production and curriculum development, family life education, community and youth outreach, medical and clinical childcare, and the development of women.

POPULATION CONCERNS: To bring down the population growth rate, and to reduce teenage pregnancy and births among women over the age of 35.

SPECIFIC POPULATION ACTIVITIES: Education, counseling, contraceptive research and the delivery of services, include: Sterilization, pill, IUD, diaphragm, foam and Depo-Provera.

FORWARD-LOOKING STRATEGIES IMPLEMENTATIONS: Development of women and family planning.

OBSTACLES TO THE IMPLEMENTATION OF FORWARD-LOOKING STRATEGIES:

NOTES:

Ministre de la Sante*　　# MAURITIUS

ADDRESS:

Rue Jules Koenig, Port Louis, Ile Maurice, Muritius

EXECUTIVE OFFICER:

Dr. B. Radha Keesoon, Interim Chief Medical Officer

BRANCH OFFICES:

TELEPHONE NUMBER:	TELEX NUMBER:
01-1905	

APPROX. STAFF SIZE:	VOLUNTEER STAFF:	YEAR ESTABLISHED:
415		1972

NUMBER OF INDIVIDUAL MEMBERS:

415

FUNDING: Government funding.

PRINCIPAL PURPOSE: To promote family planning and maternal and infant protection.

MAIN ACTIVITIES: Distribution of contraceptives, education on primary health care, health research and evaluation of family planning and maternal/infant protection.

POPULATION CONCERNS: Maintaining the fertility rate at replacement level.

SPECIFIC POPULATION ACTIVITIES: Education, demographic research, counselling, delivery of services: sterilization, pill, IUD, diaphragm, Depo-Provera and natural family planning.

FORWARD-LOOKING STRATEGIES IMPLEMENTATIONS: None.

OBSTACLES TO THE IMPLEMENTATION OF FORWARD-LOOKING STRATEGIES: None.

NOTES: *Ministry of Health

Economic and Customs Union of Central Africa

REPUBLIC OF CENTRAL AFRICA

ADDRESS:

Department des Etudes de Population, B.P. 1418, Bangui (RCA)

EXECUTIVE OFFICER:

Jean Nkounkou, Head of Dept. of Pop. Studies

BRANCH OFFICES:

TELEPHONE NUMBER:	TELEX NUMBER:
61.09.22	5252RC

APPROX. STAFF SIZE:	VOLUNTEER STAFF:	YEAR ESTABLISHED:
10		1975

NUMBER OF INDIVIDUAL MEMBERS:

10

FUNDING: Member nation fees.

PRINCIPAL PURPOSE: To promote demographic projects in the member countries of UDEAC, to provide technical assistance and consultation, to organize seminars for information exchange.

MAIN ACTIVITIES: Collection and analysis of demographic data and population policy.

POPULATION CONCERNS: Concerned with the importance of population variables in development programs.

SPECIFIC POPULATION ACTIVITIES: Demographic research.

FORWARD-LOOKING STRATEGIES IMPLEMENTATIONS: None.

OBSTACLES TO THE IMPLEMENTATION OF FORWARD-LOOKING STRATEGIES: None.

NOTES:

Family Life Association of Swaziland

SWAZILAND

ADDRESS:

P.O. Box 1051, Manzini, Swaziland

EXECUTIVE OFFICER:

Khetsiwe Dlamini, Executive Director

BRANCH OFFICES:

PO Box 1286
Mbabane, SWAZILAND

TELEPHONE NUMBER:	TELEX NUMBER:
53586	

APPROX. STAFF SIZE:	VOLUNTEER STAFF:	YEAR ESTABLISHED:
25	15	1979

NUMBER OF INDIVIDUAL MEMBERS:

300

FUNDING: Local and international donors.

PRINCIPAL PURPOSE: Family life education and family planning.

MAIN ACTIVITIES: Delivery of family health services, family life education and community based family planning services.

POPULATION CONCERNS: None indicated.

SPECIFIC POPULATION ACTIVITIES: Education, advocacy, counselling and delivery of services including sterilization, the pill and diaphragm.

FORWARD-LOOKING STRATEGIES IMPLEMENTATIONS: Were not aware of the Strategies but are interested in beginning to implement them.

OBSTACLES TO THE IMPLEMENTATION OF FORWARD-LOOKING STRATEGIES: None.

NOTES:

Family Planning Association of Uganda

UGANDA

ADDRESS:

P.O. Box 30030, Kampala, Uganda

EXECUTIVE OFFICER:

Mr. E.M. Mugoya

BRANCH OFFICES:

TELEPHONE NUMBER:

258300/230260

TELEX NUMBER:

APPROX. STAFF SIZE:

VOLUNTEER STAFF:

YEAR ESTABLISHED:

1957

NUMBER OF INDIVIDUAL MEMBERS:

500+ and 16 affiliated chapters

FUNDING: By the International Planned Parenthood Federation (IPPF).

PRINCIPAL PURPOSE: To educate the public about the advantages of family planning and to provide family planning services.

MAIN ACTIVITIES: Information, education and communication activities through home visits, public meetings, mass media, etc. Provision of clinic based as well as community based family planning services.

POPULATION CONCERNS: Adolescent fertility problems, fertility rates, child spacing and infant and maternal mortality rates.

SPECIFIC POPULATION ACTIVITIES: Education, counselling, advocacy and delivery of services: pill, IUD, diaphragm, foam and Depo-Provera.

FORWARD-LOOKING STRATEGIES IMPLEMENTATIONS: None.

OBSTACLES TO THE IMPLEMENTATION OF FORWARD-LOOKING STRATEGIES: None.

NOTES:

<table>
<tr><td colspan="3">ORGANIZATION:</td></tr>
<tr><td colspan="2">University of Zimbabwe</td><td>ZIMBABWE</td></tr>
<tr><td colspan="3">ADDRESS:
Dept. of Sociology, P.O. Box MP 167 MT, Pleasant Harare, Zimbabwe</td></tr>
<tr><td colspan="2">EXECUTIVE OFFICER:</td><td>BRANCH OFFICES:</td></tr>
<tr><td>TELEPHONE NUMBER:
303211 ext. 734</td><td>TELEX NUMBER:</td><td></td></tr>
</table>

ORGANIZATION:		
University of Zimbabwe		**ZIMBABWE**
ADDRESS: Dept. of Sociology, P.O. Box MP 167 MT, Pleasant Harare, Zimbabwe		
EXECUTIVE OFFICER:		BRANCH OFFICES:
TELEPHONE NUMBER: 303211 ext. 734	TELEX NUMBER:	
APPROX. STAFF SIZE:	VOLUNTEER STAFF:	YEAR ESTABLISHED:
NUMBER OF INDIVIDUAL MEMBERS: 2		

FUNDING: Government.

PRINCIPAL PURPOSE: To teach and perform research in Sociology.

MAIN ACTIVITIES: Teaching and research.

POPULATION CONCERNS: Research in fertility, family planning, and infant and child health.

SPECIFIC POPULATION ACTIVITIES: Education, demographic and contraceptive research.

FORWARD-LOOKING STRATEGIES IMPLEMENTATIONS: None.

OBSTACLES TO THE IMPLEMENTATION OF FORWARD-LOOKING STRATEGIES: None.

NOTES:

Zimbabwe National Family Planning Council

ZIMBABWE

ADDRESS:

Z.N.F.P.C., Box Street 220, Southerton, Harare Zimbabwe

EXECUTIVE OFFICER:			BRANCH OFFICES:
Dr. Mugagwa			

TELEPHONE NUMBER:		TELEX NUMBER:	
67656			

APPROX. STAFF SIZE:	VOLUNTEER STAFF:	YEAR ESTABLISHED:
30	0	1984

NUMBER OF INDIVIDUAL MEMBERS:

2000

FUNDING: Population Council and the Ford Foundation, self help.

PRINCIPAL PURPOSE: To promote the socio-economic status of women through provision of adult literacy classes, loans for small scale industries and education in family planning.

MAIN ACTIVITIES: Generation of income for member groups; information for encouragement of women to use family planning services; and adult literacy classes.

POPULATION CONCERNS: To ensure a decreased fertility rate.

SPECIFIC POPULATION ACTIVITIES: Education and advocacy.

FORWARD-LOOKING STRATEGIES IMPLEMENTATIONS: Adult education, as a lack of education contributes to women's poor socio-economic status and dependency.

OBSTACLES TO THE IMPLEMENTATION OF FORWARD-LOOKING STRATEGIES: Men's traditional attitude toward family size. Inability of women, due to their economic dependency, to make decisions concerning their own lives.

NOTES:

Women's Organizations

UN Photo 154,715/John Isaac

Business and Professional
Women's Club of Gaborone

BOTSWANA

ADDRESS:

P.O. Box 654, Gaborone, Botswana

EXECUTIVE OFFICER:	BRANCH OFFICES:
Mrs. N.A. Mabe, President	

TELEPHONE NUMBER:	TELEX NUMBER:

APPROX. STAFF SIZE:	VOLUNTEER STAFF:	YEAR ESTABLISHED:
		1972

NUMBER OF INDIVIDUAL MEMBERS:

31

FUNDING: Government grants, membership subscriptions and fundraising.

PRINCIPAL PURPOSE: To promote the interest of business and professional women and secure combined action by them on economical and social development of their country.

MAIN ACTIVITIES: Sponsering school groups for children whose parents are destitute; organinzing workshops to discuss issues remaining to women of national concern.

POPULATION CONCERNS: High population growth—white economic growth rates in Africa are declining this implies continued poverty of the people, especially in rural areas.

SPECIFIC POPULATION ACTIVITIES:

FORWARD LOOKING-STRATEGIES IMPLEMENTATIONS: Are aware of the strategies, are not implementing any directly, but are collborating with other organizations which are better equipped both financially and man-power.

OBSTACLES TO THE IMPLEMENTATION OF FORWARD-LOOKING STRATEGIES:

NOTES:

African Training and Research Center for Women

ETHIOPIA

ADDRESS:

P.O. Box 3001, Addis Ababa, Ethiopia

EXECUTIVE OFFICER:			BRANCH OFFICES:
Mary Tadesse, Chief			

TELEPHONE NUMBER:		TELEX NUMBER:	
1-251-44 77 22 ext 301		21029 ECA et	

APPROX. STAFF SIZE:	VOLUNTEER STAFF:	YEAR ESTABLISHED:
12		1975

NUMBER OF INDIVIDUAL MEMBERS:

FUNDING: UN regular budget, bilateral, multilateral and private sources.

PRINCIPAL PURPOSE: Research, training, publications and dissemination of information.

MAIN ACTIVITIES:

POPULATION CONCERNS: Population issues are handled through the population division at the Economic Commission for Africa.

SPECIFIC POPULATION ACTIVITIES: None.

FORWARD-LOOKING STRATEGIES IMPLEMENTATIONS: We have the responsibility for implementing the Strategies addressed to the regional commissions of the UN.

OBSTACLES TO THE IMPLEMENTATION OF FORWARD-LOOKING STRATEGIES: Lack of human and material resources.

NOTES:

Federation of Ghana Business and Professional Women

GHANA

ADDRESS:

c/o Box 36, Madina, Ghana

EXECUTIVE OFFICER:			BRANCH OFFICES:
Hannah Agyeman, Executive Secretary			Box 10052 Accra-North Ghana

TELEPHONE NUMBER:	TELEX NUMBER:	
777923		

APPROX. STAFF SIZE:	VOLUNTEER STAFF:	YEAR ESTABLISHED:
6	10 field workers	1979

NUMBER OF INDIVIDUAL MEMBERS:

1000 in 5 chapters

FUNDING: Voluntary fund for Women's Decade (UNIFEM) and membership donations.

PRINCIPAL PURPOSE: Improving the economic status of women, especially at the grassroots level.

MAIN ACTIVITIES: Farming, fish smoking and literacy training.

POPULATION CONCERNS: None indicated.

SPECIFIC POPULATION ACTIVITIES: None indicated.

FORWARD-LOOKING STRATEGIES IMPLEMENTATIONS: Advancement of women and raising the standard of their businesses.

OBSTACLES TO THE IMPLEMENTATION OF FORWARD-LOOKING STRATEGIES: None indicated.

NOTES:

Ismailia Women's Association

KENYA

P.O. Box 40190, Nairobi, Kenya

Mrs. Gulshankara, Chairman

20928

16

1926

FUNDING: Self funded.

PRINCIPAL PURPOSE: To provide a common forum for Ismailia women, to take an active part in national activities with other women's organizations and to enhance the development of women in Kenya.

MAIN ACTIVITIES: Organization of lectures, cooking demonstrations, recreational programs for senior citizens and other functions.

POPULATION CONCERNS: None indicated.

SPECIFIC POPULATION ACTIVITIES: None indicated.

FORWARD-LOOKING STRATEGIES IMPLEMENTATIONS: Are aware of the Strategies but are not implementing them.

OBSTACLES TO THE IMPLEMENTATION OF FORWARD-LOOKING STRATEGIES: None indicated.

NOTES:

Sierra Leone Muslim Women Benevolent Organization

SIERRA LEONE

ADDRESS:

P.M.B. 473,Makeni, Sierra Leone

EXECUTIVE OFFICER: Haja Hawa Kanu			BRANCH OFFICES:
TELEPHONE NUMBER:	**TELEX NUMBER:**		
APPROX. STAFF SIZE: 20	**VOLUNTEER STAFF:** 5	**YEAR ESTABLISHED:** 1970	
NUMBER OF INDIVIDUAL MEMBERS: 1675 in 15 chapters			

FUNDING: Contributions from members and donations.

PRINCIPAL PURPOSE: To serve the needy, the poor and orphans.

MAIN ACTIVITIES: Opening of educational institutions, health care for the poor, care of orphans and the building of mosques and bridges.

POPULATION CONCERNS: None indicated.

SPECIFIC POPULATION ACTIVITIES: None indicated.

FORWARD-LOOKING STRATEGIES IMPLEMENTATIONS: Were not aware of the Strategies.

OBSTACLES TO THE IMPLEMENTATION OF FORWARD-LOOKING STRATEGIES: None indicated.

NOTES:

Zimbabwe Women's Bureau

ZIMBABWE

ADDRESS:

98 Cameron Street, 2nd flr. Munndix House, Harare Zimbabwe

EXECUTIVE OFFICER:			BRANCH OFFICES:
Esinath Mapoudera, President			43 Hillside Road Harare Zimbabwe Phone: 04205
TELEPHONE NUMBER: 703376 also 790159		**TELEX NUMBER:**	
APPROX. STAFF SIZE: 20	**VOLUNTEER STAFF:** 3	**YEAR ESTABLISHED:** 1978	
NUMBER OF INDIVIDUAL MEMBERS: 11 Chapters			

FUNDING: Donor agencies.

PRINCIPAL PURPOSE: Advancement of women (especially at the grassroots level, both in rural and poor urban areas) in social, economic and legal terms. Awareness raising among women about their position in society.

MAIN ACTIVITIES: Help women's groups start and run income generating projects; training workshops to teach knowledge and skills to enable women to participate more fully in the economic and social development of the country. Collection, production and distribution of information about women in Zimbabwe.

POPULATION CONCERNS: Unspecified.

SPECIFIC POPULATION ACTIVITIES: Education and demographic research.

FORWARD-LOOKING STRATEGIES IMPLEMENTATIONS: Making women aware of their legal and land rights. Adult education, dissemination of information and networking.

OBSTACLES TO THE IMPLEMENTATION OF FORWARD-LOOKING STRATEGIES: Lack of resources, qualified personnel and funds. The government takes too long to implement some of the recommendations concerning women.

NOTES:

Europe:
Eastern Europe & the Soviet Union

TASS Moscow, USSR

Eastern Europe
and the Soviet Union

Since World War II, Eastern Europe and the Soviet Union have shared low birth rates, aging populations, and (with the exception of Yugoslavia), pro-natalist policies. The population of the Soviet Union is roughly 280 million; the Eastern European countries (Albania, Bulgaria, Czechoslovakia, the German Democratic Republic, Hungary, Poland, Rumania and Yugoslavia), have a combined population of 125.4 million. The Eastern European countries range in size from 2.8 million in Muslim Albania to 36 million in Catholic Poland. The nine countries also share one-party political systems, centrally-managed economies (again with the exception of Yugoslavia), and the socialist belief in the political equality of men and women.

As there is limited or no immigration into most of the countries, populations grow through natural increases. Like the other industrialized countries, the socialist states experienced a "baby boom" after World War II. Due to the liberalization of abortion laws in seven countries between 1955 and 1960, however, the boom ended earlier than in Western Europe and North America. The two hold-outs were the German Democratic Republic, which liberalized abortion laws in 1972, and Albania, which still prohibits it. By the 1960s, birth rates had fallen so low (14 per 1,000 in Hungary) that governments, fearful of future labor shortages, restricted abortion in four countries and approved strong pro-natalist policies in eight. These policies include economic incentives such as birth grants; paid maternity leave; monthly family and childcare allowances; subsidies for nurseries, kindergartens, school meals, transportation and housing; and even low-interest loans for newly-weds which are progressively written off with the birth of each child. Yugoslavia, whose constitution claims that "it is a human right to decide freely on childbirth" is the one exception. Albania, on the other hand, not only prohibits abortion, but also the sale of contraceptives and offers no economic incentive.

Romania has the most coercive policy. Legal abortions and the importation of contraceptives were severely curtailed in 1966. In 1967 the birth rate rose, but by 1983 it had dropped again, prompting the state to undertake new measures: doctors who perform abortions for any reasons other than the strict terms of the 1966 law are subject to 25 years imprisonment; the minimum age of marriage has been lowered to 15; an extra tax is levied on childless couples, and all women aged 20-30 are forced to undergo a monthly pregnancy test. Romania's official goal is four children per woman.

With the adoption of pro-natalist policies, birth rates also rose briefly in Czechoslovakia, Hungary and Bulgaria, but dropped again by the mid-1980s. In the USSR and Poland pro-natalist measures stopped fertility declines. All in all, the Soviet Union's fertility rate has been more stable than that of its neighbors, primarily due to the high birth rate of its rural

Muslim republics. At the same time, however, infant mortality rate in the Soviet Union rose during 1970s, to above 15 deaths for infants under one year per one thousand births.

In the years ahead, the socialist states will have to reconcile the problem of slow population growth and resultant future labor shortages, on the one hand, with the negative aspects of rapid industrialization and rapid population growth. These aspects include acute shortages of housing and other services and severe environmental pollution and degradation, particularly in the Soviet Union, the German Democratic Republic, Poland and Czechoslovakia. Despite government goals, there is little evidence that the average family size in most countries will increase beyond two children.

The status of women in Eastern Europe and the Soviet Union is key to understanding why population growth is low and why pro-natalist policies have not been more successful. Although women are fully emancipated legally and share equal rights with men, the passage of laws alone does not change deeply ingrained cultural attitudes. Sexism persists. Participation of women in the labor force is extremely high. In 1980, 90 percent of all women worked, but women are also still primarily responsible for childcare and domestic chores. The pressures of the double day are exacerbated by crowded housing conditions, lack of time- and energy-saving devices and the absence of modern shopping facilities and services. Women may spend up to two hours per day waiting in lines at shops. While awareness of the reasons why women are not willing to have more children has grown, there has been little cultural pressure on men to share the burden.

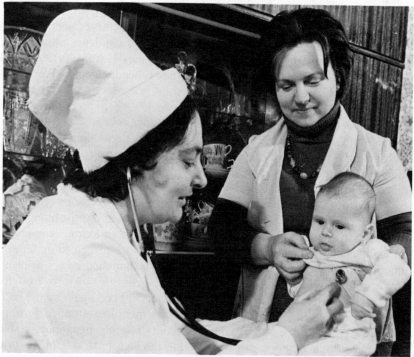

TASS Moscow, USSR

Women's Organizations in Population

TASS, Moscow USSR

Movement of Bulgarian Women

Bulgaria

ADDRESS:

SOFIA-1463, Blvd. Patriarche evtimit, 82, Bulgaria

EXECUTIVE OFFICER:			BRANCH OFFICES:
Elena Atanasova Lagadinova, President			

TELEPHONE NUMBER:		TELEX NUMBER:	
52-13-56			

APPROX. STAFF SIZE:	VOLUNTEER STAFF:	YEAR ESTABLISHED:
60		1857

NUMBER OF INDIVIDUAL MEMBERS:

FUNDING: Sale of the magazine *WOMEN TODAY*.

PRINCIPAL PURPOSE: To promote social activity of the Bulgarian woman and to enhance her role in social development.

MAIN ACTIVITIES: Education and aiding state, economic and public authorities in the development and implementation of policies related to women, children and the family.

POPULATION CONCERNS: Concerned with the implementation of the state policy for regulating family planning in conformity with the demands for quantitative and qualitative reproduction of the population.

SPECIFIC POPULATION ACTIVITIES: Education, demographic research, counselling, advocacy, Depo-Provera and natural family planning.

FORWARD-LOOKING STRATEGIES IMPLEMENTATIONS: The basic recommendations of the Strategies are laid down in Bulgarian legislation and the social policy with respect to women, children and the family is subject to continuous improvement.

OBSTACLES TO THE IMPLEMENTATION OF FORWARD-LOOKING STRATEGIES: None.

NOTES:

Hungarian Scientific Society for Family and Women's Welfare

HUNGARY

ADDRESS:

1525 Budapest, Keleti Karoly u.5-7, Hungary

EXECUTIVE OFFICER:

Dr. Andras Klinger, Secretary-General

BRANCH OFFICES:

TELEPHONE NUMBER:

159-240

TELEX NUMBER:

APPROX. STAFF SIZE:

VOLUNTEER STAFF:

YEAR ESTABLISHED:

1975

NUMBER OF INDIVIDUAL MEMBERS:

FUNDING: Membership fees.

PRINCIPAL PURPOSE:

MAIN ACTIVITIES: To increase popular knowledge in the field of family and women's welfare. To increase the scientific knowledge of the members. To promote theoretical and methodological development of research and the practical application of the results in Hungary and abroad.

POPULATION CONCERNS: The promotion of population research, information sharing among researchers, and information dissemination among the people.

SPECIFIC POPULATION ACTIVITIES: Education, demographic and contraceptive research and counselling.

FORWARD-LOOKING STRATEGIES IMPLEMENTATIONS: Analyzing the theoretical aspects of prospective Strategies in the field of women's welfare.

OBSTACLES TO THE IMPLEMENTATION OF FORWARD-LOOKING STRATEGIES: None.

NOTES:

Europe:
Western Europe

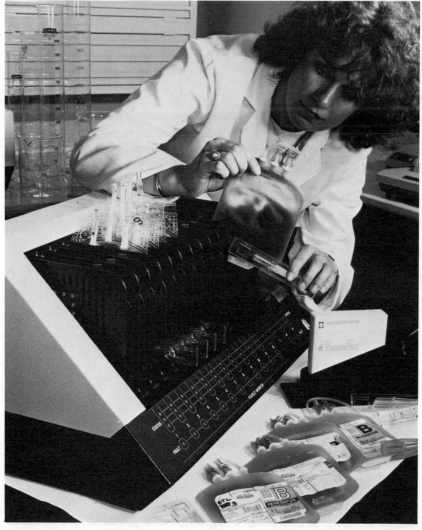

Western Europe

Western Europe has the slowest population growth rate in the world. Like North America, demographic patterns reflect a post-war "baby boom," declining fertility, heavy immigration and concerns about future health care and social security systems. In 1986 the population of the 19 countries of Western Europe was 350 million. Sixty percent of the people live in the five most populous countries: United Kingdom (57 million), France (55 million), Federal Republic of Germany (61 million), Italy (57 million) and Spain (39 million). The population will grow to only 361 million by the year 2000, with no increase in northern and western Europe, and only a slight increase in southern Europe. Birth rates are highest in Ireland and lowest in the Federal Republic of Germany.

The "baby boom" began to decline in 1965, following a general decline in birth and death rates that began around the turn of the century. This decline was brought out by industrialization, urbanization (which made children more expensive) and an increased interest of couples in practicing family planning. Unlike North America, immigration has had a limited impact on recent population growth since most countries placed severe restrictions on immigration following the oil crisis in 1973 and the subsequent recession.

Historically, Europe has been a continent of emigration , particularly to Australia, New Zealand, Canada and the United States, but in the 1960s Western Europe began to attract immigrants from all over the world drawn by social welfare systems and higher wages and incomes than in their own countries. These male "guest workers," mostly male, recruited by industry, began arriving in the major industrialized countries in the early 1960s. During that period they came primarily from Italy, Spain, Portugal and Yugoslavia, but later from Greece, Turkey and North Africa as well. Other streams of immigrants came from former colonies—Algerians and West Africans to France, Indonesians and Surinamese to the Netherlands, and Caribbeans, Pakistanis, and Indians to England. In the early 1970s large numbers of immigrants returned to Spain, Portugal and Greece, because socio-economic conditions in those countries had improved. Although Western Europe also has a substantial number of undocumented migrants (estimate at one million in Italy alone), restrictions on immigration have cut the numbers since 1980. In addition, Western Europe continues to receive a goodly number of refugees; close to 700,000 currently reside in 17 countries. Because of age composition and marital status, fertility rates among immigrants are higher—42.9 percent of total births in Luxembourg.

Western Europe faces a range of challenges because of low population growth. These include: a shift in health care services toward the needs of the aging, a shrinking labor force to support the social security system, high unemployment of young people because of persistent economic stagnation and serious environmental stress due to primarily urban industrialized societies, in particular air pollution, destruction of the forests and water pollution caused by the dumping of industrial wastes.

Concerns about population decline are more pronounced in some countries than in others. France, for example, has long been preoccupied with its low birth rate and has a pro-natalist policy. The Netherlands, on the other hand welcomes an end to population growth. Proponents of pro-natalist measures are concerned about the continued vitality of populations that do not reproduce themselves, the waning of regional power and the future of the welfare state. Opponents counter that economic integration is the way to maintain regional power, and they question the wisdom of a larger population when unemployment rates are so high and believe that greater investment in the young is the key to the future.

The status of women in the Western Europe has vastly improved since World War II, as it has in North America. The Scandinavian countries in particular are among the world's most egalitarian. Still the problems that plague North American women—low-paying sales and service jobs, higher unemployment rates and primary responsibility for domestic chores and childcare—continue to plague most Western European women as well. In 1982, the European Economic Community established a three-year program to improve women's, including immigrant women's, status by increasing educational and training opportunities, reforming tax systems that discriminate against women's employment and changing attitudes toward working women. This program is surely one result of the UN Decade for Women, as are the voting, labor and increased legal rights that Western European Women have gained through their own struggles and through organizational efforts.

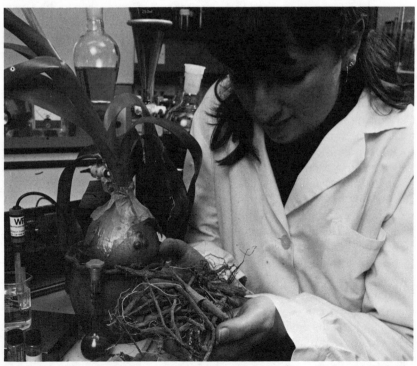

Courtesy of British Embassy

Fury's Field

Where do you go with your fury,
child,
when the roads are blocked with words
you don't understand
and your fear is worse
than the punishment.

Where do you go with your hate
when your mother
thoughtlessly
misconstrues your sincerity
and strangers laugh
at your games.

Do you then beat flat a field
in a box's amenable sand
and sow
the first seed of your fury.
Do you play a game
of dead dolls.

Say to the upright men
in the world
that they must harvest
your ripened hate
and plough the field of your fury
before they will see your face.

Cecil Bodker
Translator:
Nadia Christensen

Birth

Feeling the urge my mother
made for the privy at the far end of the courtyard
and strained strained with all her might
plagued by her painful constipation.
"It's like giving birth," she kept saying to herself
and strained strained harder
broad forehead dripping sweat
bluegreen eyes full of tears
veins swollen on the white neck
untouched by real or imitation jewels.
The kerchief slipped off
showing her dark hair;
with both hands she held onto the swollen belly with me inside.
To readjust her head-covering
like a good Orthodox Jew she let go of her belly
and kept straining straining.
The next thing was cry a long-drawn-out wail:
my head almost grazed the pit full of excrement.
A busy neighbor woman
ran to her aid and that's how I was born.
According to the gypsies a lucky future was in store for me;
for my father I was another mouth to feed
for my mother an unavoidable calamity
that befalls poor religious couples who make love
as a gesture of peace after months of quarrels
for my five not seven brothers
(luckily two died young)
a real toy that squealed
sucked at the wrinkled nipples
clung to the skin of mama's empty breasts
a mother undernourished like the mothers
of Asia Africa India South
or North America of yesterday today and tomorrow . . .

EDITH BUCK

Reprinted from *Italian Poetry Today*. Translated by Ruth Feldman and Brian Swann. Published in 1979 by New Rivers Press, St. Paul, MN.

Women's Organizations in Population

Courtesy of British Embassy Crown Copyright

Center for Research on European Women

BELGIUM

ADDRESS:

38 Stevin St., 1040 Brussels, Belgium

EXECUTIVE OFFICER:

Rebecca Franceskides and Francoise Stewart, President

BRANCH OFFICES:

TELEPHONE NUMBER:	TELEX NUMBER:
(02) 2305158	

APPROX. STAFF SIZE:	VOLUNTEER STAFF:	YEAR ESTABLISHED:
2	5	1981

NUMBER OF INDIVIDUAL MEMBERS:

72

FUNDING: Revenue from publications and research.

PRINCIPAL PURPOSE: Provide information for women on employment opportunities in Europe in all types of fields (education, technology . . . etc.).

MAIN ACTIVITIES: Publications, research, and consultations.

POPULATION CONCERNS: Family planning and reproduction in Europe and the Third World.

SPECIFIC POPULATION ACTIVITIES: Education regarding family planning options.

FORWARD-LOOKING STRATEGIES IMPLEMENTATIONS:

OBSTACLES TO THE IMPLEMENTATION OF FORWARD-LOOKING STRATEGIES:

NOTES:

The European Young Women's Christian Associations (YWCAs)

BELGUIM

ADDRESS:

94 Avenue Brugmann, B 1060-Brussels, Belgium

EXECUTIVE OFFICER:

Benita Johanson, European Liaison

BRANCH OFFICES:

TELEPHONE NUMBER:

02/344.98.61

TELEX NUMBER:

APPROX. STAFF SIZE:	VOLUNTEER STAFF:	YEAR ESTABLISHED:
1	10	1971

NUMBER OF INDIVIDUAL MEMBERS:

FUNDING: National European quotas, European Special Appeal, Friends of the European YWCAs and EEC Grants On Programmes.

PRINCIPAL PURPOSE: To enable asssociations in Europe which are affiliated to The World Young Women's Christian Association to meet together to discuss questions of mutual interest and to promote in Europe the programme of the world YWCA.

MAIN ACTIVITIES: Conducting European seminars involving an east/west programme and regional meetings; Representation in the form of consultative status to the council of Europe and attendance at Cee meetings; Coordination of National European Associations.

POPULATION CONCERNS: Women and girls associated with YWCAs in Europe.

SPECIFIC POPULATION ACTIVITIES: Education

FORWARD-LOOKING STRATEGIES IMPLEMENTATIONS: Providing information on health matters through an adult education programme.

OBSTACLES TO THE IMPLEMENTATION OF FORWARD-LOOKING STRATEGIES: Lack of women's awareness regarding Nairobi conference.

NOTES:

St. John's International Alliance   BELGIUM

ADDRESS:

Quai Churchill 19/061, 4020 Liege, Belgium

EXECUTIVE OFFICER:

Anne-Marie Pelzer

BRANCH OFFICES:

TELEPHONE NUMBER:

041/42.04.71

TELEX NUMBER:

APPROX. STAFF SIZE:

VOLUNTEER STAFF:

YEAR ESTABLISHED:

1911

NUMBER OF INDIVIDUAL MEMBERS:

FUNDING: Contributions from members

PRINCIPAL PURPOSE: To achieve equal rights between men and women in society and in church (especially Roman Catholic Church). To establish improvements in the mentalities and customs commensurate with improved laws.

MAIN ACTIVITIES: Studies; research and dialogue on questions of rights of women; theological basis for access of women to religious ministries; request to church authorities for participation of women in theological debate, in cultural organizations, and in religious press and TV.

POPULATION CONCERNS: Recognize population as a concern for the future of the world and as a primary women's issue. Concentrate efforts on attainment of equal rights between men and women.

SPECIFIC POPULATION ACTIVITIES: None.

FORWARD-LOOKING STRATEGIES IMPLEMENTATIONS: Working for the attainment of equal status of women.

OBSTACLES TO THE IMPLEMENTATION OF FORWARD-LOOKING STRATEGIES: Grave difficulty to achieve equality and promotion of women expecially in religious circles, with respect to religious thinking, ecclesiastical structures and practices. Sexist practices/thinking in religions are profound.

NOTES:

Universite des Femmes*

BELGIUM

ADDRESS:

Place Quetelet 1A, 1030 Bruxelles, Belgium

EXECUTIVE OFFICER:	BRANCH OFFICES:
Nadine Plateau, President	

TELEPHONE NUMBER:	TELEX NUMBER:
02.2196107	

APPROX. STAFF SIZE:	VOLUNTEER STAFF:	YEAR ESTABLISHED:
5	2	1979

NUMBER OF INDIVIDUAL MEMBERS:

350

FUNDING: Ministere de la Communaute Francaise**.

PRINCIPAL PURPOSE: To perform feminist research and organize to promote equality between women and men in the professional, social and family spheres.

MAIN ACTIVITIES: Sponsorship of courses, maintainence of library and documentation center and publication of bi-monthly magazine.

POPULATION CONCERNS: Issues related to women.

SPECIFIC POPULATION ACTIVITIES: Education, demographic and contraceptive research.

FORWARD-LOOKING STRATEGIES IMPLEMENTATIONS: Support of the basic human right to control fertility.

OBSTACLES TO THE IMPLEMENTATION OF FORWARD-LOOKING STRATEGIES: None indicated.

NOTES: *University of Women
**Community Ministry of French Women

ORGANIZATION:	
Vie Feminine Mouvement Chretien* d'Action Culturelly et Sociale	**BELGIUM**

ADDRESS:

rue de la Poste, 111, 1210 Brussels, Belgium

EXECUTIVE OFFICER:	BRANCH OFFICES:
Andree Delcourt, National President	

TELEPHONE NUMBER:	TELEX NUMBER:
02/217.29.52	

APPROX. STAFF SIZE:	VOLUNTEER STAFF:	YEAR ESTABLISHED:
135	6000	1920

NUMBER OF INDIVIDUAL MEMBERS:

+/- 90,000

FUNDING: Membership dues and subsidies from different ministries.

PRINCIPAL PURPOSE: To bring together and educate the working women of the world; to promote their active participation in the social, cultural, economic, political and religious life; and to work for equality between men and women.

MAIN ACTIVITIES: Participate in many cultural and social activities. Consciousness raising is a major focus.

POPULATION CONCERNS: Maternal and child health, daycare, school services and family and senior aid programs.

SPECIFIC POPULATION ACTIVITIES: Education and contraceptive research.

FORWARD-LOOKING STRATEGIES IMPLEMENTATIONS: None.

OBSTACLES TO THE IMPLEMENTATION OF FORWARD-LOOKING STRATEGIES: None.

NOTES: *Women's Christian Life Movement for Social and Cultural Action.

Women's Organization for Equality   BELGIUM

ADDRESS:

29, Rue Blanche, B-1050, Brussels, Belgium

EXECUTIVE OFFICER:	BRANCH OFFICES:
Wendy Pamay, Jennifer Connel and Rita Temmermans	

TELEPHONE NUMBER: 538.47.73

TELEX NUMBER:

APPROX. STAFF SIZE:	VOLUNTEER STAFF:	YEAR ESTABLISHED:
	10	1971

NUMBER OF INDIVIDUAL MEMBERS:

100

FUNDING: Membership fees.

PRINCIPAL PURPOSE: To raise women's consciousness about their position in society and to implement change.

MAIN ACTIVITIES: Hold regular meetings, publish a monthly newsletter, maintain a feminist library, support the battered women's refuge, sponsor social activities, offer courses/training in various subjects, support national or international feminist issues.

POPULATION CONCERNS: Those linked to feminism, such as the freedom and means for women to control their bodies, their fertility and their rights.

SPECIFIC POPULATION ACTIVITIES: Education, counselling, research and meetings regarding the history and situation of women.

FORWARD-LOOKING STRATEGIES IMPLEMENTATIONS: Endeavor to establish equal rights for all, in developed and in developing countries. Work to improve women's situation, perform women's studies, form networks, lobby for these causes.

OBSTACLES TO THE IMPLEMENTATION OF FORWARD-LOOKING STRATEGIES: The traditional resistance to equality for moral, religious and/or legal reasons; fear of organizing for economic reasons.

NOTES:

Associated Country Women of the World

ENGLAND

ADDRESS:

Vincent House, Vincent Square, London SWIP 2NB England

EXECUTIVE OFFICER:

Miss Jennifer Pearce, General Secretary

BRANCH OFFICES:

TELEPHONE NUMBER:

(01) 834-8635

TELEX NUMBER:

APPROX. STAFF SIZE:

12

VOLUNTEER STAFF:

YEAR ESTABLISHED:

1930

NUMBER OF INDIVIDUAL MEMBERS:

aprox. 9 million and 370 affiliated chapters

FUNDING: Subscriptions, voluntary donations, and international aid agencies for joint projects.

PRINCIPAL PURPOSE: To improve the status of women. To relieve poverty. To promote education and skill training for income generating schemes. And to encourage cultural exchange and friendship.

MAIN ACTIVITIES: Education - formal and non-formal, skill training through leadership development programmes, relief of poverty, promoting freindship and cultural exchange.

POPULATION CONCERNS: Nutrition and family health programmes.

SPECIFIC POPULATION ACTIVITIES: Education and counselling.

FORWARD-LOOKING STRATEGIES IMPLEMENTATIONS: Training women as entrepreneurs and managers. Maintaning co-action projects with UN agencies. Collaborating where possible with other international groups.

OBSTACLES TO THE IMPLEMENTATION OF FORWARD-LOOKING STRATEGIES: Some difficulties are identified in some of the developing countries where women are not included in the decision-making processes.

NOTES:

CHANGE

ENGLAND

ADDRESS:

P.O. Box 824 London S.E.24 9JX, United Kingdom

EXECUTIVE OFFICER:			BRANCH OFFICES:
Georgina Ashworth			

TELEPHONE NUMBER:		TELEX NUMBER:	

APPROX. STAFF SIZE:	VOLUNTEER STAFF:	YEAR ESTABLISHED:
3	3	1979

NUMBER OF INDIVIDUAL MEMBERS:

FUNDING: Sales of publications, consultancy fees, grants and donations.

PRINCIPAL PURPOSE: To research and publish reports on the condition and status of women all over the world. To lobby for women's human rights.

MAIN ACTIVITIES: Publishing and seeing recommendations put into effect, providing research and consultancy services to other organizations, maintaining a research and information archive.

POPULATION CONCERNS: Reproductive rights for women.

SPECIFIC POPULATION ACTIVITIES: Advocacy.

FORWARD-LOOKING STRATEGIES IMPLEMENTATIONS: Have persuaded the British government to begin implementing the Strategies and are monitoring this implementation. Have also persuaded European NGO's to recognize and implement the Strategies.

OBSTACLES TO THE IMPLEMENTATION OF FORWARD-LOOKING STRATEGIES: The traditional resistance to equality for moral, religious and/or legal reasons, fear of organizing for economic reasons.

NOTES:

*Business Address: % Institute of Education, Redford Way, London WCI UNITED KINGDOM

National Abortion Campaign　　**ENGLAND**

ADDRESS:

Leonora House, 70 Great Queen Street, London WC2B 5AX, Great Britain

EXECUTIVE OFFICER:			BRANCH OFFICES:
Leonora Lloyd, National Coordinator			

TELEPHONE NUMBER:	TELEX NUMBER:	
01 405 4801		

APPROX. STAFF SIZE:	VOLUNTEER STAFF:	YEAR ESTABLISHED:
	5	1975

NUMBER OF INDIVIDUAL MEMBERS:

175

FUNDING: Membership fees, sales of literature, and donations.

PRINCIPAL PURPOSE: To campaign to defend the current abortion law when it is threatened and to replace it with a law that recognizes women's right to abortion, which ensures that adequate free facilities are provided country-wide.

MAIN ACTIVITIES: Campaigning, speaking to schools, labor movement organizations, women's and students' groups, producing literature, publishing a quarterly magazine (NAC News).

POPULATION CONCERNS: The belief that women must determine if and when to have children.

SPECIFIC POPULATION ACTIVITIES: Advocacy and Education.

FORWARD-LOOKING STRATEGIES IMPLEMENTATIONS: Were aware of the Strategies but did not indicate implementations.

OBSTACLES TO THE IMPLEMENTATION OF FORWARD-LOOKING STRATEGIES: None indicated.

NOTES:

National Council of Women of Great Britain

ENGLAND

ADDRESS:

34 Lower Sloane Street, London SWIW 8BP, Great Britain

EXECUTIVE OFFICER:			BRANCH OFFICES:
Mrs. E. Marten, President			

TELEPHONE NUMBER:	TELEX NUMBER:	

APPROX. STAFF SIZE:	VOLUNTEER STAFF:	YEAR ESTABLISHED:
1	varies	1895

NUMBER OF INDIVIDUAL MEMBERS:

3003

FUNDING: Member's subscriptions.

PRINCIPAL PURPOSE: To promote human rights in the U.K. and improve quality of life for all. To stop discrimination against women and promote their participation in national affairs. To liaison with societies having similar purpose, especially the international council of women.

MAIN ACTIVITIES: Studying current legislation, especially that which affects women and families to campaign and lobby Parliament for changes in accordance with the principal purpose.

POPULATION CONCERNS: Lobbying for more of British government's foreign aid to be channelled into population programs in developing countries.

SPECIFIC POPULATION ACTIVITIES: Advocacy and education.

FORWARD LOOKING-STRATEGIES IMPLEMENTATIONS: Implementing Forward-Looking Strategies, but there is no elaboration.

OBSTACLES TO THE IMPLEMENTATION OF FORWARD-LOOKING STRATEGIES:

NOTES:

National Federation of Women's Institutes

ENGLAND

ADDRESS:

39 Eccleston Street, London, SW1W9NT, UK

EXECUTIVE OFFICER:			BRANCH OFFICES:
Mrs. Anne Ballard, General Secretary			

TELEPHONE NUMBER:	TELEX NUMBER:	
017307212		

APPROX. STAFF SIZE:	VOLUNTEER STAFF:	YEAR ESTABLISHED:
52		1915

NUMBER OF INDIVIDUAL MEMBERS:

352,000

FUNDING: Membership fees, grants and revenue from commercial activities.

PRINCIPAL PURPOSE: To improve rural living conditions.

MAIN ACTIVITIES: Providing social and education opportunities for women in home economics, crafts, music, drama, citizenship, health, welfare, consumer affairs, environmental matters and co-operative enterprise.

POPULATION CONCERNS: Since 1972, the NFWI has campaigned for a statutory full free family planning service.

SPECIFIC POPULATION ACTIVITIES: Education, and delivery of services.

FORWARD LOOKING-STRATEGIES IMPLEMENTATIONS: Working in health issues and promoting the representation of women in public life.

OBSTACLES TO THE IMPLEMENTATION OF FORWARD-LOOKING STRATEGIES: Slowness on part of government to follow up on FLS.

NOTES:

Scarlett Epstein Social Assessment Counsultant (SESAC) ENGLAND

ADDRESS:

"Hethersett", North Bank, Hassocks BN6 8JG, England

EXECUTIVE OFFICER:

Professor T. Scarlett Epstein

BRANCH OFFICES:

TELEPHONE NUMBER:	TELEX NUMBER:
07918-5579	

APPROX. STAFF SIZE:	VOLUNTEER STAFF:	YEAR ESTABLISHED:
2		1977

NUMBER OF INDIVIDUAL MEMBERS:

11

FUNDING: Donor contributions.

PRINCIPAL PURPOSE: Action oriented studies of the roles of rural women in development.

MAIN ACTIVITIES: Action research, consultancies, lectures, and publications.

POPULATION CONCERNS: Demographic structures, grassroots level interests in family planning and those of traditional family planning.

SPECIFIC POPULATION ACTIVITIES: Education, counselling, demographic and contraceptive research.

FORWARD-LOOKING STRATEGIES IMPLEMENTATIONS: Are aware of the Strategies but are not implementing them.

OBSTACLES TO THE IMPLEMENTATION OF FORWARD-LOOKING STRATEGIES: None indicated.

NOTES:

World Association of Girl Guides and Girl Scouts

ENGLAND

ADDRESS:

World Bureau, Olave Centre, 12C Lyndhurst Road, London NW3 5PQ, England

EXECUTIVE OFFICER:			BRANCH OFFICES:
Ellen Clark, Director			

TELEPHONE NUMBER:		TELEX NUMBER:
794-1181		

APPROX. STAFF SIZE:	VOLUNTEER STAFF:	YEAR ESTABLISHED:
28	30	1928

NUMBER OF INDIVIDUAL MEMBERS:

More than 8 million in 108 countries

FUNDING: Two main sources of income - the Quata, which is the annual contribution paid by every member organization, and the Thinking Day Fund.

PRINCIPAL PURPOSE: To promote unity of purpose and understanding in principles of Girl Guide/Girl Scout Movement and to encourage international and national friendship among girls. Particular concerns are that guiding/scouting meet the development needs of the countries and keep abreast of constantly changing world conditions.

MAIN ACTIVITIES: Organize international meetings, trainings and seminars; operate a Mutual Aid Scheme for national organizations; promote international education through above activities and *It's Our World: A Program for International Education*; encourage international awareness and friendship through Thinking Day (Feb. 22); cooperates with U.N. and special agencies and international non-governmental organizations.

POPULATION CONCERNS: Many member organizations are involved in some sort of family life education project, which might include maternal and child health care, family planning activities, work to help adolescents become responsible adults.

SPECIFIC POPULATION ACTIVITIES: Education.

FORWARD-LOOKING STRATEGIES IMPLEMENTATIONS: Encouraging member organizations to help in the implementation. Disseminated information on Nairobi Conference to member organizations; included this information in special publication devoted to strategies and in newsletter.

OBSTACLES TO THE IMPLEMENTATION OF FORWARD-LOOKING STRATEGIES: None indicated.

NOTES:

The Women and Development Program
of the Commonwealth Secretariat ENGLAND

ADDRESS:

Marlborough House, Pall Mall, London SW1Y 5HX, England

EXECUTIVE OFFICER:			BRANCH OFFICES:
Dorienne Wilson-Smillie, Director			

TELEPHONE NUMBER:	TELEX NUMBER:	
839.3411	27678	

APPROX. STAFF SIZE:	VOLUNTEER STAFF:	YEAR ESTABLISHED:
over 400		1965

NUMBER OF INDIVIDUAL MEMBERS:

49 member states

FUNDING: Commonwealth fund for Technical Cooperation and subscriptions from member governments.

PRINCIPAL PURPOSE: To foster development of commonwealth countries through exchange of experience and mutual assistance.

MAIN ACTIVITIES: Acts as a focal point for identifying the needs and priorities of commonwealth women and ensures that these are reflected in all Secretariat programs and Commonwealth policy discussions. Works to advance the interests of women through training programs, research and exchange of experience.

POPULATION CONCERNS: Those related to women's issues, such as child care services, education on reproduction and reproductive rights.

SPECIFIC POPULATION ACTIVITIES: Education, demographic research, and advocacy.

FORWARD-LOOKING STRATEGIES IMPLEMENTATIONS: Those which relate to international agencies, to development of women's organizations, bureaus and education.

OBSTACLES TO THE IMPLEMENTATION OF FORWARD-LOOKING STRATEGIES: Translating the Strategies into guidelines that senior policy makers can use to affect change.

NOTES:

Svenska Kvinnoforbundet r.f.   # FINLAND

ADDRESS:

Bulevarden 7A, 00120 Helsingfors, FINLAND

EXECUTIVE OFFICER:	BRANCH OFFICES:
Margareta Pietikainen, FM Chairperson	

TELEPHONE NUMBER:	TELEX NUMBER:
90-640313	

APPROX. STAFF SIZE:	VOLUNTEER STAFF:	YEAR ESTABLISHED:
3		1907

NUMBER OF INDIVIDUAL MEMBERS:

2700

FUNDING: Swedish People's Party. Suenska Kvinnoforbundet is the women's organization of the party.

PRINCIPAL PURPOSE: To help and support women to participate in all sectors (economic, political, cultural) and at all levels of community.

MAIN ACTIVITIES: Arranging meetings and seminars about themes that are of interest to our members. For example about the situation in the underdeveloped countries, the political life in Finland, women and education, women and work, women and helath, etc.

POPULATION CONCERNS: Fertility control as relates to women's equality.

SPECIFIC POPULATION ACTIVITIES: Education.

FORWARD-LOOKING STRATEGIES IMPLEMENTATIONS: Will implement when the version for Finland is ready.

OBSTACLES TO THE IMPLEMENTATION OF FORWARD-LOOKING STRATEGIES:

NOTES:

Union of Finnish Women's Movement   **FINLAND**

ADDRESS:

Bulevardi 11A1, 00120, Helsinki, Finland

EXECUTIVE OFFICER:			BRANCH OFFICES:
Arja Laine, President			

TELEPHONE NUMBER:		TELEX NUMBER:	
90-643158			

APPROX. STAFF SIZE:	VOLUNTEER STAFF:	YEAR ESTABLISHED:
1	20	1892

NUMBER OF INDIVIDUAL MEMBERS:

2,000

FUNDING: Not indicated

PRINCIPAL PURPOSE: To increase women's influence on all parts of society.

MAIN ACTIVITIES: Sponsoring meetings seminars. Publishing reports.

POPULATION CONCERNS:

SPECIFIC POPULATION ACTIVITIES: Education and counselling.

FORWARD LOOKING-STRATEGIES IMPLEMENTATIONS:

OBSTACLES TO THE IMPLEMENTATION OF FORWARD-LOOKING STRATEGIES:

NOTES:

International Council of Women **FRANCE**

ADDRESS:

13 rue Caumartin, 75009 Paris, France

EXECUTIVE OFFICER:			BRANCH OFFICES:
Dr. Sookja Hong, President			

TELEPHONE NUMBER:		TELEX NUMBER:
47 42 19 40		

APPROX. STAFF SIZE:	VOLUNTEER STAFF:	YEAR ESTABLISHED:
4	1	1888

NUMBER OF INDIVIDUAL MEMBERS:

75 Nat'l Councils

FUNDING:

PRINCIPAL PURPOSE: To promote equal rights and responsibilities for both men and women in all spheres by removing all forms of discrimination based on race, sex, language or religion. To promote recognition and respect for human rights. To support all efforts to achieve peace through negotiation and arbitration. To encourage the integration of women in development and in decision-making bodies.

MAIN ACTIVITIES: Organize international meetings and regional, sub-regional and national seminars and workshops. Participate in development programs in cooperation with other organizations.

POPULATION CONCERNS: ICW has a large Project Development program and has set health as a priority for the post-decade era.

SPECIFIC POPULATION ACTIVITIES: Education, counselling, health care projects.

FORWARD-LOOKING STRATEGIES IMPLEMENTATIONS: The ICW urges its affiliated councils to actively implement the Strategies most urgent and appropriate to the needs of the women of their country.

OBSTACLES TO THE IMPLEMENTATION OF FORWARD-LOOKING STRATEGIES: Inadequate financial support.

NOTES:

Ligue du Droit des Femmes*

FRANCE

ADDRESS:

54, Avenue de Choisy, 75013 Paris, France

EXECUTIVE OFFICER:			BRANCH OFFICES:
Anne Zelensky, President			

TELEPHONE NUMBER:	TELEX NUMBER:	
45851137		

APPROX. STAFF SIZE:	VOLUNTEER STAFF:	YEAR ESTABLISHED:
	yes	1974

NUMBER OF INDIVIDUAL MEMBERS:

2000

FUNDING: Through the French Association Law 1901.

PRINCIPAL PURPOSE: The struggle against sexism and violence against women.

MAIN ACTIVITIES: Homes for women and children victims of domestic violence, bringing attention to sexism in the media, the workplace, and the law.

POPULATION CONCERNS: None indicated.

SPECIFIC POPULATION ACTIVITIES: Advocacy, contraceptive research and the delivery of services.

FORWARD-LOOKING STRATEGIES IMPLEMENTATIONS: Promotion of women's rights.

OBSTACLES TO THE IMPLEMENTATION OF FORWARD-LOOKING STRATEGIES: None indicated.

NOTES: *League for the Rights of Women

Union de Femmes Francaise*

FRANCE

ADDRESS:

146 rue du Faubourg Poissonniere, 75010 Paris, France

EXECUTIVE OFFICER:

Denise Breton, President

BRANCH OFFICES:

TELEPHONE NUMBER:

452-6033

TELEX NUMBER:

APPROX. STAFF SIZE:	VOLUNTEER STAFF:	YEAR ESTABLISHED:
20	Over 100	1945

NUMBER OF INDIVIDUAL MEMBERS:

190,000

FUNDING: Member donations.

PRINCIPAL PURPOSE: Equality for women in law and fact, in work, family, and all of society. Action for international peace and solidarity.

MAIN ACTIVITIES: 3500 local countries unite women for action to create jobs, open day care centers, raise family allocations. Social and cultural activities, including cultural outings, gym and cooking classes.

POPULATION CONCERNS: That conditions in life and work favor the woman's choice of having a child: longer maternal leave, more day care centers, family allocations to begin after the first child.

SPECIFIC POPULATION ACTIVITIES: None indicated.

FORWARD-LOOKING STRATEGIES IMPLEMENTATIONS: Equality for women especially in the workplace.

OBSTACLES TO THE IMPLEMENTATION OF FORWARD-LOOKING STRATEGIES: Currently, the government is not encouraging the implementation of the Strategies.

NOTES: *Union of French Women

World Movement of Mothers **FRANCE**

ADDRESS:

56 rue de Passy, 75016 Paris, France

EXECUTIVE OFFICER:			BRANCH OFFICES:
Ms. Monique de VAUBLANC, Gen. Sec.			

TELEPHONE NUMBER:	TELEX NUMBER:	
(1) 45-20-55-80		

APPROX. STAFF SIZE:	VOLUNTEER STAFF:	YEAR ESTABLISHED:
	5	1947

NUMBER OF INDIVIDUAL MEMBERS:

50 NGOs

FUNDING: Membership fees.

PRINCIPAL PURPOSE: To represent mothers in international plans, to help them assume their duties to family and society and to make known the social functions of motherhood.

MAIN ACTIVITIES: Organizing seminars on parenting and family life; administering opinion surveys; engaging in information and documentation exchanges and participating in international meetings, especially within the framework of the UN and its agencies for which WMM is a consultant.

POPULATION CONCERNS: Interested in parenting, the quality of life and the welfare of children.

SPECIFIC POPULATION ACTIVITIES: Education and services such as documentation and dissemination of information.

FORWARD-LOOKING STRATEGIES IMPLEMENTATIONS: Strategies related to the activities described are being implemented.

OBSTACLES TO THE IMPLEMENTATION OF FORWARD-LOOKING STRATEGIES: Ignorance and tradition.

NOTES:

World Union of Catholic Women's Organizations

FRANCE

ADDRESS:

20 rue Notre Dame des Champs, 75006 Paris, France

EXECUTIVE OFFICER:		BRANCH OFFICES:
Eleanor E. Aitken		

TELEPHONE NUMBER:	TELEX NUMBER:
45.44.27.65	

APPROX. STAFF SIZE:	VOLUNTEER STAFF:	YEAR ESTABLISHED:
3		1910

NUMBER OF INDIVIDUAL MEMBERS:

FUNDING: Through membership fees, gifts from member organizations, subsidies from funding agencies who support our programmes and project for education, development and self-sufficiency.

PRINCIPAL PURPOSE: To promote the contribution of Catholic women to the ecclesiastical and human community; study problems of general interest in international affairs; promote action to enable women to better fulfil their role in churce and society; represent the opinion of Catholic women before international organizations; coordinate on the international level the activities of Catholic women's organizations and serve as a link between them.

MAIN ACTIVITIES: Creating awareness of women's rights and responsibilities; encouraging solidarity among women; bonding of women through international and regional conferences and seminars; providing information to and circulating information from official international organizations; support of women and their projects through education, practical assistance and funding.

POPULATION CONCERNS: Responsible family planning; stable family relationships; guidance and training of youth; provision for the elderly; help to refugees.

SPECIFIC POPULATION ACTIVITIES: Education and counselling.

FORWARD-LOOKING STRATEGIES IMPLEMENTATIONS: Next General Assembly in 1987 will include Study Days on Education, family, human dignity, technology, communications, decision-making, development.

OBSTACLES TO THE IMPLEMENTATION OF FORWARD-LOOKING STRATEGIES: The scope is vast. Have circulated a questionnaire to member organizations asking them to choose specific aspects of above concerns which are of vital interest to them e.g. literacy, family planning, skills training, prostitution, pornography, and advocacy.

NOTES:

ORGANIZATION:

Mediterranean Women's Studies Institute

GREECE

ADDRESS:

192b, Leof. Alexandras, Athens, GR-115 21, GREECE

EXECUTIVE OFFICER:			BRANCH OFFICES:
Eleni Arnopoulos-Stamiris, Director			

TELEPHONE NUMBER:	TELEX NUMBER:
01-6436604/01-6436436	

APPROX. STAFF SIZE:	VOLUNTEER STAFF:	YEAR ESTABLISHED:
6	5-8	1982

NUMBER OF INDIVIDUAL MEMBERS:

40

FUNDING: By national or international organizations on a project basis.

PRINCIPAL PURPOSE: To produce, collect and disseminate information on Mediterranean Women.

MAIN ACTIVITIES: Performing feminist research and publishing results, maintaining information and documentation center, sponsoring women's studies and training program, promoting feminist methodology for conflict resolution and promoting peace in the region, sponsoring symposia.

POPULATION CONCERNS: Concerned with population research, demographic data and information on Mediterranean Women.

SPECIFIC POPULATION ACTIVITIES: Education, demographic research, teaching women's studies and demographic issues.

FORWARD-LOOKING STRATEGIES IMPLEMENTATIONS: Women's studies and research and the promotion of peace and conflict resolution.

OBSTACLES TO THE IMPLEMENTATION OF FORWARD-LOOKING STRATEGIES: Inadequate funding for research.

NOTES:

Young Women's Christian Association (YWCA) of Greece

GREECE

ADDRESS:

11 Amerikis Street, 106 72 Athens, Greece

EXECUTIVE OFFICER:

Voula Lagou, National General Secretary

BRANCH OFFICES:

TELEPHONE NUMBER:

3624293

TELEX NUMBER:

APPROX. STAFF SIZE:	VOLUNTEER STAFF:	YEAR ESTABLISHED:
5	1	1923

NUMBER OF INDIVIDUAL MEMBERS:

15,000

FUNDING: Membership dues and participation fees.

PRINCIPAL PURPOSE: To promote the development of women and young girls.

MAIN ACTIVITIES: Adult education programs.

POPULATION CONCERNS: Family planning education and improving services for women.

SPECIFIC POPULATION ACTIVITIES: Education and advocacy.

FORWARD-LOOKING STRATEGIES IMPLEMENTATIONS: Promoting health education.

OBSTACLES TO THE IMPLEMENTATION OF FORWARD-LOOKING STRATEGIES: Difficulties in changing people's attitudes.

NOTES:

Federation Internationale des*
Femmes des Carrieres Juridiques

ITALY

ADDRESS:

Via R. Giovagnoli 6, 00152 Roma, Italy

EXECUTIVE OFFICER:			BRANCH OFFICES:
Teresa A. Brugiatelli, President			

TELEPHONE NUMBER:	TELEX NUMBER:
06-5818107	

APPROX. STAFF SIZE:	VOLUNTEER STAFF:	YEAR ESTABLISHED:
18		1928

NUMBER OF INDIVIDUAL MEMBERS:

150

FUNDING: Membership fees.

PRINCIPAL PURPOSE: To promote human rights.

MAIN ACTIVITIES: Research, meetings and cultural exchanges.

POPULATION CONCERNS: Issues related to women's concerns.

SPECIFIC POPULATION ACTIVITIES: Counselling and advocacy.

FORWARD-LOOKING STRATEGIES IMPLEMENTATIONS: Promoting women's rights.

OBSTACLES TO THE IMPLEMENTATION OF FORWARD-LOOKING STRATEGIES: Economic and political crises.

NOTES: *International Federation of Women with Legal Careers.

Isis International

ITALY

ADDRESS:

Santa Maria dell'anima 30, 00186 Roma, Italy

EXECUTIVE OFFICER:			BRANCH OFFICES:

EXECUTIVE OFFICER:

Marilee Karl

BRANCH OFFICES:

Isis InternationalCasilla 2067, Correo
    CentralSantiago, CHILE
746-097

TELEPHONE NUMBER:	TELEX NUMBER:
6565842	

APPROX. STAFF SIZE:	VOLUNTEER STAFF:	YEAR ESTABLISHED:
6	1	1974

Via Santa Maria dell'Anima 30, 00186 Roma, Italy

NUMBER OF INDIVIDUAL MEMBERS:

FUNDING: Grants

PRINCIPAL PURPOSE: To serve as a women's information and communication service. To emphasize communication among women, especially in Third World countries.

MAIN ACTIVITIES: Maintains an expanding network of over 10,000 contracts in 150 countries. Provides information and referral services, produces regular publications, coordinates regional and international networks, and offers training and technical assistance in communication and information skills.

POPULATION CONCERNS: Women's health and women's reproductive freedom, as well as any other organizing issues for women.

SPECIFIC POPULATION ACTIVITIES: Education.

FORWARD-LOOKING STRATEGIES IMPLEMENTATIONS: Communication media and networking.

OBSTACLES TO THE IMPLEMENTATION OF FORWARD-LOOKING STRATEGIES: None.

NOTES:

Dutch Section of Women's International League of Peace & Freedom **THE NETHERLANDS**

ADDRESS:

Kometeulaaee 31, 3721 JA Billuoveu, The Netherlands

EXECUTIVE OFFICER:			BRANCH OFFICES:
Board of Members			

TELEPHONE NUMBER:	TELEX NUMBER:	
030-761545		

APPROX. STAFF SIZE:	VOLUNTEER STAFF:	YEAR ESTABLISHED:
280	3	1984

NUMBER OF INDIVIDUAL MEMBERS:

150

FUNDING: Member Contributions.

PRINCIPAL PURPOSE: To bring together women from different backgrounds who are united by the determination to study and make known the causes of war and to work for constructive peace.

MAIN ACTIVITIES: Research and advocacy.

POPULATION CONCERNS: Complete reproductive freedom for women.

SPECIFIC POPULATION ACTIVITIES: Advocacy.

FORWARD LOOKING-STRATEGIES IMPLEMENTATIONS: Implementing the strategies concerning peace, equality, and development.

OBSTACLES TO THE IMPLEMENTATION OF FORWARD-LOOKING STRATEGIES: The strategies are not widely known and governments have not supported them a great deal.

NOTES:

ORGANIZATION:

The Netherlands Council
of Women   THE NETHERLANDS

ADDRESS:

Laan van Meerdervoort 30, 2517 Al Den Haag, The Netherlands

EXECUTIVE OFFICER:			BRANCH OFFICES:
Drs. K.M. Stoelinga-Coomans, President			

TELEPHONE NUMBER:	TELEX NUMBER:	
070-469304		

APPROX. STAFF SIZE:	VOLUNTEER STAFF:	YEAR ESTABLISHED:
21		1975

NUMBER OF INDIVIDUAL MEMBERS:

500,000

FUNDING: By the Dutch government.

PRINCIPAL PURPOSE: To make women aware of their position in society and of their possibilities. To stimulate women to actually take full and equal share in responsibilities in all fields of society.

MAIN ACTIVITIES: NVR is an umbrella organization of 40 independent women's organizations. The general board of the NVR concentrates on: equal rights and opportunities as a process of change in mentality; labor, both paid and unpaid, as a central factor in the structure of society.

POPULATION CONCERNS: The NVR organized a seminar "Population growth in the Third World." In 1987 several activities planned within the framework of the IVSH: a congress on women and habitat.

SPECIFIC POPULATION ACTIVITIES: Education.

FORWARD-LOOKING STRATEGIES IMPLEMENTATIONS: Participated in Nairobi Conference, which resulted in publications, workshops and seminars for NVR to promote strategies put forth at the conference.

OBSTACLES TO THE IMPLEMENTATION OF FORWARD-LOOKING STRATEGIES: Principally financial obstacles.

NOTES:

Research & Documentation Centre
Women and Autonomy **THE NETHERLANDS**

ADDRESS:

Rijksuniversiteit Leiden Statonsplein 10, 2312 AK LEIDEN, The Netherlands

EXECUTIVE OFFICER:			BRANCH OFFICES:
Dr. E. Postel/Costen			

TELEPHONE NUMBER:	TELEX NUMBER:
071-148333 ext. 4106	

APPROX. STAFF SIZE:	VOLUNTEER STAFF:	YEAR ESTABLISHED:
6	5	1976

NUMBER OF INDIVIDUAL MEMBERS:

FUNDING: Funded by the University and by the Dutch government.

PRINCIPAL PURPOSE: Documentation and research on ''Women and Development.'' Improvement of expertise on WID through education inside and outside the University. Dissemination of knowledge and information.

MAIN ACTIVITIES: Documentation centre. Research activities and consulting work.

POPULATION CONCERNS: Education on population.

SPECIFIC POPULATION ACTIVITIES: Education.

FORWARD LOOKING-STRATEGIES IMPLEMENTATIONS: Not in the position of implementing these Strategies.

OBSTACLES TO THE IMPLEMENTATION OF FORWARD-LOOKING STRATEGIES:

NOTES:

WEMOS/HAI International Women's Network on Pharmaceuticals **THE NETHERLANDS**

ADDRESS:

P.O. Box 4263, 1009 AG Amsterdam

EXECUTIVE OFFICER:

Marlein Van Rooy

BRANCH OFFICES:

TELEPHONE NUMBER:

020-653115

TELEX NUMBER:

APPROX. STAFF SIZE:	VOLUNTEER STAFF:	YEAR ESTABLISHED:
1	10	1984

NUMBER OF INDIVIDUAL MEMBERS:

FUNDING: Grants from development organizations.

PRINCIPAL PURPOSE: To support Third World women and women's organizations with information on hormonal drugs and contraceptives.

MAIN ACTIVITIES: Producing scientific, education and action material. Taking action against western industries and lobbying for legislation and education. Building women's network to exchange information. Carrying out and promoting contraceptive research.

POPULATION CONCERNS: Making cheap and safe contraceptives available to all women. Promoting reproductive freedom. Promoting access to information on pharmaceuticals produced especially for women.

SPECIFIC POPULATION ACTIVITIES:

FORWARD LOOKING-STRATEGIES IMPLEMENTATIONS:

OBSTACLES TO THE IMPLEMENTATION OF FORWARD-LOOKING STRATEGIES:

NOTES:

Women's Global Network on Reproductive Rights **THE NETHERLANDS**

ADDRESS:

Minahassastraat 1, 1009 AB Amsterdam, The Netherlands

EXECUTIVE OFFICER:			BRANCH OFFICES:
Elizabeth van Zoetendaal, Network Coordinator			

TELEPHONE NUMBER:	TELEX NUMBER:	
(20) 92 39 00		

APPROX. STAFF SIZE:	VOLUNTEER STAFF:	YEAR ESTABLISHED:
4	5	1978

NUMBER OF INDIVIDUAL MEMBERS:

600 groups & individuals

FUNDING: Grants from various national and international funding agencies/governments, membership fees, and subscriptions.

PRINCIPAL PURPOSE: To work for and support women's right to decide if, when and how to have children, regardless of nationality, class, race, age, religion, disability, sexuality, or marital status.

MAIN ACTIVITIES: Networking and strengthening national, regional and international links between reproductive rights and women's health activists/groups/clinics. Exchanging information and ideas for grassroots work, campaigning and solidarity work. Producing a quarterly newsletter in English and Spanish. Monitoring and contributing to research on reproductive health issues.

POPULATION CONCERNS: Supporting improvements in women's health, social and economic position as the only just form of affecting population, and making a distinction between demographic issues and family planning. Promoting policies, laws and services which empower women to have the children they want, neither more nor fewer. Opposing policies, laws and services which take the decision about childbearing out of women's hands, either through incentives or coercion, as abuses of women's need for family planning.

SPECIFIC POPULATION ACTIVITIES: Education, advocacy, information, campaigning, social/medical research by some member groups/individuals, and delivery of services by some member clinics and groups: sterilization, pill, IUD, diaphragm, foam, Norplant, Depo-Provera, natural family planning.

FORWARD-LOOKING STRATEGIES IMPLEMENTATIONS: Working to insure women's right to control their own fertility as outlined in the FLS.

OBSTABLES TO THE IMPLEMENTION OF FORWARD-LOOKING STRATEGIES: Poverty, lack of health care services that meet women's needs, restrictive laws, religious opposition, male domination of women, abuses and discriminatory practices in many population and family planning programmes.

NOTES:

Comissao da Condicao Feminina
(Commission on the Femine Condition)
PORTUGAL

ADDRESS:

Av. da Republica, 32-1, 1093 Lisbon, Portugal

EXECUTIVE OFFICER:			BRANCH OFFICES:
Regina Tavares da Silva, President			Rue Dr. Magalames Lemos 109-2, 4000 Porto, Portugal

TELEPHONE NUMBER:	TELEX NUMBER:
776081	

APPROX. STAFF SIZE:	VOLUNTEER STAFF:	YEAR ESTABLISHED:
40	3	1974

NUMBER OF INDIVIDUAL MEMBERS:

FUNDING: Public Administration funds.

PRINCIPAL PURPOSE: Official commission attached to the Prime Minister's office to contribute towards a change of attitudes of both women and men, so that every person may achieve full human dignity; to promote co-responsibility of men and women in all sectors of Portuguese life, and to encourage society to regard this maturity as a fundamental social importance.

MAIN ACTIVITIES: Research and action in all sectors related to the status of women; education, work, health, political and public participation. Coordination of a counselling service and library open to the public, publications and media campaigns.

POPULATION CONCERNS: Family planning is of fundamental importance to the status of women and special attention is paid to it as a human right and health issue.

SPECIFIC POPULATION ACTIVITIES: Education and advocacy.

FORWARD-LOOKING STRATEGIES IMPLEMENTATIONS: We are working on all the Strategies.

OBSTACLES TO THE IMPLEMENTATION OF FORWARD-LOOKING STRATEGIES: Many, among them economic hardships and low education levels.

NOTES:

ORGANIZATION:

Mujeres Por Europa

SPAIN

ADDRESS:

Consejo Federal del Movimiento Europeo, Calle Gran Via, 43, 3rdF, Madrid 13, Spain

EXECUTIVE OFFICER:			BRANCH OFFICES:
Francisca Tarazaga Segues, President			

TELEPHONE NUMBER:		TELEX NUMBER:	
248.08.69			

APPROX. STAFF SIZE:	VOLUNTEER STAFF:	YEAR ESTABLISHED:	
1	yes	1982	

NUMBER OF INDIVIDUAL MEMBERS:	
50	

FUNDING: Did not specify.

PRINCIPAL PURPOSE: Unification of the objectives of all the women of Europe.

MAIN ACTIVITIES: Seminars, conferences, public events and the attainment of concrete objectives related to the situation of women.

POPULATION CONCERNS: None indicated.

SPECIFIC POPULATION ACTIVITIES: Education and advocacy.

FORWARD-LOOKING STRATEGIES IMPLEMENTATIONS: Are aware of the Strategies but did not indicate implementations.

OBSTACLES TO THE IMPLEMENTATION OF FORWARD-LOOKING STRATEGIES: None indicated.

NOTES:

Moderate Women's Association

SWEDEN

ADDRESS:

Box 1243, 111 82 Stockholm, Sweden

EXECUTIVE OFFICER:

Ann Cathrine Haglund, Chairperson

BRANCH OFFICES:

TELEPHONE NUMBER:

08-236180

TELEX NUMBER:

APPROX. STAFF SIZE:	VOLUNTEER STAFF:	YEAR ESTABLISHED:
3		1920

NUMBER OF INDIVIDUAL MEMBERS:

54,000

FUNDING: Membership fees and contributions from the state and the mother party.

PRINCIPAL PURPOSE: To educate women for political tasks.

MAIN ACTIVITIES: Education and political activities.

POPULATION CONCERNS: Interested in issues related to improving the status of women in politics and in society as a whole.

SPECIFIC POPULATION ACTIVITIES: Education and political activities that are related to issues important to women, such as family policy.

FORWARD-LOOKING STRATEGIES IMPLEMENTATIONS: Promoting equal rights and opportunities for women in all fields.

OBSTACLES TO THE IMPLEMENTATION OF FORWARD-LOOKING STRATEGIES:

NOTES:

*Business Address: Lilia Nygatan 13, 111 28 Stockholm, Sweden

Women's International League for Peace & Freedom, Swedish Section **SWEDEN**

ADDRESS:

Packhusgrand 6, 11130, Stockholm, Sweden

EXECUTIVE OFFICER:

Elisabeth Gerle

BRANCH OFFICES:

IUFF-Goreborg Box 7280
Goteborg, Sweden
031-120044

TELEPHONE NUMBER:

08-211720

TELEX NUMBER:

APPROX. STAFF SIZE:	VOLUNTEER STAFF:	YEAR ESTABLISHED:
3	3	1915

NUMBER OF INDIVIDUAL MEMBERS:

2,000

FUNDING: Membership fees, government grants and fundraising projects.

PRINCIPAL PURPOSE: To work for peace.

MAIN ACTIVITIES: Demonstrations, meetings, seminars, lobbying by mail and exhibitions.

POPULATION CONCERNS: Human rights.

SPECIFIC POPULATION ACTIVITIES: Education and counselling.

FORWARD-LOOKING STRATEGIES IMPLEMENTATIONS: Working for peace, education for peace and human rights.

OBSTACLES TO THE IMPLEMENTATION OF FORWARD-LOOKING STRATEGIES: Gaining political support.

NOTES:

Women for Equality, Development and Peace

SPAIN

ADDRESS:

MIDEP, C. Fontanella, 14, Barcelona, Spain

EXECUTIVE OFFICER:

BRANCH OFFICES:

TELEPHONE NUMBER:
93-301-3990

TELEX NUMBER:

APPROX. STAFF SIZE:

VOLUNTEER STAFF:

YEAR ESTABLISHED:
1985

NUMBER OF INDIVIDUAL MEMBERS:

FUNDING: United Nations

PRINCIPAL PURPOSE: Promotion of women through a Federation of Women's associations.

MAIN ACTIVITIES: Campaigning against sexual stereotypes, promoting women's organizations, working for disarmament, coordinating action.

POPULATION CONCERNS:

SPECIFIC POPULATION ACTIVITIES: Education, contraceptive research, abortion concerns.

FORWARD-LOOKING STRATEGIES IMPLEMENTATIONS: Although the organization is implementing the Strategies, no specific ones have been targeted.

OBSTACLES TO THE IMPLEMENTATION OF FORWARD-LOOKING STRATEGIES: Social difficulties and resistance from professional groups.

NOTES:

Alliance des Societes Feminines Suisses

SWITZERLAND

ADDRESS:

Postfach 101 3048 Worblaufen, Switzerland

EXECUTIVE OFFICER:

Magrit Siegenthaler-Reusser, General Secretary

BRANCH OFFICES:

TELEPHONE NUMBER:

31584848

TELEX NUMBER:

APPROX. STAFF SIZE:	VOLUNTEER STAFF:	YEAR ESTABLISHED:
1		1900

NUMBER OF INDIVIDUAL MEMBERS:

319

FUNDING: Membership contributions, donations, subsidies from different authorities, capital and estate revenues.

PRINCIPAL PURPOSE: To promote the cooperation between Swiss women in handling tasks and problems of common interest and in defending the interests of women with the authorities.

MAIN ACTIVITIES: Organization of seminars, workshops and presidents' conferences to encourage member organizations to form their own opinions. Consultations for the Federal Authorities in important matters of legislation and public life.

POPULATION CONCERNS: Worked ten years ago for family planning clinics, now they are required in every canton. Currently involved in studies of in vitro fertilization and embryo transfer.

SPECIFIC POPULATION ACTIVITIES: Advocacy.

FORWARD-LOOKING STRATEGIES IMPLEMENTATIONS: We ask our affiliates to implement the Strategies concerning equality, employment, education, and peace.

OBSTACLES TO THE IMPLEMENTATION OF FORWARD-LOOKING STRATEGIES: It will take time for every member to become aware of the Strategies.

NOTES:

ORGANIZATION:

Association Internationale pour la Sante de la Meve et du Nouveau-Ne* SWITZERLAND

ADDRESS:

Kurbergstr, 1, 8049 Zurich, Switzerland

EXECUTIVE OFFICER:

Dr. A. Caflisch, Executive Director

BRANCH OFFICES:

13, Cours de Rive,

TELEPHONE NUMBER:

(01)565 38 00

TELEX NUMBER:

1204 Geneva, Switzerland

APPROX. STAFF SIZE:	VOLUNTEER STAFF:	YEAR ESTABLISHED:
2	0	1977

NUMBER OF INDIVIDUAL MEMBERS:

3000 in 31 national sections

FUNDING: The Herbert and Elisa de Watteville Foundation.

PRINCIPAL PURPOSE: To improve the health of mothers and newborns throughout the world.

MAIN ACTIVITIES: Secretariat, research and advocacy of knowledge about and improvement of the medical quality in the Third World; the elaboration of maternal and neonatal projects; family planning.

POPULATION CONCERNS: Family planning is an integral part of our activities.

SPECIFIC POPULATION ACTIVITIES: Education, demographic and contraceptive research, counselling, sterilization (non-surgical, using Quinacrine), pill, diaiphragm, Norplant, Depo-Provera, natural family planning.

FORWARD LOOKING-STRATEGIES IMPLEMENTATIONS: Aware, but not currently implementing.

OBSTACLES TO THE IMPLEMENTATION OF FORWARD-LOOKING STRATEGIES: None, in particular, except the usual ones given by religion, tradition or customs.

NOTES: *International Association for Maternal and Neonatal Health

Association Suisse pour les Droits de la Femme*

SWITZERLAND

ADDRESS:

1111 Romanel, s/Morges, Switzerland

EXECUTIVE OFFICER:

Christiane Langenberger-Jaeger, President

BRANCH OFFICES:

TELEPHONE NUMBER:	TELEX NUMBER:
021/87.93.68	

APPROX. STAFF SIZE:	VOLUNTEER STAFF:	YEAR ESTABLISHED:
1		1909

NUMBER OF INDIVIDUAL MEMBERS:

4000

FUNDING: Donations from members.

PRINCIPAL PURPOSE: Equal rights for men and women: equal development, equal opportunity in employment, political spheres, pay equity, maternal protection.

MAIN ACTIVITIES: Seminars, media work and publications, work with political representatives.

POPULATION CONCERNS: None indicated.

SPECIFIC POPULATION ACTIVITIES: Education, counselling and lobby of the government for reproductive rights.

FORWARD-LOOKING STRATEGIES IMPLEMENTATIONS: Are aware of the Strategies, but did not indicate implementations.

OBSTACLES TO THE IMPLEMENTATION OF FORWARD-LOOKING STRATEGIES: None indicated.

NOTES: *Swiss Association for the Rights of Women

Isis-Women's International Cross-Cultural Exchange

SWITZERLAND

ADDRESS:

P.O. Box 2471, 1211 Geneva, Switzerland

EXECUTIVE OFFICER:

Collective

BRANCH OFFICES:

TELEPHONE NUMBER:

(22) 33 6746

TELEX NUMBER:

APPROX. STAFF SIZE:	VOLUNTEER STAFF:	YEAR ESTABLISHED:
10		1976

NUMBER OF INDIVIDUAL MEMBERS:

FUNDING: Grants and donations from various development agencies and NGO'S; subscriptions to *Women's World* and sales of other publications.

PRINCIPAL PURPOSE: To improve women's situation through information exchange; to promote ideas and actions that contirbute to the eradiction of injustice based on sex discrimination, and to promote international information and communication networks designed to help women combat discrimination and injustice against them and to strengthen them in these actions.

MAIN ACTIVITIES: The Cross-Cultural Exchange Program, annual training and learning programs for women worldwide; *Women's World*, a publication; and a documentation centre and information service.

POPULATION CONCERNS: Emphasis on women's health as a fundamental to women's rights and social change.

SPECIFIC POPULATION ACTIVITIES: Education, advocacy and dissemination of information.

FORWARD-LOOKING STRATEGIES IMPLEMENTATIONS: Our work is in the direction of the Strategies. On the population concerns, the recommendations are almost entirely to governments; we are an NGO.

OBSTACLES TO THE IMPLEMENTATION OF FORWARD-LOOKING STRATEGIES: No specific obstacles, but omissions: it is extremely important that contraceptive research be carried out from a feminist perspective by women-oriented groups.

NOTES:

*Business Address: 29 Rue de Gares, 1201 Geneva, SWITZERLAND

Young Women's Christian Association World (YWCA)

SWITZERLAND

ADDRESS:

37 Quai Wilson, 1201 Geneva, Switzerland

EXECUTIVE OFFICER:			BRANCH OFFICES:
Elaine Greif, General Secretary			

TELEPHONE NUMBER:		TELEX NUMBER:	
022-32-31-000			

APPROX. STAFF SIZE:	VOLUNTEER STAFF:	YEAR ESTABLISHED:
20		1894

NUMBER OF INDIVIDUAL MEMBERS:

FUNDING: National contributions and grants. Specific projects are financed independently.

PRINCIPAL PURPOSE: To work towards a more just and participatory world. To promote the well-being and equality of women worldwide. Current priorities: health, refugees and migrants, peace, energy, environment, and human rights.

MAIN ACTIVITIES: As a coordinating office, World YWCA supports the 84 national associations. It informs them of international and inter-regional events and encourages the national groups to participate. It also engages in specific projects as mandated by the Executive committee.

POPULATION CONCERNS: World YWCA is interested in family life education and supports women's rights to be informed and able to take action in health issues.

SPECIFIC POPULATION ACTIVITIES: Education, training and dissemination of information about family life education.

FORWARD LOOKING-STRATEGIES IMPLEMENTATIONS: Forward-Looking Strategies are used as guidelines in the work of World YWCA and the national associations are encouraged to use them the same way.

OBSTACLES TO THE IMPLEMENTATION OF FORWARD-LOOKING STRATEGIES:

NOTES:

Medical Women's International Association

WEST GERMANY

ADDRESS:

Association Internationale des Femmes Medecins, Herbert-Lewin St. 1 D-5000, Cologne 41, FRG

EXECUTIVE OFFICER:

Beverly L. Tamboline, M.D.

BRANCH OFFICES:

TELEPHONE NUMBER:

0221-40041

TELEX NUMBER:

APPROX. STAFF SIZE:

2

VOLUNTEER STAFF:

YEAR ESTABLISHED:

1919

NUMBER OF INDIVIDUAL MEMBERS:

FUNDING: membership dues

PRINCIPAL PURPOSE:

MAIN ACTIVITIES:

POPULATION CONCERNS: Health of mother and child and family planning.

SPECIFIC POPULATION ACTIVITIES: Education, pill, IUD, natural family planning.

FORWARD-LOOKING STRATEGIES IMPLEMENTATIONS:

OBSTACLES TO THE IMPLEMENTATION OF FORWARD-LOOKING STRATEGIES: Ideas change slowly—financial difficulties—disinterest at governmental levels.

NOTES:

Population, Development & Health Organizations

Belgian Federation for Family Planning and Sex Education

BELGIUM

ADDRESS:

51 Rue du Tuone, 1050 Brussels, Belgium

EXECUTIVE OFFICER:

Solange Romainville, Sec. Gen.

BRANCH OFFICES:

TELEPHONE NUMBER:	TELEX NUMBER:
02/513.72.64	

APPROX. STAFF SIZE:	VOLUNTEER STAFF:	YEAR ESTABLISHED:
8		1969

NUMBER OF INDIVIDUAL MEMBERS:

8

FUNDING: Government subsidies and dues from centers.

PRINCIPAL PURPOSE: To serve as a permanent education service; the Federation administers 38 Family Planning Centers.

MAIN ACTIVITIES: Defending the centers from public suits, proposing and coordinating initiatives of centers and promoting women's right to abortion.

POPULATION CONCERNS: Concerned about the prevention of unwanted pregnancies and sexually transmitted diseases such as AIDS.

SPECIFIC POPULATION ACTIVITIES: Education and delivery of services: pill, IUD, diaphragm, Depo-Provera, natural family planning and abortion.

FORWARD-LOOKING STRATEGIES IMPLEMENTATIONS: None.

OBSTACLES TO THE IMPLEMENTATION OF FORWARD-LOOKING STRATEGIES: None.

NOTES:

Institute of Cultural Affairs International

BELGIUM

ADDRESS:

rue Amedee Lynen 8, B-1030 Brussels, Belgium

EXECUTIVE OFFICER:

R. Alton, Director of International Development Funding

BRANCH OFFICES:

TELEPHONE NUMBER:	TELEX NUMBER:
(32-2) 219008617	62035 ICA BRUB

APPROX. STAFF SIZE:	VOLUNTEER STAFF:	YEAR ESTABLISHED:
23	23	1977

NUMBER OF INDIVIDUAL MEMBERS:

556 in 35 chapters

FUNDING: Grants and donations.

PRINCIPAL PURPOSE: To develop and test methods of comprehensive community renewal and motivate cooperation in support of local development, with an emphasis on the human factor. To promote self-development in local communities and organizations. To facilitate the activities of autonomous national member institutes (ICAs).

MAIN ACTIVITIES: ICA country offices serve many purposes, depending upon the particular location. These include community meetings, research and training, youth and women's forums, project planning and documentation.

POPULATION CONCERNS: Interested in population matters only where they form part of a broader program, such as primary health care.

SPECIFIC POPULATION ACTIVITIES: No answer.

FORWARD-LOOKING STRATEGIES IMPLEMENTATIONS: None.

OBSTACLES TO THE IMPLEMENTATION OF FORWARD-LOOKING STRATEGIES: None.

NOTES:

Centre for Development Research   DENMARK

ADDRESS:

NY Kongensgade 9, DK - 1472 Copenhagen K, DENMARK

EXECUTIVE OFFICER:			BRANCH OFFICES:
Professor Knud E. Svendsen, Director			

TELEPHONE NUMBER:		TELEX NUMBER:	
45 1 14 57 00			

APPROX. STAFF SIZE:	VOLUNTEER STAFF:	YEAR ESTABLISHED:
27		1969

NUMBER OF INDIVIDUAL MEMBERS:

FUNDING: All research is funded on an individual project basis upon application.

PRINCIPAL PURPOSE: To perform social science and development research projects.

MAIN ACTIVITIES: Performing research, organizing seminars and conferences and publishing materials.

POPULATION CONCERNS: Concerned about population issues as they relate to development.

SPECIFIC POPULATION ACTIVITIES: Contraceptive research and research on the status of women and their role in production.

FORWARD-LOOKING STRATEGIES IMPLEMENTATIONS: Implementation of the Strategies through research and dissemination of information.

OBSTACLES TO THE IMPLEMENTATION OF FORWARD-LOOKING STRATEGIES:None.

NOTES:

Institute for Social Medicine

DENMARK

ADDRESS:

Kobenhauns Universitett, Panum Inst., Blegdamsvej3, 2200 Kobenhaun, Denmark

EXECUTIVE OFFICER:			BRANCH OFFICES:
TELEPHONE NUMBER:	**TELEX NUMBER:**		
APPROX. STAFF SIZE: 30	**VOLUNTEER STAFF:**	**YEAR ESTABLISHED:**	
NUMBER OF INDIVIDUAL MEMBERS:			

FUNDING: Mostly by government grants.

PRINCIPAL PURPOSE: To perform contraceptive research and provide contraceptive services.

MAIN ACTIVITIES: Health and health services research.

POPULATION CONCERNS: Education and access to contraception in Denmark and developing countries, especially in Africa.

SPECIFIC POPULATION ACTIVITIES: Education, contraceptive research and delivery of services (most modern methods and natural family planning).

FORWARD-LOOKING STRATEGIES IMPLEMENTATIONS:

OBSTACLES TO THE IMPLEMENTATION OF FORWARD-LOOKING STRATEGIES:

NOTES:

Nordic Alternative Campaign   **DENMARK**

ADDRESS:

Hqjleddet 12, 2840 Holte, Denmark

EXECUTIVE OFFICER:			BRANCH OFFICES:

EXECUTIVE OFFICER:
Hildur Jackson

BRANCH OFFICES:
Alternative Future
Hausmausgatan 27
0260 Oslo 7 Norway

TELEPHONE NUMBER:
02 804447

TELEX NUMBER:

Matsfriberg
Knapehall, 43600
Askim Sweden

APPROX. STAFF SIZE:

VOLUNTEER STAFF:

YEAR ESTABLISHED:
1981

NUMBER OF INDIVIDUAL MEMBERS:

FUNDING: Varies among different branches.

PRINCIPAL PURPOSE: To research, our major problems: The global, ecological and social problems.

MAIN ACTIVITIES: Research, experiments and communication.

POPULATION CONCERNS: Research on global problems.

SPECIFIC POPULATION ACTIVITIES:

FORWARD-LOOKING STRATEGIES IMPLEMENTATIONS: Our purpose is to implement all the Forward-Looking Strategies that we know.

OBSTACLES TO THE IMPLEMENTATION OF FORWARD-LOOKING STRATEGIES: The western civilization built on power and control of people and nature. Our main concern is therefore to change our own culture and leave the rest of the world in peace.

NOTES:

World Assembly of Youth (WAY)   **DENMARK**

ADDRESS:

4 Ved Bellahoj, 2700 Bronshoj, Copenhagen, Denmark

EXECUTIVE OFFICER:

Shiv Khare

BRANCH OFFICES:

TELEPHONE NUMBER:

01-607770

TELEX NUMBER:

APPROX. STAFF SIZE:	VOLUNTEER STAFF:	YEAR ESTABLISHED:
5	3	1949

NUMBER OF INDIVIDUAL MEMBERS:

FUNDING: Donation and grants

PRINCIPAL PURPOSE: To coordinate national youth councils and organizations, to provide development program support to youths and youth organizations, to provide training for young leaders in the development field.

MAIN ACTIVITIES:

POPULATION CONCERNS: Educating young people about controlling reproduction.

SPECIFIC POPULATION ACTIVITIES: Education, counseling, advocacy, natural family planning services.

FORWARD-LOOKING STRATEGIES IMPLEMENTATIONS: Provide information and training to young women about limiting fertility.

OBSTACLES TO THE IMPLEMENTATION OF FORWARD-LOOKING STRATEGIES: Lack of funds.

NOTES:

Family Planning Association

ENGLAND

ADDRESS:

27-35 Mortimer St., Longon W1N7RJ

EXECUTIVE OFFICER:

Alastair Service, General Secretary

BRANCH OFFICES:

TELEPHONE NUMBER:

01-636-7866

TELEX NUMBER:

APPROX. STAFF SIZE:

50

VOLUNTEER STAFF:

6

YEAR ESTABLISHED:

1930

NUMBER OF INDIVIDUAL MEMBERS:

FUNDING: Donations and government grant.

PRINCIPAL PURPOSE: To provide information and education on all aspects of family planning and reproductive health care.

MAIN ACTIVITIES: Providing information and education.

POPULATION CONCERNS: Providing information and education to ensure that every child is a wanted child.

SPECIFIC POPULATION ACTIVITIES: Education, demographic research, contraceptive research and dissemination of information, (on birth control methods and other population issues.)

FORWARD-LOOKING STRATEGIES IMPLEMENTATIONS: None yet, considering for future

OBSTACLES TO THE IMPLEMENTATION OF FORWARD-LOOKING STRATEGIES:

NOTES:

International Confederation Of Midwives

ENGLAND

ADDRESS:

57 Lower Belgrave Street, London SWIW OLR, UK

EXECUTIVE OFFICER:

Frances Cowper-Smith, Executive Director

BRANCH OFFICES:

TELEPHONE NUMBER:	TELEX NUMBER:
01 730 6137	

APPROX. STAFF SIZE:	VOLUNTEER STAFF:	YEAR ESTABLISHED:
		1922

NUMBER OF INDIVIDUAL MEMBERS:

60,000

FUNDING: Membership fees, congress proceeds and donations.

PRINCIPAL PURPOSE: To advance education in midwifery and to spread knowledge of the art and science of midwifery. To improve the standard of care provided to mothers, babies and families throughout the world.

MAIN ACTIVITIES: Triennial international congresses, regional meetings, local activities organized by member associations, collaborative activities with other organizations.

POPULATION CONCERNS:

SPECIFIC POPULATION ACTIVITIES: Education, information sharing, collaboration with other organizations.

FORWARD-LOOKING STRATEGIES IMPLEMENTATIONS:

OBSTACLES TO THE IMPLEMENTATION OF FORWARD-LOOKING STRATEGIES:

NOTES:

International Federation of Gynecology and Obstetrics

ENGLAND

ADDRESS:

27 Sussex Place, Regents Park, London, NW1 4RG, UK

EXECUTIVE OFFICER:			BRANCH OFFICES:
Professor D.V.I. Fairweather			

TELEPHONE NUMBER:		TELEX NUMBER:
(01) 7232951		

APPROX. STAFF SIZE:	VOLUNTEER STAFF:	YEAR ESTABLISHED:
1		1954

NUMBER OF INDIVIDUAL MEMBERS:

FUNDING: Membership fees and percentage of Congress registration fees.

PRINCIPAL PURPOSE: To promote and assist in research pertaining to obstetrics, gynecology and human reproduction. To improve the physical and mental health of mothers and children.

MAIN ACTIVITIES: Organization of World Congresses.

POPULATION CONCERNS: Improving the health of mother and child.

SPECIFIC POPULATION ACTIVITIES: Education

FORWARD-LOOKING STRATEGIES IMPLEMENTATIONS: None

OBSTACLES TO THE IMPLEMENTATION OF FORWARD-LOOKING STRATEGIES:

NOTES:

International Planned Parenthood Federation (IPPF)*

ENGLAND

ADDRESS:

Regent's College, Inner Circle, Regent's Park, London NW1 4NS England

EXECUTIVE OFFICER:			BRANCH OFFICES:
Mr. Bradman Weerakoon			

TELEPHONE NUMBER:	TELEX NUMBER:	
01-486-0741	919573 IPEPEE G	

APPROX. STAFF SIZE:	VOLUNTEER STAFF:	YEAR ESTABLISHED:
130		1952

NUMBER OF INDIVIDUAL MEMBERS:

FUNDING: Governments, grants and donations

PRINCIPAL PURPOSE: Family Planning

MAIN ACTIVITIES: Clinic services, community outreach services, education, information and training, youth projects, planned parenthood and women's development.

POPULATION CONCERNS: All.

SPECIFIC POPULATION ACTIVITIES: Education, counseling, advocacy, monitoring contraceptive and demographic research, delivery of services.

FORWARD-LOOKING STRATEGIES IMPLEMENTATIONS: IPPF advocates the implementation of all the FLS and concentrates on those dealing with the reproductive health of women.

OBSTACLES TO THE IMPLEMENTATION OF FORWARD-LOOKING STRATEGIES: Lack of awareness, lack of governmental support and lack of resources.

NOTES: *Also listed in the Appendix.

Institute of Population Studies

ENGLAND

ADDRESS:

Hoopern House, 101 Pennsylvania Road, Exeter EX4 6DT, Devon

EXECUTIVE OFFICER:

Dr. Robert Snowden

BRANCH OFFICES:

TELEPHONE NUMBER:	TELEX NUMBER:
(0392) 57936	42894

APPROX. STAFF SIZE:	VOLUNTEER STAFF:	YEAR ESTABLISHED:
10	1	1971

NUMBER OF INDIVIDUAL MEMBERS:

FUNDING: International grants.

PRINCIPAL PURPOSE: To perform research and provide research-training in reproductive behavior with an international context.

MAIN ACTIVITIES: Research into delivery of family planning services and training for professionals concerned with this research.

POPULATION CONCERNS: Micro-determinants of reproductive research.

SPECIFIC POPULATION ACTIVITIES: Education, contraceptive research, counseling, delivery of services (sterilization, pill, IUD, diaphragm, foam, Norplant, Depo-Provera, natural family planning, and infertility services).

FORWARD-LOOKING STRATEGIES IMPLEMENTATIONS: None.

OBSTACLES TO THE IMPLEMENTATION OF FORWARD-LOOKING STRATEGIES:

NOTES:

Minority Rights Group

ENGLAND

ADDRESS:

29 Craven Street, London WC2N 5NT, United Kingdom

EXECUTIVE OFFICER:			BRANCH OFFICES:
Ben Whitaker, Executive Officer			

TELEPHONE NUMBER:		TELEX NUMBER:	
930-6659			

APPROX. STAFF SIZE:	VOLUNTEER STAFF:	YEAR ESTABLISHED:	
13	1	1966	

NUMBER OF INDIVIDUAL MEMBERS:

FUNDING: Donations, grants and sales of publications.

PRINCIPAL PURPOSE: To achieve justice for all people through education and publicity. To research inter-ethnic conflict and ways of solving it. To promote human rights and minority education, especially for young people.

MAIN ACTIVITIES: Publishing, especially material on minorities. Education activities in schools. Human rights advocacy, especially at the U.N.

POPULATION CONCERNS: Concerned with eliminating female circumcision and genital mutilation, forced sterilization and abortion.

SPECIFIC POPULATION ACTIVITIES: Education.

FORWARD-LOOKING STRATEGIES IMPLEMENTATIONS: None.

OBSTACLES TO THE IMPLEMENTATION OF FORWARD-LOOKING STRATEGIES: None.

NOTES:

Oxfam

ENGLAND

ADDRESS:

274 Banbury Road, Oxford, OX2 7QJ, England

EXECUTIVE OFFICER:			BRANCH OFFICES:
Frank Judd, Director			

TELEPHONE NUMBER:		TELEX NUMBER:	
0865 577		83610	

APPROX. STAFF SIZE:	VOLUNTEER STAFF:	YEAR ESTABLISHED:
725	20,000 +	1942

NUMBER OF INDIVIDUAL MEMBERS:

FUNDING: Private donations, proceeds of 800 charity shops, government funds (16%).

PRINCIPAL PURPOSE: The relief of poverty worldwide.

MAIN ACTIVITIES: Funding non-operational overseas programme. Education and campaigning in U.K.

POPULATION CONCERNS:

SPECIFIC POPULATION ACTIVITIES: Education, counselling, research on availability of services, women's news, etc., delivery of services.

FORWARD-LOOKING STRATEGIES IMPLEMENTATIONS: Yes, unspecified.

OBSTACLES TO THE IMPLEMENTATION OF FORWARD-LOOKING STRATEGIES: None.

NOTES:

Population Concerns

ENGLAND

ADDRESS:

231 Totlenham Court Rd., London W1P 0HX

EXECUTIVE OFFICER:			BRANCH OFFICES:

TELEPHONE NUMBER:		TELEX NUMBER:	
01-637-9582			

APPROX. STAFF SIZE:	VOLUNTEER STAFF:	YEAR ESTABLISHED:
5	2	1974

NUMBER OF INDIVIDUAL MEMBERS:

FUNDING: Donation and grants.

PRINCIPAL PURPOSE: To raise funds for population and development programs around the world. To increase awareness about the nature, size and complexity of the world population, especially as it affects social and economic development.

MAIN ACTIVITIES: Education, fund raising and project work.

POPULATION CONCERNS: Reducing maternal mortality and morbidity.

SPECIFIC POPULATION ACTIVITIES: Education and delivery of services.

FORWARD-LOOKING STRATEGIES IMPLEMENTATIONS: Income-generating activities and improving womens' health.

OBSTACLES TO THE IMPLEMENTATION OF FORWARD-LOOKING STRATEGIES:

NOTES:

Population Investigation Committee

ENGLAND

ADDRESS:

LSE Houghton Street, Aldwych, London WC2A 2AE, United Kingdom

EXECUTIVE OFFICER:

Prof. E.A. Wrigley, Chairman

BRANCH OFFICES:

TELEPHONE NUMBER:	TELEX NUMBER:
01-405-7686	

APPROX. STAFF SIZE:	VOLUNTEER STAFF:	YEAR ESTABLISHED:
3	0	1936

NUMBER OF INDIVIDUAL MEMBERS:

17

FUNDING: Grants and sales of *Pop Studies*.

PRINCIPAL PURPOSE: To perform research, teaching and publishing in the field of population.

MAIN ACTIVITIES: Research and publishing a journal, *Pop Studies*.

POPULATION CONCERNS: Demographic research and dissemination of demographic data.

SPECIFIC POPULATION ACTIVITIES: Education and demographic research. Training in population studies.

FORWARD-LOOKING STRATEGIES IMPLEMENTATIONS: None.

OBSTACLES TO THE IMPLEMENTATION OF FORWARD-LOOKING STRATEGIES: None.

NOTES:

ADDRESS:	
4 Provost Road, London NW3 4ST	

EXECUTIVE OFFICER:	BRANCH OFFICES:
D.F. Hubback, Chairman	

TELEPHONE NUMBER:	TELEX NUMBER:
01 586 4341	

APPROX. STAFF SIZE:	VOLUNTEER STAFF:	YEAR ESTABLISHED:
1		

NUMBER OF INDIVIDUAL MEMBERS:

FUNDING: Trust and private contributions.

PRINCIPAL PURPOSE: To promote relief of poverty and the improvement of standards of health throughout the world thereby making possible a better life for mankind by promoting a better understanding of the world, population resources; and encouraging such research, education or other action in any part of the world as may contribute to due adjustment of population to resources.

MAIN ACTIVITIES: Medical research (including male and female sterilization and abortion), demographic, social and economic research.

POPULATION CONCERNS: Exploring the need for and the acceptability of new methods of birth control.

SPECIFIC POPULATION ACTIVITIES: Education, demographic and contraceptive research.

FORWARD LOOKING-STRATEGIES IMPLEMENTATIONS: Are aware of the Strategies but did not indicate implementations.

OBSTACLES TO THE IMPLEMENTATION OF FORWARD-LOOKING STRATEGIES: None.

NOTES:

The Population Research Institute   **FINLAND**

ADDRESS:

Kalevankatu 16, 00100, Helsinki 10, Finland

EXECUTIVE OFFICER:

Riitta Auvinen

BRANCH OFFICES:

TELEPHONE NUMBER:

90-640235

TELEX NUMBER:

APPROX. STAFF SIZE:

6

VOLUNTEER STAFF:

YEAR ESTABLISHED:

1946

NUMBER OF INDIVIDUAL MEMBERS:

FUNDING: The Finnish Population and Family Welfare Federation and the Ministry of Education allocate money annually.

PRINCIPAL PURPOSE: To study the Finnish population, including nativity, mortality and migration.

MAIN ACTIVITIES: Research.

POPULATION CONCERNS: Demographic trends and family welfare.

SPECIFIC POPULATION ACTIVITIES: Demographic and contraceptive research.

FORWARD-LOOKING STRATEGIES IMPLEMENTATIONS: Contraceptive and family policy improvements.

OBSTACLES TO THE IMPLEMENTATION OF FORWARD-LOOKING STRATEGIES:

NOTES:

TELEPHONE NUMBER:		TELEX NUMBER:
(358-0) 640235		123682 fam sf

APPROX. STAFF SIZE:	VOLUNTEER STAFF:	YEAR ESTABLISHED:
40		1941

NUMBER OF INDIVIDUAL MEMBERS:
22 affiliated chapters

FUNDING: Slotmachine Association's aid, by state aid and aid from local authorities as well as by our own fundraising.

PRINCIPAL PURPOSE: Act for the benefit of families and children and for the promotion of a balanced population policy.

MAIN ACTIVITIES: To take initiative to reform legislation and strive to direct social planning, housing policy and social services to meet the needs of families with children. Serves families by conducting social and medical research work, educating people who work in close contact with families to meet their problems by giving family and genetical counselling and family planning as well as psycho-social and medical aid to childless couples.

POPULATION CONCERNS: The Population political aim is to obtain a demographically balanced society.

SPECIFIC POPULATION ACTIVITIES: Education, demographic research, contraceptive research, counselling, advocacy, information, contact service and delivery of services which include: Pill, IUD, Norplant and Condoms.

FORWARD-LOOKING STRATEGIES IMPLEMENTATIONS:

OBSTACLES TO THE IMPLEMENTATION OF FORWARD-LOOKING STRATEGIES:

, **NOTES:**

Actually

FRANCE

ADDRESS:

295 rue St. Jacques, 75005 Paris, France

EXECUTIVE OFFICER:

C. Goldet

BRANCH OFFICES:

TELEPHONE NUMBER:

4354.5807

TELEX NUMBER:

APPROX. STAFF SIZE:	VOLUNTEER STAFF:	YEAR ESTABLISHED:
3	3	1986

NUMBER OF INDIVIDUAL MEMBERS:

FUNDING: Research and training.

PRINCIPAL PURPOSE: Population and development, especially in Africa.

MAIN ACTIVITIES: Education, demographic research, contraceptive research and counseling.

POPULATION CONCERNS: Yes, but no elaboration.

SPECIFIC POPULATION ACTIVITIES:

FORWARD-LOOKING STRATEGIES IMPLEMENTATIONS: Social opposition, due partly to economic hardship and partly to historical attitudes.

OBSTACLES TO THE IMPLEMENTATION OF FORWARD-LOOKING STRATEGIES:

NOTES:

ORGANIZATION:	
INODEP	**FRANCE**

ADDRESS:
49 ruede la Glaciere, 750 13 Paris, France

EXECUTIVE OFFICER:			BRANCH OFFICES:
TELEPHONE NUMBER: 45 35 67 40	**TELEX NUMBER:**		
APPROX. STAFF SIZE: 10	**VOLUNTEER STAFF:**	**YEAR ESTABLISHED:** 1971	
NUMBER OF INDIVIDUAL MEMBERS:			

FUNDING: One third national and international funds, one third private funds and one third sell.

PRINCIPAL PURPOSE: Education to development.

MAIN ACTIVITIES: Training sessions and education to development (economics, politics, foreign relations, people's culture, education, etc.)

POPULATION CONCERNS:

SPECIFIC POPULATION ACTIVITIES: Education, women's problems just one of many activities.

FORWARD-LOOKING STRATEGIES IMPLEMENTATIONS:

OBSTACLES TO THE IMPLEMENTATION OF FORWARD-LOOKING STRATEGIES:

NOTES:

International Union for Health Education

FRANCE

ADDRESS:

9 rue Newton, 75116 Paris, France

EXECUTIVE OFFICER:

Dr. Harry Crawley, Pres. Health Education Bureau

BRANCH OFFICES:

TELEPHONE NUMBER:	TELEX NUMBER:
(33)-(1) 47209793	UNIONINTER

APPROX. STAFF SIZE:	VOLUNTEER STAFF:	YEAR ESTABLISHED:
4	unspecified no.	1951

NUMBER OF INDIVIDUAL MEMBERS:

640 in 5 regional offices

FUNDING: Member contributions and sales of publications.

PRINCIPAL PURPOSE: To contribute towards the improvement of health and well-being by encouraging the participation of individuals, families and communities in the promotion of their own health.

MAIN ACTIVITIES: Periodic world conferences on health education, promotion of regional programs through regional offices, organization of regional seminars, publication of International Journal of Health Education, development of activities and projects within the framework of its Technical Development Board.

POPULATION CONCERNS: Education, development, health status, family planning.

SPECIFIC POPULATION ACTIVITIES: Education.

FORWARD-LOOKING STRATEGIES IMPLEMENTATIONS: Education for family planning.

OBSTACLES TO THE IMPLEMENTATION OF FORWARD-LOOKING STRATEGIES: Not answered.

NOTES:

AIM Group for Family Law Reform   **IRELAND**

ADDRESS:

64 Lower Mount Street, Dublin 2, Ireland

EXECUTIVE OFFICER:			BRANCH OFFICES:
Trisha McKay, Administrator			

TELEPHONE NUMBER:	TELEX NUMBER:
605478	

APPROX. STAFF SIZE:	VOLUNTEER STAFF:	YEAR ESTABLISHED:
25	24	1972

NUMBER OF INDIVIDUAL MEMBERS:

4 chapters

FUNDING: Donations and grants.

PRINCIPAL PURPOSE: To offer support, legal information, and a referral service for people with problems arising out of marriage breakdown. To campaign for reform in certain areas of family law and social welfare.

MAIN ACTIVITIES: Advocating legal and social reform, non-directive counselling and referral, publishing magazines, newsletters and information leaflets, lecturing at schools and clubs.

POPULATION CONCERNS: Interest in the social and legal aspects of population.

SPECIFIC POPULATION ACTIVITIES: Education, and counselling.

FORWARD-LOOKING STRATEGIES IMPLEMENTATIONS: Some strategies being implemented through CSW Ireland.

OBSTACLES TO THE IMPLEMENTATION OF FORWARD-LOOKING STRATEGIES: None.

NOTES:

Irish Family Planning Association

IRELAND

ADDRESS:

P.O. Box 908, 15 Mountjoy Square, Dublin, Ireland

EXECUTIVE OFFICER:			BRANCH OFFICES:
Dr. Shiela Jones, Chairperson			

TELEPHONE NUMBER:	TELEX NUMBER:
740723	

APPROX. STAFF SIZE:	VOLUNTEER STAFF:	YEAR ESTABLISHED:
60	25	1969

NUMBER OF INDIVIDUAL MEMBERS:
250

FUNDING: Income from contraceptive sales.

PRINCIPAL PURPOSE: To promote family planning in Ireland.

MAIN ACTIVITIES: Two family planning clinics, a resource center and courses in health, sex education, women's health issues and family planning.

POPULATION CONCERNS: Promote and provide family planning services.

SPECIFIC POPULATION ACTIVITIES: Education, advocacy, counselling, delivery of services: male sterilization, pill, IUD, diaphragm, foam, natural family planning.

FORWARD-LOOKING STRATEGIES IMPLEMENTATIONS: Education, clinical services and political lobbying.

OBSTACLES TO THE IMPLEMENTATION OF FORWARD-LOOKING STRATEGIES: Political and religious opposition to family planning. Adverse publicity on individual methods of birth control. Difficulty in educating and serving young women and women from rural areas and lower socio-economic backgrounds.

NOTES:

International Federation for Preventive & Social Medicine

ITALY

ADDRESS:

Via Salaria 237, 00199 Roma, Italy

EXECUTIVE OFFICER:			BRANCH OFFICES:
Prof. G.A. Canaperia			

TELEPHONE NUMBER:	TELEX NUMBER:
8457928	

APPROX. STAFF SIZE:	VOLUNTEER STAFF:	YEAR ESTABLISHED:
6	5	1950

NUMBER OF INDIVIDUAL MEMBERS:

145 in 31 chapters

FUNDING: Membership fees and special contributions.

PRINCIPAL PURPOSE: To support and promote the creation of national association of hygiene and preventive and social medicine. To contribute to the advancement of hygiene, preventive and social medicine through the promotion of study, research and training.

MAIN ACTIVITIES: International meetings and conferences, regional meetings and seminars, publishing periodicals and other publications and providing scholarships.

POPULATION CONCERNS: Issues related to maternal and child health.

SPECIFIC POPULATION ACTIVITIES: Education.

FORWARD-LOOKING STRATEGIES IMPLEMENTATIONS: None.

OBSTACLES TO THE IMPLEMENTATION OF FORWARD-LOOKING STRATEGIES: None.

NOTES:

Unione Italiana Centri Educazione Matrimoniale Prematrimoniale (U.I.C.E.M.P.) ITALY

ADDRESS:

20122 MILANO, Via Eugenio Chiesa 1, Italy

EXECUTIVE OFFICER:

Tullia Carettoni, President

BRANCH OFFICES:

TELEPHONE NUMBER:	TELEX NUMBER:
783915	

APPROX. STAFF SIZE:	VOLUNTEER STAFF:	YEAR ESTABLISHED:
3	5	1966

NUMBER OF INDIVIDUAL MEMBERS:

FUNDING: Client fees.

PRINCIPAL PURPOSE: To promote family planning as a basic human right and to promote sex education.

MAIN ACTIVITIES: Run ten family planning centers, organize conferences and courses, produce educational material.

POPULATION CONCERNS: Promotion of family planning rights and reduction of the incidence of legal and clandestine abortions.

SPECIFIC POPULATION ACTIVITIES: Education, counselling, advocacy and delivery of services: pill, IUD, diaphragm, foam, condom, natural family planning and abortion referral.

FORWARD-LOOKING STRATEGIES IMPLEMENTATIONS: None.

OBSTACLES TO THE IMPLEMENTATION OF FORWARD-LOOKING STRATEGIES: None.

NOTES:

ORGANIZATION:

European Association for Population Studies THE NETHERLANDS

ADDRESS:

P.O. Box 11676, 2502 AR, The Hague, The Netherlands

EXECUTIVE OFFICER:		BRANCH OFFICES:
Dr. Nico van Nimwegen		

TELEPHONE NUMBER:	TELEX NUMBER:
0(70) 409482 Ex. 22	31138 NIDI NL

APPROX. STAFF SIZE:	VOLUNTEER STAFF:	YEAR ESTABLISHED:
		1983

NUMBER OF INDIVIDUAL MEMBERS:

350

FUNDING: Individual and institutional members.

PRINCIPAL PURPOSE: To promote study of population in Europe by fostering the co-operation between people who are interested in European Population Studies and by stimulating their interest in population matters among governments and the public.

MAIN ACTIVITIES: Organizes conferences, seminars, workshops and working groups. Publishes and disseminates information dealing with population.

POPULATION CONCERNS: To study European population and promote this study.

SPECIFIC POPULATION ACTIVITIES: Demographic and contraceptive research.

FORWARD LOOKING-STRATEGIES IMPLEMENTATIONS:

OBSTACLES TO THE IMPLEMENTATION OF FORWARD-LOOKING STRATEGIES:

NOTES:

Norwegian Nurses Association NORWAY

ADDRESS:

P.O. Box 2633, St. Hanshaugen, N-0131 Oslo 1, Norway

EXECUTIVE OFFICER:			BRANCH OFFICES:
Aud Blankholm, President			

TELEPHONE NUMBER:		TELEX NUMBER:
(02)382000		

APPROX. STAFF SIZE:	VOLUNTEER STAFF:	YEAR ESTABLISHED:
65		1912

NUMBER OF INDIVIDUAL MEMBERS:

35,000

FUNDING: Membership fees.

PRINCIPAL PURPOSE: Professional and trade union for nurses in Norway. To improve socio-economic conditions for nurses and the quality and quantity of nursing care through improved nursing education.

MAIN ACTIVITIES: Professional seminars and courses, negotiation at all levels, international representation, professional advisory committments.

POPULATION CONCERNS: Family planning.

SPECIFIC POPULATION ACTIVITIES: Supports the activities of the National Family Planning Organization through membership and representation at the meetings.

FORWARD-LOOKING STRATEGIES IMPLEMENTATIONS: None.

OBSTACLES TO THE IMPLEMENTATION OF FORWARD-LOOKING STRATEGIES: None.

NOTES:

*Business Address: Collettsgate 54, Oslo 4, NORWAY

Senterkvinnene

NORWAY

ADDRESS:

boks 6890 St. Olavs Plass, 0130 Oslo 1, Norway

EXECUTIVE OFFICER:

Leder Anne Lise Folsvik

BRANCH OFFICES:

TELEPHONE NUMBER:	TELEX NUMBER:
02 206720	

APPROX. STAFF SIZE:	VOLUNTEER STAFF:	YEAR ESTABLISHED:
	1	

NUMBER OF INDIVIDUAL MEMBERS:

15,000

FUNDING:

PRINCIPAL PURPOSE:

MAIN ACTIVITIES: .

POPULATION CONCERNS:

SPECIFIC POPULATION ACTIVITIES: Education and demographic research.

FORWARD-LOOKING STRATEGIES IMPLEMENTATIONS: None.

OBSTACLES TO THE IMPLEMENTATION OF FORWARD-LOOKING STRATEGIES: None.

NOTES:

*Business Address: Peder Claussonsqt. 2, 0130 Oslo 1, NORWAY

ORGANIZATION:

Worldview International Foundation

NORWAY

ADDRESS:

Skippergaten 21, 0154 Oslo 1, Norway

EXECUTIVE OFFICER:

Arne Fjortoft, General Secretary

BRANCH OFFICES:

TELEPHONE NUMBER:	TELEX NUMBER:
472-427776	74023 OSIPSN

APPROX. STAFF SIZE:	VOLUNTEER STAFF:	YEAR ESTABLISHED:
160	7	1979

NUMBER OF INDIVIDUAL MEMBERS:

200in 7 media centers

FUNDING: Donations, government and U.N. grants and income from professional service.

PRINCIPAL PURPOSE: To use communication in support of human development and for meeting basic needs in the development process.

MAIN ACTIVITIES: Training people in communication techniques at the media centers, using audio-visual equipment.

POPULATION CONCERNS: Several population programs concerning population and development.

SPECIFIC POPULATION ACTIVITIES: Education, advocacy and communication.

FORWARD-LOOKING STRATEGIES IMPLEMENTATIONS: Organizing seminars, such as "Population and the Role of the Family" and "Women as Managers and Entrepreneurs."

OBSTACLES TO THE IMPLEMENTATION OF FORWARD-LOOKING STRATEGIES: The feeling that more energy was spent on preparing the strategies than is left to put them in motion.

NOTES:

---

*Business Address: 10 Kinross Avenue, Colombo, SRI LANKA, tel: 583109, telex: 21282 CREST CE

International Sociological Association

SPAIN

ADDRESS:

Consejo Superior de Investigaciones Cientificas, Pinar 25, 28006

EXECUTIVE OFFICER:

Prof. Margaret Andres, President

BRANCH OFFICES:

TELEPHONE NUMBER:

TELEX NUMBER:

APPROX. STAFF SIZE:	VOLUNTEER STAFF:	YEAR ESTABLISHED:
6		1948

NUMBER OF INDIVIDUAL MEMBERS:

1000, 40 National Associations

FUNDING: Membership fees, UNESCO, subventions from country hosting the secretariat.

PRINCIPAL PURPOSE: Promoting sociology internationally, in the widest possible sense.

MAIN ACTIVITIES: Organizing four-yearly World Congresses of Sociology, stimulating the activities (individual congress) of some 40 Research Committees, publishing a book series.

POPULATION CONCERNS: Sociology of Population.

SPECIFIC POPULATION ACTIVITIES: Demographic Research.

FORWARD LOOKING-STRATEGIES IMPLEMENTATIONS:

OBSTACLES TO THE IMPLEMENTATION OF FORWARD-LOOKING STRATEGIES:

NOTES:

Swedish International Development Authority (SIDA)

SWEDEN

ADDRESS:

S-105 25 Stockholm, Sweden

EXECUTIVE OFFICER:			BRANCH OFFICES:
Carl Tham, Director General			

TELEPHONE NUMBER:		TELEX NUMBER:	
08-15.01.00			

APPROX. STAFF SIZE:	VOLUNTEER STAFF:	YEAR ESTABLISHED:
500		1965

NUMBER OF INDIVIDUAL MEMBERS:

FUNDING: Government funding.

PRINCIPAL PURPOSE: To provide bilateral development assistance.

MAIN ACTIVITIES: Bilateral support to about 20 countries in the areas of health, education, rural development and industry.

POPULATION CONCERNS: Population issues as related to the activities above are considered a priority.

SPECIFIC POPULATION ACTIVITIES: None.

FORWARD-LOOKING STRATEGIES IMPLEMENTATIONS: Giving support to other organizations, such as the Women's Global Network on Reproductive Rights and the Committee for a Health Quarterly by and for Women Worldwide.

OBSTACLES TO THE IMPLEMENTATION OF FORWARD-LOOKING STRATEGIES: None so far.

NOTES:

Centre Medico-Social Pro Familia

SWITZERLAND

ADDRESS:

Av. du Theatre 7, 1003 Lausanne, Switzerland

EXECUTIVE OFFICER:

Mme. Madeleine Duvoisin-Julmy, Director

TELEPHONE NUMBER:

22 25 93

TELEX NUMBER:

BRANCH OFFICES:

Planning Familial
CMS Pro Familia
Georgette 1
1003 Lausanne
Switzerland

APPROX. STAFF SIZE:	VOLUNTEER STAFF:	YEAR ESTABLISHED:
19		1966

NUMBER OF INDIVIDUAL MEMBERS:

70 in 3 sectors

FUNDING: 1/3 remuneration for services, 2/3 subsidies from public.

PRINCIPAL PURPOSE: Medical/Social prevention of problems in relationships, social and sexual.

MAIN ACTIVITIES: Family planning consultation, marriage counselling and sex education for youth.

POPULATION CONCERNS: To offer the time, assistance, dialogue, help and counsel in matters dealing with procreation, communication within couples and youth sexuality.

SPECIFIC POPULATION ACTIVITIES: Education, contraceptive research, counselling , counselling for sterilization, delivery of services which include: Pill, IUD, Diaphragm, Depo-Provera, Natural Family Planning, Day After Pill, tracking down sexually transmitted diseases.

FORWARD LOOKING-STRATEGIES IMPLEMENTATIONS:

OBSTACLES TO THE IMPLEMENTATION OF FORWARD-LOOKING STRATEGIES:

NOTES:

International Council of Voluntary Agencies

SWITZERLAND

ADDRESS:

13 rue Gautier, 1201 Geneva, Switzerland

EXECUTIVE OFFICER:

Anthony Kazlowski, Executive Director

BRANCH OFFICES:

TELEPHONE NUMBER:	TELEX NUMBER:
31.66.02	22891 ICVACH

APPROX. STAFF SIZE:	VOLUNTEER STAFF:	YEAR ESTABLISHED:
7	0	1962

NUMBER OF INDIVIDUAL MEMBERS:

75

FUNDING: Membership fees and grants.

PRINCIPAL PURPOSE: To promote NGO activities in the fields of humanitarian assistance and development cooperation.

MAIN ACTIVITIES: Communication and collaboration among NGOs, promotion of voluntary agency networks, liaison with governments and intergovernmental organizations, publishing a bi-monthly newsletter, advising voluntary agencies on improving management and maintaining a documentation center on voluntary agencies.

POPULATION CONCERNS: Those issues related to the environment and to development. ICVA has a Subgroup on Population, Environment and Sustainable Development.

SPECIFIC POPULATION ACTIVITIES: Education and advocacy.

FORWARD-LOOKING STRATEGIES IMPLEMENTATIONS: None.

OBSTACLES TO THE IMPLEMENTATION OF FORWARD-LOOKING STRATEGIES: None.

NOTES:

ORGANIZATION:

Inter-Parliamentary Union   SWITZERLAND

ADDRESS:

P.O. Box 438, CH-1211, Geneva, 19, Switzerland

EXECUTIVE OFFICER:			BRANCH OFFICES:
Pierre Cornillion, Secretary General			

TELEPHONE NUMBER:		TELEX NUMBER:	
34.41.50		289-784-IPU	

APPROX. STAFF SIZE:	VOLUNTEER STAFF:	YEAR ESTABLISHED:
24	0	1889

NUMBER OF INDIVIDUAL MEMBERS:

107 national parliaments

FUNDING: Contributions from national groups.

PRINCIPAL PURPOSE: To promote personal contacts between members of all Parliaments and to unite them in common action to promote international peace and cooperation.

MAIN ACTIVITIES: Meetings and conferences bringing together members of Parliament from different countries and ideological trends, to study political, social, economic, parliamentary and cultural problems of international significance. Gathering and dissemination of information through publications, and programs of technical cooperation.

POPULATION CONCERNS: Study population issues in worldwide context at conferences and gives attention to population component in studies of other questions at the regional level.

SPECIFIC POPULATION ACTIVITIES: Resolutions to ensure the creation of the appropriate climate, machinery and funding programs for family planning and family health.

FORWARD-LOOKING STRATEGIES IMPLEMENTATIONS: Urging of parliaments to action to formulate initiatives that will achieve equal rights and responsibilities for men and women.

OBSTACLES TO THE IMPLEMENTATION OF FORWARD-LOOKING STRATEGIES: None.

NOTES:

International Research Institute for Reproduction   WEST GERMANY

ADDRESS:

Kaiser-Wilhelm-Ring 22, 4000 Dusseldorf-II, Federal Republic of Germany

EXECUTIVE OFFICER:

Karl H. Kurz, M.D., Executive Officer

BRANCH OFFICES:

TELEPHONE NUMBER:	TELEX NUMBER:
0211/588288, 0211/572957, 0211/480074	8586569 IRIRD

APPROX. STAFF SIZE:	VOLUNTEER STAFF:	YEAR ESTABLISHED:
11/2	2-5	1981

NUMBER OF INDIVIDUAL MEMBERS:

28

FUNDING: Funded by two founders of Institute, individual donors and a judge who orders compensation for IRIR.

PRINCIPAL PURPOSE: To find new contraceptive methods and improve existing ones; to educate and train medical and paramedical personnel in all methods of fertility regulation including prevention, diagnosis and treatment of S.T.D. and fertility; to provide medical means such as instruments, ultrasound machines, teaching material, educational phantoms, and means for contraception; to make the public in industrialized countries aware of the unmet needs concerning child spacing and women's health in developing countries.

MAIN ACTIVITIES: Invention and research in means, instruments and methods for reproductive health care.

POPULATION CONCERNS: Present contraceptive technology seems to hamper the wider spread of birth spacing due to discipline, price and side effects of the means. Population issues may only be solved in the future if improved long-acting, reversible contraception becomes a substantial part of popualtion activities.

SPECIFIC POPULATION ACTIVITIES: Education, counselling of personnel, delivery of services: IUD, natural family planning.

FORWARD-LOOKING STRATEGIES IMPLEMENTATIONS: Implementing strategies by working to provide appropriate methods of family planning and to improve standards of quality, efficiency and safety of fertility control methods.

OBSTACLES TO THE IMPLEMENTATION OF FORWARD-LOOKING STRATEGIES: Disinterest of Europeans in population issues thus non-funding of reproductive health care. Opposition of certain industries against improved long-acting methods for contraception and the related technology.

NOTES:

Pro Familia

WEST GERMANY

ADDRESS:

Pro Familia-Bundesverband, Cronstettenstrasse 30, D-6000 Frankfurt am Main 1, FRG

EXECUTIVE OFFICER:

Elke Thoss, Executive Director

BRANCH OFFICES:

TELEPHONE NUMBER:

069-550901

TELEX NUMBER:

APPROX. STAFF SIZE:	VOLUNTEER STAFF:	YEAR ESTABLISHED:
9	33	1952

NUMBER OF INDIVIDUAL MEMBERS:

6018 in 10 branches

FUNDING: Central level: Ministry of Youth, Family, Women and Health. Federal level: federal/local governments, selling of services, private funds.

PRINCIPAL PURPOSE: To provide counselling, education and clinical servicesd related to sex and family planning.

MAIN ACTIVITIES: Providing sexual counselling, sex education and family planning and abortion service.

POPULATION CONCERNS: Dissemination of services, education and counselling for a range of family planning and sexual issues.

SPECIFIC POPULATION ACTIVITIES: Education, contraceptive research, counselling, advocacy, human rights, delivery of services: sterilization, pill, IUD, diaphragm, foam, natural family planning, condom, infertility counselling, abortion.

FORWARD-LOOKING STRATEGIES IMPLEMENTATIONS: For many years, paragraphs 156-159 have been leading guidelines for Pro Familia's activities.

OBSTACLES TO THE IMPLEMENTATION OF FORWARD-LOOKING STRATEGIES: The "Pro-life" position of the government as well as the Catholic Church.

NOTES:

Women's Organizations

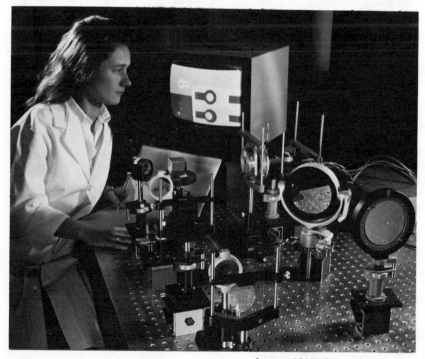

Comite de Liaison des Femmes* **BELGIUM**

ADDRESS:

1a place Quetelet , 1030 Bruxelles, Belgium

EXECUTIVE OFFICER:

Co-Presidents: Mrs. H. Peemans-Poullet and Mrs. R. Dury

BRANCH OFFICES:

TELEPHONE NUMBER:

02/219 2802

TELEX NUMBER:

APPROX. STAFF SIZE:	VOLUNTEER STAFF:	YEAR ESTABLISHED:
	10	1980

NUMBER OF INDIVIDUAL MEMBERS:

150

FUNDING: Donations, dues, EEC subsidies, and publication sales.

PRINCIPAL PURPOSE: To promote and defend the social, economic and political rights of women.

MAIN ACTIVITIES: Sponsoring pressure groups and complaints bureau.

POPULATION CONCERNS: None.

SPECIFIC POPULATION ACTIVITIES: None.

FORWARD-LOOKING STRATEGIES IMPLEMENTATIONS: None.

OBSTACLES TO THE IMPLEMENTATION OF FORWARD-LOOKING STRATEGIES: None.

NOTES: *Communication Board for Women

Norwegian Council for Women, Development Information Unit

NORWAY

ADDRESS:

Fr. Nansens pl. 6, Oslo 1, Norway

EXECUTIVE OFFICER:	BRANCH OFFICES:
Hege Berg-Nielsen, Information Secretary	

TELEPHONE NUMBER:	TELEX NUMBER:	

APPROX. STAFF SIZE:	VOLUNTEER STAFF:	YEAR ESTABLISHED:
2	5	1904

NUMBER OF INDIVIDUAL MEMBERS:

FUNDING: Government support and membership fees.

PRINCIPAL PURPOSE: To provide information about women in the developing world to Norwegian women's organizations.

MAIN ACTIVITIES: Publishing papers, holding seminars and organizing study tours.

POPULATION CONCERNS: None.

SPECIFIC POPULATION ACTIVITIES: None.

FORWARD-LOOKING STRATEGIES IMPLEMENTATIONS: None.

OBSTACLES TO THE IMPLEMENTATION OF FORWARD-LOOKING STRATEGIES: None.

NOTES:

Norges Husmorforbund*

NORWAY

ADDRESS:

Oscars GT. 43, 0258 Oslo 2, Norway

EXECUTIVE OFFICER:			BRANCH OFFICES:
Ingunn Birkeland			

TELEPHONE NUMBER:		TELEX NUMBER:	
02-557907			

APPROX. STAFF SIZE:	VOLUNTEER STAFF:	YEAR ESTABLISHED:	
13		1915	

NUMBER OF INDIVIDUAL MEMBERS:

30,000

FUNDING: Almost all work is done by volunteers.

PRINCIPAL PURPOSE: Educate and encourage housewives in their work; spread information on family laws, cultural activities, housework, raising children; strengthen economic position of the family; maintain education in domestic science and family relationship subjects for boys and girls; work for mutual understanding between the people of the world.

MAIN ACTIVITIES: Education, spread information.

POPULATION CONCERNS:

SPECIFIC POPULATION ACTIVITIES: None.

FORWARD-LOOKING STRATEGIES IMPLEMENTATIONS: Paragraphs 215-220, 120.

OBSTACLES TO THE IMPLEMENTATION OF FORWARD-LOOKING STRATEGIES: None.

NOTES: *Norwegian Housewife Association

The Federation of Liberal Women (FLW)

SWEDEN

ADDRESS:

FLW, Box 6508, 11383 Stockholm, Sweden

EXECUTIVE OFFICER:			BRANCH OFFICES:
Anita Amlen			

TELEPHONE NUMBER:		TELEX NUMBER:	
011-46-8/15 10 30		19545-Liberal 5	

APPROX. STAFF SIZE:	VOLUNTEER STAFF:	YEAR ESTABLISHED:	
2		1936	

NUMBER OF INDIVIDUAL MEMBERS:

FUNDING:

PRINCIPAL PURPOSE: Equality between men and women in politics, in family and at the employment market.

MAIN ACTIVITIES: Recruit women into politics and educate women for political tasks.

POPULATION CONCERNS:

SPECIFIC POPULATION ACTIVITIES:

FORWARD-LOOKING STRATEGIES IMPLEMENTATIONS:

OBSTACLES TO THE IMPLEMENTATION OF FORWARD-LOOKING STRATEGIES:

NOTES:

Federation International des Femmes*
Diplomees des Universites SWITZERLAND

ADDRESS:

37 Quai Wilson, 1201 Geneva, Switzerland

EXECUTIVE OFFICER:			BRANCH OFFICES:
Alice Paquier			

TELEPHONE NUMBER:		TELEX NUMBER:	
022-312380			

APPROX. STAFF SIZE:	VOLUNTEER STAFF:	YEAR ESTABLISHED:
6		1919

NUMBER OF INDIVIDUAL MEMBERS:

FUNDING: Membership subscriptions

PRINCIPAL PURPOSE: To encourage understanding and friendship between university women worldwide, international cooperation, education, and women to use their talents and knowledge at solving problems at the local, national and international level.

MAIN ACTIVITIES: Education on the condition of women, seminars, regional and international meetings, publications and scholarships.

POPULATION CONCERNS: Population is related to the status of women, but the FFDU has no specific population activities.

SPECIFIC POPULATION ACTIVITIES:

FORWARD-LOOKING STRATEGIES IMPLEMENTATIONS: Encouragement of women to participate in local and international affairs.

OBSTACLES TO THE IMPLEMENTATION OF FORWARD-LOOKING STRATEGIES:

NOTES: *International Federation of University Graduate Women

International Council of Nurses

SWITZERLAND

ADDRESS:

Place Jean-Marteau 3, 1201 Geneve, Switzerland

EXECUTIVE OFFICER:	BRANCH OFFICES:
Constance Holleran	

TELEPHONE NUMBER:	TELEX NUMBER:
31.29.60	

APPROX. STAFF SIZE:	VOLUNTEER STAFF:	YEAR ESTABLISHED:
16		1899

NUMBER OF INDIVIDUAL MEMBERS:

FUNDING: Memberships

PRINCIPAL PURPOSE:

MAIN ACTIVITIES:

POPULATION CONCERNS:

SPECIFIC POPULATION ACTIVITIES:

FORWARD-LOOKING STRATEGIES IMPLEMENTATIONS:

OBSTACLES TO THE IMPLEMENTATION OF FORWARD-LOOKING STRATEGIES:

NOTES:

Americas:
Latin America & the Carribean

Latin America
and the Caribbean

Latin America and the Caribbean have changed enormously since World War II. Declining death rates and rising birth rates have been accompanied by higher incomes, rapid urbanization and the growth of megacities, heavy internal and external migration, large shifts of labor out of agriculture and into manufacturing and services, increased education for men and women and greater participation of women in the labor force. In 1950 the population of Latin America and the Caribbean was 165 million, roughly equal to the 166 million who lived in the United States and Canada. By 1986 the region had 417 million people whereas North America had 267 million. Long-range projections suggest that the population of Latin America and the Caribbean could exceed one billion by the time it stabilizes in the 21st century.

To a large extent the decline in death rates has been brought about by improved health measures: control of infectious diseases, vaccinations, antibiotics and the eradication of malaria. High birth rates, however, have produced a youthful population (45 percent is under 15 years of age in all countries of the region save Argentina, Cuba and Uruguay) that strains existing education and health systems and limits the capacity of depressed economies crippled by external debt to generate sufficient employment. In Mexico alone over one million young people enter the labor force each year. High unemployment and underemployment, in turn, has led to the growth of a large informal sector economy in all countries.

Although population in some countries has grown slowly or even declined (such as Argentina and Uruguay), the six poorest countries (Bolivia, El Salvador, Guatemala, Haiti, Honduras and Nicaragua) have experienced rapid population growth (2.5–3.4 percent). In Central America in particular, rapid population growth has increased pressures on land, labor markets and on the ability of governments to provide services to meet the needs of the people, thus nurturing social-political violence among the increasing ranks of unemployed struggling to survive.

Population declines have taken place in urban rather than rural areas. Crowded living conditions and increased incomes during the 1960s and 1970s spurred couples to limit the number of children. In addition, women in urban areas have had greater educational and employment opportunities and greater access to family planning services.

The persistence of mortality differences between high and low income groups highlights the tremendous disparities between rich and poor throughout the region. Antiquated land tenure patterns such as in Central America, and the shift to export crops and labor-saving technologies in agriculture have displaced peasant farmers and created a growing class of poor landless wage laborers, further stimulating the massive migrations from rural to urban areas and across national borders. The resultant continuing uncontrolled growth of megacities such as Mexico City, Sao Paulo, Rio de Janeiro and Buenos Aires (all of which have populations ranging from 10 million to 17 million) has eviscerated the ability of municipal and federal authorities to provide social and other services, and has caused serious environmental problems.

There have been three major influences on Latin America. The "structuralists" believe that the unequal distribution of political power and wealth, particularly land and other productive resources, is the principal obstacle to progress and more equitable societies. Secondly, the offical teachings of the Catholic Church prohibit abortion and the use of contraceptives. Lastly, the military has long viewed family planning as an attempt by foreigners to weaken a nation's power. As a result, only eight countries have specific Government policy goals to reduce their populations: Barbados, Colombia, Dominican Republic, El Salvador, Guatemala, Jamaica and Mexico. Eleven others support family planning programs for health reasons. Four have no policy or are pro-natalist: Bolivia, Chile, Argentina and Uruguay.

In spite of women's gains in education and their increasing incorporation into the wage labor force, their status in Latin America and the Caribbean is still closely linked to motherhood. Although women's employment rates are higher than in other regions of the Third World, the overall participation rate is low primarily because their work in agriculture and the informal sector is rarely represented in government labor-force statistics. Yet an estimated 40 percent of women work in agriculture, and where male out-migration is high, women assume responsibility for subsistence crops. Women who farm, however, receive little technical assistance from government extension services and have difficulty gaining access to land. And since they do not own land that can serve as collateral, they do not qualify for credit. Agrarian reforms in Latin America have not benefitted women. Although one in five households in Latin America and between 30-50 percent in the Caribbean are headed by a woman, the legal structure of many countries favors women who are or have been legally married. Machismo, the belief that women are naturally subordinate, belong in the home and should obey men, still prevails.

There is, however, a large and active women's movement throughout Latin America and the Caribbean working through a wide variety of organizations to change legal structures and to increase women's access to resources. Their growing ability to form coalitions and to take collective action across class lines bodes well for the future.

I Just Lightning

I just lightning, *says*
I just shout, *says*
I just whistle, *says*
I am a lawyer woman, *says*
I am a woman of transactions, *says*
Holy Father, *says*
That is his clock, *says*
That is his lord eagle, *says*
That is his opossum, *says*
That is his lord hawk, *says*
Holy Father, *says*
Mother, *says*
I am a mother woman beneath the water, *says*
I am a woman wise in medicine, *says*
Holy Father, *says*
I am a saint woman, *says*
I am a spirit woman, *says*
She is woman of light, *says*
She is woman of the day, *says*
Holy Father, *says*
I am a shooting star woman, *says*
I am a shooting star woman, *says*
I am a whirling woman of colors, *says*
I am a whirling woman of colors, *says*
I am a clean woman, *says*
I am a clean woman, *says*
I am a woman who whistles, *says*
I am a woman who looks into the insides of things, *says*
I am a woman who investigates, *says*
I am a woman wise in medicine, *says*
I am a mother woman, *says*
I am a spirit woman, *says*
I am a woman of light, *says*
I am a woman of the day, *says*
I am a Book woman, *says*
I am a woman who looks into the insides of things, *says*

Maria Sabina   Reprinted with permission of Latin American Literary Review Press.
Translators:
Eloina Estrada de Gonzalez &
Henry Munn

I'm a Mirror

The water glistens
on my skin
and I don't feel it
The water streams
down my back
I don't feel it
I towel myself
pinch my own arm
feel nothing
terrified, I stare into the mirror
she pinches herself
I start dressing hastily
in the corners appear
crazed eyes
glints of screams
scurrying of rats
teeth
still I feel nothing
I wander through the streets:
dirty-faced children
begging for pennies
teen-aged prostitutes
the streets are running sores
rumbling tanks
flashing bayonets
bodies falling
the sound of sobbing
I finally feel my arm
I've stopped being a phantom

I hurt
therefore I exist
I look again at the scene:
boys who run
bleeding
women with panic
in their faces
now it hurts less
I pinch myself again
now I feel nothing
I simply reflect
what happens around me
the tanks
aren't tanks
and the screams
aren't screams
I'm a flat mirror
in which nothing penetrates
my surface
is hard
brilliant
polished
I've turned into a mirror
I am bloodless
I scarcely retain
a vague memory
of pain.

Claribel Alegria
Translator:
Darwin J. Flakoll

Reprinted with permission of Latin
American Literary Review Press.

Women's Organizations in Population

The Population Institute

The Population Institute

The Population Institute

292

Asociacion Ayuda Materna Ñuñu* ARGENTINA

ADDRESS:

Ave. San Martin 1450, 1638 Vicente Lopez, Buenos Aires, Argentina

EXECUTIVE OFFICER:			BRANCH OFFICES:
Nora Baldrich de Blanchetti			

TELEPHONE NUMBER:		TELEX NUMBER:	
795-6802			

APPROX. STAFF SIZE:	VOLUNTEER STAFF:	YEAR ESTABLISHED:	
2	71	1974	

NUMBER OF INDIVIDUAL MEMBERS:

348

FUNDING: Member's contributions.

PRINCIPAL PURPOSE: To advise and guide the mother in the successful nursing of her child, and to improve the mother-child relationship.

MAIN ACTIVITIES: Meetings, discussions, conferences, telephone and written counselling.

POPULATION CONCERNS:

SPECIFIC POPULATION ACTIVITIES: Education, Natural Family Planning and Counselling.

FORWARD-LOOKING STRATEGIES IMPLEMENTATIONS:

OBSTACLES TO THE IMPLEMENTATION OF FORWARD-LOOKING STRATEGIES:

NOTES: *Maternal Help Association

Centro de Estudios
de la Mujer*

ARGENTINA

ADDRESS:

Olleros 2554, Buenos Aires (1426), Argentina

EXECUTIVE OFFICER:

Gloria Bonder, Director

BRANCH OFFICES:

TELEPHONE NUMBER:	TELEX NUMBER:
72-0142	

APPROX. STAFF SIZE:	VOLUNTEER STAFF:	YEAR ESTABLISHED:
5	25	1979

NUMBER OF INDIVIDUAL MEMBERS:

55

FUNDING: National and international research funds.

PRINCIPAL PURPOSE: Publications on women's status in Argentna and the world, advanced programs on women's studies, research in areas of women and education, work, and health; programs of action and enablement of women.

MAIN ACTIVITIES: Publications on women's status in Argentina and the world, advanced programs on women's studies, research in areas of women and education, work, and health; programs of action and enablement of women.

POPULATION CONCERNS:

SPECIFIC POPULATION ACTIVITIES: Education, counselling, courses to enable and sensitize health workers with respect to the basic health problems of women.

FORWARD-LOOKING STRATEGIES IMPLEMENTATIONS: None.

OBSTACLES TO THE IMPLEMENTATION OF FORWARD-LOOKING STRATEGIES: None.

NOTES: *Center on the Study of Women

Centro Multinacional de la Mujer* ARGENTINA

ADDRESS:

Avda. Velez Sarsfield 153, 5000 Cordoba, Argentina

EXECUTIVE OFFICER:

Dra. Alicia Malanca de Rodriguez Rojas

BRANCH OFFICES:

TELEPHONE NUMBER:
45750

TELEX NUMBER:

APPROX. STAFF SIZE:
10

VOLUNTEER STAFF:

YEAR ESTABLISHED:
1978

NUMBER OF INDIVIDUAL MEMBERS:

FUNDING: Through the Argentinian government, CIM, and OEA.

PRINCIPAL PURPOSE: Advancement of women for the development of Latin American countries.

MAIN ACTIVITIES: Research and workshops.

POPULATION CONCERNS: Not indicated.

SPECIFIC POPULATION ACTIVITIES: Education, research in nutrition in the Indian population of north Argentina and natural family planning.

FORWARD-LOOKING STRATEGIES IMPLEMENTATIONS: Currently implementing the strategies.

OBSTACLES TO THE IMPLEMENTATION OF FORWARD-LOOKING STRATEGIES: Not indicated.

NOTES: *Multinational Center for Women

Women & Development Unit

BARBADOS

ADDRESS:

Extra Mural Dept., Pinelands, St. Michael, Barbados

EXECUTIVE OFFICER:	BRANCH OFFICES:
Peggy Antrobus, Tutor/Coordinator	

TELEPHONE NUMBER:	TELEX NUMBER:
(809) 436-6312	2257 UNIVADOS WB

APPROX. STAFF SIZE:	VOLUNTEER STAFF:	YEAR ESTABLISHED:
17		1978

NUMBER OF INDIVIDUAL MEMBERS:

FUNDING: International sources.

PRINCIPAL PURPOSE: Consciousness raising on women in development issues, training, technical assistance and communications networking.

MAIN ACTIVITIES: Training, networking, and technical assistance for organizations and rural development programs.

POPULATION CONCERNS: Women and health related issues and reproductive rights.

SPECIFIC POPULATION ACTIVITIES: Education, counselling and advocacy.

FORWARD-LOOKING STRATEGIES IMPLEMENTATIONS: Networking with peace groups regionally and internationally in promoting peace and social justice. Education to change attitudes and perceptions towards women and their roles in Caribbean society.

OBSTACLES TO THE IMPLEMENTATION OF FORWARD-LOOKING STRATEGIES: Prevalence of resistance and conservative attitudes, especially at policy-making levels. Trivialization of issues on women and development.

NOTES:

ORGANIZATION:	
Cabo Women Center	**BRAZIL**

ADDRESS:

Rua Padre Antonio Alves, 20 centro Cabo, Brasil

EXECUTIVE OFFICER:

Efigenia Maria de Oliveira, President

BRANCH OFFICES:

TELEPHONE NUMBER:	TELEX NUMBER:
(081) 521-0785	

APPROX. STAFF SIZE:	VOLUNTEER STAFF:	YEAR ESTABLISHED:
9	3	1984

NUMBER OF INDIVIDUAL MEMBERS:

4000

FUNDING: Member fees, funds from Interamerica.

PRINCIPAL PURPOSE: To organize working women; women health programs.

MAIN ACTIVITIES: Health programs, handwork education.

POPULATION CONCERNS: Family planning through health education.

SPECIFIC POPULATION ACTIVITIES: Education, counselling, demographic research, natural family planning.

FORWARD-LOOKING STRATEGIES IMPLEMENTATIONS: Strengthen women's organizations, women's civil rights, access to family planning.

OBSTACLES TO THE IMPLEMENTATION OF FORWARD-LOOKING STRATEGIES: Lack of human resources, lack of financial resources.

NOTES:

CEMICAMP-Center for Research & Control of Maternal-Infant Diseases

BRAZIL

ADDRESS:

C.P. 6181, 13.081 Campinas, Sao Paulo, Brasil

EXECUTIVE OFFICER:

BRANCH OFFICES:

TELEPHONE NUMBER:

(0192) 392856

TELEX NUMBER:

APPROX. STAFF SIZE:

35

VOLUNTEER STAFF:

0

YEAR ESTABLISHED:

NUMBER OF INDIVIDUAL MEMBERS:

0

FUNDING: Grants.

PRINCIPAL PURPOSE: To promote the control of diseases particular to women and children in the region of Campinas. This includes the prevention and early detection of diseases, especially those that are categorized as problems of public health.

MAIN ACTIVITIES: Research into family planning, contraceptives, breast cancer and breastfeeding.

POPULATION CONCERNS: Family planning.

SPECIFIC POPULATION ACTIVITIES: Education, contraceptive research and delivery of services (sterilization, pill, IUD, diaphragm and Norplant).

FORWARD-LOOKING STRATEGIES IMPLEMENTATIONS: The promotion of adequate contraceptive research, provision of family planning services and educatiion.

OBSTABLES TO THE IMPLEMENATION OF FORWARD-LOOKING STRATEGIES: Difficulties with certain governmental agencies.

NOTES:

Rede Mulher

BRAZIL

ADDRESS:

CX Postal 1803, Sao Paulo, Brazil

EXECUTIVE OFFICER:

Moema Viezzer

BRANCH OFFICES:

TELEPHONE NUMBER:	TELEX NUMBER:
2629407	(011) 23059 CANN

APPROX. STAFF SIZE:	VOLUNTEER STAFF:	YEAR ESTABLISHED:
11	2000	1980

NUMBER OF INDIVIDUAL MEMBERS:

FUNDING: Fundraising projects.

PRINCIPAL PURPOSE: To promote the popular education of women and communication among women. To perform participatory research and documentation.

MAIN ACTIVITIES: Engaged in support and advisory work for women's groups of Sao Paulo City, in both the Eastern and Southern Zones. Sponsor a women's popular theatre and courses on women's rights. Publish and distribute materials.

POPULATION CONCERNS: Concerned about population issues that interest organized groups of women in Brazil.

SPECIFIC POPULATION ACTIVITIES: Education.

FORWARD-LOOKING STRATEGIES IMPLEMENTATIONS: None.

OBSTACLES TO THE IMPLEMENTATION OF FORWARD-LOOKING STRATEGIES: None.

NOTES:

Servçio de Aleitamento Materno*

BRAZIL

ADDRESS:

II Centro de Saude-Breastfeeding Service, Prace Maravilha-Poco-Maceio, AL, Brasil

EXECUTIVE OFFICER:
Dr. Ib Gatto, Health Secretary

BRANCH OFFICES:

TELEPHONE NUMBER:

TELEX NUMBER:

APPROX. STAFF SIZE:
3

VOLUNTEER STAFF:

YEAR ESTABLISHED:
1979

NUMBER OF INDIVIDUAL MEMBERS:

FUNDING: State Health System.

PRINCIPAL PURPOSE: To promote the practice of breastfeeding.

MAIN ACTIVITIES: To educate low-income mothers about breastfeeding, infant nutrition, infant health and family plannning. Counselling and providing services to mothers.

POPULATION CONCERNS: Family planning. Exclusive breastfeeding is encouraged in the first few months and natural barrier methods are promoted.

SPECIFIC POPULATION ACTIVITIES: Counselling, education and advocacy.

FORWARD-LOOKING STRATEGIES IMPLEMENTATIONS: Providing information that will allow women to make educated choices.

OBSTACLES TO THE IMPLEMENTATION OF FORWARD-LOOKING STRATEGIES: The public health system has many shortcomings. Doctors and other service providers lack motivation, responsibility and enthusiasm.

NOTES: *Breastfeeding Service

SOS CORPO-Grupo de Saude da Mulher*

BRAZIL

ADDRESS:

Rua Do Hospicio, 859 - Apto. 14 - Recife - PE., 50.050 Brazil

EXECUTIVE OFFICER:			BRANCH OFFICES:
Dolores Wandscheer			

TELEPHONE NUMBER:	TELEX NUMBER:	
(081) 221.30 18	811328 MMTTBR	

APPROX. STAFF SIZE:	VOLUNTEER STAFF:	YEAR ESTABLISHED:
8		1982

NUMBER OF INDIVIDUAL MEMBERS:

14

FUNDING: Grants from European and American foundations and NGOs.

PRINCIPAL PURPOSE: To carry out activities related to women's health.

MAIN ACTIVITIES: Providing health education to women and young adults, producing didactic materials, counselling, etc.

POPULATION CONCERNS: Interested in promoting family planning as a basic human right.

SPECIFIC POPULATION ACTIVITIES: Education, contraceptive research and counselling.

FORWARD-LOOKING STRATEGIES IMPLEMENTATIONS: Were not aware of the strategies.

OBSTACLES TO THE IMPLEMENTATION OF FORWARD-LOOKING STRATEGIES: None.

NOTES: *Women's Health Group

Women's Studies Centre, PUC-Rio BRAZIL

ADDRESS:

Rua Marques Aau Vicente 225, Rio de Janeiro 22453, Brasil

EXECUTIVE OFFICER:			BRANCH OFFICES:
Dr. Fanny Tabak			

TELEPHONE NUMBER:		TELEX NUMBER:	
(021) 274-9922 ext. 288		(021) 31048	

APPROX. STAFF SIZE:	VOLUNTEER STAFF:	YEAR ESTABLISHED:
7	6	1981

NUMBER OF INDIVIDUAL MEMBERS:

20

FUNDING: Domestic and international funding agencies.

PRINCIPAL PURPOSE: Teaching and research.

MAIN ACTIVITIES: Teaching, research, documentation, publications.

POPULATION CONCERNS: Low-income and migrant women: to circulate information and training of professional skills.

SPECIFIC POPULATION ACTIVITIES: Education, demographic research and counselling.

FORWARD-LOOKING STRATEGIES IMPLEMENTATIONS: None.

OBSTACLES TO THE IMPLEMENTATION OF FORWARD-LOOKING STRATEGIES: Lack of funding.

NOTES:

CEDE

COLOMBIA

ADDRESS:

Facultad de Economia, Universidad de los Andes, AA 4976, Bogota, Colombia

EXECUTIVE OFFICER:			BRANCH OFFICES:
Dr. Augusto Cano, Director			

TELEPHONE NUMBER:		TELEX NUMBER:	
2410377			

APPROX. STAFF SIZE:	VOLUNTEER STAFF:	YEAR ESTABLISHED:
		1958

NUMBER OF INDIVIDUAL MEMBERS:

FUNDING: Tuitions and research grants.

PRINCIPAL PURPOSE: To study Colombian problems in the following areas; women's studies, family and socio-economic development; employment and poverty; population and development; rural and agricultural development; industrial development; projects evaluation. There are other areas more strictly economic oriented in the classical terms.

MAIN ACTIVITIES: Research and teaching.

POPULATION CONCERNS: According to the population involved in the areas listed in questions.

SPECIFIC POPULATION ACTIVITIES: Education; Demographic Research, we are not interested in family planning but in womens problems within the family and at the social level especially in education, labor, ideology.

FORWARD-LOOKING STRATEGIES IMPLEMENTATIONS:

OBSTACLES TO THE IMPLEMENTATION OF FORWARD-LOOKING STRATEGIES:

NOTES:

Corporacion Casa de la Mujer*　　COLOMBIA

ADDRESS:

Cra. 18 No. 59–60, Apartado 36151, Bogota, Colombia

EXECUTIVE OFFICER:	BRANCH OFFICES:
Olga Amparo Sanchez G.	

TELEPHONE NUMBER:	TELEX NUMBER:
2482469	

APPROX. STAFF SIZE:	VOLUNTEER STAFF:	YEAR ESTABLISHED:
12		1982

NUMBER OF INDIVIDUAL MEMBERS:

12

FUNDING:

PRINCIPAL PURPOSE: To provide various workshops and services to women.

MAIN ACTIVITIES: Carrying out workshops on Health and Sexuality, Woman and Family, Creativity for women and children and preparation for childbirth. Providing legal, psychological, informational and therapy services. Providing medical consulting and support activities such as forums, roundtables and conferences.

POPULATION CONCERNS: Health and sexuality, preparation for childbirth.

SPECIFIC POPULATION ACTIVITIES: Education, contraceptive research, counselling, delivery of services.

FORWARD-LOOKING STRATEGIES IMPLEMENTATIONS:

OBSTACLES TO THE IMPLEMENTATION OF FORWARD-LOOKING STRATEGIES:

NOTES: *House of Women Corporation

Desarrollo Economico Laboral Femenino Integral*

COSTA RICA

ADDRESS:

Apdo. 49: Centro Colon, San Jose, Costa Rica

EXECUTIVE OFFICER:

BRANCH OFFICES:

TELEPHONE NUMBER:

33-56-10

TELEX NUMBER:

APPROX. STAFF SIZE:	VOLUNTEER STAFF:	YEAR ESTABLISHED:
12	40	1974

NUMBER OF INDIVIDUAL MEMBERS:

FUNDING: Government funding, donations.

PRINCIPAL PURPOSE: Women's group with emphasis on employment and training programs, promote awareness of women's role within family and society, stimulate attitudinal changes with respect to legal and social reforms.

MAIN ACTIVITIES: Non-formal education (radio), rural and urban projects.

POPULATION CONCERNS: Information, social.

SPECIFIC POPULATION ACTIVITIES: Counselling, education, demographic research, contraceptive research.

FORWARD-LOOKING STRATEGIES IMPLEMENTATIONS: None.

OBSTACLES TO THE IMPLEMENTATION OF FORWARD-LOOKING STRATEGIES: None.

NOTES: *Women's Integration in Ecomonic Development

Federation of Cuban Women

CUBA

ADDRESS:

Paseo #260, Vedado, Ciudad Habana, Cuba

EXECUTIVE OFFICER:

Vilma Espin, President

BRANCH OFFICES:

TELEPHONE NUMBER:	TELEX NUMBER:
3-9940	FMC-CU 511270

APPROX. STAFF SIZE:	VOLUNTEER STAFF:	YEAR ESTABLISHED:
100		1960

NUMBER OF INDIVIDUAL MEMBERS:

3,100,000

FUNDING: Membership fees, donations and grants from international organizations.

PRINCIPAL PURPOSE: To achieve full equality for women and integration in the process of economic and social development.

MAIN ACTIVITIES: Involved in: education, healthcare, social work, employment solidarity, mass media, fundraising, rural women, research, training, international relations.

POPULATION CONCERNS: Education and research on: family planning, sex education, teenage pregnancy, maternal and child health, parental responsibilities and demography.

SPECIFIC POPULATION ACTIVITIES: Education, demographic research, contraceptive research, counselling and delivery of services: pill, IUD, diaphragm and natural family planning.

FORWARD-LOOKING STRATEGIES IMPLEMENTATIONS: Organizing a National Seminar with the participation of governmental and non-governmental organizations involved in the implementation of the Strategies.

OBSTACLES TO THE IMPLEMENTATION OF FORWARD-LOOKING STRATEGIES: More time is needed to identify the obstacles.

NOTES:

Mujeres en Desarrollo Dominicana, Inc.* DOMINICAN REPUBLIC

ADDRESS:

Av. Maximo Gomez #70, Santo Domingo, D.N., A.P. 325, Republica Dominicana

EXECUTIVE OFFICER:

Luz Maria Abreu L.

BRANCH OFFICES:

TELEPHONE NUMBER:	TELEX NUMBER:
685-8111, A.C. (809)	ITT 0597

APPROX. STAFF SIZE:	VOLUNTEER STAFF:	YEAR ESTABLISHED:
40	26	1977

NUMBER OF INDIVIDUAL MEMBERS:

160

FUNDING:

PRINCIPAL PURPOSE: Development of rural women.

MAIN ACTIVITIES: Enablement, technical assistance, financing of productive projects, legal aid and ecological education.

POPULATION CONCERNS: 175 groups that encompass 5000 rural women.

SPECIFIC POPULATION ACTIVITIES: Education.

FORWARD-LOOKING STRATEGIES IMPLEMENTATIONS: None.

OBSTACLES TO THE IMPLEMENTATION OF FORWARD-LOOKING STRATEGIES: Lack of funding.

NOTES: *Dominican Women in Development

Asociacion de Mujeres
Profesionales y de Negocios*

ECUADOR

ADDRESS:

Casilla 260 Suc. 15, Quito ECUADOR

EXECUTIVE OFFICER:

Irene Ayarza Salazar

BRANCH OFFICES:

TELEPHONE NUMBER:

237-549

TELEX NUMBER:

APPROX. STAFF SIZE:	VOLUNTEER STAFF:	YEAR ESTABLISHED:
	36	1973

NUMBER OF INDIVIDUAL MEMBERS:

36

FUNDING: Membership dues.

PRINCIPAL PURPOSE: To empower women in their work. To work for equality in opportunities and conditions for women in politics, economy and other aspects of life.

MAIN ACTIVITIES: Infant malnutrition program to improve children's diets. The use of waste as fertilizers to grow home vegetable gardens. Discussions and talks on the many new roles of women.

POPULATION CONCERNS: Informing women who are making decisions about motherhood and family planning.

SPECIFIC POPULATION ACTIVITIES: Education and contraceptive research.

FORWARD-LOOKING STRATEGIES IMPLEMENTATIONS:

OBSTACLES TO THE IMPLEMENTATION OF FORWARD-LOOKING STRATEGIES: Lack of economic means.

NOTES: *Professional & Business Women's Association

Union Nacional de Mujeres del Ecuador*

ECUADOR

ADDRESS:

Versalles 1103, Quito, Ecuador

EXECUTIVE OFFICER:			BRANCH OFFICES:
Dra. Irene Paredes			

TELEPHONE NUMBER:	TELEX NUMBER:	
237796		

APPROX. STAFF SIZE:	VOLUNTEER STAFF:	YEAR ESTABLISHED:
	unspecified no.	1961

NUMBER OF INDIVIDUAL MEMBERS:

2000 in 30 affiliates

FUNDING:

PRINCIPAL PURPOSE: Community education, family health, production co-ops, nutrition education, community store and rural housing.

MAIN ACTIVITIES: Family health and nutritional education of rural women. Workshops (high quality handicrafts). Citizen civic education.

POPULATION CONCERNS: Work with 20,000 rural women and poor urban women on a national level.

SPECIFIC POPULATION ACTIVITIES: None.

FORWARD-LOOKING STRATEGIES IMPLEMENTATIONS: None.

OBSTACLES TO THE IMPLEMENTATION OF FORWARD-LOOKING STRATEGIES: None.

NOTES: *Ecuatorian National Women's Union

Women's Affairs Bureau

GUYANA

ADDRESS:

237 Camp Street, South Cummingsburg, Georgetown, Guyana

EXECUTIVE OFFICER:

Cde. Urmia Johnson, Director

BRANCH OFFICES:

TELEPHONE NUMBER:	TELEX NUMBER:
65871	

APPROX. STAFF SIZE:	VOLUNTEER STAFF:	YEAR ESTABLISHED:
9	75	1981

NUMBER OF INDIVIDUAL MEMBERS:

FUNDING: Government of Guyana

PRINCIPAL PURPOSE: To work towards the removal of all discriminations against women, to promote development of their potential and to ensure their integration in the national development of the country.

MAIN ACTIVITIES: Formulation of policies for the integration of women in development. Develop proposals to government in relation to legislation and legal reforms with reference to women. Assist in designing and organizing training programs for women aimed at dissminating information and upgrading skills of women in all spheres of activities.

POPULATION CONCERNS: Child spacing, family life education women's health problems and information.

SPECIFIC POPULATION ACTIVITIES: Education, demographic research, counselling, advocacy and delivery of services.

FORWARD LOOKING-STRATEGIES IMPLEMENTATIONS: Institutionalization of legal forms, ensuring that the employment legislation provides for equal pay, regular treatment and benefits to women.

OBSTACLES TO THE IMPLEMENTATION OF FORWARD-LOOKING STRATEGIES: Lack of finances, administration lags and attitudinal problems.

NOTES:

Women's Progressive Organization   GUYANA

ADDRESS:

Freedom House, 41 Robb Street, Lacytown, Georgetown Guyana

EXECUTIVE OFFICER:			BRANCH OFFICES:
Mrs. Janet Jagan, Pres.; Mrs. Indra Chandarpal, Gen. Sec.			

TELEPHONE NUMBER:		TELEX NUMBER:	
02-72095 or 72096 or 51479			

APPROX. STAFF SIZE:	VOLUNTEER STAFF:	YEAR ESTABLISHED:
3	yes	1953

NUMBER OF INDIVIDUAL MEMBERS:

5000

FUNDING: From membership dues and fund-raising activities and the sale of our quarterly newspaper "Women Unite".

PRINCIPAL PURPOSE: To champion the rights of women in particular and to struggle for the restoration of democracy, which is the major pre-requisite for the achievement towards equality and development for our women.

MAIN ACTIVITIES: Consciousness raising activities with emphasis in the rural areas; educational work through seminars, 3 week live-in classes; representation of women on individual and collective levels; agitation and protest work; international solidarity and emphasis on peace.

POPULATION CONCERNS: In the area of the right of women to choose; provision of legal abortions (therapeutic) subsidized by the state; availability of birth control with proper family planning education to all women; provision of pap smears and proper and accurate diagnostic analysis; education of parents in family and child care; accurate facilities for primary health care.

SPECIFIC POPULATION ACTIVITIES: Education; Contraceptive Research; Counselling, Campaigns against the use of Depo-Provera and Copper T.

FORWARD-LOOKING STRATEGIES IMPLEMENTATIONS: We are struggling for the restoration of democracy. Development so that there would be more employment for all and a higher standard of living. Putting pressure on the government to implement the forward looking strategies in the area of Health, education, employment and civil rights.

OBSTACLES TO THE IMPLEMENTATION OF FORWARD-LOOKING STRATEGIES: The refusal of the government to allow the people to take part in the decision making processes whether at the level of elections, trade unions, political policies or womens organizations. Lack of access to the state owned media and inability to move the government.

NOTES:

Women's Revolutionary Socialist Movement

GUYANA

ADDRESS:

44 Public Rd., Kitty, Georgetown, Guyana

EXECUTIVE OFFICER:

Viola Burnham, National Chairperson

BRANCH OFFICES:

TELEPHONE NUMBER:

72122

TELEX NUMBER:

APPROX. STAFF SIZE:

12

VOLUNTEER STAFF:

100+

YEAR ESTABLISHED:

1957

NUMBER OF INDIVIDUAL MEMBERS:

3000 + 35 affiliated chapters

FUNDING: Fundraising and contributions.

PRINCIPAL PURPOSE: To serve as a women's political arm of the ruling party in government. To organize and mobilize women for political activities and fundraising projects.

MAIN ACTIVITIES: Political, economic and social activities.

POPULATION CONCERNS: Concerned about increases in population.

SPECIFIC POPULATION ACTIVITIES: Education, counselling, delivery of services: pill, IUD, diaphragm, foam and natural family planning.

FORWARD-LOOKING STRATEGIES IMPLEMENTATIONS: Interested in creating employment opportunities for women and educating and training them for integration in national development.

OBSTACLES TO THE IMPLEMENTATION OF FORWARD-LOOKING STRATEGIES: None.

NOTES:

Jamaica Federation of Women

JAMAICA

ADDRESS:

74 Arnold Rd. Kingston 5, Jamaica, WI

EXECUTIVE OFFICER:			BRANCH OFFICES:
Mrs. Lucille V. Miller, Chairwoman			

TELEPHONE NUMBER:		TELEX NUMBER:	
926-7726			

APPROX. STAFF SIZE:	VOLUNTEER STAFF:	YEAR ESTABLISHED:	
5	91	1944	

NUMBER OF INDIVIDUAL MEMBERS:

1500 and 75 affiliated chapters

FUNDING: Fundraising, grants, donations and funding for projects by affiliated organizations.

PRINCIPAL PURPOSE: To foster cultural, educational and civic development among women of Jamaica.

MAIN ACTIVITIES: Early childhood education(sponsor 56 basic schools throughout the island). Primary health care with an emphasis on family planning. Involvement in community efforts: health clinics, disaster preparedness boards, etc.

POPULATION CONCERNS: Family planning, family size and child spacing.

SPECIFIC POPULATION ACTIVITIES: Education, contraceptive research and counselling.

FORWARD-LOOKING STRATEGIES IMPLEMENTATIONS: None.

OBSTACLES TO THE IMPLEMENTATION OF FORWARD-LOOKING STRATEGIES: Lack of funds and poor leadership.

NOTES:

Sistren

JAMAICA

ADDRESS:

20 Kensington Crescent, Kingston 5, Jamaica

EXECUTIVE OFFICER:			BRANCH OFFICES:

EXECUTIVE OFFICER:

Lana Finikin

TELEPHONE NUMBER:	TELEX NUMBER:

TELEPHONE NUMBER:

9292457

APPROX. STAFF SIZE:	VOLUNTEER STAFF:	YEAR ESTABLISHED:
18	20	1977

NUMBER OF INDIVIDUAL MEMBERS:

12

FUNDING: Funding agencies and local contributions.

PRINCIPAL PURPOSE: Popular education aiming to create threatre which challenges and stimulates questions about the situation of women and offer workshops where drama is used as a tool for problem-solving and women's organizing.

MAIN ACTIVITIES: Theatre, popular education on issues of concern to women and Newsmagazine.

POPULATION CONCERNS: Indirectly as is related to sexuality, reproductive rights and allocation of resources which are treated by our popular education project and newsmagazine.

SPECIFIC POPULATION ACTIVITIES: Education and advocacy.

FORWARD-LOOKING STRATEGIES IMPLEMENTATIONS: As they relate to our education programme.

OBSTABLES TO THE IMPLEMENATION OF FORWARD-LOOKING STRATEGIES: Lack of human and material resources. Government policy and time.

NOTES:

Women's Centres Programme for Adolescent Mothers

JAMAICA

ADDRESS:

42 Trafalgar Road, Kingston 10, Jamaica WI

EXECUTIVE OFFICER:			BRANCH OFFICES:
Pamela McNeil, National Coordinator			

TELEPHONE NUMBER:	TELEX NUMBER:	
929-3512		

APPROX. STAFF SIZE:	VOLUNTEER STAFF:	YEAR ESTABLISHED:
36	6	1978

NUMBER OF INDIVIDUAL MEMBERS:

FUNDING: Jamaican government and foreign funding agencies.

PRINCIPAL PURPOSE: To assist teenage mothers to complete their education. To delay second pregnancies until mother has begun her career.

MAIN ACTIVITIES: Teaching (academic subjects), counselling (social), family planning and day nursery.

POPULATION CONCERNS: Problems associated with teenage motherhood and repeat pregnancies during teen years.

SPECIFIC POPULATION ACTIVITIES: Education, counselling, advocacy, and delivery of the pill and IUD.

FORWARD-LOOKING STRATEGIES IMPLEMENTATIONS: Prepare young women for careers and thereby limiting their dependence on men.

OBSTACLES TO THE IMPLEMENTATION OF FORWARD-LOOKING STRATEGIES: Mainly economic obstacles.

NOTES:

Young Women's Christian Association of Jamaica (YWCA)

JAMAICA

ADDRESS:

2h Camp Road, Kingston 5, Jamaica W.I.

EXECUTIVE OFFICER:

Miss Minna McLeod, National Gen. Secretary

BRANCH OFFICES:

TELEPHONE NUMBER:	TELEX NUMBER:
92-83023	

APPROX. STAFF SIZE:	VOLUNTEER STAFF:	YEAR ESTABLISHED:
6		1923

NUMBER OF INDIVIDUAL MEMBERS:

800

FUNDING: Revenue from 7 flats, small Government subvention, special effort rental space by Branches and membership dues.

PRINCIPAL PURPOSE: To promote the welfare of women and girls through physical, mental, social, economic and spiritual development.

MAIN ACTIVITIES: Continuing education for girls 16–19 years old, youth work, family life education, skill, training, and leisure time activities.

POPULATION CONCERNS: High incidence of teenage pregnancies, high level of unemployment, low level of skills, and negative attitudes.

SPECIFIC POPULATION ACTIVITIES: Education, counselling and delivery of services which include: Pill, Foam and Condom on request.

FORWARD-LOOKING STRATEGIES IMPLEMENTATIONS:

OBSTACLES TO THE IMPLEMENTATION OF FORWARD-LOOKING STRATEGIES:

NOTES:

Grupo de Estudios de la Mujer Paraguaya*

PARAGUAY

ADDRESS:

CPES Eligio Ayala 973, C.C. 2157, Asuncion, Paraguay

EXECUTIVE OFFICER:

Graziella Corvalan, Coordinator

BRANCH OFFICES:

TELEPHONE NUMBER:	TELEX NUMBER:
4-3734	

APPROX. STAFF SIZE:	VOLUNTEER STAFF:	YEAR ESTABLISHED:
6	unspecified no.	1985

NUMBER OF INDIVIDUAL MEMBERS:

FUNDING: International agencies.

PRINCIPAL PURPOSE: Research on women's studies. Research on women in Paraguay. Publications.

MAIN ACTIVITIES: Research and publications.

POPULATION CONCERNS: Education and Migration.

SPECIFIC POPULATION ACTIVITIES: Education and demographic research.

FORWARD-LOOKING STRATEGIES IMPLEMENTATIONS: None.

OBSTACLES TO THE IMPLEMENTATION OF FORWARD-LOOKING STRATEGIES: None.

NOTES: *Studies on the Paraguayan Women's Group

Asociacion para el Desarrollo e Integracion de la Mujer*

PERU

ADDRESS:

Apartado #41-0097, Lima 41, Peru

EXECUTIVE OFFICER:

Gabriela Canepa Perez Albela

BRANCH OFFICES:

TELEPHONE NUMBER:

37-1997

TELEX NUMBER:

APPROX. STAFF SIZE:	VOLUNTEER STAFF:	YEAR ESTABLISHED:
26	10	1979

NUMBER OF INDIVIDUAL MEMBERS:

32

FUNDING: U.S. organizations, government and NGOs.

PRINCIPAL PURPOSE: To promote women's advancement and intergration into the socio-economic activities with equal opportunities.

MAIN ACTIVITIES: Training, credit, IEC, health and family planning services, CBD programs and legal services.

POPULATION CONCERNS: Peru has high fertility and high population growth (2.7%), women have limited access to education, and family planning services are limited to not even 20% of WFA with high (70%) of under-employment and unemployment. Women have almost no possibilities of finding adequate jobs. Also, access to credit is almost nil.

SPECIFIC POPULATION ACTIVITIES: Education, counselling, advocacy, contraceptive research, demographic research and delivery of the pill, IUD and diaphragm.

FORWARD-LOOKING STRATEGIES IMPLEMENTATIONS: Women's health, family planning, IEC and services, advancement of women through training (non-formal) and credit availability.

OBSTACLES TO THE IMPLEMENTATION OF FORWARD-LOOKING STRATEGIES: Limited resources to expand ADIM's programs.

NOTES: *Women's Development & Integration Association

*Business Address: Calle Van Dyck 281, San Borja, Lima 41, Peru

ORGANIZATION:

Asociacion Peru-Mujer*

PERU

ADDRESS:

Apartado Postal 949, Correo Central, Lima 100, Peru

EXECUTIVE OFFICER: Blanca Figueroa			BRANCH OFFICES:
TELEPHONE NUMBER: 314416		**TELEX NUMBER:**	
APPROX. STAFF SIZE: 50	**VOLUNTEER STAFF:** 15	**YEAR ESTABLISHED:** 1979	
NUMBER OF INDIVIDUAL MEMBERS:			

FUNDING: Donations.

PRINCIPAL PURPOSE: To work through study and action to encourage the participation of women in development at all levels.

MAIN ACTIVITIES: Women and Nutrition. Communal Gardens. Breastfeeding. Women and Work: production of Andean crafts, textile work. Women and Services: childcare, legal aid. Women and Health: educational materials.

POPULATION CONCERNS: Family planning is an issue that is always in any program we have.

SPECIFIC POPULATION ACTIVITIES: Education, counselling, research about attitudes and sexuality.

FORWARD-LOOKING STRATEGIES IMPLEMENTATIONS: We work in education especially in order to change the attitudes of women to create less negative feelings about family planning.

OBSTACLES TO THE IMPLEMENTATION OF FORWARD-LOOKING STRATEGIES: Most of the input is in the use of methods and statistical research. We feel that most help is needed to finance work in order to change attitudes.

NOTES: *Peru-Women's Association

*Business Address: Larrabure y Unanue 231-803, Jesus Maria, Lima, Peru

Puerto Rican Institute for Civil Rights-Women's Rights Project PUERTO RICO

ADDRESS:

Blanco Romano Street #7,Rio Piedras, Puerto Rico 00925

EXECUTIVE OFFICER:

Charles S. Hey Maestre, General Secretary

BRANCH OFFICES:

TELEPHONE NUMBER:	TELEX NUMBER:
(809)754-7390	INSPURDEC, San Juan

APPROX. STAFF SIZE:	VOLUNTEER STAFF:	YEAR ESTABLISHED:
5	8-10	1977

NUMBER OF INDIVIDUAL MEMBERS:

FUNDING: US and European foundations, churches, private corporations and donors.

PRINCIPAL PURPOSE: To preserve, defend and expand the civil liberties and rights of the Puerto Rican people through the women's rights, peace and police brutality and governmental repression projects.

MAIN ACTIVITIES: Educational activities, such as seminars, workshops and publications, mass media programs, litigation, and legal counselling for other grassroots organizations and individuals.

POPULATION CONCERNS: Reproductive health.

SPECIFIC POPULATION ACTIVITIES: Contraceptive research, legal counselling and delivery of spermicides.

FORWARD-LOOKING STRATEGIES IMPLEMENTATIONS: Are aware of the Strategies and have future plans for implementation.

OBSTACLES TO THE IMPLEMENTATION OF FORWARD-LOOKING STRATEGIES: Lack of communication among different feminist groups in Puerto Rico.

NOTES:

Centro Flora Tristan*

PERU

ADDRESS:

Pargue Hernan Velarde 42, Lima 1, Peru

EXECUTIVE OFFICER:

Dr. Antonio J. Cisneros, Executive Director

BRANCH OFFICES:

TELEPHONE NUMBER:	TELEX NUMBER:
248008, 240839	

APPROX. STAFF SIZE:	VOLUNTEER STAFF:	YEAR ESTABLISHED:
4		1979

NUMBER OF INDIVIDUAL MEMBERS:

FUNDING: International NGOs and Solidarity Funds

PRINCIPAL PURPOSE: To advance women's rights in Peru, involving women in the feminist movement, forwarding new theoretical approaches on development issues and proposing legal changes which benefit women. Reproductive Rights Program develops a women's movement for women's health reproductive rights.

MAIN ACTIVITIES: Popular education, communication, Research, Legal Assistance to Women

POPULATION CONCERNS: To involve women in the definition of the population decisions which affect them, so as to guarantee their reproductive rights.

SPECIFIC POPULATION ACTIVITIES: education, counselling

FORWARD-LOOKING STRATEGIES IMPLEMENTATIONS:

OBSTACLES TO THE IMPLEMENTATION OF FORWARD-LOOKING STRATEGIES:

NOTES: *Flora Tristan Center

National Council of Women   ST. KITTS, WI

ADDRESS:

Dorset No. 8, P.O. Box 49, Basseterre, St. Kitts, WI

EXECUTIVE OFFICER:

Anne Liburd, President

BRANCH OFFICES:

TELEPHONE NUMBER:

2126

TELEX NUMBER:

APPROX. STAFF SIZE:

VOLUNTEER STAFF:

7

YEAR ESTABLISHED:

1974

NUMBER OF INDIVIDUAL MEMBERS:

FUNDING: Subscriptions of affilliated members organizations and fund-raising efforts.

PRINCIPAL PURPOSE: Bring together women in unity, teach skills for purpose of income generation, as well as self employment and independency. To make women aware of their role in the community.

MAIN ACTIVITIES: Education, skill training, seminars, lectures and communication skills.

POPULATION CONCERNS: Family life, responsible parenthood, maternal and child health, teenage pregnancy and family planning.

SPECIFIC POPULATION ACTIVITIES: Education and counselling.

FORWARD-LOOKING STRATEGIES IMPLEMENTATIONS: Assist with information.

OBSTACLES TO THE IMPLEMENTATION OF FORWARD-LOOKING STRATEGIES: Not indicated.

NOTES:

National Commission on the Status of Women

TRINIDAD

ADDRESS:

Riverside Plaza, Level 9, Bessor St., Port-of-Spain, Trinidad, West Indies

EXECUTIVE OFFICER:			BRANCH OFFICES:
Ms. Phyllis Augustus, Secretary			

TELEPHONE NUMBER:		TELEX NUMBER:	
627-3306			

APPROX. STAFF SIZE:	VOLUNTEER STAFF:	YEAR ESTABLISHED:
2		1980

NUMBER OF INDIVIDUAL MEMBERS:

21

FUNDING: Government of Trinidad and Tobago.

PRINCIPAL PURPOSE: To promote full civil, political, economic, social and cultural rights for the women of the country. To assist the government in integrating women into the development process. To submit findings to the government on the progress achieved by women in these areas, indicating existing problems and recommending possible solutions.

MAIN ACTIVITIES: Consciousness raising activities.

POPULATION CONCERNS: Concerned about the increase in teenage pregnancies and the growing number of unemployed young people.

SPECIFIC POPULATION ACTIVITIES: Education and support.

FORWARD-LOOKING STRATEGIES IMPLEMENTATIONS: Strategies are implemented as they fit into the Commission's annual program of activities; other agencies and organizations are more directly concerned with implementation.

OBSTACLES TO THE IMPLEMENTATION OF FORWARD-LOOKING STRATEGIES: None.

NOTES:

Population, Development & Health Organizations

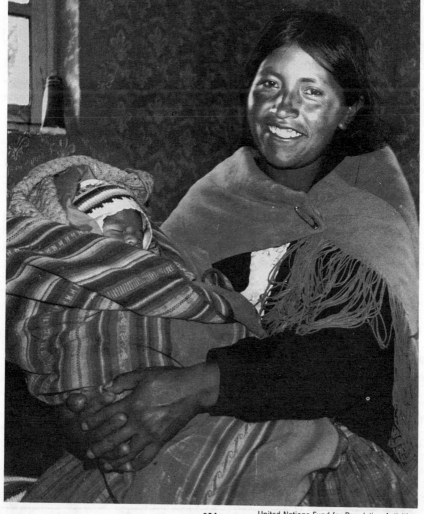

United Nations Fund for Population Activities

Centro de Estudios de Poblacion*

ARGENTINA

ADDRESS:

Casilla 4397 Correo Central, 1000 Buenos Aires, Argentina

EXECUTIVE OFFICER:

Dr. Edith Alejandra Pantelides, Director

BRANCH OFFICES:

TELEPHONE NUMBER:	TELEX NUMBER:
86-0303	

APPROX. STAFF SIZE:	VOLUNTEER STAFF:	YEAR ESTABLISHED:
18	0	1974

NUMBER OF INDIVIDUAL MEMBERS:

FUNDING: Grants, contracts.

PRINCIPAL PURPOSE: Research; training; technical assistance.

MAIN ACTIVITIES: Research; training; technical assistance.

POPULATION CONCERNS: All fields of population research.

SPECIFIC POPULATION ACTIVITIES: Education, counselling.

FORWARD-LOOKING STRATEGIES IMPLEMENTATIONS: None.

OBSTACLES TO THE IMPLEMENTATION OF FORWARD-LOOKING STRATEGIES: None.

NOTES: *Population Studies Center

Antigua Planned Parenthood Association

ANTIGUA

ADDRESS:

P.O. Box 419, St. John's, Antigua

EXECUTIVE OFFICER:

Hazelyn Benjamin, Executive Director

BRANCH OFFICES:

TELEPHONE NUMBER:	TELEX NUMBER:
462-0947	

APPROX. STAFF SIZE:	VOLUNTEER STAFF:	YEAR ESTABLISHED:
9		1972

NUMBER OF INDIVIDUAL MEMBERS:

100

FUNDING: Privately funded by IPPF Western Hemisphere Region (IPPF/WHR) and donations from other agencies.

PRINCIPAL PURPOSE: Is to promote responsible parenthood and to provide family planning services.

MAIN ACTIVITIES: Information and Education on Family Planning and Family Life Education. Contraceptive delivery services which include A Medical and Clinical and A Community based distribution component.

POPULATION CONCERNS: The number of unskilled teenagers leaving school and the rise in teenage pregnancies.

SPECIFIC POPULATION ACTIVITIES: Education, Demographic Research, Contraceptive Research, Counselling, Advocacy, Delivery of Services, Sterilization, Pill, IUD, Diaphram, Foam, Norplant, Depo-provera, and Natural Family Planning.

FORWARD-LOOKING STRATEGIES IMPLEMENTATIONS: Non-indicated

OBSTACLES TO THE IMPLEMENTATION OF FORWARD-LOOKING STRATEGIES:

NOTES:

ORGANIZATION:	
Barbados Family Planning Association	**BARBADOS**

ADDRESS:

Bay Street, St. Michael, Barbados, W.I.

EXECUTIVE OFFICER:	BRANCH OFFICES:
Charles G. Alleyne, Exec. Director	

TELEPHONE NUMBER:	TELEX NUMBER:
426-2226	

APPROX. STAFF SIZE:	VOLUNTEER STAFF:	YEAR ESTABLISHED:
30		1955

NUMBER OF INDIVIDUAL MEMBERS:

150

FUNDING: Barbados Government and International Donor Agencies.

PRINCIPAL PURPOSE: Fertility control and family development.

MAIN ACTIVITIES: Make clinical and educational services accessible to the community.

POPULATION CONCERNS: Stabilization of population.

SPECIFIC POPULATION ACTIVITIES: Education, Demographic research, Contraceptive research, Counselling, Advocacy, and Delivery of Services which include: Sterilization, Pill, IUD, Diaphragm, Foam, Depoprovera.

FORWARD LOOKING-STRATEGIES IMPLEMENTATIONS: Specifically those population-related strategies set out in paragraphs 148 and 155-159.

OBSTACLES TO THE IMPLEMENTATION OF FORWARD-LOOKING STRATEGIES:

NOTES:

Institute of Social and Economic Research (Eastern Caribbean)

BARBADOS

ADDRESS:

University of the West Indies, P.O. Box 64, Bridgetown, BARBADOS

EXECUTIVE OFFICER:			BRANCH OFFICES:
Dr. Joycelin Massiah			

TELEPHONE NUMBER:		TELEX NUMBER:	
(809) 425-1012 or 425-1310		UNIVADOS WB 2257	

APPROX. STAFF SIZE:	VOLUNTEER STAFF:	YEAR ESTABLISHED:
8		1963

NUMBER OF INDIVIDUAL MEMBERS:

FUNDING: The Institute is financed through the budget of UWI and by way of grants from funding agencies for specific research projects.

PRINCIPAL PURPOSE: To provide, where necessary, and within the context of its reosurces, independent research and information for the governments of the Eastern Caribbean sub-region, policy-oriented research and to provide a modicum of assistance to staff in the teaching departments engaged in research, to place major emphasis on inter-disciplinary research for the sub-region; to publish and disseminate the findings of the research to as wide an audience as possible.

MAIN ACTIVITIES: Research, Training, Organizing of Conferences/Seminars, Publications

POPULATION CONCERNS: General population issues, effectiveness of family planning programmes, Population and Development, Women and Population

SPECIFIC POPULATION ACTIVITIES: Demographic Research

FORWARD-LOOKING STRATEGIES IMPLEMENTATIONS: Spearheading efforts to mount Women and Development Studies Programme within the UWI

OBSTACLES TO THE IMPLEMENTATION OF FORWARD-LOOKING STRATEGIES: Funding, Administrative hurdles

NOTES:

Maternal Health & Family Planning Department

BERMUDA

ADDRESS:

Victoria St. Health Center, P.O. Box HM 1195, Hamilton, Bermuda

EXECUTIVE OFFICER:

Dr. J. Cann, Chief Medical Officer

BRANCH OFFICES:

TELEPHONE NUMBER:	TELEX NUMBER:
6 0224	

APPROX. STAFF SIZE:	VOLUNTEER STAFF:	YEAR ESTABLISHED:
6	0	1949

NUMBER OF INDIVIDUAL MEMBERS:

FUNDING: Government funding.

PRINCIPAL PURPOSE: Delivery of family planning services, and maternal health care and education of population.

MAIN ACTIVITIES: Family planning: education and service delivery. Maternal health care; cancer screening and gynecological care.

POPULATION CONCERNS: Reduction in teenage pregnancy. Maintenance of a steady birth rate.

SPECIFIC POPULATION ACTIVITIES: Education; counselling; statistics collection. Delivery of services: pill, IUD, diaphragm, foam, Depo-Provera, natural family planning.

FORWARD-LOOKING STRATEGIES IMPLEMENTATIONS: None.

OBSTACLES TO THE IMPLEMENTATION OF FORWARD-LOOKING STRATEGIES: None.

NOTES:

Centro de Orientacion Familiar*

BOLIVIA

ADDRESS:

Casilla 7522, La Paz, Bolivia

EXECUTIVE OFFICER:

Luis Llano Saavedra, Executive Director

BRANCH OFFICES:

TELEPHONE NUMBER:	TELEX NUMBER:
358348 and 370405	

APPROX. STAFF SIZE:	VOLUNTEER STAFF:	YEAR ESTABLISHED:
15	6	1978

NUMBER OF INDIVIDUAL MEMBERS:

80

FUNDING: Private funding with volunteer help.

PRINCIPAL PURPOSE: To provide family planning services.

MAIN ACTIVITIES: Family planning services.

POPULATION CONCERNS:

SPECIFIC POPULATION ACTIVITIES: Education, demographic research, delivery of services: Pill, IUD, diaphragm, foam, natural family planning.

FORWARD LOOKING-STRATEGIES IMPLEMENTATIONS: Promotion of family planning services as a basic human right.

OBSTACLES TO THE IMPLEMENTATION OF FORWARD-LOOKING STRATEGIES: Influence of religion and indifference of volunteer organizations are two obstacles.

NOTES: *Family Orientation Center

*Business Address: Av. 20 de Octubre 2332, Of. 106, La Paz-Bolivia

Centro Latinoamericano de Demografia*

CHILE

ADDRESS:

Casilla 91, Santiago, Chile

EXECUTIVE OFFICER:

Carmen Arretx, Officer in Charge

BRANCH OFFICES:

TELEPHONE NUMBER:

228-3206, 248-5051

TELEX NUMBER:

441054 (ITT), 240077(Telex Chile)

APPROX. STAFF SIZE:	VOLUNTEER STAFF:	YEAR ESTABLISHED:
65	0	1957

NUMBER OF INDIVIDUAL MEMBERS:

FUNDING: UNFPA, Canadian, French and Low Countries governments; Canadian Center of International Research.

PRINCIPAL PURPOSE: To contribute to socio-economic development of Latin America, assisting in the understanding of the demographic situation and the integration of population factors in development programs and plans.

MAIN ACTIVITIES: Research projects. Projects in intergrating population in socio-economic development. Projects in population information and technology for development. Projects in empowerment, demography and development.

POPULATION CONCERNS: Population and development, including the integration of demographic factors in the formulation of national policies and programs.

SPECIFIC POPULATION ACTIVITIES: Demographic research.

FORWARD-LOOKING STRATEGIES IMPLEMENTATIONS: Implemented indirectly. Do studies on the situation of women and the influence of demographic variables with consideration of these aspects in the political picture.

OBSTACLES TO THE IMPLEMENTATION OF FORWARD-LOOKING STRATEGIES: None.

NOTES: *Latin American Demographic Center

*Business Address: Edificio Naciones Unidas, Av. Dag Hammarskjold s/n, Santiago, Chile

Programa Regional del Empleo Para America Latina Y el Caribe*

CHILE

ADDRESS:

Casilla 618, Santiago, Chile

EXECUTIVE OFFICER:

Victor E. Tokman, Director

BRANCH OFFICES:

TELEPHONE NUMBER:	TELEX NUMBER:
486500	340382 PREALC CK

APPROX. STAFF SIZE:	VOLUNTEER STAFF:	YEAR ESTABLISHED:
27		1968

NUMBER OF INDIVIDUAL MEMBERS:

FUNDING: OIT, UNFPA, and regional governments.

PRINCIPAL PURPOSE: To promote and contribute to the application of regional and national politics expanding efforts to improve the occupational situation in Latin America and the Caribbean.

MAIN ACTIVITIES: Assistance to governments and regional organizations responsible for the definition and execution of policies and programs with direct impact on the employment level. Personnel requires national and local organizations to analyze the employment situation, define and execute policies and programs with high occupational content/context. Execution and promotion of research related to employment, income distribution and satisfying basic needs. Support national projects that incorporate demographic variables in employment planning basic needs.

POPULATION CONCERNS: Incorporation of demographic analysis in employment planning and basic needs. Formulation and implementation of population and development policies.

SPECIFIC POPULATION ACTIVITIES: Demographics

FORWARD LOOKING-STRATEGIES IMPLEMENTATIONS: Education and demographic research.

OBSTACLES TO THE IMPLEMENTATION OF FORWARD-LOOKING STRATEGIES:

NOTES: *Employment Regional Program for Latin America & the Caribbean

Business Address: Alonso de Cordova 4212, Santiago, Chile

Centro Medico de la Familia*

COLOMBIA

ADDRESS:

Apartado Aereo 24656, Bogota, Colombia

EXECUTIVE OFFICER:

Cecrilia Romero Parra, Licensed Nurse

BRANCH OFFICES:

TELEPHONE NUMBER:	TELEX NUMBER:
2852439	

APPROX. STAFF SIZE:	VOLUNTEER STAFF:	YEAR ESTABLISHED:
9		1979

NUMBER OF INDIVIDUAL MEMBERS:

FUNDING: Income through services.

PRINCIPAL PURPOSE: To promote attention in the area of reproductive medicine of high human and professional quality.

MAIN ACTIVITIES: Family medicine, early diagnosis of cervical and breast family planning cancer. Psychology, clinical laboratory and sex education.

POPULATION CONCERNS: Offer an orientation service, supply contraceptives to families of our community.

SPECIFIC POPULATION ACTIVITIES: Education, counselling, delivery of services: pill, IUD, foam, and natural family planning.

FORWARD LOOKING-STRATEGIES IMPLEMENTATIONS:

OBSTACLES TO THE IMPLEMENTATION OF FORWARD-LOOKING STRATEGIES:

NOTES: *Family Medical Center

Corporacion Centro Regional de Poblacion*

COLOMBIA

ADDRESS:

Apartado Aereo 24846, Bogota, Colombia

EXECUTIVE OFFICER:

Rodolfo A. Hereida, Exec. Director

BRANCH OFFICES:

TELEPHONE NUMBER:	TELEX NUMBER:
2559900	45722 CCRPC - Bogota

APPROX. STAFF SIZE:	VOLUNTEER STAFF:	YEAR ESTABLISHED:
20		1973

NUMBER OF INDIVIDUAL MEMBERS:

7

FUNDING: Fundraising projects.

PRINCIPAL PURPOSE: To develop, promote and support population programs and economic development.

MAIN ACTIVITIES: Research.

POPULATION CONCERNS: Concerned about the integration of population factors in development activities.

SPECIFIC POPULATION ACTIVITIES: Education, demographic and contraceptive research, counselling and Norplant.

FORWARD-LOOKING STRATEGIES IMPLEMENTATIONS: None.

OBSTACLES TO THE IMPLEMENTATION OF FORWARD-LOOKING STRATEGIES: None.

NOTES: *Regional Center for Population Corporation

Instituto Colombiano de Bienestar Familiar*

COLOMBIA

ADDRESS:
Avenida #64-01, Bogota, Colombia

EXECUTIVE OFFICER:
Dr. Jaime Benitez Tobon

BRANCH OFFICES:

TELEPHONE NUMBER:
2-31-46-07

TELEX NUMBER:
2-506600

APPROX. STAFF SIZE:
4386

VOLUNTEER STAFF:

YEAR ESTABLISHED:
1968

NUMBER OF INDIVIDUAL MEMBERS:

FUNDING: Receive two percent of the payroll of public and/or private enterprises in the sale of salt.

PRINCIPAL PURPOSE: To organize and execute activities which protect minorities and strengthen the family.

MAIN ACTIVITIES: Preventing and solving problems in the areas of nutrition, protection and legal assistance.

POPULATION CONCERNS: Concerned about population issues related to family welfare and minority assistance.

SPECIFIC POPULATION ACTIVITIES: Education and counselling.

FORWARD-LOOKING STRATEGIES IMPLEMENTATIONS: None.

OBSTACLES TO THE IMPLEMENTATION OF FORWARD-LOOKING STRATEGIES: None.

NOTES: *Colombian Institute on Family Welfare

Profamilia

COLOMBIA

ADDRESS:

Calle 34 No. 14-52, Bogota, Colombia

EXECUTIVE OFFICER:			BRANCH OFFICES:
Dr. Fernando Tamayo			

TELEPHONE NUMBER:		TELEX NUMBER:
2872100		

APPROX. STAFF SIZE:	VOLUNTEER STAFF:	YEAR ESTABLISHED:
621	8	1965

NUMBER OF INDIVIDUAL MEMBERS:

FUNDING: Donations.

PRINCIPAL PURPOSE: Providing family planning services.

MAIN ACTIVITIES: Family planning, medical services, surgical and clinical programs.

POPULATION CONCERNS: Promoting family planning and reducing the excessive birth rate.

SPECIFIC POPULATION ACTIVITIES: Education, Demographic Research, Contraceptive Research, Counselling, Sterilization, Pill, IUD, Spermicides, Norplant, Depo-provera and Natural Family Planning.

FORWARD LOOKING-STRATEGIES IMPLEMENTATIONS:

OBSTACLES TO THE IMPLEMENTATION OF FORWARD-LOOKING STRATEGIES:

NOTES:

Asociacion Centro de Orientacion Familiar*

COSTA RICA

ADDRESS:

Apartado 6806, San Jose, Costa Rica

EXECUTIVE OFFICER:

Marina de Solano, Director

BRANCH OFFICES:

TELEPHONE NUMBER:

21-15-48

TELEX NUMBER:

APPROX. STAFF SIZE:

VOLUNTEER STAFF:

YEAR ESTABLISHED:

1968

NUMBER OF INDIVIDUAL MEMBERS:

FUNDING:

PRINCIPAL PURPOSE: To contribute to the improvement of living standards of Costa Ricans, especially in the lower sectors of the country.

MAIN ACTIVITIES: Radio program "Dialogo", consulting service, direct educational activities, production and distribution of educational material, research project-action.

POPULATION CONCERNS:

SPECIFIC POPULATION ACTIVITIES: Education, psychological consulting, radio program and sale of literature.

FORWARD LOOKING-STRATEGIES IMPLEMENTATIONS:

OBSTACLES TO THE IMPLEMENTATION OF FORWARD-LOOKING STRATEGIES:

NOTES: *Family Orientation Center Association

GNTES (National Working Group on Sexual Education)

CUBA

ADDRESS:

Calle 19 #851 esq. a 4, Vedado, Ciudad Habana, Cuba

EXECUTIVE OFFICER:

Ph.D. Monika Krause Peters, Coordinator of GNTES

BRANCH OFFICES:

TELEPHONE NUMBER:	TELEX NUMBER:
30-2856 or 30-2679	

APPROX. STAFF SIZE:	VOLUNTEER STAFF:	YEAR ESTABLISHED:
25	4	1979

NUMBER OF INDIVIDUAL MEMBERS:

FUNDING: Mainly by the Ministry of Health of Cuba and international assistance (UNFPA and IPPF)

PRINCIPAL PURPOSE: Sexual education, in the sense of capacitation of the new generation for partnership, love, marriage and responsible family-raising in conditions of equality of men and women.

MAIN ACTIVITIES: Elaboration and implementation of sexual education programs for medicine, para-medical staffs, teacher-training institutions and women's capacitation centers. Research on reproductive behavior, family planning and sexual education.

POPULATION CONCERNS: Teenagers-pregnancy, insufficient usage of contraceptive products, lack of responsibility of young people, mainly lack of male responsibility.

SPECIFIC POPULATION ACTIVITIES: Education, Demographic Research, Contraceptive Research, Coun-selling, Advocacy, Delivery of Services, Sterilization, Pill, IUD, Diaphram, Foam, Promotion of the Condom.

FORWARD-LOOKING STRATEGIES IMPLEMENTATIONS: Implementation of a national programme of Family Planning according to the recommendation of Mexico 84 in Nairobi 85; implementation of a Sexual Edu-cation Programme that covers all the nation.

OBSTACLES TO THE IMPLEMENTATION OF FORWARD-LOOKING STRATEGIES: Religious traditions, taboos, prejudices remnants of male overvaluing and double moral ideology are still factors that limitate our actions.

NOTES:

Dominica Planned Parenthood Association

DOMINICA

ADDRESS:

P.O. Box 247, Gar field and Cross Lane, Roseau, Dominica, Eastern Caribbean

EXECUTIVE OFFICER:			BRANCH OFFICES:
Catherine Valerie-Solomon			

TELEPHONE NUMBER:		TELEX NUMBER:	
809-449-4043			

APPROX. STAFF SIZE:	VOLUNTEER STAFF:	YEAR ESTABLISHED:
5	20	

NUMBER OF INDIVIDUAL MEMBERS:
30

FUNDING: Funds from International Planned Parenthood Association

PRINCIPAL PURPOSE: To disseminate information on family planning and family life education to the Dominican public. To counsel teenagers on the sexuality and sexual develompent and responsibility.

MAIN ACTIVITIES: Counselling groups and secondary schools around the island.

POPULATION CONCERNS: Limiting the number of unplanned and unwanted pregnancies on the island.

SPECIFIC POPULATION ACTIVITIES: Education, Contraceptive research, counselling, advocacy, contraceptions are passed on to the health clinics and pharmacies when we receive them.

FORWARD-LOOKING STRATEGIES IMPLEMENTATIONS:

OBSTACLES TO THE IMPLEMENTATION OF FORWARD-LOOKING STRATEGIES:

NOTES:

Consejo Nacional de Poblacion y Familia* DOMINICAN REPUBLIC

ADDRESS:

Avenida Tiradentes, Esq. San Cristobal, A.P. 1803, Santo Domingo, Republica Dominicana

EXECUTIVE OFFICER:

Dr. Ramon Portes Carrasco, Executive Secretary

BRANCH OFFICES:

TELEPHONE NUMBER:

TELEX NUMBER:

APPROX. STAFF SIZE:	VOLUNTEER STAFF:	YEAR ESTABLISHED:
80	0	1968

NUMBER OF INDIVIDUAL MEMBERS:

FUNDING: U.N., International Development Agency, national government.

PRINCIPAL PURPOSE: Responsible for the National Family Planning Organization and evaluating and researching the program.

MAIN ACTIVITIES: Distribution of contraception methods. Education and information about contraceptive use. Training to the team that provides the contraceptives to the users.

POPULATION CONCERNS: Women between 15 and 49 years.

SPECIFIC POPULATION ACTIVITIES: Education; demographic research; contraceptive research; counselling. Delivery of services: pill, diaphragm, Norplant, foam, natural family planning.

FORWARD-LOOKING STRATEGIES IMPLEMENTATIONS: None.

OBSTACLES TO THE IMPLEMENTATION OF FORWARD-LOOKING STRATEGIES: None.

NOTES: *National Council on Population & Family

Asociacion Pro Bienestar
de la Familia Ecuatoriana*

ECUADOR

ADDRESS:

Noguchi 1516 y Letamendi, P.O. Box 5954, Guayaquil, Ecuador

EXECUTIVE OFFICER:			BRANCH OFFICES:
Dr. Paolo Marangoni			General Roca #359 y Bosmediano Ecuador 452-060 and 453-588

TELEPHONE NUMBER:		TELEX NUMBER:	
400888			

APPROX. STAFF SIZE:	VOLUNTEER STAFF:	YEAR ESTABLISHED:	
160	17	1965	

NUMBER OF INDIVIDUAL MEMBERS:	
25	

FUNDING: IPPF, AID, Population Council, Pathfinder, AVS and local income.

PRINCIPAL PURPOSE: Family Planning.

MAIN ACTIVITIES: To provide family planning services.

POPULATION CONCERNS: Population growth.

SPECIFIC POPULATION ACTIVITIES: Education, counselling, delivery of services: sterilization, pill, IUD, foam and Norplant.

FORWARD LOOKING-STRATEGIES IMPLEMENTATIONS:

OBSTACLES TO THE IMPLEMENTATION OF FORWARD-LOOKING STRATEGIES:

NOTES: *Ecuatorian Association for Family Welfare

Federacion Ecuatoriana de Enfermeras/os*

Ecuador

ADDRESS:

P.O. Box 3523, Quito, Ecuador

EXECUTIVE OFFICER:

Dra. Maria del Rosario Naranjo

BRANCH OFFICES:

TELEPHONE NUMBER:

524-069

TELEX NUMBER:

APPROX. STAFF SIZE:

2

VOLUNTEER STAFF:

YEAR ESTABLISHED:

1969

NUMBER OF INDIVIDUAL MEMBERS:

750

FUNDING: By 25% of the monthly fees given individually by nurses throughout provincial schools.

PRINCIPAL PURPOSE: To gather all nurses of the country to form a strong class capable of looking after its own interests, patients and community.

MAIN ACTIVITIES: Professional defense, education and research, and organization of members.

POPULATION CONCERNS: Individual issue.

SPECIFIC POPULATION ACTIVITIES: Education.

FORWARD-LOOKING STRATEGIES IMPLEMENTATIONS: Not aware.

OBSTACLES TO THE IMPLEMENTATION OF FORWARD-LOOKING STRATEGIES:

NOTES: *Ecuatorian Federation of Nurses

ORGANIZATION:

CEMAT (Mesoamerican Center on Studies for AT)

GUATEMALA

ADDRESS:

4a. avenida 2-28 zona 1, Guatemala, Guatemala, Central America

EXECUTIVE OFFICER:		BRANCH OFFICES:
Dr. Edgardo Caceres, Executive Director		

TELEPHONE NUMBER:		TELEX NUMBER:
22153		

APPROX. STAFF SIZE:	VOLUNTEER STAFF:	YEAR ESTABLISHED:
40		1976

NUMBER OF INDIVIDUAL MEMBERS:
20

FUNDING: International cooperation agencies. Mainly from Germany, Canada, USA, Switzerland.

PRINCIPAL PURPOSE: Develop and implement appropriate technology projects and training systems for popular groups; promote and systematize the transference of AT knowledge from other countries to Guatemala, and then applicating it to our rural areas.

MAIN ACTIVITIES: Experimentation and diffusion on: Non-conventional sources of energy agriculture, nutrition, health (medicinal plants), rural medicine alternative construction. Diffusion of specific appropriate technologies such as biodigesters, DAFF latrines, firewood saving stoves, etc. Information and documentation activities through our Information Center answering specific consults.

POPULATION CONCERNS: To inform people interested when consulting the Data Bank.

SPECIFIC POPULATION ACTIVITIES: Education; Demographic Research

FORWARD-LOOKING STRATEGIES IMPLEMENTATIONS: In our field projects where groups of women are starting to work their own microenterprises or specific activities (such as bakeries). Social workers teach them and show them about issues concerning population, work, rights etc.

OBSTACLES TO THE IMPLEMENTATION OF FORWARD-LOOKING STRATEGIES: Lack of graphic material, easy to understand. Although APROFAM in our country is taking such task into their specific programs.

NOTES:

Caribbean Community Secretariat   GUYANA

ADDRESS:

Bank of Guyana Building, P.O. Box 10827, Georgetown, GUYANA

EXECUTIVE OFFICER:			BRANCH OFFICES:
Mr. Roderick Rainford, Secretary-General			

TELEPHONE NUMBER:		TELEX NUMBER:
69281-9/51960-9		2263

APPROX. STAFF SIZE:	VOLUNTEER STAFF:	YEAR ESTABLISHED:
200		1973

NUMBER OF INDIVIDUAL MEMBERS:

13 member Governments

FUNDING: Member Governments and international funding agencies for programme and project activities.

PRINCIPAL PURPOSE: To promote regional cooperation among the member states of English-speaking in the Caribbean.

MAIN ACTIVITIES: Economic cooperation, foreign policy and functional cooperation.

POPULATION CONCERNS: That member governments should formulate national population policies aimed at arriving at a rational balance between population and resources; that population issues should be incorporated in development planning.

SPECIFIC POPULATION ACTIVITIES: Education, demographic research, advocacy and support to member governments in the formulation of population policy.

FORWARD-LOOKING STRATEGIES IMPLEMENTATIONS: Through activities related to data collection, publication education, strengthening of national machinery, the economic empowerment of women and technical assistance.

OBSTACLES TO THE IMPLEMENTATION OF FORWARD-LOOKING STRATEGIES: Lack of human and financial resources to the implementation of programmes in areas listed at 14 e.g. there is need for a stronger data-base, better functioning of national machinery and technical assistance.

NOTES:

Prolama

HONDURAS

ADDRESS:

Junta Nacional de Bienestar Social, Tegucipalpa, D.C. Honduras

EXECUTIVE OFFICER:

Dra. Argentina de Chavez, Technical Director

BRANCH OFFICES:

P.O. Box #512, San Pedro Sula, Honduras

TELEPHONE NUMBER:	TELEX NUMBER:
22-51-27	

APPROX. STAFF SIZE:	VOLUNTEER STAFF:	YEAR ESTABLISHED:
21		1983

NUMBER OF INDIVIDUAL MEMBERS:

14 chapters

FUNDING: U.S.A.I.D., UNICEF.

PRINCIPAL PURPOSE: To train and teach health workers about breastfeeding; to give direct services to mothers.

MAIN ACTIVITIES: Education, training and direct services.

POPULATION CONCERNS: Child spacing, and keeping breastfeeding and family planning compatible.

SPECIFIC POPULATION ACTIVITIES: Education, counselling.

FORWARD-LOOKING STRATEGIES IMPLEMENTATIONS: None.

OBSTACLES TO THE IMPLEMENTATION OF FORWARD-LOOKING STRATEGIES: None.

NOTES:

Rural Technology Project

HONDURAS

ADDRESS:

Apartado postal 1626, Tegucigolpa, Honduras

EXECUTIVE OFFICER:

Sonia Yolando Zacapa, President

BRANCH OFFICES:

TELEPHONE NUMBER:

TELEX NUMBER:

APPROX. STAFF SIZE:
300

VOLUNTEER STAFF:

YEAR ESTABLISHED:
1979

NUMBER OF INDIVIDUAL MEMBERS:

FUNDING: A.I.D.—Agency for International Development

PRINCIPAL PURPOSE: To give technical assistance to the rural population.

MAIN ACTIVITIES: Implementation and dissemination of appropriate technologies.

POPULATION CONCERNS: To improve the quality of life for the rural population.

SPECIFIC POPULATION ACTIVITIES: Education

FORWARD-LOOKING STRATEGIES IMPLEMENTATIONS: Not aware of them.

OBSTACLES TO THE IMPLEMENTATION OF FORWARD-LOOKING STRATEGIES:

NOTES:

*Business Address:** Edificio M y M, Boulivar Suyapa

ORGANIZATION:

Institute of Social and Economic Research

JAMAICA

ADDRESS:

Univ. of the West Indies, Mona, Kingston 7, JAMAICA

EXECUTIVE OFFICER:			BRANCH OFFICES:
Dr. Joycelin Massiah			Univ. of the West Indies St. Augustine Trinidad and Tobago
TELEPHONE NUMBER: (809) 425-1012/425-1310		**TELEX NUMBER:** UNIVADOS WB 2257	Univ. of the West Indies P.O. Box 64 Bridgetown Barbados
APPROX. STAFF SIZE: 8	**VOLUNTEER STAFF:**	**YEAR ESTABLISHED:** 1963	
NUMBER OF INDIVIDUAL MEMBERS:			

FUNDING: Through the budget of UWI and by way of grants from funding agencies for specific research projects.

PRINCIPAL PURPOSE: To provide independent research and information for the governments of the Eastern Caribbean sub-region; to establish policy-oriented research; to place major emphasis on inter-disciplinary research; and to publish and disseminate the findings of this research to as wide an audience as possible.

MAIN ACTIVITIES: Research, training, organization of conferences/seminars, and publications.

POPULATION CONCERNS: General population issues, effectiveness of family planning programmes, population and development, and women and population.

SPECIFIC POPULATION ACTIVITIES: Demographic research.

FORWARD-LOOKING STRATEGIES IMPLEMENTATIONS: Spearheading efforts to mount Women and Development Studies Programme within the UWI.

OBSTACLES TO THE IMPLEMENTATION OF FORWARD-LOOKING STRATEGIES: Funding and administrative hurdles.

NOTES:

Nurses Association of Jamaica

JAMAICA

ADDRESS:

4 Trevennion Park Road, Kingston 5, Jamaica W.I.

EXECUTIVE OFFICER:			BRANCH OFFICES:
Thelma Deer-Anderson, President			

TELEPHONE NUMBER:		TELEX NUMBER:	
809-92-95213			

APPROX. STAFF SIZE:	VOLUNTEER STAFF:	YEAR ESTABLISHED:	
4	21	1946	

NUMBER OF INDIVIDUAL MEMBERS:

1751

FUNDING: Membership subscriptions.

PRINCIPAL PURPOSE: To advance the status of nursing as a profession.

MAIN ACTIVITIES: Stimulate educational development of nurses, uphold the ethics of the nursing profession at both national and international levels and hold negotiation for nurses.

POPULATION CONCERNS: Population control and family life education.

SPECIFIC POPULATION ACTIVITIES: Education, counselling, advocacy and delivery of standard birth control services.

FORWARD-LOOKING STRATEGIES IMPLEMENTATIONS: None.

OBSTACLES TO THE IMPLEMENTATION OF FORWARD-LOOKING STRATEGIES: Financing and personnel.

NOTES:

Association Martiniquaise Pour L'Information et L'Orientation Familiales*   MARTINIQUE

ADDRESS:

125, 127 rue Moreau de Jonnes, 97200 Fort de France, Martinique

EXECUTIVE OFFICER:			BRANCH OFFICES:
Mr. Roger Bucher, Director			

TELEPHONE NUMBER:		TELEX NUMBER:	
71-46-01			

APPROX. STAFF SIZE:	VOLUNTEER STAFF:	YEAR ESTABLISHED:
28	9	1968

NUMBER OF INDIVIDUAL MEMBERS:

53

FUNDING: Government grants.

PRINCIPAL PURPOSE: Inform families and give them the possibilities to conceive freely when and how many children they can morally and economically raise.

MAIN ACTIVITIES: Information, contraceptive services and counselling. Information in rural areas and in schools.

POPULATION CONCERNS:

SPECIFIC POPULATION ACTIVITIES: Education, contraceptive research, counselling and delivery of services including the pill, IUD, Depo-Provera and natural family planning.

FORWARD LOOKING-STRATEGIES IMPLEMENTATIONS: All those concerning family planning.

OBSTACLES TO THE IMPLEMENTATION OF FORWARD-LOOKING STRATEGIES:

NOTES: *Martinique Association for Information and Family Orientation

Social Marketing International Association

MEXICO

ADDRESS:

Circuito Balvanera #3, 76900 Corregidora, Queretaro, Mexico

EXECUTIVE OFFICER:

Luis de la Macorra, President; Valentina Prieto, Executive Director

BRANCH OFFICES:

TELEPHONE NUMBER:	TELEX NUMBER:
(463) 654-79	121629

APPROX. STAFF SIZE:	VOLUNTEER STAFF:	YEAR ESTABLISHED:
1	5	1984

NUMBER OF INDIVIDUAL MEMBERS:

70

FUNDING: Grants from foundations; membership fees.

PRINCIPAL PURPOSE: SMI recognizes as a main organizational objective the distribution of information about results achieved by the application of social marketing techniques particularly in those areas not generally covered by other groups of publications.

MAIN ACTIVITIES: The promotion of social marketing applied to any social program anywhere in the world.

POPULATION CONCERNS: The application of social marketing can make any population program more effective.

SPECIFIC POPULATION ACTIVITIES: Social marketing

FORWARD-LOOKING STRATEGIES IMPLEMENTATIONS:

OBSTACLES TO THE IMPLEMENTATION OF FORWARD-LOOKING STRATEGIES:

NOTES:

Asociacion Panameña para el Planeamiento de la Familia*

PANAMA

ADDRESS:

Apartado 4637, Panama 5, Panama

EXECUTIVE OFFICER:	BRANCH OFFICES:
Julio Armando Lavergne, M.D.	

TELEPHONE NUMBER:	TELEX NUMBER:
67-0151	

APPROX. STAFF SIZE:	VOLUNTEER STAFF:	YEAR ESTABLISHED:
20	9	1965

NUMBER OF INDIVIDUAL MEMBERS:

60

FUNDING: 85% from IPPF, 15% are local resources.

PRINCIPAL PURPOSE: Family planning.

MAIN ACTIVITIES: Sexual and family education. Family planning services with special attention to adolescents.

POPULATION CONCERNS: Relation between population and development

SPECIFIC POPULATION ACTIVITIES: Demographic research; education; contraceptive research; counselling. Delivery of services: pill, IUD, diaphragm, foam, natural family planning.

FORWARD-LOOKING STRATEGIES IMPLEMENTATIONS: None.

OBSTABLES TO THE IMPLEMENATION OF FORWARD-LOOKING STRATEGIES: None.

NOTES: *Panamenian Association for Family Planning

Alfalit en el Peru

PERU

ADDRESS:

Apartado 3997, Lima 100, Peru

EXECUTIVE OFFICER:

Reverend Florencio Duran Bravo, Executive Secretary

BRANCH OFFICES:

TELEPHONE NUMBER:	TELEX NUMBER:
238623	

APPROX. STAFF SIZE:	VOLUNTEER STAFF:	YEAR ESTABLISHED:
10	166	1966

NUMBER OF INDIVIDUAL MEMBERS:

9

FUNDING: Lutheran Church, methodist church and projects.

PRINCIPAL PURPOSE: Popular education-literacy and basic adult education.

MAIN ACTIVITIES: Literacy, basic adult education and community development,

POPULATION CONCERNS: Education and population health in third world countries.

SPECIFIC POPULATION ACTIVITIES: Education, demographic research, contraceptive research and natural family planning.

FORWARD LOOKING-STRATEGIES IMPLEMENTATIONS: Will implement them in their plan for next year.

OBSTACLES TO THE IMPLEMENTATION OF FORWARD-LOOKING STRATEGIES:

NOTES:

*Business Address: Jr. Orbegoso 650, Lima 5, Peru

ADDRESS:

Camilo Carillo No. 114, 61. Piso, Jesus Maria, Lima, Peru

EXECUTIVE OFFICER:	BRANCH OFFICES:
Prof. J. Edgard Ibarcena Acosta, M.D.	

TELEPHONE NUMBER:	TELEX NUMBER:
230797/322410/231197	

APPROX. STAFF SIZE:	VOLUNTEER STAFF:	YEAR ESTABLISHED:
50	30	1980

NUMBER OF INDIVIDUAL MEMBERS:

24

FUNDING: Government, A.I.D. and UNFPA.

PRINCIPAL PURPOSE: To execute the population policy put forth by the Peruvian government.

MAIN ACTIVITIES: Proposing, promoting, directing, guiding and supervising government population policy. Executing policy through both the public and private sector.

POPULATION CONCERNS: Putting responsible parenthood into practice in Peru by the year 2000.

SPECIFIC POPULATION ACTIVITIES: Education, demographic research, contraceptive research, counselling, sterilization, Pill, IUD, Diaphragm, Foam, Norplant and Natural Family Planning.

FORWARD-LOOKING STRATEGIES IMPLEMENTATIONS: The Council is aware of the strategies and is working to implement them.

OBSTACLES TO THE IMPLEMENTATION OF FORWARD-LOOKING STRATEGIES: Restricted A.I.D. and UNFPA funds.

NOTES: *National Council on Population

Instituto Peruano de
Paternidad Responsable*

PERU

ADDRESS:

Apartado Postal 2191, Jesus Maria, Lima II, Peru

EXECUTIVE OFFICER:			BRANCH OFFICES:
Miguel Ramos Zambrano, Director			

TELEPHONE NUMBER:		TELEX NUMBER:
63-59-65		20330 PE-CP

APPROX. STAFF SIZE:	VOLUNTEER STAFF:	YEAR ESTABLISHED:
10	4	1976

NUMBER OF INDIVIDUAL MEMBERS:

108

FUNDING: Dues, donations and own resources.

PRINCIPAL PURPOSE: To promote acceptance in the community of responsible parenthood as a basic human right, that allows couples to decide freely the number and spacing of their children and obtain family stability and social harmony necessary to achieve authentic development and improve the access of the population to information and adequate medical services for responsible parenthood and family planning.

MAIN ACTIVITIES: Education and information, empowerment, medical-clinical services and family planning services, surgical sterilization, and community action family planning laboratory.

POPULATION CONCERNS:

SPECIFIC POPULATION ACTIVITIES: Education, demographic research, counselling, delivery of services: Sterilization only in the cases of high risk pregnancies, pill, IUD, diaphragm, foam, and Depo-Provera, natural family planning.

FORWARD LOOKING-STRATEGIES IMPLEMENTATIONS: None indicated.

OBSTACLES TO THE IMPLEMENTATION OF FORWARD-LOOKING STRATEGIES:

NOTES: *Peruvian Institute for Responsible Parenthood

*Business Address: Gregorio Escobedo 115, Jesus Maria, Lima, Peru

Talpuv Group

PERU

ADDRESS:

222 Correo Central, Huancayo, Peru

EXECUTIVE OFFICER:

Raul Santana Paucar, Director

BRANCH OFFICES:

TELEPHONE NUMBER:		TELEX NUMBER:
234549, 233785		

APPROX. STAFF SIZE:	VOLUNTEER STAFF:	YEAR ESTABLISHED:
15	40	1976

NUMBER OF INDIVIDUAL MEMBERS:

5

FUNDING: Grants and fundraising.

PRINCIPAL PURPOSE: To create alternatives for the development of rural areas.

MAIN ACTIVITIES: Research, education, lectures, seminars and skill training.

POPULATION CONCERNS: Health, family size and birth spacing.

SPECIFIC POPULATION ACTIVITIES: Education and counselling.

FORWARD-LOOKING STRATEGIES IMPLEMENTATIONS: Not aware, would like some information.

OBSTACLES TO THE IMPLEMENTATION OF FORWARD-LOOKING STRATEGIES:

NOTES:

St. Vincent Planned Parenthood Association

ST. VINCENT

ADDRESS:

P.O. Box 99, Kingstown St. Vincent, West Indies

EXECUTIVE OFFICER:	BRANCH OFFICES:
Marvis Payne, Executive Director	

TELEPHONE NUMBER:	TELEX NUMBER:
61793	

APPROX. STAFF SIZE:	VOLUNTEER STAFF:	YEAR ESTABLISHED:
5		1966

NUMBER OF INDIVIDUAL MEMBERS:

350

FUNDING: IPPF major funding agency.

PRINCIPAL PURPOSE: To give information; to educate and communicate in family life and family planning.

MAIN ACTIVITIES: Education

POPULATION CONCERNS: The overall health of our people.

SPECIFIC POPULATION ACTIVITIES: Education; Counselling; Delivery of Service; pill; foam; and other non-clinical services.

FORWARD-LOOKING STRATEGIES IMPLEMENTATIONS: Reaching out to both men and women in our education program; distribution of information by handouts, film shows, and discussions.

OBSTACLES TO THE IMPLEMENTATION OF FORWARD-LOOKING STRATEGIES: Financial constraints.

NOTES:

Caribbean Epidemiology Center (CAREC)

TRINIDAD

ADDRESS:

P.O. Box 164, Port of Spain, Trinidad

EXECUTIVE OFFICER:			BRANCH OFFICES:
Dr. Peter Diggory			

TELEPHONE NUMBER:		TELEX NUMBER:
6224261-2		

APPROX. STAFF SIZE:	VOLUNTEER STAFF:	YEAR ESTABLISHED:
50		1975

NUMBER OF INDIVIDUAL MEMBERS:

FUNDING: PAHO/WHO and governments of Caribbean countries, including the government of Trinidad & Tobago.

PRINCIPAL PURPOSE: Epidemiology and surveillance of diseases, traffic accidents and injury.

MAIN ACTIVITIES: Research

POPULATION CONCERNS: Epidemiology

SPECIFIC POPULATION ACTIVITIES: Education; Epidemiology

FORWARD-LOOKING STRATEGIES IMPLEMENTATIONS: None indicated.

OBSTACLES TO THE IMPLEMENTATION OF FORWARD-LOOKING STRATEGIES:

NOTES:

Institute of Social and Economic Research

TRINIDAD

ADDRESS:

University of the West Indies, St. Augustine, Trinidad, W.I.

EXECUTIVE OFFICER:

Head ISER

BRANCH OFFICES:

TELEPHONE NUMBER:		TELEX NUMBER:
663-1364, 1359		24520-UWI/WG

APPROX. STAFF SIZE:	VOLUNTEER STAFF:	YEAR ESTABLISHED:
12	0	1970

NUMBER OF INDIVIDUAL MEMBERS:

FUNDING: University grants committee.

PRINCIPAL PURPOSE: Research in social sciences.

MAIN ACTIVITIES: Research, training, dissemination of information.

POPULATION CONCERNS: All demographic factors.

SPECIFIC POPULATION ACTIVITIES: Education; demographic research; contraceptive research.

FORWARD-LOOKING STRATEGIES IMPLEMENTATIONS: None.

OBSTACLES TO THE IMPLEMENTATION OF FORWARD-LOOKING STRATEGIES: None.

NOTES:

Centro de Informaciones y Estudios del Uruguay*

URUGUAY

ADDRESS:

Juan Paullier 1174, Montevideo, Uruguay

EXECUTIVE OFFICER:			BRANCH OFFICES:
Arq. Mario Lombardi, Director			

TELEPHONE NUMBER:		TELEX NUMBER:	
4-3205, 40-3866			

APPROX. STAFF SIZE:	VOLUNTEER STAFF:	YEAR ESTABLISHED:
26		1975

NUMBER OF INDIVIDUAL MEMBERS:

13

FUNDING: Institutional support and specific projects from international agencies.

PRINCIPAL PURPOSE: Scientific research of social realities, promoting better understanding of national problems and providing bases of analysis for change.

MAIN ACTIVITIES: Research in the areas of sociology, demography, history, urban studies and other disciplines with social contexts.

POPULATION CONCERNS:

SPECIFIC POPULATION ACTIVITIES: Demographic research.

FORWARD-LOOKING STRATEGIES IMPLEMENTATIONS: We are preparing research proposals that focus on aspects of fertility and reproductive health.

OBSTACLES TO THE IMPLEMENTATION OF FORWARD-LOOKING STRATEGIES: None.

NOTES: *Information & Study Center on Uruguay

Centro de Investigaciones y Estudios Familiares*

URUGUAY

ADDRESS:

J.E.Rodo 2115, Montevideo, Uruguay

EXECUTIVE OFFICER:	BRANCH OFFICES:
Sra. Ana M. Gelsi	

TELEPHONE NUMBER:	TELEX NUMBER:
40.0681	

APPROX. STAFF SIZE:	VOLUNTEER STAFF:	YEAR ESTABLISHED:
17	48	1968

NUMBER OF INDIVIDUAL MEMBERS:

482

FUNDING: Contributions from ADVENIAT (Alemania) and individual donations.

PRINCIPAL PURPOSE: To research the problems that affect the family and to offer services for their solution.

MAIN ACTIVITIES: Counselling, sex education, family education, bi-monthly publication of DIGESTO FAMILIAR, psychological orientation, etc.

POPULATION CONCERNS: Concerned about controlling fertility.

SPECIFIC POPULATION ACTIVITIES: Education, demographic and contraceptive research, counselling and natural family planning.

FORWARD-LOOKING STRATEGIES IMPLEMENTATIONS: None.

OBSTACLES TO THE IMPLEMENTATION OF FORWARD-LOOKING STRATEGIES: Lack of didactic information and literature.

NOTES: *Research & Family Study Center

Centro Nacional de Planificacion Natural de la Familia*

URUGUAY

ADDRESS:

Pablo de Maria 1362, Montevideo, Uruguay

EXECUTIVE OFFICER:			BRANCH OFFICES:
Sra. Elizabeth S. Piedra			

TELEPHONE NUMBER:	TELEX NUMBER:	
40.3251		

APPROX. STAFF SIZE:	VOLUNTEER STAFF:	YEAR ESTABLISHED:
11	46	1976

NUMBER OF INDIVIDUAL MEMBERS:

321

FUNDING: Donations.

PRINCIPAL PURPOSE: To promote natural family planning.

MAIN ACTIVITIES: Consultations, organizing seminars, producing literature and teaching courses.

POPULATION CONCERNS: Interested in many population isuues, including: sex education, family planning, preparation for marriage, abortion, euthanasia, etc.

SPECIFIC POPULATION ACTIVITIES: Education, demographic and contraceptive research, counselling, advocacy and natural family planning.

FORWARD-LOOKING STRATEGIES IMPLEMENTATIONS: Not aware of them.

OBSTACLES TO THE IMPLEMENTATION OF FORWARD-LOOKING STRATEGIES: None.

NOTES: *National Center on Natural Family Planning

ORGANIZATION:

Instituto Interamericano del Niño*

URUGUAY

ADDRESS:

Av. 8 de Octubre 2904, Montevideo, Uruguay

EXECUTIVE OFFICER:

Dr. Rodrigo C. Toral, Gen. Dir.

BRANCH OFFICES:

TELEPHONE NUMBER:	TELEX NUMBER:
80-1142/80-1219	UY 23119 IIN

APPROX. STAFF SIZE:	VOLUNTEER STAFF:	YEAR ESTABLISHED:
30		1927

NUMBER OF INDIVIDUAL MEMBERS:

All OAS members

FUNDING: By the OAS.

PRINCIPAL PURPOSE: To address the problems of maternity, childhood, adolescence, and the family.

MAIN ACTIVITIES: To provide technical assistance to member countries and to support the minority protection efforts of others. To provide special and pre-school education, design statistical information, provide health and pharmaceutical education, help with legislative affairs, etc.

POPULATION CONCERNS: Health and population statistics.

SPECIFIC POPULATION ACTIVITIES: Education and demographic research.

FORWARD-LOOKING STRATEGIES IMPLEMENTATIONS: None.

OBSTACLES TO THE IMPLEMENTATION OF FORWARD-LOOKING STRATEGIES: None.

NOTES: *Children's Inter-American Institute

Women's Organizations

The Population Institute

Women In Development (W.I.D.) Limited

BARBADOS

ADDRESS:

Melbourne, Belmont Road, St. Michael, Barbados

EXECUTIVE OFFICER:

Lynn Allison, Executive Director

BRANCH OFFICES:

TELEPHONE NUMBER:

(809) 427-8154, 426-0045

TELEX NUMBER:

APPROX. STAFF SIZE:	VOLUNTEER STAFF:	YEAR ESTABLISHED:
10		1978

NUMBER OF INDIVIDUAL MEMBERS:

FUNDING: Local and international funding agencies and grants.

PRINCIPAL PURPOSE: To provide employment and income generation for low-income persons of Barbados through the WID loan program placement center, and apprenticeship scheme.

MAIN ACTIVITIES: Loan program: provides credit and technical assistance to persons commencing or expanding a small business. Placement center: links job applicants to job opportunities. Apprenticeship scheme: places on-the-job training.

POPULATION CONCERNS: None.

SPECIFIC POPULATION ACTIVITIES: Education and advocacy.

FORWARD-LOOKING STRATEGIES IMPLEMENTATIONS: None.

OBSTACLES TO THE IMPLEMENTATION OF FORWARD-LOOKING STRATEGIES: Lack of funding.

NOTES:

Cooperativa Integral de Fomento Trabajo Manual*

BOLIVIA

ADDRESS:

Apartado Postal 2577, Cochabamba, Bolivia

EXECUTIVE OFFICER:			BRANCH OFFICES:
Sr. Federico Diez de Medina B, Gerente General			

TELEPHONE NUMBER:		TELEX NUMBER:	
40567		FOTRAMA	

APPROX. STAFF SIZE:	VOLUNTEER STAFF:	YEAR ESTABLISHED:
35	1350	1962

NUMBER OF INDIVIDUAL MEMBERS:

1402

FUNDING: Before: Foreign support, today: independent.

PRINCIPAL PURPOSE: Encouragement of Manual Arts, weaving, rags, raising alpacas.

MAIN ACTIVITIES: Spinning wool, weaving cloth and sale of products.

POPULATION CONCERNS:

SPECIFIC POPULATION ACTIVITIES:

FORWARD-LOOKING STRATEGIES IMPLEMENTATIONS:

OBSTACLES TO THE IMPLEMENTATION OF FORWARD-LOOKING STRATEGIES:

NOTES: *Cooperation on the Integration of Manual Labor

Latin America Media Network, Women's Alternative Media Unit

CHILE

ADDRESS:

Casilla 16-637-Correo 9, Santiago, Chile

EXECUTIVE OFFICER:	BRANCH OFFICES:
Adriana Santa Cruz	

TELEPHONE NUMBER:	TELEX NUMBER:
2315486, 2314387	

APPROX. STAFF SIZE:	VOLUNTEER STAFF:	YEAR ESTABLISHED:
17	0	1981

NUMBER OF INDIVIDUAL MEMBERS:

FUNDING: Funding groups.

PRINCIPAL PURPOSE: Produce yearly and one monthly publication.

MAIN ACTIVITIES: Produce 20 publications per year, including one monthly distributed in Latin America.

POPULATION CONCERNS: None.

SPECIFIC POPULATION ACTIVITIES: Education.

FORWARD-LOOKING STRATEGIES IMPLEMENTATIONS: Implementing through information.

OBSTABLES TO THE IMPLEMENATION OF FORWARD-LOOKING STRATEGIES: None.

NOTES:

Unidad de Comunicacion Alternativa de la Mujer Fempress*

CHILE

ADDRESS:

Callao 3461, Santiago, Chile

EXECUTIVE OFFICER:

Adriana Santa Cruz, Directora

BRANCH OFFICES:

TELEPHONE NUMBER:

08-23-61-80

TELEX NUMBER:

APPROX. STAFF SIZE:

3

VOLUNTEER STAFF:

YEAR ESTABLISHED:

1981

NUMBER OF INDIVIDUAL MEMBERS:

FUNDING: Sweden NORAD-Norway, Canada UNIFEM—US.

PRINCIPAL PURPOSE: Alternative communication from and for women.

MAIN ACTIVITIES: Publish 12 monthly bulletins, publish 4 quarterly bulletins, detect alternative publications and detect radio programs of and for women.

POPULATION CONCERNS: Communication.

SPECIFIC POPULATION ACTIVITIES:

FORWARD-LOOKING STRATEGIES IMPLEMENTATIONS:

OBSTACLES TO THE IMPLEMENTATION OF FORWARD-LOOKING STRATEGIES:

NOTES: *Unity of Alternative Communication for Women

INSTRAW DOMINICAN REPUBLIC

ADDRESS:

Cesar Nicolas Penson 102-A, Santo Domingo, Dominican Republic

EXECUTIVE OFFICER:

Mrs. Dunja Pastizzi-Ferencic, Director

BRANCH OFFICES:

TELEPHONE NUMBER:	TELEX NUMBER:
(809) 685-2111	(326) 4280 WRA SD

APPROX. STAFF SIZE:	VOLUNTEER STAFF:	YEAR ESTABLISHED:
25		1979

NUMBER OF INDIVIDUAL MEMBERS:

FUNDING: Contributions from States, intergovernmental and non-governmental organizations, foundations and private donations.

PRINCIPAL PURPOSE: INSTRAW acts as a catalyst to promote the full participation of women in all aspects of development through research, training, and the exchange of information.

MAIN ACTIVITIES: Through research, training and informational activities, INSTRAW works to increase women's potential economic contribution to development and to integrate them into the development process. INSTRAW also works to raise awareness of women's issues worldwide and to incorporate agenda items on women into the work of relevant U.N. bodies.

POPULATION CONCERNS:

SPECIFIC POPULATION ACTIVITIES:

FORWARD-LOOKING STRATEGIES IMPLEMENTATIONS: INSTRAW is addressing the need for increased research, training, information and communication activities due to insufficient awareness and understanding of relationship between development and the advancement of women. Member states have been called upon to collaborate with INSTRAW on the implementation of the FLS.

OBSTACLES TO THE IMPLEMENTATION OF FORWARD-LOOKING STRATEGIES:

NOTES:

The Woman's Club of Jamaica

JAMAICA

ADDRESS:

101 Hope Road, Kingston 6, Jamaica

EXECUTIVE OFFICER:			BRANCH OFFICES:
Mrs. E. Ammar, President			

TELEPHONE NUMBER:	TELEX NUMBER:	
(809) 927-0678		

APPROX. STAFF SIZE:	VOLUNTEER STAFF:	YEAR ESTABLISHED:
	20	1936

NUMBER OF INDIVIDUAL MEMBERS:

137

FUNDING: Membership dues.

PRINCIPAL PURPOSE: To encourage social interaction between all Jamaican women. To promote civic municipal improvements.

MAIN ACTIVITIES: Fundraising through social functions and supporting various charities.

POPULATION CONCERNS:

SPECIFIC POPULATION ACTIVITIES:

FORWARD-LOOKING STRATEGIES IMPLEMENTATIONS:

OBSTACLES TO THE IMPLEMENTATION OF FORWARD-LOOKING STRATEGIES:

NOTES:

Americas:
North America (Canada & the U.S.)

Dick Mathews

North America:
The United States and Canada

Low fertility rates, aging populations, the maturing of the "baby boom" generation born after World War II and high immigration levels characterize the demographic patterns of the United States and Canada. In 1987 the population of United States is 243.8 million and of Canada, 25.9 million. The fertility rates of both countries are below the levels required to replace the current population in the future.

The U.S. population growth of 1.0 percent, nevertheless, is one of the highest of all industrialized nations. Immigration and the racial and ethnic makeup of the population are important factors in population growth. Fertility rates, for example, are higher for hispanic and black women. That the United States is a country of immigrants is well known; that the countries of origin have changed dramatically since 1900 (when most immigrants came from Europe) is perhaps less well known. Today the majority of immigrants come from Latin America and the Caribbean (42 percent) and Southeast Asia (39 percent). Historically in unsettled economic times, illegal immigration (now estimated at between three to four million annually) has become an issue of public concern. Thus, in 1986 the U.S. Congress passed a comprehensive bill to regulate immigration by imposing sanctions on employers of illegal aliens. The bill also gives amnesty to all aliens residing in the U.S. prior to 1982 and to aliens who worked in agriculture for 90 days prior to May 1986.

Like the United States, Canada is a country of heavy immigration. In general, Canada has favored immigrants with skills, having experienced a substantial loss of skilled citizens to the United States following World War II. The economic problems of the 1970s, however, led policymakers to question the high influx of immigrants during the 1960s and to subsequently limit their numbers. In general, however, the government sees immigration as a positive long-term economic benefit and in 1986 set targets that will gradually increase the number of immigrants in the years ahead.

The "baby boom" generation has created educational and employment challenges as it has matured, especially in Canada where 50 percent more children were born from 1940-1959 than in the previous two decades. In the United States the peak years were somewhat later, 1955-1964, when 43 million were born. The "baby boom" was caused by the prosperous post-war economy that encouraged couples to marry young and have more children. And following the entry of an unprecedented number of women into the labor force during World War II, there was also a backlash of pro-marriage, pro-natalist and pro-housewife forces.

The changing age structure of both countries holds serious implications for health care and social security. People over 65 are the fastest growing age group in both countries, and life expectancy is high, close to 75 years, with white females living longer. Since the aging suffer more from illness and chronic health conditions, increasing numbers will put greater pressures on health care facilities, the costs of which are already astronomical in the United States. Social security systems in both countries are also feeling the strain; the falling rates of workers to retirees raises questions about future solvency, particularly when the "baby boomers" reach retirement age.

By the 1970s the women's movement had made strong inroads into curbing the forces that drove women out of the factories and back into their homes after World War II. Between 1960-1985 women's participation in the labor force grew from 19 to 40 percent in Canada, and from 26 to 43 percent in the United States. The increasing numbers of women earning university degrees, making slow but steady progress into what were previously considered all-male professions and delaying marriage and childbearing is reflected in these statistics. Other factors that have contributed to the decline in fertility include: the wide availability of more effective forms of contraception and legal abortion (save in some small towns and rural areas of Canada strongly influenced by the Catholic Church), the expense of raising children, difficulties in finding good daycare services, rising divorce rates and a perception of the single life as more attractive.

In spite of the gains, income disparities persist. Women in the United States who have four or more years of university still earn an average of only $10,696 per year versus $24,833 for men with a university degree. And the majority of women still work in sex-segregated, low-paying, low-status service or sales jobs. Because of the high divorce rate and the resultant increase in families headed by women, overall family incomes have declined in both countries. In Canada, women head 83 percent of all single parent families, nearly half of which are below the poverty line. In the United States in 1981, 45 percent of all employed women were single (divorced, widowed or never married) and sole supporters of their children. The poverty rate of Blacks and Hispanics in general, and of Black and Hispanic women in particular, is higher than that of Whites. The unemployment rate of women of all races and ethnic origins is higher than among men. Among the elderly, the largest percentage of poor are women who do not live with relatives. Finally, women are still primarily responsible for domestic chores and childcare.

The large number of women's organizations in both countries actively lobbying for changes in social policies testifies to the fact that in spite of the gains of The Decade, economic equality for women in the United States and Canada is still in the future.

Let No Charitable Hope

Now let no charitable hope
Confuse my mind with images
Of eagle and of antelope:
I am in nature none of these.

I was, being human, born alone;
I am, being woman, hard beset;
I live by squeezing from a stone
The little nourishment I get.

In masks outrageous and austere
The years go by in single file;
But none has merited my fear,
And none has quite escaped my smile.

The Population Institute

Elinor Wylie

Reprinted from Elinor Wylie, *Collected Poems of Elinor Wylie*, published by Alfred A. Knopf, Inc., New York. Reprinted with permission of the publisher.

Dick Mathews

The Suburb

No time, no time,
and with so many in line to be
born or fed or made love to, there is no
excuse for staring at it, though it's spring again
and the leaves have come out looking
limp and wet like little green new born babies.

The girls have come out in their new bought dresses,
carefully, carefully. They know they're in danger.
Already there are couples crumpled under the chestnuts.
The houses crowd closer, listening to each other's radios.
Weeds have got into the window boxes. The washing hangs,
helpless. Children are lusting for ice cream.

It is my lot each May to be hot and pregnant,
a long way away from the years when I slept by myself—
the white bed by the dressing table, pious with cherry blossoms,
the flatteries and punishments of photographs and mirrors.
We walked home by starlight and he touched my breasts.
"Please, please!" Then I let him anyway. Cars
droned and flashed, sucking at the cow parsley. Later
there were teas and the engagement party. The wedding
in the rain. The hotel where I slept in the bathroom.
The night when he slept on the floor.

The ache of remembering, bitterer than a birth. Better
to lie still and let the babies run through me.
To let them possess me. They will spare me
spring after spring. Their hungers deliver me.
I grow fat as they devour me. I give them my sleep
and they absolve me from waking. Who can accuse me?
I am beyond blame.

ANNE STEVENSON

Reprinted from REVERSALS with the kind permission of Wesleyan
University Press

In Mind

There's in my mind a woman
of innocence, unadorned but

fair-featured, and smelling of
apples or grass. She wears

a utopian smock or shift, her hair
is light brown and smooth, and she

is kind and very clean without
ostentation—
but she has
no imagination.
And there's a
turbulent moon-ridden girl

or old woman, or both,
dressed in opals and rags, feathers

and torn taffeta,
who knows strange songs—

but she is not kind.

DENISE LEVERTON

Reprinted from POEMS 1960-1967.
Copyright 1963 by Denise Leverton Goodman "IN MIND" was first
printed in poetry.
Reprinted with the kind permission of New Directions Publishing Corp.

The Population Institute

Women's Organizations in Population

Canadian Research Institute for the Advancement of Women

CANADA

ADDRESS:

151 Slater Street-Suite 408, Ottawa, Ontario Canada K1P 5H3

EXECUTIVE OFFICER:

Linda Clippingdale, Ex. Dir.; Dr. Jill Vickers, Pres.

BRANCH OFFICES:

TELEPHONE NUMBER:

(613) 563-0681

TELEX NUMBER:

APPROX. STAFF SIZE:	VOLUNTEER STAFF:	YEAR ESTABLISHED:
7		1976

NUMBER OF INDIVIDUAL MEMBERS:

800

FUNDING: Government funding, publication sales, membership, donations, user fees for bank of researchers.

PRINCIPAL PURPOSE: To encourage, coordinate and disseminate research into women's experience in Canada.

MAIN ACTIVITIES: Research; communication of research results through publications and conferences; promoting of research through grants and prizes; networking.

POPULATION CONCERNS: Women's reproductive health and reproductive control.

SPECIFIC POPULATION ACTIVITIES: CRIAW is not directly involved in specific population activities, although individual members and researchers are.

FORWARD-LOOKING STRATEGIES IMPLEMENTATIONS: Implementation is being carried out through research.

OBSTACLES TO THE IMPLEMENTATION OF FORWARD-LOOKING STRATEGIES:

NOTES:

Collectif de Rinouski pour la Sante des Femmes

CANADA

ADDRESS:

167 St. Louis, Romouski, Quebec Canada G5L 5R2

EXECUTIVE OFFICER:

BRANCH OFFICES:

TELEPHONE NUMBER:

(418)722-4797

TELEX NUMBER:

APPROX. STAFF SIZE:

VOLUNTEER STAFF:

YEAR ESTABLISHED:

1977

NUMBER OF INDIVIDUAL MEMBERS:

10

FUNDING: Annual government grants

PRINCIPAL PURPOSE: Maintenance of network on all aspects of women's health; work to heighten women's awareness of health and medical fields, the right to abortion; safe, free, accessible contraception and expression of sexuality without discrimination.

MAIN ACTIVITIES: Workshops for women on health topics such as stress, self help, family planning. Work with Planned Parenthood Federation of Quebec; publish newsletter.

POPULATION CONCERNS: Women's health issues.

SPECIFIC POPULATION ACTIVITIES: Education

FORWARD-LOOKING STRATEGIES IMPLEMENTATIONS:

OBSTACLES TO THE IMPLEMENTATION OF FORWARD-LOOKING STRATEGIES:

NOTES:

Concerned Citizens for Choice on Abortion

CANADA

ADDRESS:

P.O. Box 24617, Station C, Vancouver B.C., Canada V5T 4E1

EXECUTIVE OFFICER:

Norah Hutchinson and Cheryl Wirsz, Steering Committee.

BRANCH OFFICES:

TELEPHONE NUMBER:	TELEX NUMBER:
(604) 876-9920	

APPROX. STAFF SIZE:	VOLUNTEER STAFF:	YEAR ESTABLISHED:
	20	1978

NUMBER OF INDIVIDUAL MEMBERS:

500

FUNDING: Donations.

PRINCIPAL PURPOSE: To remove abortion from the Canadian criminal code, to legalize free-standing abortion clinics and to defend women's right to choose.

MAIN ACTIVITIES: Education.

POPULATION CONCERNS: Reproductive freedom.

SPECIFIC POPULATION ACTIVITIES: Education and counselling.

FORWARD-LOOKING STRATEGIES IMPLEMENTATIONS: None.

OBSTACLES TO THE IMPLEMENTATION OF FORWARD-LOOKING STRATEGIES: None.

NOTES:

ORGANIZATION:

Conseil Consultatif Candadien de la Situation de la Femme*

CANADA

ADDRESS:

800 ouest, boul. Dorchester suite 1036 Montreal H3B IX9

EXECUTIVE OFFICER:			BRANCH OFFICES:
Sylvia Gold, President			

TELEPHONE NUMBER:	TELEX NUMBER:	
283-3123		

APPROX. STAFF SIZE:	VOLUNTEER STAFF:	YEAR ESTABLISHED:
2		

NUMBER OF INDIVIDUAL MEMBERS:

FUNDING: Federal Government.

PRINCIPAL PURPOSE: Present the government and the public with questions that preoccupy women and advise the federal gov't. on subjects relating to the status of women.

MAIN ACTIVITIES: Research, dissemination of information and documentation to the public.

POPULATION CONCERNS: All issues relating to women.

SPECIFIC POPULATION ACTIVITIES: Education.

FORWARD-LOOKING STRATEGIES IMPLEMENTATIONS: Were not aware of strategies.

OBSTACLES TO THE IMPLEMENTATION OF FORWARD-LOOKING STRATEGIES:

NOTES: *Canadian Advisory Council on the Status of Women

Montreal Health Pres/.Les Presses de la Sante

CANADA

ADDRESS:

CP 1000, Station La Cite', Montreal, Canada H2W 2N1

EXECUTIVE OFFICER:

Rosemary Byrne Huntes, Executive Director

BRANCH OFFICES:

TELEPHONE NUMBER:	TELEX NUMBER:
(514) 272-5441	

APPROX. STAFF SIZE:	VOLUNTEER STAFF:	YEAR ESTABLISHED:
2	7	1972

NUMBER OF INDIVIDUAL MEMBERS:

9

FUNDING: Through the sale of our material some funding for research from Wealth Promotion Directorate-Health & Welfare.

PRINCIPAL PURPOSE: Research, write, publish and distribute information on health and sexuality.

MAIN ACTIVITIES: Writing and updating our books on birth control, STD's sexual assault and menopause.

POPULATION CONCERNS:

SPECIFIC POPULATION ACTIVITIES:

FORWARD-LOOKING STRATEGIES IMPLEMENTATIONS: Unspecified.

OBSTACLES TO THE IMPLEMENTATION OF FORWARD-LOOKING STRATEGIES:

NOTES:

National Action Committee on the Status of Women

CANADA

ADDRESS:

344 Bloor St. W., Ste. 505, Toronto, Ont. M5S 1W9 Canada

EXECUTIVE OFFICER:			BRANCH OFFICES:
Louis Dulude			

TELEPHONE NUMBER:	TELEX NUMBER:
416-922-3246	

APPROX. STAFF SIZE:	VOLUNTEER STAFF:	YEAR ESTABLISHED:
8	45	1972

NUMBER OF INDIVIDUAL MEMBERS:

FUNDING: Federal government and direct mail fundraising.

PRINCIPAL PURPOSE: To unite women and women's groups across Canada in the struggle for equality.

MAIN ACTIVITIES: Writing briefs and visiting members of Parliament.

POPULATION CONCERNS: Birth control, and housing and immigration policies.

SPECIFIC POPULATION ACTIVITIES: Advocacy.

FORWARD-LOOKING STRATEGIES IMPLEMENTATIONS: Plan to implement Strategies in the future.

OBSTACLES TO THE IMPLEMENTATION OF FORWARD-LOOKING STRATEGIES: None.

NOTES:

National Council of Women of Canada

CANADA

ADDRESS:

270 Maclaren Street, Ste. 20, Ottawa, ONY, CANADA K2P 0M3

EXECUTIVE OFFICER:

Margaret Macgee, President

BRANCH OFFICES:

TELEPHONE NUMBER:

613-233-4953

TELEX NUMBER:

APPROX. STAFF SIZE:	VOLUNTEER STAFF:	YEAR ESTABLISHED:
1		1893

NUMBER OF INDIVIDUAL MEMBERS:

750,000 +

FUNDING: Membership fees, donations and the interest from a foundation fund.

PRINCIPAL PURPOSE: To act as an educator, a voice and a catalyst for Canadians on issues affecting the common good. Special emphasis is placed on improving the status of women.

MAIN ACTIVITIES: Action and research on issues such as: the arts, international affairs and peace, children and the family, economic topics, education, health and welfare, housing, community planning, mass media and women, and employment. Also submit findings to the government at three levels.

POPULATION CONCERNS: Support the work of Planned Parenthood Federation of Canada.

SPECIFIC POPULATION ACTIVITIES: Asked government not to allow use of Depo-Provera.

FORWARD-LOOKING STRATEGIES IMPLEMENTATIONS: Involved in researching social issues in which Canada needs improvement. There are special needs for Canada's indigenous people and a need for more women to be involved at decision-making levels.

OBSTACLES TO THE IMPLEMENTATION OF FORWARD-LOOKING STRATEGIES: Although the government of Canada supports the Strategies, it has not allocated funds or developed policies for their implementation.

NOTES:

Pacific Post-Partum Support Society **CANADA**

ADDRESS:

888 Burrard Street, Vancouver, B.C. Canada V6Z 1X9

EXECUTIVE OFFICER:

Penny Handford, Program Coordinator

BRANCH OFFICES:

TELEPHONE NUMBER:	TELEX NUMBER:
(604)689-9994	

APPROX. STAFF SIZE:	VOLUNTEER STAFF:	YEAR ESTABLISHED:
4	21	1984

NUMBER OF INDIVIDUAL MEMBERS:

25

FUNDING: Community Fund-Raising

PRINCIPAL PURPOSE: To counsel and support women who are experiencing post-partum depression and to provide community education.

MAIN ACTIVITIES: Providing a treatment program involving volunteer telephone counselling and a support group.

POPULATION CONCERNS: Unwanted pregnancy as a part of post-partum depression.

SPECIFIC POPULATION ACTIVITIES: Counseling.

FORWARD-LOOKING STRATEGIES IMPLEMENTATIONS: None.

OBSTACLES TO THE IMPLEMENTATION OF FORWARD-LOOKING STRATEGIES:

NOTES:

Pauktuutit-Inuit Women's Association of Canada

CANADA

ADDRESS:

200 Elgin Street, Suite 804, Ottawa, Ontario Canada K2L 254

EXECUTIVE OFFICER:

Eva Voisey, President

BRANCH OFFICES:

TELEPHONE NUMBER:

(613)238-3977

TELEX NUMBER:

APPROX. STAFF SIZE:

6

VOLUNTEER STAFF:

YEAR ESTABLISHED:

1984

NUMBER OF INDIVIDUAL MEMBERS:

150

FUNDING: Government and private donations.

PRINCIPAL PURPOSE: To foster a greater awareness of the needs of Inuit women and to encourage their participation in community regional and national concerns in relation to social, cultural and economic development.

MAIN ACTIVITIES: Establishing local Inuit women's groups within communities, workshops, annual general meeting, newsletter, lobbying, liason with other native & non-native groups, research.

POPULATION CONCERNS:

SPECIFIC POPULATION ACTIVITIES: Education, demographic research, contraceptive research, counselling, advocacy, delivery of services.

FORWARD-LOOKING STRATEGIES IMPLEMENTATIONS: Currently reviewing strategies.

OBSTACLES TO THE IMPLEMENTATION OF FORWARD-LOOKING STRATEGIES:

NOTES:

Regina Healthsharing Inc.   CANADA

ADDRESS:

Box 734, Regina, Saskatchewan, Canada S4P 3A8

EXECUTIVE OFFICER:

Shannon Buchan—Contact Person, President

BRANCH OFFICES:

TELEPHONE NUMBER:	TELEX NUMBER:
(306) 352-1540	

APPROX. STAFF SIZE:	VOLUNTEER STAFF:	YEAR ESTABLISHED:
4	12	1976

NUMBER OF INDIVIDUAL MEMBERS:

246

FUNDING: Our organization is funded through private donations as well as government research grants. We have no sustaining funding. We occasionally receive project funding through the Secretary of State's Women's Program for specific projects.

PRINCIPAL PURPOSE: To improve the quality of health care which women receive and to enhance the level of well-being among women in our community. The organization focuses on education, self-help, responsibility and networking, as well as lobbying for change in government policies and institutions as avenues to change.

MAIN ACTIVITIES: Regina Healthsharing has produced two women's health conferences, numerous research and lobbying documents and a variety of educational materials. We provide regular one day workshops on health issues as well as providing patient advocacy, support for self-help groups, a lending library. We lobby all levels of government as well as institutions. We are presently providing workshops designed to enhance women's political power by delineating the connections between health and women's status. These workshops are being held especially for rural, native, and women in conflict with the law.

POPULATION CONCERNS: High rate of teenage pregnancy, forced and non-informed sterilization of native women, women in conflict with the law, low-income and disabled women. Use of dangerous and non-tested contraceptives (ie. Depo-Provero). Low level of funding for contraceptive research for women, (effects, improvement, ect.). Use of violent obstetrical practices. Lack of informed consent over contraceptive use.

SPECIFIC POPULATION ACTIVITIES: Education, contraceptive research, counseling, advocacy, cultural issues and childbearing.

FORWARD-LOOKING STRATEGIES IMPLEMENTATIONS: Yes. We have been actively lobbying our federal and provincial governments to implement the Strategies, through their funding mechanisms. We have been increasing our educational efforts, and have been working for abortion access for our community.

OBSTACLES TO THE IMPLEMENTATION OF FORWARD-LOOKING STRATEGIES: Although our government agreed to the document, in reality their conviction was not there. They feel it is unwise to interfere with the provincial governments handling of the abortion issue by decriminalizing abortion and deregulating it. Women's education and advancement is not a priority, funding wise.

NOTES:

Real Women of Canada

CANADA

ADDRESS:

247 Golden Orchard Dr., Hamilton, Ontario, Canada L9C 6J4

EXECUTIVE OFFICER:			BRANCH OFFICES:
Lynne Scime			

TELEPHONE NUMBER:	TELEX NUMBER:
(416) 387-1374	

APPROX. STAFF SIZE:	VOLUNTEER STAFF:	YEAR ESTABLISHED:
12		1983

NUMBER OF INDIVIDUAL MEMBERS:

FUNDING: Memberships and donations.

PRINCIPAL PURPOSE: To educate women of Canada with regard to political and social issues which will impact on their lives. We also function as a political lobby group.

MAIN ACTIVITIES: Lobbying federal and provincial politicians/education of membership on current issues.

POPULATION CONCERNS: Concerned with sex education in our publicly-funded schools and Canada's birth rate situation.

SPECIFIC POPULATION ACTIVITIES: Education and advocacy.

FORWARD-LOOKING STRATEGIES IMPLEMENTATIONS: Aware.

OBSTACLES TO THE IMPLEMENTATION OF FORWARD-LOOKING STRATEGIES: Considerable resistance from small conservative organizations.

NOTES:

Saskatchewan Association on Human Rights

CANADA

ADDRESS:

406-245 3rd Avenue, South, Saskatoon, Sask. S7K 1M4, Canada

EXECUTIVE OFFICER:	BRANCH OFFICES:
Sherry Duncan, Executive Director, Lloyd Robertson, President	

TELEPHONE NUMBER:	TELEX NUMBER:

APPROX. STAFF SIZE:	VOLUNTEER STAFF:	YEAR ESTABLISHED:
1		1068

NUMBER OF INDIVIDUAL MEMBERS:

350

FUNDING: Federal and provincial grants, and donations.

PRINCIPAL PURPOSE:

MAIN ACTIVITIES:

POPULATION CONCERNS: Education.

SPECIFIC POPULATION ACTIVITIES: Annual participation in local international women's day committee. Disseminate varied information on family planning.

FORWARD LOOKING-STRATEGIES IMPLEMENTATIONS:

OBSTACLES TO THE IMPLEMENTATION OF FORWARD-LOOKING STRATEGIES:

NOTES:

Women's Institutes of Nova Scotia   **CANADA**

ADDRESS:

% Nova Scotia Agriculture College Box, 550, Truro Nova Scotia, Canada B2N 5E3

EXECUTIVE OFFICER:			BRANCH OFFICES:
Norma J. Mosher, Executive Director			

TELEPHONE NUMBER:		TELEX NUMBER:	
(902) 895-1571			

APPROX. STAFF SIZE:	VOLUNTEER STAFF:	YEAR ESTABLISHED:	
1		1913	

NUMBER OF INDIVIDUAL MEMBERS:
1804

FUNDING: Government grants and membership fees.

PRINCIPAL PURPOSE: Education, leadership development and community service.

MAIN ACTIVITIES: Development of program material, sponsoring conferences and seminars, school projects and aid to developing countries.

POPULATION CONCERNS: Nutrition, health care, pensions, land use, equal opportunities, food supply.

SPECIFIC POPULATION ACTIVITIES: Education.

FORWARD-LOOKING STRATEGIES IMPLEMENTATIONS: Aware of the strategies, but have not begun work on the implementation at the present.

OBSTACLES TO THE IMPLEMENTATION OF FORWARD-LOOKING STRATEGIES:

NOTES:

African-American Women's Caucus **USA**

ADDRESS:

P.O. Box 11897, Baltimore, MD 21207

EXECUTIVE OFFICER:			BRANCH OFFICES:
Noni Ford, President			

TELEPHONE NUMBER:		TELEX NUMBER:	
(301) 444-3282			

APPROX. STAFF SIZE:	VOLUNTEER STAFF:	YEAR ESTABLISHED:	
0	35		

NUMBER OF INDIVIDUAL MEMBERS:

PRINCIPAL PURPOSE: To improve the quality of life of women of African ancestry.

MAIN ACTIVITIES: Education on issues confronting African-American women.

POPULATION CONCERNS: Concerned with the unresolved debates of reproductive freedom and abortion.

SPECIFIC POPULATION ACTIVITIES: Advocacy.

FORWARD-LOOKING STRATEGIES IMPLEMENTATIONS: None.

OBSTACLES TO THE IMPLEMENTATION OF FORWARD-LOOKING STRATEGIES: None.

NOTES:

All Nation's Women's League, Inc.

USA

ADDRESS:

69 Fifth Ave. New York, NY 10003

EXECUTIVE OFFICER:

Ms. Angela Miller

BRANCH OFFICES:

TELEPHONE NUMBER:

(212) 989-0315

TELEX NUMBER:

APPROX. STAFF SIZE:	VOLUNTEER STAFF:	YEAR ESTABLISHED:
	89	1970

NUMBER OF INDIVIDUAL MEMBERS:

1008

FUNDING: Dues and donations.

PRINCIPAL PURPOSE: To promote a mutual understanding of women's problems and the need for community integration. Seeks to improve the cultural, educational, and professional status of women throughout the world. Works to broaden public awareness on women's issues.

MAIN ACTIVITIES: Sponsors cultural events, educational and health programs, and lectures. Educational children activities include classes in music, painting and crafts. Offers vocational rehabilitation programs for unemployed women, operates counseling office. Publishes newsletter and holds conventions.

POPULATION CONCERNS: None.

SPECIFIC POPULATION ACTIVITIES: Education, counseling, health and nutrition advocacy, natural family planning.

FORWARD-LOOKING STRATEGIES IMPLEMENTATIONS: None.

OBSTACLES TO THE IMPLEMENTATION OF FORWARD-LOOKING STRATEGIES: None.

NOTES:

Boston Women's Health Book Collective   **USA**

ADDRESS:

47 Nichols Avenue, Watertown, MA 02172, USA

EXECUTIVE OFFICER:

Norma Swenson & Judy Norsigian

BRANCH OFFICES:

TELEPHONE NUMBER:

(617)924-0271

TELEX NUMBER:

APPROX. STAFF SIZE:	VOLUNTEER STAFF:	YEAR ESTABLISHED:
7	1-2	1970

NUMBER OF INDIVIDUAL MEMBERS:

FUNDING: Royalties income and literature sales, donations and grants.

PRINCIPAL PURPOSE: Women's health education.

MAIN ACTIVITIES: Women's health information center, media outreach, bilingual discussion groups and workshops on health for Latin women, Tampon project, international outreach, and a women's health and learning center at the Massachusetts Correctional Institution.

POPULATION CONCERNS: These will be summarized in a forthcoming report following a meeting planned with the Population Council and the International Women's Health Coalition.

SPECIFIC POPULATION ACTIVITIES: Education.

FORWARD-LOOKING STRATEGIES IMPLEMENTATIONS: Are aware of the Strategies but are not specifically implementing them.

OBSTACLES TO THE IMPLEMENTATION OF FORWARD-LOOKING STRATEGIES: None indicated.

NOTES:

B'nai B'rith Women

USA

ADDRESS:

1640 Rhode Island Ave., NW, Washington, DC 20036

EXECUTIVE OFFICER:			BRANCH OFFICES:
Elaine Binder, Executive Director			

TELEPHONE NUMBER:		TELEX NUMBER:	
(202) 857-6675			

APPROX. STAFF SIZE:	VOLUNTEER STAFF:	YEAR ESTABLISHED:
75	85	1897

NUMBER OF INDIVIDUAL MEMBERS:

120,000

FUNDING: Membership dues.

PRINCIPAL PURPOSE: To unite Jewish women as a force for social development.

MAIN ACTIVITIES: Promoting social advancement through educational, charitable and religious programs.

POPULATION CONCERNS: Education, Advocacy.

SPECIFIC POPULATION ACTIVITIES: Working for senate consideration of the convention on the elimination of all forms of discrimination against women.

FORWARD-LOOKING STRATEGIES IMPLEMENTATIONS: Trying to get Senate to consider the Convention on the Elimination of All Forms of Discrimination Against Women.

OBSTACLES TO THE IMPLEMENTATION OF FORWARD-LOOKING STRATEGIES: Senatorial resistance to schedule hearing.

NOTES:

The Centre for Development and Population Activities (CEDPA)

USA

ADDRESS:

1717 Mass. Ave. N.W., Suite 202, Washington, DC 20036, USA

EXECUTIVE OFFICER:

Kaval Gulhati, President

BRANCH OFFICES:

TELEPHONE NUMBER:

(202) 667-1142

TELEX NUMBER:

440 384 CFPA

APPROX. STAFF SIZE:	VOLUNTEER STAFF:	YEAR ESTABLISHED:
31		1975

NUMBER OF INDIVIDUAL MEMBERS:

2000

FUNDING: Grants from public and private sources.

PRINCIPAL PURPOSE: To upgrade, through training and technical assistance, the leadership skills of Third World managers (especially women), so that they can more effectively plan and carry out community-based projects in family planning, health, and income-generation.

MAIN ACTIVITIES: CEDPA conducts management training programs in the U.S. and overseas and, as follow-up to the programs, provides technical assistance and seed-money grants to alumnae for their projects in family planning, health, and development.

POPULATION CONCERNS: To improve the effectiveness of family planning service, delivery, and education programs in the Third World by improving the management skills of the individuals (particularly women) who administer them; and to extend family planning education and services to more Third World women through community-based projects.

SPECIFIC POPULATION ACTIVITIES: Education, management training and delivery of services.

FORWARD-LOOKING STRATEGIES IMPLEMENTATIONS: Focusing on upgrading the skills of women managers of family planning programs. Recognizing that women must be planners and policy-makers at the management level. Initiation of a new project that will focus on the problem of teenage pregnancy in the Third World.

OBSTACLES TO THE IMPLEMENTATION OF FORWARD-LOOKING STRATEGIES: None indicated.

NOTES:

CHOICE Concern for Health Options: Information, Care, and Education

USA

ADDRESS:

125 South 9th St. Suite 603, Philadelphia, PA 19017

EXECUTIVE OFFICER:

Elizabeth Werthan, President

BRANCH OFFICES:

TELEPHONE NUMBER:

(215) 592-7644

TELEX NUMBER:

APPROX. STAFF SIZE:

23

VOLUNTEER STAFF:

YEAR ESTABLISHED:

1971

NUMBER OF INDIVIDUAL MEMBERS:

FUNDING: Government funding, fundraising, private donations, contracts, and grants.

PRINCIPAL PURPOSE: Focusing on individual and societal women's issues, working as an advocate for women's reproductive rights and self determination.

MAIN ACTIVITIES: Education and Advocacy. Sponsoring a family planning hotline, a childcare information and referral program, and a teen theatre company.

POPULATION CONCERNS: Family planning information, referrals, counseling, and advocacy.

SPECIFIC POPULATION ACTIVITIES: Hotline for reproductive healthcare information; teen theatre company addressing issues such as peer pressure and family planning.

FORWARD-LOOKING STRATEGIES IMPLEMENTATIONS: Aware of them. Programs already compatible with the strategies.

OBSTACLES TO THE IMPLEMENTATION OF FORWARD-LOOKING STRATEGIES:

NOTES:

Clearinghouse on Women's Issues

USA

ADDRESS:

P.O. Box 70603, Friendship Heights, MD 20906

EXECUTIVE OFFICER:

Daisy B. Fields, President

BRANCH OFFICES:

TELEPHONE NUMBER:

(301) 871-6106

TELEX NUMBER:

APPROX. STAFF SIZE:	VOLUNTEER STAFF:	YEAR ESTABLISHED:
	All workers	1974

NUMBER OF INDIVIDUAL MEMBERS:

300

FUNDING: Dues and contributions.

PRINCIPAL PURPOSE: To disseminate information on sex discrimination and policies that affect the economic and educational status of women.

MAIN ACTIVITIES: Working for equality in the workplace, equal legal rights, increased educational opportunities for women, elimination of prejudice and discrimination.

POPULATION CONCERNS: Concerned with those population issues related to the purpose described, especially women's health.

SPECIFIC POPULATION ACTIVITIES: Education.

FORWARD-LOOKING STRATEGIES IMPLEMENTATIONS: None.

OBSTACLES TO THE IMPLEMENTATION OF FORWARD-LOOKING STRATEGIES: None.

NOTES:

ORGANIZATION:

Delegation for Friendship Among Women

USA

ADDRESS:

2219 Caroline Lane, South St. Paul, MN 55075, USA

EXECUTIVE OFFICER:

Mary Barden Keegan

BRANCH OFFICES:

TELEPHONE NUMBER:

(612)455-5620

TELEX NUMBER:

APPROX. STAFF SIZE:	VOLUNTEER STAFF:	YEAR ESTABLISHED:
7	7	1970

NUMBER OF INDIVIDUAL MEMBERS:

278

FUNDING: Self-funded.

PRINCIPAL PURPOSE: To exchange information with women in developing countries.

MAIN ACTIVITIES: Exchange of information and ideas with women.

POPULATION CONCERNS: Birth control and aging.

SPECIFIC POPULATION ACTIVITIES: Education, counselling and delivery of natural family planning services.

FORWARD-LOOKING STRATEGIES IMPLEMENTATIONS: Were not aware of the Strategies.

OBSTACLES TO THE IMPLEMENTATION OF FORWARD-LOOKING STRATEGIES: None indicated.

NOTES:

Equity Policy Center

USA

ADDRESS:

4818 Drummond Avenue, Chevy Chase, MD 20815, USA

EXECUTIVE OFFICER:			BRANCH OFFICES:
Irene Tinker, Director			

TELEPHONE NUMBER:		TELEX NUMBER:	
(301)656-4475			

APPROX. STAFF SIZE:	VOLUNTEER STAFF:	YEAR ESTABLISHED:	
4	2	1978	

NUMBER OF INDIVIDUAL MEMBERS:

FUNDING: Grants from ILO, FAO, IBRD, USAID, foundations, and personal contributions.

PRINCIPAL PURPOSE: To ensure that women are included in the development programs worldwide; to collect data to bring up the importance of women's economic and social work; and to work with agencies and Congress to support these goals.

MAIN ACTIVITIES: Collect data, write papers, lecture, testify, hold and attend conferences and design and evaluate projects.

POPULATION CONCERNS: Women's right to control her own body. Interaction between family size and women's status, and population pressure and environmental degradation.

SPECIFIC POPULATION ACTIVITIES: Advocacy.

FORWARD-LOOKING STRATEGIES IMPLEMENTATIONS: We are aware of the Strategies and are trying to implement them.

OBSTACLES TO THE IMPLEMENTATION OF FORWARD-LOOKING STRATEGIES: None indicated.

NOTES:

International Black Women's Congress

USA

ADDRESS:

P.O. Box 4250, Newark, NJ 07112, USA

EXECUTIVE OFFICER:			BRANCH OFFICES:
Dr. La Francis Rodgers-Rose, International President			

TELEPHONE NUMBER:		TELEX NUMBER:
(201)926-0570		

APPROX. STAFF SIZE:	VOLUNTEER STAFF:	YEAR ESTABLISHED:
5	3	1983

NUMBER OF INDIVIDUAL MEMBERS:

1800

FUNDING: Not indicated.

PRINCIPAL PURPOSE: International, grassroots, networking organization of women of African descent for support in solving mutual problems.

MAIN ACTIVITIES: Holding annual international and national conferences, support groups, workshops and training.

POPULATION CONCERNS: Teen pregnancy, child spacing and safe birth control.

SPECIFIC POPULATION ACTIVITIES: Education, counselling and advocacy.

FORWARD-LOOKING STRATEGIES IMPLEMENTATIONS: Understanding development from an Afro-centric perspective; working on women's work-training.

OBSTACLES TO THE IMPLEMENTATION OF FORWARD-LOOKING STRATEGIES: None indicated.

NOTES:

*Business Address: 1081 Bergen Street, Suite 200, Newark, NJ 07112

International Center for Research on Women USA

1717 Massachusetts Avenue, NW, Suite 501, Washington, DC 20036

Mayra Buvinic, Director

(202) 797-0007

15

1976

FUNDING: Government funds, foundations, corporations, U.N. agencies.

PRINCIPAL PURPOSE: To improve the productivity and incomes of poor women in developing countries worldwide. By providing women with access to training, credit and technical assistance, ICRW enhances their earning power, strengthens their significant participation in agriculture, industry and commerce, and expands their contribution to economic development.

MAIN ACTIVITIES: Technical services to development agencies. Research on women's economic participation in developing countries. Public education that improves understanding of the contribution that women make.

POPULATION CONCERNS: ICRW programs address the dual economic and family responsibilities of Third World women. We are interested in women's fertility as it impacts on women's economic roles. We are especially interested in women headed households.

SPECIFIC POPULATION ACTIVITIES: Demographic research.

FORWARD-LOOKING STRATEGIES IMPLEMENTATIONS: ICRW provides technical services to AID missions with reference to the economic roles of women. ICRW is studying how poor women combine their responsibilities as income earners and mothers.

OBSTACLES TO THE IMPLEMENTATION OF FORWARD-LOOKING STRATEGIES: Funding constraints, unwilllingness of national governments to implement programs for women; the right-to-life movement.

NOTES:

Inter-American Commission of Women $\qquad$ USA

ADDRESS:

1889 F Street, NW, Suite 880, Washington, DC 20006

EXECUTIVE OFFICER:			BRANCH OFFICES:

BRANCH OFFICES:
Centro Multinacional de la Mujer, Avenida Velez Sarsfield 153, 5000 Cordoba, Argentina

TELEPHONE NUMBER:	TELEX NUMBER:
(202) 789-6085	OAS64128

APPROX. STAFF SIZE:	VOLUNTEER STAFF:	YEAR ESTABLISHED:
		1928

NUMBER OF INDIVIDUAL MEMBERS:

FUNDING: Organization of American States.

PRINCIPAL PURPOSE: Ensuring the recognition of civil and political rights of women.

MAIN ACTIVITIES: Analyzing problems of women in the Americas; training and organizing women for participation in development programs; urging governments to comply with resolutions and mandates approved by inter-American or international conferences. Serving as advisory body of OAS; establishing cooperation among various organizations and agencies whose activities affect women; informing governments of the status of women in the Americas.

POPULATION CONCERNS: Maternal and child health care; expansion of government family planning programs.

SPECIFIC POPULATION ACTIVITIES: Education & Advocacy.

FORWARD-LOOKING STRATEGIES IMPLEMENTATIONS: Promotion of increased political participation; improved educational opportunities; equal job opportunities and legal equality, improved health and nutrition programs; increased funding for low-income housing and the establishment of the appropriate machinery with sufficient resources and authority to ensure the inclusion of women in development policies and programs.

OBSTACLES TO THE IMPLEMENTATION OF FORWARD-LOOKING STRATEGIES: None.

NOTES:

International Council of African Women

USA

ADDRESS:

P.O. Box 55076, Washington, DC 20011, USA

EXECUTIVE OFFICER:

Loretta Ross, Coordinator

BRANCH OFFICES:

TELEPHONE NUMBER:

(301)565-9313

TELEX NUMBER:

APPROX. STAFF SIZE:	VOLUNTEER STAFF:	YEAR ESTABLISHED:
	8	1982

NUMBER OF INDIVIDUAL MEMBERS:

200

FUNDING: Not indicated.

PRINCIPAL PURPOSE: Networking and information sharing among women of African descent. Support services for rape crisis centers and battered women's shelters; education on reproductive rights for women of color.

MAIN ACTIVITIES: Publication of a newsletter, holding conferences and educational forums and visiting women's organizations in other countries.

POPULATION CONCERNS: Need for appropriate information to combat use of unsafe reproductive technologies on women of color in both the US and around the world. Lack of involvement of color communities in reproductive rights issues.

SPECIFIC POPULATION ACTIVITIES: Education, advocacy and organizing.

FORWARD-LOOKING STRATEGIES IMPLEMENTATIONS: Working with the District of Columbia's Commission for women to encourage local government response to the Strategies dealing with family planning.

OBSTACLES TO THE IMPLEMENTATION OF FORWARD-LOOKING STRATEGIES: Government administrators not considering the Strategies as serious policy recommendations. Low awareness level of the Nairobi Conference and limited resources of our organization.

NOTES:

International Projects Assistance Services

USA

ADDRESS:

P.O. Box 100, Carrboro, NC 27510, USA

EXECUTIVE OFFICER:			BRANCH OFFICES:
Katie McLaurin, Executive Director			

TELEPHONE NUMBER:		TELEX NUMBER:	
(919) 967-7052, 1-(800) 334-8446		5101-000-435	

APPROX. STAFF SIZE:	VOLUNTEER STAFF:	YEAR ESTABLISHED:	
13		1973	

NUMBER OF INDIVIDUAL MEMBERS:

FUNDING: Private donations and foundations.

PRINCIPAL PURPOSE: To help women achieve their fertility goals by providing a safe, inexpensive and effective approach to delivery of comprehensive family planning services.

MAIN ACTIVITIES: Developing and funding hospital-based physician training programs in the use of manual vacuum aspiration technique for the treatment of septic and incomplete abortion, menstrual regulation and endometrial biopsy.

POPULATION CONCERNS: Maternal mortality due to contraceptive failure, including incomplete and septic abortion. Availability of safe, effective, low-trauma treatment.

SPECIFIC POPULATION ACTIVITIES: Education, counselling. Delivery of services: Pill, IUD.

FORWARD LOOKING-STRATEGIES IMPLEMENTATIONS: Paragraphs 156 and 159 from FLS.

OBSTACLES TO THE IMPLEMENTATION OF FORWARD-LOOKING STRATEGIES:

NOTES:

International Women's Rights Action Watch

USA

ADDRESS:

Development, Law and Policy Center for Population and Family Health, Columbia University, 60 Haven Avenue, New York, NY 10032, USA

EXECUTIVE OFFICER:			BRANCH OFFICES:
Arvonne Fraser & Steven Isaacs, Co-Directors			Women Public Policy and Development Project
TELEPHONE NUMBER:	**TELEX NUMBER:**		Hubert Humphrey Institute of Public Affairs
(212)305-6980	POPFAMHLTH971913		University of Minnesota
APPROX. STAFF SIZE:	**VOLUNTEER STAFF:**	**YEAR ESTABLISHED:**	301 19th Avenue
10	varies	1985	South Minneapolis, MN 55455
NUMBER OF INDIVIDUAL MEMBERS:			Tele:(612)625-2505

FUNDING: Grants form private foundations.

PRINCIPAL PURPOSE: To facilitate education and implementation of international women's rights, using the United Nations convention of the elimination of all forms of discrimination as a women's bill of rights.

MAIN ACTIVITIES: Legal and policy analysis, networking and a clearinghouse of information.

POPULATION CONCERNS: Provide legal information and technical assistance as well as act as a clearing-house and network on numerous population issues, laws and policies around the world.

SPECIFIC POPULATION ACTIVITIES: Education and technical legal advice.

FORWARD-LOOKING STRATEGIES IMPLEMENTATIONS: To aid their implementation through legal apparati as best as possible.

OBSTACLES TO THE IMPLEMENTATION OF FORWARD-LOOKING STRATEGIES: None indicated.

NOTES:

ORGANIZATION:

Ms. Foundation for Women   **USA**

ADDRESS:

370 Lexington Avenue, New York, 10017

EXECUTIVE OFFICER:			BRANCH OFFICES:
Marie C. Wilson, Exec. Director			

TELEPHONE NUMBER:	TELEX NUMBER:	
(212) 689-3475		

APPROX. STAFF SIZE:	VOLUNTEER STAFF:	YEAR ESTABLISHED:
8		1978

NUMBER OF INDIVIDUAL MEMBERS:

FUNDING: Individual contributions.

PRINCIPAL PURPOSE: To provide services to groups concerned with survival issues.

MAIN ACTIVITIES: To provide funding for grassroots groups concerned with survival issues, priority given to projects of low income, racial or ethnic or geographic groups whose access to funding or organizing has been limited to projects that bring women together across racial, ethnic, or economic lines.

POPULATION CONCERNS: Reproduction rights.

SPECIFIC POPULATION ACTIVITIES: Education and advocacy.

FORWARD-LOOKING STRATEGIES IMPLEMENTATIONS: Aware of Strategies.

OBSTACLES TO THE IMPLEMENTATION OF FORWARD-LOOKING STRATEGIES:

NOTES:

National Council of Negro Women, Inc.

USA

ADDRESS:

701 North Fairfax Street, Suite 330, Alexandria, VA 22314, USA

EXECUTIVE OFFICER:		BRANCH OFFICES:
Dorothy I. Height, National President		

TELEPHONE NUMBER:	TELEX NUMBER:
(703)648-5740	

APPROX. STAFF SIZE:	VOLUNTEER STAFF:	YEAR ESTABLISHED:
20		1935

NUMBER OF INDIVIDUAL MEMBERS:

30,000

FUNDING: Contributions from members and organizations, grants and contracts.

PRINCIPAL PURPOSE: To improve the quality of life for black women and their families in the U.S., the Caribbean, and Africa.

MAIN ACTIVITIES: Programs addressing women's education and career advancement, family life, preventive and service programs in teenage pregnancy, juvenile delinquency, health, hunger and malnutrition, and skills trainings. International activities focus on working with women in developing countries in the areas of agriculture, food production, family health and income generation.

POPULATION CONCERNS: Teenage pregnancy and family health.

SPECIFIC POPULATION ACTIVITIES: Education.

FORWARD-LOOKING STRATEGIES IMPLEMENTATIONS: Providing information to members and others who participated on study tour to NGO forum. Integration of some of the issues into our field projects.

OBSTACLES TO THE IMPLEMENTATION OF FORWARD-LOOKING STRATEGIES: Difficulty in institutionalizing changes into existing societal and governmental structures.

NOTES:

National Council for Research on Women

USA

ADDRESS:

Roosevelt House, 47-49 East 65th Street, New York, NY 10021, USA

EXECUTIVE OFFICER:	BRANCH OFFICES:
Mariam Chamberlain, President	

TELEPHONE NUMBER:	TELEX NUMBER:
(212)570-5001	

APPROX. STAFF SIZE:	VOLUNTEER STAFF:	YEAR ESTABLISHED:
5		1981

NUMBER OF INDIVIDUAL MEMBERS:

50

FUNDING: Grants from the Ford Foundation.

PRINCIPAL PURPOSE: To facilitate collaborative research and exchange of information, personnel and technical assistance among members. To monitor and coordinate current information on public policy and funding resources, and to make resources available to a broad national and international audience.

MAIN ACTIVITIES: Programs including *A Woman's Thesaurus* providing women-centered, standardized terms; a national council database project coodinating the development and application of current technology, software and index standards to improve access of existing research programs and work-in-progress; seminars on collaborative research topics and roundtables bringing together researchers and practitioners in a broad range of social concerns.

POPULATION CONCERNS: All women-centered research being done on population issues.

SPECIFIC POPULATION ACTIVITIES: Education, advocacy, demographic and contraceptive research.

FORWARD-LOOKING STRATEGIES IMPLEMENTATIONS: All strategies relating to women's studies research and education functions.

OBSTACLES TO THE IMPLEMENTATION OF FORWARD-LOOKING STRATEGIES: None indicated.

NOTES:

National Institute for Women of Color

USA

ADDRESS:

P.O. Box 50583, Washington, DC 20004

EXECUTIVE OFFICER:			BRANCH OFFICES:
Sharon Porter			

TELEPHONE NUMBER:	TELEX NUMBER:
(202) 828-0735	

APPROX. STAFF SIZE:	VOLUNTEER STAFF:	YEAR ESTABLISHED:
		1981

NUMBER OF INDIVIDUAL MEMBERS:

FUNDING: Contributions from individuals and foundations.

PRINCIPAL PURPOSE: To assist women of color in achieving economic and educational equity.

MAIN ACTIVITIES: Networking vehicle for women of color, advocacy and information generation and dissemination.

POPULATION CONCERNS: The welfare and health of women of color.

SPECIFIC POPULATION ACTIVITIES: Education and advocacy.

FORWARD-LOOKING STRATEGIES IMPLEMENTATIONS: Monitoring status of U.S. women of color. Building and strengthening alliances among women. Promoting global perspective. National Conference for Women of Color in 1987.

OBSTACLES TO THE IMPLEMENTATION OF FORWARD-LOOKING STRATEGIES: None.

NOTES:

National Organization for Women (NOW)   **USA**

ADDRESS:

1401 New York Avenue, Northwest, Suite 800, Washington, DC 20005, USA

EXECUTIVE OFFICER:			BRANCH OFFICES:
Molly Yard, President			

TELEPHONE NUMBER:	TELEX NUMBER:	
(202)347-2279		

APPROX. STAFF SIZE:	VOLUNTEER STAFF:	YEAR ESTABLISHED:
32	20	1966

NUMBER OF INDIVIDUAL MEMBERS:

250,000

FUNDING: Membership and donor support.

PRINCIPAL PURPOSE: Advocacy for women's legal rights and defense of reproductive choices, lobbying for these purposes.

MAIN ACTIVITIES: Providing information on abortion and contraceptives; organizing mass demonstrations, lobbying; sponsorships of national campaigns; support of women political candidates.

POPULATION CONCERNS: Keeping abortions safe and legal in the U.S. and encouraging other countries to provide safe and legal abortions for women and access to family planning information.

SPECIFIC POPULATION ACTIVITIES: Education and advocacy.

FORWARD-LOOKING STRATEGIES IMPLEMENTATIONS: Emphasis on encouraging chapters to work with their local governments to establish school-based health clinics and defend abortion clinics from attacks.

OBSTACLES TO THE IMPLEMENTATION OF FORWARD-LOOKING STRATEGIES: Strong anti-choice sentiment at local level, lack of unity among pro-choice groups, low level of consciousness about the Strategies.

NOTES:

*Business Address: Loretta Ross, Women of Color Director

National Women's Health Network

USA

224 7th Street, SE, Washington, DC 20003, USA

Victoria Leonard, Executive Director

(202)543-9222

APPROX. STAFF SIZE:	VOLUNTEER STAFF:	YEAR ESTABLISHED:
8	4	1976

8000

FUNDING: Membership, fundraisers, foundation grants, donations and publications.

PRINCIPAL PURPOSE: To give women a voice in the health care system in the U.S.

MAIN ACTIVITIES: Functions as a clearinghouse for information on women's health. Encourages and sponsors action-oriented programs in the areas of organizing, public education and legal advocacy.

POPULATION CONCERNS: Contraception; hunger and health; environment and women's rights.

SPECIFIC POPULATION ACTIVITIES: Education, advocacy, demographic and contraceptive research.

FORWARD-LOOKING STRATEGIES IMPLEMENTATIONS: We are implementing the Strategies.

OBSTACLES TO THE IMPLEMENTATION OF FORWARD-LOOKING STRATEGIES: We have been working on informing women on the destruction caused by use of the Dalkon Shield and IUD, but the governments have not been very cooperative in disseminating this information.

NOTES:

U.N. Decade for Women Committee of the U.N.A.*—U.S.A. Mid Peninsula Chapter

USA

ADDRESS:

552 Emerson Street, Palo Alto, CA 94301

EXECUTIVE OFFICER:			BRANCH OFFICES:
Laddie Hughes, Chairperson			

TELEPHONE NUMBER:	TELEX NUMBER:	
(415) 494-1352		

APPROX. STAFF SIZE:	VOLUNTEER STAFF:	YEAR ESTABLISHED:
		1982

NUMBER OF INDIVIDUAL MEMBERS:

3

FUNDING: We charge for some of our public meetings. Grants from the Skaggs Foundation of Oakland Ca. Use our own monies.

PRINCIPAL PURPOSE: Emphasize the role of the United Nations as an advocate in advancing the status of women. Promote ratification by the US of the UN Convention on the Elimination of All forms of Discrimination Against Women (CEDAW).

MAIN ACTIVITIES: Hold public meetings with expert speakers on various women's issues. Disseminate information on the UN convention EDAW. Developed a survey "Progress of Women Towards Full Equality" for use by local women's groups; gave workshop on survey at NGO Forum 85.

POPULATION CONCERNS: None directly. Only in as much as childbearing and child rearing done excessively prevents women from achieveing equality with men.

SPECIFIC POPULATION ACTIVITIES:

FORWARD-LOOKING STRATEGIES IMPLEMENTATIONS: Individual committee members are working on different issues, e.g. one promotes the participation of females in science and enginering; another ran in primary for local congressional seat and lost.

OBSTACLES TO THE IMPLEMENTATION OF FORWARD-LOOKING STRATEGIES: Lack of monies to fund projects; cultural attitudes regarding what is appropriate for women to do in the workplace, in politics etc.

NOTES: *United Nations Association

Washington Women's Self-Help

USA

ADDRESS:

P.O. Box 777011, Washington, DC 20013-7011

EXECUTIVE OFFICER:

Karen Milgate

BRANCH OFFICES:

TELEPHONE NUMBER:	TELEX NUMBER:
462-3224	

APPROX. STAFF SIZE:	VOLUNTEER STAFF:	YEAR ESTABLISHED:
2		

NUMBER OF INDIVIDUAL MEMBERS:

20

FUNDING: Fees for services, donations and grants.

PRINCIPAL PURPOSE: To de-mystify and de-medicalize western medicine in the area of women's reproductive health care. At the same time to develop alternative health care models.

MAIN ACTIVITIES: We provide the cervical cap, and do research on it. We have developed a model for self-help prenatal care, we also do phone counseling, referrals and information.

POPULATION CONCERNS: We work for women to have health options, both in preventing and maintaining pregnancy.

SPECIFIC POPULATION ACTIVITIES: Education, Contraceptive Research, Counselling, Advocacy, Delivery of Service, Foam, and Natural Family Planning.

FORWARD-LOOKING STRATEGIES IMPLEMENTATIONS: Aware.

OBSTACLES TO THE IMPLEMENTATION OF FORWARD-LOOKING STRATEGIES: Lack of monetary support and the brainwashed consciousness of the western world which says lay health workers are irresponsible and only the Doctor knows best.

NOTES:

Women's Action Alliance

USA

ADDRESS:

370 Lexington Avenue, New York, NY 10017, USA

EXECUTIVE OFFICER:			BRANCH OFFICES:
Sylvia Kramer			

TELEPHONE NUMBER:		TELEX NUMBER:	
(212)532-8330			

APPROX. STAFF SIZE:	VOLUNTEER STAFF:	YEAR ESTABLISHED:
5	4	1971

NUMBER OF INDIVIDUAL MEMBERS:

FUNDING: Foundations, coporate foundations, U.S.government, sales, fundraising and private donations.

PRINCIPAL PURPOSE: To promote equality for women through educational programs and services.

MAIN ACTIVITIES: National information, referral services and library; networking and coalition building; action towards sex equity in education.

POPULATION CONCERNS: Teenage pregnancy.

SPECIFIC POPULATION ACTIVITIES: Education and advocacy.

FORWARD-LOOKING STRATEGIES IMPLEMENTATIONS: Are aware of the Strategies but did not specify implementations.

OBSTACLES TO THE IMPLEMENTATION OF FORWARD-LOOKING STRATEGIES: None indicated.

NOTES:

Women for Guatemala

USA

ADDRESS:

P.O. Box 53421, Washington, DC 20009, USA

EXECUTIVE OFFICER:	BRANCH OFFICES:
Maricela Vargas & Kay Studer, Co-coordinators	

TELEPHONE NUMBER:	TELEX NUMBER:
(202) 234-6037	

APPROX. STAFF SIZE:	VOLUNTEER STAFF:	YEAR ESTABLISHED:
4	10	1983

NUMBER OF INDIVIDUAL MEMBERS:

75

FUNDING: By foundations and personal contributions.

PRINCIPAL PURPOSE: To promote understanding among non-American women about the struggle of Guatemalan women and children. To generate a network of moral and active support for Guatemalan women. To link women of both countries in their common struggle for self-determination. To channel material help for refugee women in and outside Guatemala through groups that work for that cause.

MAIN ACTIVITIES: Compile and distribute information about Guatemalan women to women in the USA; publish a quarterly bulletin; sponsor tours of Guatemalan women; sponsor activities to awaken North-american interest and solicit aid.

POPULATION CONCERNS:

SPECIFIC POPULATION ACTIVITIES: Education, contraceptive research and research and provision of information on sterilization.

FORWARD-LOOKING STRATEGIES IMPLEMENTATIONS: Not Aware.

OBSTACLES TO THE IMPLEMENTATION OF FORWARD-LOOKING STRATEGIES:

NOTES:

The Women's Institute **USA**

ADDRESS:

P.O. Box 6005, Silver Spring, MD 20906, USA

EXECUTIVE OFFICER:			BRANCH OFFICES:
Rita Z. Johnson, President			

TELEPHONE NUMBER:	TELEX NUMBER:
(301)871-6106	

APPROX. STAFF SIZE:	VOLUNTEER STAFF:	YEAR ESTABLISHED:
	2	1975

NUMBER OF INDIVIDUAL MEMBERS:

FUNDING: Contributions and profits from conferences and seminars.

PRINCIPAL PURPOSE: To address the issues of the International Women's Year and the U.N. Decade for Women.

MAIN ACTIVITIES: Education through the publication of documents of interest to women, scholars and students.

POPULATION CONCERNS: Those relating to women's issues.

SPECIFIC POPULATION ACTIVITIES: Education.

FORWARD-LOOKING STRATEGIES IMPLEMENTATIONS: Publication of relevent materials.

OBSTACLES TO THE IMPLEMENTATION OF FORWARD-LOOKING STRATEGIES: None indicated.

NOTES:

*Business Address: ℅ D. Fields, Vice President, 13905 North Gate Drive, Silver Spring, MD 20906

Women's International Network

USA

187 Grant Street, Lexington, MA 02173

Fran P. Hosken, Editor

617-862-9431

APPROX. STAFF SIZE:	VOLUNTEER STAFF:	YEAR ESTABLISHED:
	Yes	1982

FUNDING: Subscriptions.

PRINCIPAL PURPOSE: Provides a worldwide open communication system by, for, and about women of all age groups, backgrounds, beliefs and nationalities.

MAIN ACTIVITIES: Publishes WIN news which disseminates information about worldwide status of women.

POPULATION CONCERNS: Women and Health is a special column that reports on family planning, nutrition, abortion, childbirth, fertility and more.

SPECIFIC POPULATION ACTIVITIES: Education.

FORWARD-LOOKING STRATEGIES IMPLEMENTATIONS: Through the dissemination of information about the strategies and the U.N. decade for women on a global basis.

OBSTACLES TO THE IMPLEMENTATION OF FORWARD-LOOKING STRATEGIES: Identifying sponsors for women's organizations in the Third World.

NOTES:

Women's Research and Education Institute of the Congressional Caucus for Women's Issues USA

ADDRESS:

1700 18th St., NW, Ste. 400, Washington, DC 20009

EXECUTIVE OFFICER:

Betty P. Dooley, Exec. Director

BRANCH OFFICES:

TELEPHONE NUMBER:

(202) 328-7070

TELEX NUMBER:

APPROX. STAFF SIZE:

6

VOLUNTEER STAFF:

YEAR ESTABLISHED:

1977

NUMBER OF INDIVIDUAL MEMBERS:

FUNDING:

PRINCIPAL PURPOSE: To channel sound research on women into the policymaking process.

MAIN ACTIVITIES: Research. Also administer a fellowship program for graduate students that places them in congressional offices or on congressional committees.

POPULATION CONCERNS: Concerned with virtually all issues that affect women and families.

SPECIFIC POPULATION ACTIVITIES: Demographic research.

FORWARD-LOOKING STRATEGIES IMPLEMENTATIONS: None.

OBSTACLES TO THE IMPLEMENTATION OF FORWARD-LOOKING STRATEGIES: None.

NOTES:

Women, Public Policy & Dev. Project of the Humphrey Institute of Public Affairs, University of MN　USA

ADDRESS:

Humphrey Center, 301 19th Avenue South, Minneapolis, MN 55455

EXECUTIVE OFFICER:	BRANCH OFFICES:
Arvonne S. Fraser, Senior Fellow and Project Director	

TELEPHONE NUMBER:	TELEX NUMBER:	
(612) 625-2505		

APPROX. STAFF SIZE:	VOLUNTEER STAFF:	YEAR ESTABLISHED:
8	1	1981

NUMBER OF INDIVIDUAL MEMBERS:

FUNDING: Grant from the Carnegie Corp. of New York; local Minnesota foundations; and individual donors.

PRINCIPAL PURPOSE: To monitor, analyze, and encourage law and policy reform in accordance with the principles of the U.N. Convention on the Elimination of All Forms of Discrimination Against Women.

MAIN ACTIVITIES: Serves as the international, non-governmental clearinghouse and source of information on the Convention and its implementation; monitor and support the work of CEDAW; help form, strengthen and assist national coalitions working on law and policy reform; provide technical guidelines for monitoring compliance; training education.

POPULATION CONCERNS: Education.

SPECIFIC POPULATION ACTIVITIES: Education.

FORWARD-LOOKING STRATEGIES IMPLEMENTATIONS: Forward-Looking Strategies are being implemented.

OBSTACLES TO THE IMPLEMENTATION OF FORWARD-LOOKING STRATEGIES:

NOTES:

Women's Studies Research Center

USA

ADDRESS:

University of Wisconsin, 209 North Brooks Street, Madison, WI 53715, USA

EXECUTIVE OFFICER:			BRANCH OFFICES:
Dr. Janet Hyde, Director			

TELEPHONE NUMBER:		TELEX NUMBER:	
(608)263-2051			

APPROX. STAFF SIZE:	VOLUNTEER STAFF:	YEAR ESTABLISHED:
2		1977

NUMBER OF INDIVIDUAL MEMBERS:

10

FUNDING: University of Wisconsin.

PRINCIPAL PURPOSE: To promote research on women and women's issues by faculty at the University of Wisconsin.

MAIN ACTIVITIES: Obtaining research grants for research on women, sponsoring a colloquium series and Honorary Fellows.

POPULATION CONCERNS: Research projects on motherhood and maternity leave issues.

SPECIFIC POPULATION ACTIVITIES: Education and research on social issues.

FORWARD-LOOKING STRATEGIES IMPLEMENTATIONS: Are not implementing the Strategies.

OBSTACLES TO THE IMPLEMENTATION OF FORWARD-LOOKING STRATEGIES: None.

NOTES:

World Federation of Methodist Women — **USA**

ADDRESS:

7100 Grey Oaks Drive, New Orleans, LA 70126

EXECUTIVE OFFICER:		BRANCH OFFICES:
Mrs. Edith Ming, President		

TELEPHONE NUMBER:	TELEX NUMBER:

APPROX. STAFF SIZE:	VOLUNTEER STAFF:	YEAR ESTABLISHED:
	4	1956

NUMBER OF INDIVIDUAL MEMBERS:

6,000,000

FUNDING: Contributions.

PRINCIPAL PURPOSE: To encourage members to grow in Christian experience and to use this commitment to serve men, women & children. To serve and educate at the national level and in developing countries through programs relating to development and women's and children's rights.

MAIN ACTIVITIES: Supporting representatives to U.N., holding conferences and seminars, supporting and organizing education and development programs.

POPULATION CONCERNS: Encouraging women and families to limit family size and use family planning programs.

SPECIFIC POPULATION ACTIVITIES: Education and Advocacy

FORWARD-LOOKING STRATEGIES IMPLEMENTATIONS:

OBSTACLES TO THE IMPLEMENTATION OF FORWARD-LOOKING STRATEGIES:

NOTES:

ZONTA INTERNATIONAL

USA

ADDRESS:

35 East Wacker Drive, Ste. 2040, Chicago, IL 60601

EXECUTIVE OFFICER:			BRANCH OFFICES:
Valerie F. Levitan, Exec. Director			

TELEPHONE NUMBER:		TELEX NUMBER:	
(312) 346-1445		190200UT	

APPROX. STAFF SIZE:	VOLUNTEER STAFF:	YEAR ESTABLISHED:	
17		1919	

NUMBER OF INDIVIDUAL MEMBERS:

35,000 approx.

FUNDING: Membership dues and fees and contributions.

PRINCIPAL PURPOSE: To improve the legal, political, economic and professional status of women and to work for the advancement of world understanding, goodwill and peace.

MAIN ACTIVITIES: To provide access to education and basic training for women and girls; to improve employment opportunities and conditions for women and girls; to support the world community of aging women and to improve the basic health of women and children.

POPULATION CONCERNS: Zonta believes that strategies aimed at improving the condition of the family should take into account the development and economy of a country, governmental policies and the status of women. In recognizing the family as a basic foundation of society, Zonta believes that women must be involved in making family planning decisions for themselves.

SPECIFIC POPULATION ACTIVITIES: Education, regular representation at meetings of The Population Institute and NGO committees on population and family issues and international service projects promoting the improved education and health of women and children.

FORWARD-LOOKING STRATEGIES IMPLEMENTATIONS: Zonta supports a number of income-generating projects for women in cooperation with the United Nations Development Fund for Women (UNIFEM). The projects are aimed at improving the living conditions, skills and health of women and their children. Zonta also works with aging women on a community level.

OBSTACLES TO THE IMPLEMENTATION OF FORWARD-LOOKING STRATEGIES: Ignorance of the specific, important issues affecting women. Education is a slow process, made up of victories and set-backs.

NOTES:

Population, Development & Health Organizations

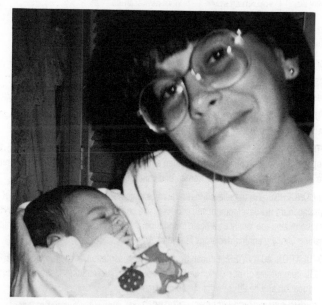

The Population Institute

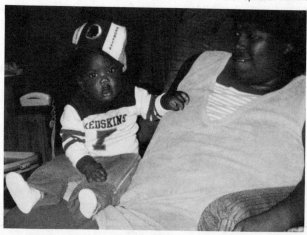

422 The Population Institute

EDPRA Consulting Inc.

CANADA

ADDRESS:

#803–200 Elgin Street, Ottawa Ontario Canada K2P 1L5

EXECUTIVE OFFICER:

Dr. Theodora Carroll-Foster, Vice President

BRANCH OFFICES:

TELEPHONE NUMBER:

(613)233-7731

TELEX NUMBER:

APPROX. STAFF SIZE: 8

VOLUNTEER STAFF:

YEAR ESTABLISHED: 1981

NUMBER OF INDIVIDUAL MEMBERS:

FUNDING: Fees & Grants.

PRINCIPAL PURPOSE: To provide sound population policy, research and analysis for public and private sectors. To develop, implement, monitor and evaluate population projects and programs.

MAIN ACTIVITIES: Research Studies and Briefs; Policy Development and Analysis; Project & Program Development; Management; Evaluation; Demographic Analysis.

POPULATION CONCERNS: The relationship of population to our global environment and sustainable development. The impact of religion on women, family planning and development.

SPECIFIC POPULATION ACTIVITIES: Education; Demographic Research; population projects development; population policy and analysis; community animation and participation; social marketing.

FORWARD-LOOKING STRATEGIES IMPLEMENTATIONS: Working with Canadian Governments (federal & provincial), womens organizations and NGO's (non-government orgs.) on issues under FLS paragraphs 156–159, which discuss a women's right to control her own fertility.

OBSTACLES TO THE IMPLEMENTATION OF FORWARD-LOOKING STRATEGIES: The unwillingness to consider or the lack of awareness among many donor agencies' staff of the interrelationships between environment, population and development issues, and the key role of women in all three.

NOTES:

ORGANIZATION:

Edmonton Board of Health

CANADA

ADDRESS:

500, 10216-124 Street, Edmonton T5N4A3, Canada

EXECUTIVE OFFICER:

BRANCH OFFICES:

TELEPHONE NUMBER:

(403) 482-1965

TELEX NUMBER:

APPROX. STAFF SIZE:

8

VOLUNTEER STAFF:

YEAR ESTABLISHED:

1969

NUMBER OF INDIVIDUAL MEMBERS:

FUNDING: Provincial government funding.

PRINCIPAL PURPOSE: Birth control information and services to young women.

MAIN ACTIVITIES: Clinical and educational services related to family planning.

POPULATION CONCERNS: Prevention of unwanted pregnancies.

SPECIFIC POPULATION ACTIVITIES: Education; contraceptive research; counselling; advocacy; delivery of services: pill, IUD, diapharm, foam, natural family planning.

FORWARD LOOKING-STRATEGIES IMPLEMENTATIONS:

OBSTACLES TO THE IMPLEMENTATION OF FORWARD-LOOKING STRATEGIES:

NOTES:

Global Citizens

CANADA

ADDRESS:

Box 49, Stanstead, Quebec JOB3E0

EXECUTIVE OFFICER:			BRANCH OFFICES:
Duncan Graham			

TELEPHONE NUMBER:		TELEX NUMBER:
(819) 876-5438		

APPROX. STAFF SIZE:	VOLUNTEER STAFF:	YEAR ESTABLISHED:
	1	1975

NUMBER OF INDIVIDUAL MEMBERS:

100

FUNDING: Donations and membership fees.

PRINCIPAL PURPOSE:

MAIN ACTIVITIES: 1986 promoting a study by the U.N. on the concept of a second house or chamber at the U.N. which would be democratically representative of the world community. Supporting a World Federalist, Canada legal action on nuclear weapons.

POPULATION CONCERNS: Family planning education as part of a World development package.

SPECIFIC POPULATION ACTIVITIES:

FORWARD LOOKING-STRATEGIES IMPLEMENTATIONS:

OBSTACLES TO THE IMPLEMENTATION OF FORWARD-LOOKING STRATEGIES:

NOTES:

Oxfam-Canada

CANADA

ADDRESS:

251 Laurier Avenue W., rm 301, Ottawa, Ontario, Canada, K1P 5J6

EXECUTIVE OFFICER:			BRANCH OFFICES:
Lawrence Cummings, National Secretary			

TELEPHONE NUMBER:		TELEX NUMBER:
613-237-5236		053-4358

APPROX. STAFF SIZE:	VOLUNTEER STAFF:	YEAR ESTABLISHED:
30	100	1963

NUMBER OF INDIVIDUAL MEMBERS:

FUNDING: Private contributions (mostly individuals). Projects receive matching contributions from government.

PRINCIPAL PURPOSE: To combat poverty, hunger and injustice in the world through development projects abroad and development education at home.

MAIN ACTIVITIES: Development projects, development education, public policy advocacy, fundraising in support of all of the above.

POPULATION CONCERNS: Mainly education programs around general public health and against use of Depo-Provera in Third World communities.

SPECIFIC POPULATION ACTIVITIES: Education.

FORWARD LOOKING-STRATEGIES IMPLEMENTATIONS: We are not implementing the Forward-Looking Strategies.

OBSTACLES TO THE IMPLEMENTATION OF FORWARD-LOOKING STRATEGIES: Not indicated.

NOTES:

Planned Parenthood
Newfoundland/Labrador

CANADA

ADDRESS:

203 Merrymeeting Rd., St. John's NFLD Canada

EXECUTIVE OFFICER:			BRANCH OFFICES:
Wendy Williams			

TELEPHONE NUMBER:		TELEX NUMBER:	
(709) 579-1009			

APPROX. STAFF SIZE:	VOLUNTEER STAFF:	YEAR ESTABLISHED:	
2	30	1972	

NUMBER OF INDIVIDUAL MEMBERS:	
100	

FUNDING: Donations and fees for services.

PRINCIPAL PURPOSE: To operate a birth control clinic.

MAIN ACTIVITIES: To operate a birth control clinic, information telephone line, and educational programmes.

POPULATION CONCERNS: Adolescent pregnancies.

SPECIFIC POPULATION ACTIVITIES: Education; counselling; delivery of services: Pill, IUD, diaphram, foam, and natural family planning.

FORWARD LOOKING-STRATEGIES IMPLEMENTATIONS: Not indicated.

OBSTACLES TO THE IMPLEMENTATION OF FORWARD-LOOKING STRATEGIES:

NOTES:

Sex Information and Education Council of Canada

CANADA

ADDRESS:

41 Marchmount Rd., Toronto, Ontario M6G 2A8, Canada

EXECUTIVE OFFICER:

Dr. Barry Martin, Executive Coordinator

BRANCH OFFICES:

TELEPHONE NUMBER:	TELEX NUMBER:
(416) 533-9029	

APPROX. STAFF SIZE:	VOLUNTEER STAFF:	YEAR ESTABLISHED:
1	0	1966

NUMBER OF INDIVIDUAL MEMBERS:

800

FUNDING: We are a non-profit organization funded by our membership dues.

PRINCIPAL PURPOSE:

MAIN ACTIVITIES: We publish a journal and a newsletter. We organize and present education workshops and seminars on various aspects of education, counselling, therapy and research.

POPULATION CONCERNS: Concerned with human sexuality. To promote, encourage and assist in public and professional education about sexuality.

SPECIFIC POPULATION ACTIVITIES: Education and counselling concerning methods of birth control: pill, IUD, diaphragm, foam, natural family planning.

FORWARD LOOKING-STRATEGIES IMPLEMENTATIONS: Unaware of strategies.

OBSTACLES TO THE IMPLEMENTATION OF FORWARD-LOOKING STRATEGIES:

NOTES:

Academy for Educational Development

USA

ADDRESS:

1255 23rd Street NW, Washington, DC 20037, USA

EXECUTIVE OFFICER:			BRANCH OFFICES:
Stephen Moseley			

TELEPHONE NUMBER:	TELEX NUMBER:
(202)862-1900	197601 ACADED WSH

APPROX. STAFF SIZE:	VOLUNTEER STAFF:	YEAR ESTABLISHED:
150		1962

NUMBER OF INDIVIDUAL MEMBERS:

FUNDING: USAID, foreign governments, foundations and other U.S. government agencies.

PRINCIPAL PURPOSE: To promote social development in the areas of education, population, health, training, agriculture and nutrition in less developed countries.

MAIN ACTIVITIES: Management and implementation of development projects in developing countries.

POPULATION CONCERNS: Operates several projects in the area of population and family planning.

SPECIFIC POPULATION ACTIVITIES: Education, contraceptive reseach and delivery of services.

FORWARD LOOKING-STRATEGIES IMPLEMENTATIONS: Are aware of the Strategies but did not indicate implementations.

OBSTACLES TO THE IMPLEMENTATION OF FORWARD-LOOKING STRATEGIES: None.

NOTES:

Africare, Inc.

USA

ADDRESS:

1601 Conn. Avenue N.W., Washington, DC 20009, USA

EXECUTIVE OFFICER:			BRANCH OFFICES:
C. Payne Lucas			

TELEPHONE NUMBER:		TELEX NUMBER:	
(202)462-3614			

APPROX. STAFF SIZE:	VOLUNTEER STAFF:	YEAR ESTABLISHED:	
80	3	1971	

NUMBER OF INDIVIDUAL MEMBERS:

FUNDING: Private donations and government aid.

PRINCIPAL PURPOSE: Private voluntary organization involved in rural development in Africa.

MAIN ACTIVITIES: Food, agriculture, rural health and refugee assistance. Water resource development and reforestation.

POPULATION CONCERNS: Improving the health of mothers and infants. Reducing the number of deaths associated with child bearing.

SPECIFIC POPULATION ACTIVITIES: Education, training of health workers in family planning services.

FORWARD LOOKING-STRATEGIES IMPLEMENTATIONS:

OBSTACLES TO THE IMPLEMENTATION OF FORWARD-LOOKING STRATEGIES:

NOTES:

African-American Institute (AAI) USA

ADDRESS:

833 United Nations Plaza, New York, NY 10017

EXECUTIVE OFFICER:	BRANCH OFFICES:
Amb. Donald Easum, Pres., Dr. Randolph Nugent, Chair. of Board	Branch offices located in Africa.

TELEPHONE NUMBER:	TELEX NUMBER:
(212) 949-5666	666-565

APPROX. STAFF SIZE:	VOLUNTEER STAFF:	YEAR ESTABLISHED:
60	5	1954

NUMBER OF INDIVIDUAL MEMBERS:

FUNDING: Funded by USAID, U.S. Department of State, Corporate contributers.

PRINCIPAL PURPOSE: To increase awareness about African development and about U.S.-African relations, and to respond to African development needs with concrete programs of assistance.

MAIN ACTIVITIES: Administering education and training programs. Administering international visitors programs. Publishing *African Report* organizing conferences, seminars and other forums for dialogue between African and American policy makers. Presenting exhibitions of African art.

POPULATION CONCERNS: The women in the African Development Program have organized workshops on healthcare in Africa, which have included discussions of reproductive health care.

SPECIFIC POPULATION ACTIVITIES: Education.

FORWARD LOOKING-STRATEGIES IMPLEMENTATIONS: Increasing number of educational opportunities for African women. Increasing attention given by African and American policy makers to women's issues. Disseminating information on Women in development to women's groups in Africa. Disseminating results of research on African women who have participated in AAI.

OBSTACLES TO THE IMPLEMENTATION OF FORWARD-LOOKING STRATEGIES: Lack of knowledge of what other U.S. non-governmental organizations are doing.

NOTES:

Alan Guttmacher Institute (AGI) **USA**

2010 Massachusetts Avenue, N.W., Washington, DC 20036, USA

EXECUTIVE OFFICER:			BRANCH OFFICES:
Jeannie I. Rosoff, President			

TELEPHONE NUMBER:	TELEX NUMBER:
(202) 296-4012	

APPROX. STAFF SIZE:	VOLUNTEER STAFF:	YEAR ESTABLISHED:
50	0	1974

NUMBER OF INDIVIDUAL MEMBERS:

FUNDING: Private foundations and contributions.

PRINCIPAL PURPOSE: Public information, education and advocacy concerning broad issues of reproductive health—domestically and internationally.

MAIN ACTIVITIES: Publications: *Family Planning Perspectives*—scientific journal, *Washington Memo*—biweekly newsletter.

POPULATION CONCERNS: Assuring policies that enhance access to safe, high quality, effective voluntary reproductive health services for those who want and need them in U.S. and through international population programs.

SPECIFIC POPULATION ACTIVITIES: Education, demographic research, contraceptive research and advocacy.

FORWARD LOOKING-STRATEGIES IMPLEMENTATIONS: We are implementing the FLS through public information and advocacy at the national level.

OBSTACLES TO THE IMPLEMENTATION OF FORWARD-LOOKING STRATEGIES: Unspecified.

NOTES:

The Asia Foundation USA

550 Kearny St., San Francisco, CA 94108

Dr. Haydn Williams, President

Box 7072 Airmail
Distribution Center
Manila International
Airport, THE PHILIPPINES

415-982-4640

50 | | 1954

FUNDING: Private, corporate, foundation, and government.

PRINCIPAL PURPOSE: To assist Asians in the growth and development of their own societies and strengthen Asian-American understanding, cooperation and friendship.

MAIN ACTIVITIES: The strengthening and assisting of Asian private voluntary organizations, professional societies and regional organizations in the fields of education and human resource development; law and judicial administration; public administration and civil service training; international relations studies programs; communications, publications and library development; private community development programs; business administration, management and private entrepreneurship.

POPULATION CONCERNS: Varies with country and funding.

SPECIFIC POPULATION ACTIVITIES:

FORWARD-LOOKING STRATEGIES IMPLEMENTATIONS:

OBSTACLES TO THE IMPLEMENTATION OF FORWARD-LOOKING STRATEGIES:

NOTES:

Association for Voluntary Surgical Contraception (AVSC)

USA

ADDRESS:

122 East 42nd Street, New York, New York 10168

EXECUTIVE OFFICER:			BRANCH OFFICES:
Hugo Hoogenboom			

TELEPHONE NUMBER:	TELEX NUMBER:	
(212) 531-2500		

APPROX. STAFF SIZE:	VOLUNTEER STAFF:	YEAR ESTABLISHED:
90		1943

NUMBER OF INDIVIDUAL MEMBERS:

FUNDING: USAID.

PRINCIPAL PURPOSE: AVSC seeks to make permanent contraceptions available to all adults on the basis of free and fully informed choice.

MAIN ACTIVITIES: International level: working toward making surgical contraception services a basic component of health programs throughout the world. Domestic level: education and information programs directed toward public and professional communities.

POPULATION CONCERNS: Public awareness which allows adults to make free and informed choices.

SPECIFIC POPULATION ACTIVITIES: Education, advocacy, contraceptive research, and sterilization.

FORWARD-LOOKING STRATEGIES IMPLEMENTATIONS: Place women in managerial positions and include women in planning process.

OBSTACLES TO THE IMPLEMENTATION OF FORWARD-LOOKING STRATEGIES: Obstacles of change and new cultures adapting.

NOTES:

ORGANIZATION:	
CARE	**USA**

ADDRESS:
660 First Avenue, New York, NY 10016, USA

EXECUTIVE OFFICER:	BRANCH OFFICES:
Dr. Philip Johnston	

TELEPHONE NUMBER:	TELEX NUMBER:
(212) 686-3110	

APPROX. STAFF SIZE:	VOLUNTEER STAFF:	YEAR ESTABLISHED:
225	5775 Int'l staff	1945

NUMBER OF INDIVIDUAL MEMBERS:

FUNDING: USAID, foreign governments, foundations and other U.S. government agencies.

PRINCIPAL PURPOSE: To promote social development in the areas of education, population, health, training, agriculture and nutrition in less developed countries.

MAIN ACTIVITIES: Management and implementation of development projects in developing countries.

POPULATION CONCERNS: Operates several projects in the area of population and family planning.

SPECIFIC POPULATION ACTIVITIES: Education, contraceptive research and delivery of services.

FORWARD LOOKING-STRATEGIES IMPLEMENTATIONS: Are aware of the Strategies but did not indicate implementations.

OBSTACLES TO THE IMPLEMENTATION OF FORWARD-LOOKING STRATEGIES: None.

NOTES:

Carolina Population Center

USA

University of North Carolina, University Square East, Chapel Hill, NC 27514-3397

EXECUTIVE OFFICER: J. Richard Udry, Director	BRANCH OFFICES:

TELEPHONE NUMBER: (919) 966-2157	TELEX NUMBER: 510 920 0766

APPROX. STAFF SIZE: 55	VOLUNTEER STAFF:	YEAR ESTABLISHED: 1966

NUMBER OF INDIVIDUAL MEMBERS:

FUNDING: United Institutes of Child Health and Human Development.

PRINCIPAL PURPOSE: Established to provide coordination for a university-wide program in population. Unlike academic departments, the Center does not admit students or award degrees but serves the University community through the facilitation of interdisciplinary and multidisciplinary research and research training.

MAIN ACTIVITIES: Holds a weekly research seminar designed to encourage and facilitate cross-disciplinary discussion and input to resolution of problems encountered at various stages in the conduct of research. Reports of new, on-going, and completed research projects of the center are distributed in the form of an annual report and in the CPC Working Paper Series.

POPULATION CONCERNS: Have been involved in projects on an international basis on topics such as population change; population policy; mortality, migration, and population distribution, fertility, contraception, abortion and sterilization; marriage, divorce and the family.

SPECIFIC POPULATION ACTIVITIES: Education.

FORWARD-LOOKING STRATEGIES IMPLEMENTATIONS:

OBSTACLES TO THE IMPLEMENTATION OF FORWARD-LOOKING STRATEGIES:

NOTES:

Center for Population Communications-International

USA

ADDRESS:

777 United Nations Plaza, New York, New York 10017

EXECUTIVE OFFICER:

David O. Poindexter

BRANCH OFFICES:

TELEPHONE NUMBER:

(212) 687-3366

TELEX NUMBER:

APPROX. STAFF SIZE:	VOLUNTEER STAFF:	YEAR ESTABLISHED:
6		1970

NUMBER OF INDIVIDUAL MEMBERS:

FUNDING: Private foundations and individuals.

PRINCIPAL PURPOSE: Seeks to foster cooperation on more effective use of broadcast and other media and to provide technical assistance to media professionals in developing countries.

MAIN ACTIVITIES: Provides coordination for the U.N. NGO community and technical assistance to media professionals.

POPULATION CONCERNS: International awareness of overpopulation.

SPECIFIC POPULATION ACTIVITIES: Education and advocacy.

FORWARD-LOOKING STRATEGIES IMPLEMENTATIONS: Implementation in a general way.

OBSTACLES TO THE IMPLEMENTATION OF FORWARD-LOOKING STRATEGIES: None.

NOTES:

Center for Population and Family Health of Columbia University

USA

ADDRESS:

60 Haven Avenue, B-3, New York, New York 10032, USA

EXECUTIVE OFFICER:			BRANCH OFFICES:
Dr. Allan Rosenfield			

TELEPHONE NUMBER:	TELEX NUMBER:
(212) 305-6960	

APPROX. STAFF SIZE:	VOLUNTEER STAFF:	YEAR ESTABLISHED:
100		1975

NUMBER OF INDIVIDUAL MEMBERS:

FUNDING: The center is funded by a variety of public agencies and private foundations, including among others, DHHS, USAID, New York Department of Health, Carnegie and Rockefeller foundations.

PRINCIPAL PURPOSE: To provide education and services, conduct research in maternal and child health and family planning in both international and domestic settings.

MAIN ACTIVITIES: International primary health care and family planning services and research in developing countries. Women's health services in Washington Heights area of NYC. Graduate degree program in public health.

POPULATION CONCERNS: CPFH is primarily concerned with issues of mortality and fertility as they affect women and children in the U.S. and overseas.

SPECIFIC POPULATION ACTIVITIES: Education; democratic research; advocacy; operations research; International training; delivery of services: sterilization, pill, IUD, diaphragm, foam, ORT, and other primary health care technologies.

FORWARD LOOKING-STRATEGIES IMPLEMENTATIONS: CPFH has long played an advocacy role in support of access to family planning information and services as a basic human right.

OBSTACLES TO THE IMPLEMENTATION OF FORWARD-LOOKING STRATEGIES: Conservative political attitudes toward family planning, particularly with regard to services for adolescents, are a continuing obstacle to ensuring access to quality services for all.

NOTES:

Center for Population Options

USA

ADDRESS:

1012 14th Street, NW, Suite 1200, Washington, DC 20005, USA

EXECUTIVE OFFICER:

Judith Senderowitz, Executive Director

BRANCH OFFICES:

TELEPHONE NUMBER:		TELEX NUMBER:
(202)347-5700		

APPROX. STAFF SIZE:	VOLUNTEER STAFF:	YEAR ESTABLISHED:
20	2	1980

NUMBER OF INDIVIDUAL MEMBERS:

FUNDING: Private foundations and individual contributions.

PRINCIPAL PURPOSE: Teenage pregnancy prevention.

MAIN ACTIVITIES: Works through education, research, media relations and public policy initiatives to reduce the incidence of unintended adolescent pregnancies. The International Clearinghouse on Adolescent Fertility (ICAF) collects and disseminates information on adolescent fertility programming worldwide to a broad network of organizations. Beginning in 1987, ICAF will support developing country projects through a small grants program and technical assistance.

POPULATION CONCERNS: Concerned with the impact that too-early childbearing has on the health and education of young women, on the well-being of children and on societies which must support the rapid population growth caused, in part by shortened time between generations resulting from adolescent pregnancies.

SPECIFIC POPULATION ACTIVITIES: Education and advocacy.

FORWARD LOOKING-STRATEGIES IMPLEMENTATIONS: ICAF's activities support all of the concerns emphasized in the Strategies through education, the provision of family planning services and support for public policy which encourages delayed childbearing.

OBSTACLES TO THE IMPLEMENTATION OF FORWARD-LOOKING STRATEGIES: None.

NOTES:

Committee to Defend Reproductive Rights

USA

ADDRESS:

2845 24th Street, San Francisco, CA 94110, USA

EXECUTIVE OFFICER:		BRANCH OFFICES:
Colette Patt & Sharon Page, Coordinators		

TELEPHONE NUMBER:	TELEX NUMBER:
(415) 826-2100	

APPROX. STAFF SIZE:	VOLUNTEER STAFF:	YEAR ESTABLISHED:
15	13	1977

NUMBER OF INDIVIDUAL MEMBERS:

600

FUNDING: Membership contributions and foundation support.

PRINCIPAL PURPOSE: To safeguard the reproductive rights and freedom of all women and men through grassroots organization on the local, state, and national level.

MAIN ACTIVITIES: Education and activism on women's reproductive rights and related issues.

POPULATION CONCERNS: Reproductive rights.

SPECIFIC POPULATION ACTIVITIES: Education and advocacy.

FORWARD-LOOKING STRATEGIES IMPLEMENTATIONS: Protection of reproductive rights.

OBSTACLES TO THE IMPLEMENTATION OF FORWARD-LOOKING STRATEGIES: None indicated.

NOTES:

Church World Service

USA

475 Riverside Drive, New York, New York 10115, USA

EXECUTIVE OFFICER:			BRANCH OFFICES:
J. Richard Butler			

TELEPHONE NUMBER:		TELEX NUMBER:
(212) 870-2426		

APPROX. STAFF SIZE:	VOLUNTEER STAFF:	YEAR ESTABLISHED:
60	2	1946

NUMBER OF INDIVIDUAL MEMBERS:

FUNDING: Contributions from Protestant and orthodox demoninations.

PRINCIPAL PURPOSE: Disaster, relief and rehabilitaion.

MAIN ACTIVITIES: Development programs involved with disaster relief, rehabilitation, refugees and immigration.

POPULATION CONCERNS:

SPECIFIC POPULATION ACTIVITIES: There is an office responsible for population, family planning and health care issues.

FORWARD LOOKING-STRATEGIES IMPLEMENTATIONS: Unspecified

OBSTACLES TO THE IMPLEMENTATION OF FORWARD-LOOKING STRATEGIES: The status of women in general especially in developing countries.

NOTES:

East-West Population Institute

USA

ADDRESS:

1777 East-West Road, Honolulu, HI 96848, USA

EXECUTIVE OFFICER:			BRANCH OFFICES:
Dr. Lee-Jay Cho			

TELEPHONE NUMBER:		TELEX NUMBER:	
(808)944-7444		230989171	

APPROX. STAFF SIZE:	VOLUNTEER STAFF:	YEAR ESTABLISHED:	
42		1969	

NUMBER OF INDIVIDUAL MEMBERS:	
373	

FUNDING: U.S. Information agency. U.S. Agency for International and Development. Private foundations and contracts.

PRINCIPAL PURPOSE: To develop and disseminate knowledge in the field of population.

MAIN ACTIVITIES: Conducts programs of research and professions; education on population with emphasis on the analysis of demographic trends, their social and economic causes and consequences, and their policy implications in Asia, The Pacific and the Unites States.

POPULATION CONCERNS: Population trends and demographics estimation. Fertility and the family in transition. Economic development and human resources. Urbanization, migration and development.

SPECIFIC POPULATION ACTIVITIES: Education and demographic research.

FORWARD LOOKING-STRATEGIES IMPLEMENTATIONS:

OBSTACLES TO THE IMPLEMENTATION OF FORWARD-LOOKING STRATEGIES:

NOTES:

Family Health International

USA

1 Triangle Drive, Research Triangle Park, North Carolina, 22709, USA

EXECUTIVE OFFICER:			BRANCH OFFICES:
Malcom Potts, President			

TELEPHONE NUMBER:		TELEX NUMBER:	
(919) 549-0517		579442	

APPROX. STAFF SIZE:	VOLUNTEER STAFF:	YEAR ESTABLISHED:	
125	0	1971	

NUMBER OF INDIVIDUAL MEMBERS:

FUNDING: U.S. Government contracts, foundation grants and individual donations.

PRINCIPAL PURPOSE: To increase the safety, effectiveness, acceptibility, and ease of using family planning methods, and to improve the delivery of voluntary fertility planning and primary health care services.

MAIN ACTIVITIES: Conducting, analyzing and disseminating research on contraception and distribution of family planning services; evaluating mother-child health programs and training clinical researchers and primary health care providers.

POPULATION CONCERNS: Availability of safe and effective contraceptives in order that every woman can chose the method that is most appropriate. We are concerned with maternal mortality during the reproductive years and how inadequate health care facilities and availability of contraceptive methods impact maternal mortality.

SPECIFIC POPULATION ACTIVITIES: Demographic research and contraceptive research. Delivery of services: sterilization, pill, IUD, diaphragm, foam, Norplant, Depo-Provera and natural family planning.

FORWARD LOOKING-STRATEGIES IMPLEMENTATIONS: Work to seek families benefits by assessing the long term safety of contraceptive methods.

OBSTACLES TO THE IMPLEMENTATION OF FORWARD-LOOKING STRATEGIES:

NOTES:

Global Committee of Parliamentarians on Population & Development

USA

ADDRESS:

304 E. 45th Street, (12th Flr), New York, NY 10017, USA

EXECUTIVE OFFICER:			BRANCH OFFICES:
Akio Matsumura			

TELEPHONE NUMBER:	TELEX NUMBER:	
(212)953-7947	4994118 GCPPD	

APPROX. STAFF SIZE:	VOLUNTEER STAFF:	YEAR ESTABLISHED:
8		1982

NUMBER OF INDIVIDUAL MEMBERS:

FUNDING: United Nations and other International agencies.

PRINCIPAL PURPOSE: To serve as a worldwide forum for parlimentarians interested in Population and development issues for the exchange of information and experience and to coordinate their activites accordingly.

MAIN ACTIVITIES: Forum for information exchange.

POPULATION CONCERNS: We are especially interested in the links between population and development and the way that parliamentarians can concretely act on making these links.

SPECIFIC POPULATION ACTIVITIES: Education and advocacy.

FORWARD LOOKING-STRATEGIES IMPLEMENTATIONS: Through our *Statement on Popualtion Stabilization by World Leaders*, we are directly implementing the paragraphs relevent to the population strategies.

OBSTACLES TO THE IMPLEMENTATION OF FORWARD-LOOKING STRATEGIES: We sometimes encounter difficulties to get the world leaders to sign the same statement without changing the wording and to understand that this is a document signifying consensus on the importance of population and development.

NOTES:

International Center for Training in Population and Family Health

USA

ADDRESS:

14130 W. 9th Street, Zion, Il. 60099, USA

EXECUTIVE OFFICER:			BRANCH OFFICES:
Andre Singleton, President			

TELEPHONE NUMBER:		TELEX NUMBER:	
(312) 746-8352			

APPROX. STAFF SIZE:	VOLUNTEER STAFF:	YEAR ESTABLISHED:	
4	0	1980	

NUMBER OF INDIVIDUAL MEMBERS:

FUNDING: Contracts and fees.

PRINCIPAL PURPOSE: INCENPFH is a private, minority-owned corporation organized to provide training, consultancy and technical assistance to government agencies and private organizations of developing countries in the following areas: 1)Family Planning 2)Adolescent fertility management 3)Population education 4)Program Planning and Development.

MAIN ACTIVITIES:

POPULATION CONCERNS: Adolescent fertility management.

SPECIFIC POPULATION ACTIVITIES: Education, counselling and program development.

FORWARD LOOKING-STRATEGIES IMPLEMENTATIONS:

OBSTACLES TO THE IMPLEMENTATION OF FORWARD-LOOKING STRATEGIES:

NOTES:

The International Child Resource Institute **USA**

1810 Hopkins Street, Berkeley, CA 94707

Ken Jaffe, Executive Director

TELEPHONE NUMBER:	TELEX NUMBER:
(415) 644-1000	

APPROX. STAFF SIZE:	VOLUNTEER STAFF:	YEAR ESTABLISHED:
7	5	1981

NUMBER OF INDIVIDUAL MEMBERS:

250

FUNDING: Foundations

PRINCIPAL PURPOSE: Information services and technical assistance to providers of services to children, women and families.

MAIN ACTIVITIES: Information services (computer based child resource information bank) and technical service.

POPULATION CONCERNS: Poor or disadvantaged children, families and women worldwide.

SPECIFIC POPULATION ACTIVITIES: Advocacy; information services; technical assistance to childrens programs e.g. childcare, child health, daycare.

FORWARD-LOOKING STRATEGIES IMPLEMENTATIONS:

OBSTACLES TO THE IMPLEMENTATION OF FORWARD-LOOKING STRATEGIES:

NOTES:

International Population Institute **USA**

ADDRESS:

6020 Rossmore Drive, Bethesda, Md 20814, USA

EXECUTIVE OFFICER:

Dr. Joseph A. Cavanaugh

BRANCH OFFICES:

TELEPHONE NUMBER:

(301) 530-0867

TELEX NUMBER:

APPROX. STAFF SIZE:	VOLUNTEER STAFF:	YEAR ESTABLISHED:
2	0	1975

NUMBER OF INDIVIDUAL MEMBERS:

FUNDING: Private funds.

PRINCIPAL PURPOSE: Promote substantial population decrease; discourage immigration; research in population dynamics in U.S.; provide technical assistance in foreign countries on population problems.

MAIN ACTIVITIES: Volunteer services in demography; preparation on book length manuscript on U.S. population problems and policies.

POPULATION CONCERNS: Population growth in the U.S. Population policies and their formulation. Urbanization in foreign countries.

SPECIFIC POPULATION ACTIVITIES: Demographic research.

FORWARD LOOKING-STRATEGIES IMPLEMENTATIONS: We are not implementing the FLS.

OBSTACLES TO THE IMPLEMENTATION OF FORWARD-LOOKING STRATEGIES:

NOTES:

Maricopa County Organizing Project

USA

ADDRESS:

12225 Grand Ave., El Mirge, AZ 85335

EXECUTIVE OFFICER:		BRANCH OFFICES:
Francisca Cavazos		

TELEPHONE NUMBER:	TELEX NUMBER:	

APPROX. STAFF SIZE:	VOLUNTEER STAFF:	YEAR ESTABLISHED:
5	2	1977

NUMBER OF INDIVIDUAL MEMBERS:	
50,000	

FUNDING: Private foundation.

PRINCIPAL PURPOSE: To protect and promote the civil rights of farm workers.

MAIN ACTIVITIES: Involved in pesticide and legal projects.

POPULATION CONCERNS: Concerned with those population issues that affect farm workers.

SPECIFIC POPULATION ACTIVITIES: Demographic research and natural family planning services.

FORWARD-LOOKING STRATEGIES IMPLEMENTATIONS: Involved in promoting the right to organize.

OBSTACLES TO THE IMPLEMENTATION OF FORWARD-LOOKING STRATEGIES: Political problems.

NOTES:

National Abortion Federation **USA**

ADDRESS:

900 Pennsylvania Avenue, S.E., Washington, DC 20003, USA

EXECUTIVE OFFICER:

Barbara Radford, Executive Director

BRANCH OFFICES:

TELEPHONE NUMBER:	TELEX NUMBER:
(202) 546-9060	

APPROX. STAFF SIZE:	VOLUNTEER STAFF:	YEAR ESTABLISHED:
7	0	1977

NUMBER OF INDIVIDUAL MEMBERS:

150

FUNDING: Foundation support, individual contributions, and membership dues.

PRINCIPAL PURPOSE: NAF is an organization of providers with a mission to preserve and enhance the quality and accessibility of abortion services.

MAIN ACTIVITIES: Education, Publications.

POPULATION CONCERNS: Ensuring Reproductive Freedom.

SPECIFIC POPULATION ACTIVITIES: Education; advocacy; referral to abortion providers.

FORWARD LOOKING-STRATEGIES IMPLEMENTATIONS:

OBSTACLES TO THE IMPLEMENTATION OF FORWARD-LOOKING STRATEGIES:

NOTES:

National Family Planning and Reproductive Health Association

USA

ADDRESS:

122 C Street, N.W., Suite 380, Washington, DC 20001, USA

EXECUTIVE OFFICER:			BRANCH OFFICES:
Scott R. Swirling, Executive Director			

TELEPHONE NUMBER:		TELEX NUMBER:	
(202) 628-3535			

APPROX. STAFF SIZE:	VOLUNTEER STAFF:	YEAR ESTABLISHED:	
8	0	1971	

NUMBER OF INDIVIDUAL MEMBERS:

982

FUNDING: Membership dues, foundations, and private contributions.

PRINCIPAL PURPOSE: To promote and protect the public commitment to comprehensive, high quality family planning and reproductive health care in the U.S. and abroad.

MAIN ACTIVITIES: Publish newsletter 10 times a year. Annual meeting of family planning professionals. Advocacy, government relations, lobbying, legislative alerts and 24 hour hotline. Monitor domestic and International family planning developments.

POPULATION CONCERNS: Family Planning, teenage pregnancy, infant mortality, contraceptive research, sexually transmitted diseases, maternal and child health.

SPECIFIC POPULATION ACTIVITIES: Education, litigation when necessary.

FORWARD LOOKING-STRATEGIES IMPLEMENTATIONS: NFPRHA works primarily to protect and enhance family planning services provided through Title X to the Public Health Service Act. The primary government-funded family planning program for low-income women.

OBSTACLES TO THE IMPLEMENTATION OF FORWARD-LOOKING STRATEGIES: A hostile Republican administration has attempted to undermine access to all methods of family planning for some women in need, especially teenagers. Also, some grassroots groups have attacked the national family planning program.

NOTES:

National Organization on Adolescent Pregnancy and Parenting

USA

ADDRESS:

P.O. Box 2365, Reston, VA 22090, USA

EXECUTIVE OFFICER:			BRANCH OFFICES:
Sharon Rodine, Director, Toni Brown, President			

TELEPHONE NUMBER:		TELEX NUMBER:
(703) 435-3948		

APPROX. STAFF SIZE:	VOLUNTEER STAFF:	YEAR ESTABLISHED:
Varies	20	1979

NUMBER OF INDIVIDUAL MEMBERS:

800

FUNDING: Government grants, foundations, corporate contributions.

PRINCIPAL PURPOSE: To provide a national membership-based network of medical, education and social service professionals, plus local, state and national leaders concerned with issues related to adolescent pregacy and parenting, including primary pregnancy prevention.

MAIN ACTIVITIES: Provide resources - sharing opportunities, newsletters, conferences and workshops. Coalition building and networking. Advocacy and public awareness.

POPULATION CONCERNS: Problems and consequences of unplanned adolescent pregnancy, early child-bearing and parenting for females and males. The significant "Costs" in terms of money and human potential. Education, technical assistance, program models and conferences.

SPECIFIC POPULATION ACTIVITIES: Education and Advocacy.

FORWARD LOOKING-STRATEGIES IMPLEMENTATIONS: None indicated.

OBSTACLES TO THE IMPLEMENTATION OF FORWARD-LOOKING STRATEGIES:

NOTES:

Office of Population Research, Princeton University

USA

ADDRESS:

21 Prospect Avenue, Princeton, NJ 08544, USA

EXECUTIVE OFFICER:

Charles F. Westoff, Director

BRANCH OFFICES:

TELEPHONE NUMBER:	TELEX NUMBER:
(609) 452-5510	

APPROX. STAFF SIZE:	VOLUNTEER STAFF:	YEAR ESTABLISHED:
10	0	1936

NUMBER OF INDIVIDUAL MEMBERS:

50

FUNDING: Foundations, university and goverment-grants.

PRINCIPAL PURPOSE: Demographic research and training.

MAIN ACTIVITIES: Research on fertility, mortality, nuptiality, demographic theory and teaching.

POPULATION CONCERNS: Research only.

SPECIFIC POPULATION ACTIVITIES: Education, demographic research, contraceptive research.

FORWARD LOOKING-STRATEGIES IMPLEMENTATIONS:

OBSTACLES TO THE IMPLEMENTATION OF FORWARD-LOOKING STRATEGIES:

NOTES:

The Population Council*

USA

One Dag Hammarskjold Plaza, New York, NY 10017, USA

George Zeidenstein, President

See apendix

(212)644-1300

200

1952

FUNDING: Grants and donations:

PRINCIPAL PURPOSE: To perform population research, advise and assist governments and international agencies and disseminate information on population issues.

MAIN ACTIVITIES: Research in three areas: biomedical, social science and family planning programs; publishing on population issues and support of advance training for population specialists.

POPULATION CONCERNS: Contraception, population growth and its relationship to family planning policies.

SPECIFIC POPULATION ACTIVITIES: Education, advocacy and the dissemination of information.

FORWARD LOOKING-STRATEGIES IMPLEMENTATIONS: None indicated.

OBSTACLES TO THE IMPLEMENTATION OF FORWARD-LOOKING STRATEGIES: None.

NOTES:

*Also listed in the Appendix.

Population Crisis Committee (PCC)

USA

1120 19th St., N.W., Suite 550, Washington, DC 20036

EXECUTIVE OFFICER:			BRANCH OFFICES:
J. Joseph Speidel, M.D.			

TELEPHONE NUMBER:		TELEX NUMBER:
(202) 659-1833		440450

APPROX. STAFF SIZE:	VOLUNTEER STAFF:	YEAR ESTABLISHED:
25	6	1965

NUMBER OF INDIVIDUAL MEMBERS:

FUNDING: Grants and individual donors

PRINCIPAL PURPOSE: Promote understanding and action to solve world population crisis.

MAIN ACTIVITIES: Public policy, education through media and publications, diplomatic liaison and special projects.

POPULATION CONCERNS: Focused on international population issues.

SPECIFIC POPULATION ACTIVITIES: Education and advocacy.

FORWARD-LOOKING STRATEGIES IMPLEMENTATIONS: Funding and advocacy for international Family Planning programs.

OBSTACLES TO THE IMPLEMENTATION OF FORWARD-LOOKING STRATEGIES: Current political climate.

NOTES:

ADDRESS:
110 Maryland Avenue, N.E., Suite 207, Washington, DC 20002

EXECUTIVE OFFICER:		BRANCH OFFICES:
Werner Fornos, President		Apartado Aereo 89112 Bogota, Columbia Phone: 236-7695

TELEPHONE NUMBER:	TELEX NUMBER:
(202) 544-3300	

Av. Fr. Rooseveloan
1050 Bruxelle, Brussel
Phone: 649-24.649

APPROX. STAFF SIZE:	VOLUNTEER STAFF:	YEAR ESTABLISHED:
20	5	1969

NUMBER OF INDIVIDUAL MEMBERS:
60,000

FUNDING: Private foundations and individual donors

PRINCIPAL PURPOSE: To educate U.S. public on Global overpopulation and foster leadership to resolve the problem.

MAIN ACTIVITIES: Publish monthly newspaper, *POPLINE*, coordinates U.S. citizens network. Launches individual World Population Days throughout the year and organizes World Population Awareness Week recognized annually in the United States and abroad.

POPULATION CONCERNS: International population and family planning issues, and the inter-relationship of population, the environment and the status of women.

SPECIFIC POPULATION ACTIVITIES: Education, Advocacy, Demographic Research.

FORWARD-LOOKING STRATEGIES IMPLEMENTATIONS: Dissemenation of information about population strategies and publication of global directory.

OBSTACLES TO THE IMPLEMENTATION OF FORWARD-LOOKING STRATEGIES: Ignorance and misconceptions among many U.S. citizens and government officials about population and women's issues. Present political climate in U.S.A. also contributes to some of these misconceptions.

NOTES:

Population Reference Bureau, Inc. (PRB)   USA

Suite 800, 777 14th Street, N.W., Washington, DC 20005

Thomas W. Merrick, Ph.D.

(202) 639-8040

31   1929

FUNDING: Private contributions, memberships, publication sales, and contracts.

PRINCIPAL PURPOSE: Gathers, interprets, and disseminates information on the facts and implications of national and global population trends.

MAIN ACTIVITIES: Educational material, organizes conferences, seminars, workshops, operates reference library and offers consultant services.

POPULATION CONCERNS: Population awareness.

SPECIFIC POPULATION ACTIVITIES: Regular publications: Population Bulletin, Population Today, the Population Data Sheet and U.S. Population Data sheet wall charts; the Population Trends and Public Policy Series: and interchange newsletter and teachers guide IMPACT (Innovative Materials for Population Action).

FORWARD-LOOKING STRATEGIES IMPLEMENTATIONS: Implementation in a general way.

OBSTACLES TO THE IMPLEMENTATION OF FORWARD-LOOKING STRATEGIES: None.

NOTES:

Population Services International

USA

ADDRESS:

1030 15th Street, NW, Suite 330, Washington, DC 20005, USA

EXECUTIVE OFFICER: William P. Schellstede	**BRANCH OFFICES:**

TELEPHONE NUMBER:	TELEX NUMBER:
(202)789-1551	197885 PSIW-UT

APPROX. STAFF SIZE:	VOLUNTEER STAFF:	YEAR ESTABLISHED:
10		1970

NUMBER OF INDIVIDUAL MEMBERS:

FUNDING: Contracts and grants from private foundations and donor organizations contributions.

PRINCIPAL PURPOSE: International family planning.

MAIN ACTIVITIES: Delivery of non-clinical contraceptives through contraceptive social marketing.

POPULATION CONCERNS: Promotion of contraceptives through advertising. Delivery of non-clinical contraceptives.

SPECIFIC POPULATION ACTIVITIES: Education; advertising and promotion; delivery of services: Pill, Noristerat, condom, ORS, vaginal tablets, safe delivery kits.

FORWARD LOOKING-STRATEGIES IMPLEMENTATIONS: Ongoing motivational campaigns on benefits of family planning generally and specific non-clinical product information, distribution of ORT.

OBSTACLES TO THE IMPLEMENTATION OF FORWARD-LOOKING STRATEGIES: Government attitudes that hinder advancement of new project activities; funding limitations for new project implementation.

NOTES:

Population Studies & Training Center, Brown University

USA

ADDRESS:

Box 1916 Maxcy Hall, Providence, RI 02912, USA

EXECUTIVE OFFICER:	BRANCH OFFICES:
Dr. Sidney Goldstein, Director	

TELEPHONE NUMBER:	TELEX NUMBER:
(401)863-2668	

APPROX. STAFF SIZE:	VOLUNTEER STAFF:	YEAR ESTABLISHED:
20		1965

NUMBER OF INDIVIDUAL MEMBERS:

40

FUNDING: Brown University, grants from National Institute of Child Health and Human development, Ford Foundation and William and Flora Hewlett Foundation. The American Express Foundation and the National Institute on Aging.

PRINCIPAL PURPOSE: To facilitate and strengthen research and graduate training in Population studies.

MAIN ACTIVITIES: Research by faculty and trainees on population issues in the United States and developing countries.

POPULATION CONCERNS: Demographic variables - fertility, mortality and migration. Migration, urbanization, population change, ethnicity, and demographic behavior. Family and demographic research.

SPECIFIC POPULATION ACTIVITIES: Demographic research & Education.

FORWARD LOOKING-STRATEGIES IMPLEMENTATIONS:

OBSTACLES TO THE IMPLEMENTATION OF FORWARD-LOOKING STRATEGIES:

NOTES:

Program for the Introduction and Adaptation of Contraceptive Technology (PIACT)

USA

ADDRESS:

4 Nickerson Street, Seattle, WA 98109, USA*

EXECUTIVE OFFICER:			BRANCH OFFICES:
Gordon W. Perkin, MD			P.O. Box 981MT

TELEPHONE NUMBER:	TELEX NUMBER:
(206) 285-3500	4740049 PATHUI

Jakarta Pusat
Indonesia

P.O. Box 22-36
Ramindra, Bankok
Thailand

APPROX. STAFF SIZE:	VOLUNTEER STAFF:	YEAR ESTABLISHED:
70	1	1976

NUMBER OF INDIVIDUAL MEMBERS:

FUNDING:

PRINCIPAL PURPOSE: To improve the availability, effectiveness, safety, and acceptance of contraceptive and health products in developing countries.

MAIN ACTIVITIES: Research and development. Field studies. Information, education, and communication. Technology transfer.

POPULATION CONCERNS: Delivery of services through technical assistance.

SPECIFIC POPULATION ACTIVITIES: Education.

FORWARD LOOKING-STRATEGIES IMPLEMENTATIONS: In a general way.

OBSTACLES TO THE IMPLEMENTATION OF FORWARD-LOOKING STRATEGIES:

NOTES: *WASHINGTON OFFICE
1990 M Street, N.W.
Suite 720
Washington, D.C. 20036
Tele: (202) 822-0033

The Population Resource Center   **USA**

ADDRESS:

622 Third Ave., New York, New York 10017

EXECUTIVE OFFICER:			**BRANCH OFFICES:**
Irving S. Friedman Ph.D.			110 Maryland Ave., N.E. Suite 302
TELEPHONE NUMBER:		**TELEX NUMBER:**	Washington, D.C. 20002
(212) 687-6020			(202) 546-5030
APPROX. STAFF SIZE:	**VOLUNTEER STAFF:**	**YEAR ESTABLISHED:**	
10		1975	
NUMBER OF INDIVIDUAL MEMBERS:			

FUNDING: Private foundations, corporations, individuals and The Population Association of America.

PRINCIPAL PURPOSE: Resource for officials in government, corporations and the nonprofit sector on the relationship between demographic trends and socioeconomic policy issues.

MAIN ACTIVITIES: Briefing and analyses for policymakers.

POPULATION CONCERNS: Demographic trends and socioeconomic policy issues.

SPECIFIC POPULATION ACTIVITIES: Education.

FORWARD-LOOKING STRATEGIES IMPLEMENTATIONS: Aware.

OBSTACLES TO THE IMPLEMENTATION OF FORWARD-LOOKING STRATEGIES: None.

NOTES:

TransAfrica

USA

545 8th Street, S.E., Suite 200, Washington, DC 20003

EXECUTIVE OFFICER:			BRANCH OFFICES:
Randall Robinson, Executive Director			

TELEPHONE NUMBER:		TELEX NUMBER:	
(202)547-2550			

APPROX. STAFF SIZE:	VOLUNTEER STAFF:	YEAR ESTABLISHED:	
12	3	1975	

NUMBER OF INDIVIDUAL MEMBERS:

FUNDING: Foundation support and private donations.

PRINCIPAL PURPOSE: Black American lobby, research and educational group on foreign policy in Africa and the Carribean.

MAIN ACTIVITIES: Lobby work; research; writing and publications.

POPULATION CONCERNS: Dissemination of information about women and population.

SPECIFIC POPULATION ACTIVITIES: Education.

FORWARD LOOKING-STRATEGIES IMPLEMENTATIONS: Attaining the full freedom and self determination of women and children under apartheid, and meeting development goals.

OBSTACLES TO THE IMPLEMENTATION OF FORWARD-LOOKING STRATEGIES: U.S. public lack of knowledge of the issues and the failure of policymakers to see political benefit for their support of these issues.

NOTES:

FUNDING: Mostly through contracts and partly by member schools of Public Health.

PRINCIPAL PURPOSE: Contribute to the health of the people of U.S. and the world.

MAIN ACTIVITIES: Technical assistance and training in health and population programs.

POPULATION CONCERNS: The relationship between population and health; population and development; policy issues.

SPECIFIC POPULATION ACTIVITIES: Education and training. Technical assistance and consulting.

FORWARD LOOKING-STRATEGIES IMPLEMENTATIONS: We are implementing the FLS by teaching graduate students and in developing agencies policies.

OBSTACLES TO THE IMPLEMENTATION OF FORWARD-LOOKING STRATEGIES: There is a tendency for some health professionals to narrowly define the field and to avoid dealing with women's education and literacy which seems the most important variable to health and population programs.

NOTES:

World Federation of Health Agencies for the Advancement of Voluntary Surgical Contraception USA

ADDRESS:

122 East 42nd Street, New York, NY 10168, USA

EXECUTIVE OFFICER:

Ms. Beth S. Atkins

BRANCH OFFICES:

TELEPHONE NUMBER:	TELEX NUMBER:
(212)351-2525	425604 AVS-UI

APPROX. STAFF SIZE:	VOLUNTEER STAFF:	YEAR ESTABLISHED:
6		1975

NUMBER OF INDIVIDUAL MEMBERS:

FUNDING: Major Source of funding is U.S. Agency for International Development. This is supplemented by private donations and membership dues.

PRINCIPAL PURPOSE: The Federation provides a unifying forum for its members to set policies and standards relevant to various aspects of voluntary surgical contraception programs. It also provides a means of communication with other international organizations which are working in the public health and family planning movement.

MAIN ACTIVITIES: Works with local, national, regional and international organizations to include voluntary surgical contraception as a method of fertility management; examines social and medical issues related to voluntary surgical contraception and encourages interaction and discussion among health and family planning agencies; develops within countries a leadership base of key professionals in positions to influence policy and bring about changes.

POPULATION CONCERNS: The federation pursues activities designed to promote worldwide recognition and use of voluntary surgical contraception by both professionals and individuals in their fertility management decisions.

SPECIFIC POPULATION ACTIVITIES: Education, advocacy, sterilization and Norplant.

FORWARD LOOKING-STRATEGIES IMPLEMENTATIONS: Working to increase women's roles as service providers and policy makers in the voluntary surgical contraception field; working to prevent maternal morbidity and mortality by encouraging use of effective family planning.

OBSTACLES TO THE IMPLEMENTATION OF FORWARD-LOOKING STRATEGIES: Obstacles are widespread and the impetus provided by the women's decade is no longer apparent.

NOTES:

World Vision International

USA

ADDRESS:

919 West Huntington Drive, Monrovia, Ca. 91016

EXECUTIVE OFFICER:			BRANCH OFFICES:
Rev. Thomas Houston, President			

TELEPHONE NUMBER:	TELEX NUMBER:	
(818) 303-8811	67-5341	

APPROX. STAFF SIZE:	VOLUNTEER STAFF:	YEAR ESTABLISHED:
300		1978

NUMBER OF INDIVIDUAL MEMBERS:

4,269

FUNDING: Contributions from individuals and organizations.

PRINCIPAL PURPOSE: The Key Objective of World Vision's ministry of children and families is to find the most needy children and families, enlist the most appropriate sponsors and donors, and manage the resources released to meet the most need in the best way at the least cost.

MAIN ACTIVITIES: Relief and development in the Third World.

POPULATION CONCERNS: World Vision has accepted the Primary Health Care Alma Alta Declaration and approach, including the concern for accessible and affordable safe family planning options. It recognizes the inherent social limitations resulting from a population growth rate which is beyond the ability of the local government to properly service its population. Individual project decisions on family planning are decentralized to Regional and Country Advisors.

SPECIFIC POPULATION ACTIVITIES: Education, and Counseling. Individual family planning activity is based on the decisions of Regional and Country PHC advisors working in collaboration with the MOH. Family planning activities are not a major activity of our programs.

FORWARD-LOOKING STRATEGIES IMPLEMENTATIONS: Yes. Child Spacing is encouraged in most health projects. Delivery of family commodities is usually left to the local Ministry of Health, with World Vision health workers referring women. Health education on the importance of child spacing, is always performed in collaboration with local MOH.

OBSTACLES TO THE IMPLEMENTATION OF FORWARD-LOOKING STRATEGIES: Organizationally, family planning is not a high priority objective. Family planning falls under our "Health Sector" which in turn falls under the "Ministering to Children and Families" and "Developing Self Reliance" objectives.

NOTES:

Worldwatch Institute

USA

1776 Massachusetts Avenue, NW, Washington, DC 20036, USA

Lester R. Brown

(202) 452-1999

APPROX. STAFF SIZE:	VOLUNTEER STAFF:	YEAR ESTABLISHED:
16	0	1974

FUNDING: Fifty-five percent from publication sales and the remainder is from foundations, donations and corporations.

PRINCIPAL PURPOSE: Research and publication on issues dealing with economic, demographic and natural resources and social trends. Both a worldwide and regional focus.

MAIN ACTIVITIES: Research, publication and outreach.

POPULATION CONCERNS: Economic and ecological connections to population growth rates and population size. Relationship between health, income and agriculture.

SPECIFIC POPULATION ACTIVITIES: Demographic research and contraceptive research.

FORWARD LOOKING-STRATEGIES IMPLEMENTATIONS: We are implementing the FLS within the realm of our publications.

OBSTACLES TO THE IMPLEMENTATION OF FORWARD-LOOKING STRATEGIES: Unspecified.

NOTES:

Zero Population Growth

USA

ADDRESS:

1601 Connecticut Avenue, NW, Washington, DC 20009, USA

EXECUTIVE OFFICER:

Susan Weber, Executive Director

BRANCH OFFICES:

TELEPHONE NUMBER:	TELEX NUMBER:
(202)332-2200	

APPROX. STAFF SIZE:	VOLUNTEER STAFF:	YEAR ESTABLISHED:
12		1968

NUMBER OF INDIVIDUAL MEMBERS:

20,000

FUNDING: Approximately 80% by membership dues and contributions, and 20% by private foundations.

PRINCIPAL PURPOSE: ZPG works to stabilize population growth and to restore a sustainable balance between people, resources, and the environment both in the U.S. and worldwide.

MAIN ACTIVITIES: Publications; teacher training; Government relations; media education.

POPULATION CONCERNS: Development of a Sustainable Society.

SPECIFIC POPULATION ACTIVITIES: Public education; Advocacy.

FORWARD LOOKING-STRATEGIES IMPLEMENTATIONS: Not indicated.

OBSTACLES TO THE IMPLEMENTATION OF FORWARD-LOOKING STRATEGIES:

NOTES:

Women's Organizations

Dick Mathews

The Population Institute

ORGANIZATION:

Emunah Women of Canada

CANADA

ADDRESS:

5775 Victoria Av., Rm. 107, Montreal, Quebec, H3W 2R4 CANADA

EXECUTIVE OFFICER:			BRANCH OFFICES:
Roslyn Schneidman			

TELEPHONE NUMBER:		TELEX NUMBER:	
514-735-3919			

APPROX. STAFF SIZE:	VOLUNTEER STAFF:	YEAR ESTABLISHED:
4		

NUMBER OF INDIVIDUAL MEMBERS:

FUNDING: Donations and membership fees.

PRINCIPAL PURPOSE: To strengthen religious consciousness. To provide social care and religious and secular education for children and young people.

MAIN ACTIVITIES: Programs for education and entertainment. Leadership seminars and fundraising events.

POPULATION CONCERNS: None.

SPECIFIC POPULATION ACTIVITIES: None.

FORWARD-LOOKING STRATEGIES IMPLEMENTATIONS: None.

OBSTACLES TO THE IMPLEMENTATION OF FORWARD-LOOKING STRATEGIES: None.

NOTES:

Ontario Native Women's Association   CANADA

ADDRESS:

278 Bay Street, Thunder Bay 'P', Ontario, Canada P7B 1R8

EXECUTIVE OFFICER:			BRANCH OFFICES:
Shirley O'Conner, President			

TELEPHONE NUMBER:	TELEX NUMBER:
(807) 345-9821 or 6862	

APPROX. STAFF SIZE:	VOLUNTEER STAFF:	YEAR ESTABLISHED:
5	1	1972

NUMBER OF INDIVIDUAL MEMBERS:

varied

FUNDING: Provincial Core Funding

PRINCIPAL PURPOSE: The main concern of the Association is the presevation and promotion of native Indian culture, language and heritage.

MAIN ACTIVITIES: Employment coordination; representation and advocacy; research; leadership training; summer employment program for Students; Information Services; Public Relations; Legislative Interpretation; Justice Development Program; Youth Corps Internship; Community Organizational Development Training Program.

POPULATION CONCERNS:

SPECIFIC POPULATION ACTIVITIES:

FORWARD-LOOKING STRATEGIES IMPLEMENTATIONS: Not implementing and unaware of strageties.

OBSTACLES TO THE IMPLEMENTATION OF FORWARD-LOOKING STRATEGIES:

NOTES:

ORGANIZATION:	
Church Women United	**USA**

ADDRESS:

475 Riverside Drive, Rm. 812, New York, NY 10115

EXECUTIVE OFFICER: Doris A. Younger, Director	BRANCH OFFICES:

TELEPHONE NUMBER: (212) 870-2359	TELEX NUMBER:

APPROX. STAFF SIZE: 20	VOLUNTEER STAFF: 2-3	YEAR ESTABLISHED: 1941

NUMBER OF INDIVIDUAL MEMBERS:

1500 affiliated chapters

FUNDING: Contributions.

PRINCIPAL PURPOSE: To unite women of different religious beliefs.

MAIN ACTIVITIES: Ecumenical celebrations and a variety of actions.

POPULATION CONCERNS: The welfare of women and children.

SPECIFIC POPULATION ACTIVITIES: None.

FORWARD-LOOKING STRATEGIES IMPLEMENTATIONS: CWU is implementing the Bill of Rights for Women.

OBSTACLES TO THE IMPLEMENTATION OF FORWARD-LOOKING STRATEGIES:

NOTES:

Coalition for Women in International Development

USA

ADDRESS:

2101 L St., NW, Ste. 916, Washington, DC 20037

EXECUTIVE OFFICER:

Nancy Rubin, Chair

BRANCH OFFICES:

TELEPHONE NUMBER:

(202) 466-3430

TELEX NUMBER:

APPROX. STAFF SIZE:	VOLUNTEER STAFF:	YEAR ESTABLISHED:
112		1976

NUMBER OF INDIVIDUAL MEMBERS:

150

FUNDING:

PRINCIPAL PURPOSE: To inform and influence United States policymakers about issues affecting women and their families in the developing world. To mobilize support throughout the U.S. for policies that recognize women as partners in both the work and the benefits of development.

MAIN ACTIVITIES: Information-sharing, quarterly luncheon meetings.

POPULATION CONCERNS: Any concerns that are related to the purpose described.

SPECIFIC POPULATION ACTIVITIES: None.

FORWARD-LOOKING STRATEGIES IMPLEMENTATIONS: None.

OBSTACLES TO THE IMPLEMENTATION OF FORWARD-LOOKING STRATEGIES: None.

NOTES:

Ecumenical Women's Center

USA

ADDRESS:

5253 N. Kenmore Av., Chicago, IL 60640

EXECUTIVE OFFICER:			BRANCH OFFICES:
Ms. Elizabeth Okayama			

TELEPHONE NUMBER:	TELEX NUMBER:	
312-728-1850		

APPROX. STAFF SIZE:	VOLUNTEER STAFF:	YEAR ESTABLISHED:
1	1	1972

NUMBER OF INDIVIDUAL MEMBERS:

400

FUNDING: Allocations from church denominations, individual and organizational memberships, subscriptions to newsletter, and contributions.

PRINCIPAL PURPOSE: The Ecumenical Women's Center addresses social justice issues of concern to women in the church and society through education, advocacy and service.

MAIN ACTIVITIES: Referral service for counselling, employment and crisis situations; Computer Data Base of services and resources for women in prison on a national scale; resources for women and men in the church: inclusive Language Hymnal, Songbook, and Meditation Book.

POPULATION CONCERNS: None.

SPECIFIC POPULATION ACTIVITIES: None.

FORWARD-LOOKING STRATEGIES IMPLEMENTATIONS: None.

OBSTACLES TO THE IMPLEMENTATION OF FORWARD-LOOKING STRATEGIES:

NOTES:

ORGANIZATION:

"Forward-Looking" Strategies Committee
*UNA-USA Midpenisula Chapter

USA

ADDRESS:

552 Emerson Street, Palo Alto, CA 94301

EXECUTIVE OFFICER:			BRANCH OFFICES:
Laddie Hughes, Chairperson			

TELEPHONE NUMBER:		TELEX NUMBER:	
(415) 494-1352			

APPROX. STAFF SIZE:	VOLUNTEER STAFF:	YEAR ESTABLISHED:
3 Com. mem.		1982

NUMBER OF INDIVIDUAL MEMBERS:

FUNDING: Charge for public meetings, grant from the Skaggs Foundation.

PRINCIPAL PURPOSE: Emphasize the role of the U.N. as an advocate in advancing the status of women. Promote ratification by the U.S. of the U.N. Convention on the Elimination of All Forms of Discrimination against women.

MAIN ACTIVITIES: Hold public meetings with expert speakers on various women's issues. Disseminate information on the U.N. convention. Developed a survey "Progress of Women Towards Full Equality" for use by local women's groups.

POPULATION CONCERNS: Concerned with those child-bearing and child-rearing issues that hinder women in achieving equality with men.

SPECIFIC POPULATION ACTIVITIES: None.

FORWARD-LOOKING STRATEGIES IMPLEMENTATIONS: Individual committee members are working on different issues. One promotes the participation of women in science and engineering. Another ran for a local congressional seat.

OBSTACLES TO THE IMPLEMENTATION OF FORWARD-LOOKING STRATEGIES: Lack of funds for projects and cultural attitudes related to women's role in the workforce.

NOTES:

*United Nations Association

International Women's Tribune Centre

USA

ADDRESS:

777 UN Plaza, New York, NY 10017

EXECUTIVE OFFICER:			BRANCH OFFICES:
Dr. Anne G. Walker, Exec. Director			

TELEPHONE NUMBER:	TELEX NUMBER:
(212) 687-8633	

APPROX. STAFF SIZE:	VOLUNTEER STAFF:	YEAR ESTABLISHED:
	8	1976

NUMBER OF INDIVIDUAL MEMBERS:

FUNDING:

PRINCIPAL PURPOSE: To ensure that women in Third World countries have the information, training technology and tools they need to become active participants in development plans, policies and projects.

MAIN ACTIVITIES: Provide educational and training materials in French, Spanish, and English to 14,000 individuals and groups working on behalf of women in 160 countries.

POPULATION CONCERNS: No direct population concerns.

SPECIFIC POPULATION ACTIVITIES:

FORWARD-LOOKING STRATEGIES IMPLEMENTATIONS: IWTC is developing a community action resource manual based on the Forward-Looking Strategies to assist community activists working at the local level.

OBSTACLES TO THE IMPLEMENTATION OF FORWARD-LOOKING STRATEGIES: Lack of awareness among women regarding the Strategies and how they can use them in their own activities.

NOTES:

National Federation of
Business and Professional Women's Clubs **USA**

ADDRESS:

2012 Mass. Ave., NW, Washington, DC 20036

EXECUTIVE OFFICER:			BRANCH OFFICES:
Irma F. Brosseau			

TELEPHONE NUMBER:		TELEX NUMBER:	
(202) 293-1100			

APPROX. STAFF SIZE:	VOLUNTEER STAFF:	YEAR ESTABLISHED:	
26		1919	

NUMBER OF INDIVIDUAL MEMBERS:

140,000

FUNDING:

PRINCIPAL PURPOSE: To promote equal rights and economic self-sufficiency for working women.

MAIN ACTIVITIES: BPW/USA helps women assume civic leadership positions and prominence in the workplace. Under the guidance of a national legislative platform, BPW advocates legislation supporting working women.

POPULATION CONCERNS: Concerned with those population issues that are important to women who work outside the home.

SPECIFIC POPULATION ACTIVITIES: None.

FORWARD-LOOKING STRATEGIES IMPLEMENTATIONS: BPW enacted a resolution at the July 1986 convention calling for a national plan in the U.S. to promote the Strategies. It also resolved that each State Federation appoint a chairperson to develop ways to implement the Strategies in their states.

OBSTACLES TO THE IMPLEMENTATION OF FORWARD-LOOKING STRATEGIES: None.

NOTES:

Women's International League for Peace and Freedom

USA

ADDRESS:

1213 Race St., Philadelphia, PA 19107

EXECUTIVE OFFICER:			BRANCH OFFICES:
Anne Ivey, President			

TELEPHONE NUMBER:		TELEX NUMBER:	
(215) 563-7110			

APPROX. STAFF SIZE:	VOLUNTEER STAFF:	YEAR ESTABLISHED:
10-15	10+	

NUMBER OF INDIVIDUAL MEMBERS:

FUNDING: Membership dues.

PRINCIPAL PURPOSE: To promote equality of all people in a world free of racism and sexism and to build constructive peace through world disarmament. To change social priorities to meet human needs.

MAIN ACTIVITIES: Promoting grassroots action and social change toward the above goals.

POPULATION CONCERNS: None.

SPECIFIC POPULATION ACTIVITIES: None.

FORWARD-LOOKING STRATEGIES IMPLEMENTATIONS: Working for peace and freedom.

OBSTACLES TO THE IMPLEMENTATION OF FORWARD-LOOKING STRATEGIES: None.

NOTES:

Women Strike for Peace

USA

ADDRESS:

145 S. 13th Street, Room 706, Philadelphia, PA 19107

EXECUTIVE OFFICER:			BRANCH OFFICES:
Ethel Taylor			

TELEPHONE NUMBER:	TELEX NUMBER:
(215) 923-0861	

APPROX. STAFF SIZE:	VOLUNTEER STAFF:	YEAR ESTABLISHED:
7	20	

NUMBER OF INDIVIDUAL MEMBERS:

FUNDING: Members and contributors.

PRINCIPAL PURPOSE: To educate and lobby on the issues of nuclear disarmament and non-intervention and to empower women to start the process of change where they live.

MAIN ACTIVITIES: Lobby; produce newsletters and educational materials; hold rallies, demonstrations and conferences; work in coalitions; develop specific campaigns around current arms control and disarmament issues.

POPULATION CONCERNS: It is hoped that by diverting money from military uses to human needs, the status of women and children will improve.

SPECIFIC POPULATION ACTIVITIES: None.

FORWARD-LOOKING STRATEGIES IMPLEMENTATIONS: Working to promote the Strategy that calls for women's unpaid labor in the home and in agriculture to be included in national GNP's.

OBSTACLES TO THE IMPLEMENTATION OF FORWARD-LOOKING STRATEGIES: There is no evidence that governments take this idea seriously.

NOTES:

APPENDIX:
Suggestions for Further Information

International Planned Parenthood Federation (IPPF) International Office

IPPF, which has been a leader in private world-wide efforts in family planning, is an international federation of autonomous national family planning associations (FPAs) in 121 countries dedicated to the belief that knowledge of family planning is a basic human right and that a balance between the population of the world and its natural resources is a necessary condition of human happiness, prosperity and peace.

The IPPF encourages the formation of national associations to pioneer family planning services in each country of the world and to bring about a favorable climate of public opinion in which governments can be persuaded to accept responsibility. Family planning associations offer contraceptive services, set and maintain high clinical standards, train all levels of personnel, and carry out education programmes to inform and teach people about the personal health, social and economic benefits of family planning.

Regents College Inner Circle
Regent's Park
London NW 1 4NS
England

Telephone: 468-0741
Cable: IPEPEE LONDONSW1
Telex: 919573 IPEPEE LDN

IPPF Regional Bureaus are located in London at the International Office. Field Offices can be reached at the addresses below:

AFRICA REGION

Kenya
IPPF Field Office
P.O. Box 30234
Nairobi

Telex: 22703 INFED
Tele: 720280

Senegal
IPPF Field Office
BP 1553
109 Rue Carnot X Denain
Dakar

Telex: 3393 DAKAFIL
Tele: 223952/223749

Swaziland
IPPF Field Office
Box A 30
Mbabane

Telex: 2242 WD
Tele: 4331

Togo
IPPF Field Office
BP 4101
Lome

Telex: 5046
Tele: 210716

WESTERN HEMISPHERE REGION

USA
IPPF Regional Field Office
105 Madison Avenue (30th Street)
New York, NY 10016

Telex: 620661
Tele: (212)679 2230

EAST & SOUTHEAST ASIA & OCEANIA REGION

Malaysia
IPPF Field Office
246 Jalan Ampang
Kuala Lumpur 16-03

Telex: 30638

INDIAN OCEAN REGION

Nepal
IPPF Field Office
P.O. Box 3274
GA 2-979 Battisputali
Kathmandu 1
Telex: 2270

ARAB WORLD REGION

Jordan
IPPF Field Office
P.O. Box 926520
Amman
Telex: 23046

Egypt
IPPF Field Office
P.O. Box 113
Giza
Telex: 21537 CSUN
Tele: 724330

Local Offices are located on the
following pages.

AFGHANISTAN
Afghan Family Guidance Association
P.O. Box 545
Kabul
Cable: FAMILYGUIDE
Tele: 22659

ARGENTINA
Asociacion Argentina de Proteccion Familiar
Aguero 1566/1568
1425 Buenos Aires
Tele: 821-4990
      821-6155

AUSTRALIA
The Australian Federation of Family Planning
   Associations
Suite 603, 6th Floor
Roden Cutler House
24 Campbell Street
Sydney NSW 2000
Tele: 211 1944

AUSTRIA
Osterreichische Gesellschaft fur Familienplanung
Universitatsfrauenklinik II
Spitalgasse 23
A-1090 Wien
Tele: 4800/2942

BOLIVIA
Centro de Orientacion Familiar
Edificio Guadalquivir
Oficina No. 106, Primer Piso
Mezzanine, Avenida 20 de Octubre
esq. Rosen Gutierrez
Casilla Expresa 7522
La Paz
Tele: 370 405
      358 348

BOTSWANA
MCH/FP Family Health Unit
Ministry of Health
P.O. Box 992
Gaborone
Telex: 2345 BOOTH BD
Attention: Family Health Unit

BRAZIL
Sociedade Civil de Bem Estar Familiar Brasil
   (BEMFAM)
Rua Esmeraldino Banderia 120
Na Estacao do Riachuelo
CEP 20961 Engemho Novo
Rio de Janeiro
Telex: 2130634 BEMF BR
Cable: SOBEMFA
Tele: 261-6658
      261-2499
      201-9849/201-6212

BULGARIA
Family Development Council of Bulgaria
Institute of Obstetrics & Gynecology
Medical Academy
Zdrave Street 2
Sofia 1431
Telex: 22797 RES VIT BG

CANADA
Planned Parenthood Federation of Canada
   (PPFC)
151 Slater Street, Suite 200
Ottawa, Ont. K1P 5H3
Cable: FAMPLAN
Tele: 238-4474

CARIBBEAN
Caribbean Family Planning Affiliation
P.O. Box 419
St. Mary's Street
St. John's
Antigua
Telex: 2145 CWTXAGY AK
Tele: 24170
      24171

CHILE

Asociacion Chilena de Proteccion de la Familia
Casilla 16504, Correo 9—Providencia
Avenida Santa Maria 0494
Santiago de Chile

Cable: APROFA
Tele: 370478
    371307
    371384

CHINA, PEOPLE'S REPUBLIC OF

China Family Planning Association
2 Nan Chun Cheng Street
Xi Zhi Men
Beijing

Cable: FPASSO

COLOMBIA

Asociacion Pro-Bienestar de la Familia
Colombiana (PROFAMILIA)
Calle 34, No. 14-52
Bogota

Cable: PROFAMILIA
Tele: 287-2100

COSTA RICA

Asociacion Demografica Costarricense
Apartado Postal 10203
Paseo Colon No. 1811
    Frente al Hospital Nacional de Ninos)
San Jose

Cable: ASDECO
TELEX: 2604 ASDECO
Tele: 225629

CUBA

Sociedad Cientifica Cubana para el Desarrollo de
    la Familia (SOCUDEF)
Calle 4 Numero 307
E/ 3a. y 5a. Miramar
La Habana

CYPRUS

Family Planning Association of Cyprus
Boumboulina Street 25
Nicosia

Telegraphis: FAMPLAN
Tele: 42093

DENMARK

Foreningen for Familieplanlaegning
Aurehojvej 2
2900 Hellerup

Tele: 625688

DOMINICAN REPUBLIC

Asociacion Dominicana
Pro-Bienestar de la Familia, Inc.
Apartado Postal 1053
Calle Socorro Sanchez No. 64
Zona Postal 1
Santo Domingo DN

Cable DOMBIEFA
Tele: 689 2723
    682 9611

ECUADOR

Asociacion Pro-Bienestar de la Familia
    Ecuatoriana
Apartado Postal 5954
Noguchi 1516 y Letamendi
Guayaquil

Cable: APROFE
Tele: 400386/406957

EGYPT, ARAB REPUBLIC OF

Egyptian Family Planning Association
5 Talaat Harb Street
Cairo

Cable: GEFPLAN
Telex: 92000 MERZ UN
Tele: 32742

EL SALVADOR

Asociacion Domografica Salvadorena
Apartado Postal 06 1338
19 Calle Poniente 4
7a Avenida Norte
Edificio K
San Salvador

Cable: DEMOSAL
Tele: 266 206
    266 313
    266 413
    266 618

ETHIOPIA

Family Guidance Association of Ethiopia
P.O. Box 5716
Addis Ababa

Cable: BETESEB
Tele: 154111
    154368

FIJI

Family Planning Association of Fiji
P.O. Box 619
Suva

Cable: FAMPLAN
Tele: 23091/25543

FINLAND

Vaestoliitto
Kalevankatu 16
00100 Helsinki 10

Tele: 640 235

FRANCE
Mouvement Francais pour le Planning Familial
4 Square St-Irenee
75011 Paris

Tele: 807 2910

GAMBIA
Family Planning Association of The Gambia
P.O. Box 325
Kanifing
Banjul

Cable: FAMPLANASS
Tele: Sava Kunda 2463

GERMAN DEMOCRATIC REPUBLIC
Ehe und Familie
Sektion der Gesellschaft fur sozialhygiene der
  DDR
Leninallee
25 Rostock

Tele: 37261/396943

GERMANY, FEDERAL REPUBLIC OF
Pro Famailia: Deutsche Gesellschaft
Sexualbergtung und Familienplanung e.v.
Cronstettendstrasse 30
6 Frankfurt am Main 1

Tele: 550901

GHANA
Planned Parenthood Association of Ghana
P.O. Box 5756
Accra

Cable: PPAGHANA
Tele: 27073

GRENADA
Grenada Planned Parenthood Association
P.O. Box 127
Scott Street
St. George's

Cable: GPPA
Tele: 2636

GREECE
The Family Planning Association
c/o 137 Vas.Sophias Avenue
Athens 618

Tele: 6438100

GUATEMALA
Asociacion Pro-Bienstar de la Familia de
  Guatemala (APROFAM)
Apartado Postal 1004
9a Calle 0-57
Zona 1
Ciudad de Guatemala

Cable: ASOFAMGUA
Tele: 29188
     81586
     81069

HONDURAS
Asociacion Hondurena de Planificacion de la
  Familia
Apartado Postal 625
Avenida Principal entre:
Colonias Alameda y Ruben Dario
Tegucigalpa DC

Cable: ASHONPLAFA
Telex: 1395 APLAMF HO
Tele: 323959
     323225
     326449

HONG KONG
Family Planning Association of Hong Kong
184–192 Lockhart Road, 3/F
Hong Kong

Cable: FAMPLAN
Tele: 5-754477

HUNGARY
Hungarian Scientific Society for Family and
  Women's Welfare
Buday Laszlo u. 1–3
1024 Budapest

Tele: 351-576

INDIA
Family Planning Association of India
Bajaj Bhavan
Nariman Point
Bombay 400 021

Cable: FAMPLAN
Telex: 4428 CBCO IN
     2589
Tele: 202 9080/202 5174

INDONESIA
The Indonesian Planned Parenthood Association
P.O. Box 18 KBYB
Jalan Hang Jebat III/F.3
Kebayoran Baru
Jakarta Selatan

Cable: IPPA
Tele: 775903
     775904

IRAQ
The Iraq Family Planning Association
P.O. Box 6028
Maari Street
Mansour City
Baghdad

Cable: ALMANSOUR
Tele: 37575

IRELAND
Irish Family Planning Association
15 Mountjoy Square
Dublin 1

Tele: 740 723

ISRAEL

Israel Family Planning Association
P.O. Box 11595
66 Bograshov Street
Tel-Aviv 63429

Tele: 281228
    63429

ITALY

Unione Italiana Centri Educazione Matrimoniale e
    Prematrimoniale
Via Eugenio Chiesa 1
20122 Milano

Tele: 783915

JAMAICA

Jamaica Family Planning Association Ltd.
P.O. Box 92
14 King Street
St. Ann's Bay

Cable: JFPA
Tele: 9722515

JAPAN

Family Planning Federation of Japan, Inc.
Hoken Kaikan Bekkan
1-1 Sadohara-Cho
Ichigaya, Shinjuku-ku
Tokoyo 162

Cable: FAMPLAF
Tele: 262 2101

JORDAN

Jordan Family Planning and Protection
    Association (West Bank)
P.O. Box 19999
Jerusalem

Tele: 83636

Jordan Family Planning and Protection
    Association (East Bank)
Jabel El Hussein
Khalid Ibn El Waleed Street
P.O. Box 8066
Amman

Cable: FAMPLAN
Tele: 30139

KENYA

Family Planning Association of Kenya
P.O. Box 30581
Nairobi

Cable: FAMPLAN
Tele: 28029
    25695/22125

KIRIBATI

Family Planning Association of Kiribati
c/o Ministry of Health & Family Planning
P.O. Box 268
Bikenibeu
Tarawa

Cable: MEDICAL BIKENIBEU

KOREA, REPUBLIC OF

Planned Parenthood Federation of Korea
CPO Box 3360
Seoul

Cable: PPFKOREA
Tele: 634 5152
    8211/2

LEBANON

P.O. Box 118240
Corniche Mazraa
Al Maskan Building
Beirut

Telex: 43390 LFPA
Tele: 311978

LESOTHO

Lesotho Planned Parenthood Association
P.O. Box 340
Maseru

Tele: 23645/326278

LIBERIA

Family Planning Association of Liberia
P.O. Box 938
Monrovia

Cable: FPAL
Tele: 262008/262243

LUXEMBOURG

Mouvement Luxembourgeois pour le Planning
    Familial et l'Education
    Sexuelle
18–20 rue Glesener
Luxembourg-Ville

Tele: 53931

MADAGASCAR, DEMOCRATIC REPUBLIC OF

Fianakaviana Sambatra
BP 703
Tananarive

Telex: 22519 KOBAMA FISA
Tele: 24498

MALAYSIA, WEST

Federation of Family Planning Associations,
    Malaysia
81A Jalan SS 15/5A
Subang Jaya
Selangor

Tele: 769409

MALAYSIA SABAH
Sabah Family Planning Association
P.O. Box 1361, Jalan Kabajikan
Kota Kinabalu
Sabah
East Malaysia

Cable: SAFAPA
Tele: 55202

MALAYSIA-SARAWAK
Sarawak Family Planning Association
P.O. Box 788 (Jalan Jawa) Kuching
Sarawak
East Malaysia

Cable: SAFAPA KUCHING
Tele: 24629
     26982

MALI
Association Malienne pour la Protection et la
   Promotion de la Famille
BP 105
Bamako

Telex: 992 AMPPF
Tele: 224494

MARTINIQUE
AMIOF
125–127 Rue Moreau de Jonnes
Fort-de-France
Martinique, FWI

MAURITIUS
The Mauritius Family Planning Association
30 Sir Seewoosagur Ramgoolam Street
Port Louis

Telex: 4364
Tele: 08316/084184/082784

MEXICO
Fundacion Mexicana para Planificacion Familiar
Calle Juarez 208
Tlalpan
Mexico 22 DF

Cable: FEPAC
Tele: 5737268
    5737070/5737100

MONTSERRAT
Montserrat Planned Parenthood Association
P.O. Box 118
Haney Street
Plymouth

Tele: 2736

MOROCCO
Association Marocaine de la Planification
   Familiale
P.O. Box 1217
6 Ion El-Cadi
Quartier des Orangers
Rabat R.P.

Cable: FAMPLAN
Telex: 32833 AMPFM
Tele: 20362

NEPAL
Family Planning Association of Nepal
P.O. Box 486
Katmandu

Cable: NEPFAPLAS
Telex: 2307 FPAN NP
Tele: 13107/15497/15534/15961

NETHERLANDS
Rutgers Stichting
Correspondence:
   Postbus 17430, 2502 CK
   s'Gravenhage
Street Address:
   Groot Hertoginnelaan 201
   2517 ES, s'Gravenhage

Tele: 631750

ARUBA
Foundation for the Promotion of Responsible
   Parenthood
P.O. Box 269
Bernhardstraat 75
San Nicholas

Cable: FAMIA PLANEA
Tele: 48833

CURACAO
Foundation for the Promotion of Responsible
   Parenthood
Parllelweg 38
Julianadorp

Cable: PLANFAM
Tele: 611487
    611323

ST. MAARTEN
Foundation for the Promotion of Responsible
   Parenthood
Section St. Maarten
P.O. Box 322
Philipsburg

Tele: 22818

NEW ZEALAND
The New Zealand Family Planning Association,
Inc.
P.O. Box 68200
214 Karangahape Road
Newton
Auckland 1

Cable: FAMPLAN

NICARAGUA
Asociacion Demografica Nicaraguense
Apartado Postal 4220
Iglesia del Carmen 1 Cuadra al Norte y una
Cuadra Abajo
Managua

Cable: ADNIC
Tele: 25967
25303
22588

NIGERIA
Planned Parenthood Federation of Nigeria
PMB 12657
Lagos

Cable: PLANFED
Tele: 960129
960133

NORWAY
Norsk Forening for Familieplanlaegging
c/o Kari Kromann
Department of Social Medicine
Rikshopitalet
Pilestredet
Oslo 1

Cable: NORAD, OSLO
Telex: 16548 NORAD-N
Tele: 22 2077

PAKISTAN
Family Planning Association of Pakistan
Family Planning House
3-A Temple Road
Lahore

Cable: FAMPLANAS
Tele: 21299

PANAMA
Asociacion Panamena para el Planeamiento de la
Familia
Apartado Postal 4637
Edificio Multifamiliar No. 2a
Panama 5

Cable: APLAFA
Tele: 67 1990
67 0181/2

PAPUA NEW GUINEA
Family Planning Association of Papua New
Guinea
Correspondence:
P.O. Box 7123, Boroko
Street Address:
Bombax Street, Hohola

Tele: 255112/21299

PARAGUAY
Centro Paraguayo de Estudios de Poblacion
Edificio ''El Dorado'' 8o piso
Juan E. O'Leary y Manduvira
Asuncion

Cable: CEPEP
Tele: 44842

PERU
Instituto Peruano de Paternidad Responsible
(INPARES)
Casilla Postal 2191
Gregorio Escobedo 115
Jesus Maria
Lima

Telex: 20339 PE CP
Tele: 233296

PHILIPPINES
Family Planning Organization of the Philippines,
Inc.
Correspondence:
P.O. Box 1279, Manila
Street Address:
50 Dona M. Hemady St.
New Manila
Quezon City
Metro Manila

Cable: FOPPHIL
Tele: 721-40-67
721-73-02
721-71-01

POLAND
Towarzystwo Rozwoju Rodziny
U1. Karowa 31
Warsaw

Tele: Warsaw 268825

PORTUGAL
Associacao para o Planeamento da Familia
Rua Artilharia Um, 38-2o, Dto.
1200 Lisbon
Tele: 653993

PUERTO RICO

Asociacion Puertorriquena Pro-Bienestar de la
   Familia
Apartado Postal 2221
Calle Padre las Casas No. 117
El Vedado
Hato Rey
Puerto Rico 00919

Cable: ASOPROFAM
Tele: 765 7373
     765 7374
     765 7350
     765 7304
     765 7341

REUNION

Association Orientation Familiale du Departement
   de la Reunion (AROF)
BP 93
5 rue des Marguiers
Saint Denis 97400

ROMANIA

Filantropia Hospital
Bucharest

RWANDA

Office National de la Population (ONAPO)
BP 914
Kigali

ST. KITTS-NEVIS

St. Kitts-Nevis Family Planning Association
P.O. Box 358
Basseterre

Tele: 3230

ST. LUCIA

St. Lucia Planned Parenthood Association
32 Victoria Street
Castries

Cable: PARENTHOOD
Tele: 4335

ST. VINCENT

St. Vincent Planned Parenthood Association
P.O. Box 99
Victoria Park (West)
Kingstown

Cable: VINPLAM
Tele: 61793

SENEGAL

Association Senegalaise pour le Bien-Etre
   Familial
BP 6084
Dakar

Tele: 227602

SEYCHELLES

Seychelles Family Planning Association
P.O. Box 590
Mahe

SIERRA LEONE

Planned Parenthood Association of Sierra Leone
P.O. Box 1094
22 Pultney Street
Freetown

Tele: 22774

SINGAPORE

Family Planning Association of Singapore
Singapore Council of Social Service Building
11 Penang Lane, #05-02
Singapore 0923

Tele: 338 5155

SOLOMON ISLANDS

Solomon Islands Planned Parenthood
   Association
P.O./ Box 554
Honiara

Tele: 22991

SOMALIA

Somali Family Health Care Association
P.O. Box 3783
Mogadishu

SOUTH AFRICA

Family Planning Association of South Africa
412 York House
46 Kerk Street
Johannesburg 2001

Tele: 838-1440
    834-3981

SRI LANKA

Family Planning Association of Sri Lanka
P.O. Box 365
37/27 Bullers Lane
Colombo 7

Cable: FAMPLAN
Telex: 2238 TRUST CE 'attention FPA'
Tele: 84157
    84203
    84269

SUDAN

Sudan Family Planning Association
P.O. Box 170
Khartoum

Cable: FAMPLAN
Tele: 43460

SURINAM

Stichting LOBI
P.O. Box 9267
Fajalobiestraat 13
Paramaribo

Cable: LOBI
Tele: 97111—Office
    99304
    77311—Clinic

SWAZILAND
Ministry of Health
P.O. Box 5
Mbabane

Family Life Association of Swaziland
P.O. Box 1051
Manzini

SWEDEN
Riksforbundet for Sexuell Upplysning
Box 17006
Rosenlundsgatan 13
Stockholm 17

Tele: 680940

SWITZERLAND
Familienplanungstelle
Universitatsfrauenklinik
4000 Basel

Centre Medico-Social de Pro Familia
Avenue Georgette 1
1003 Lausanne

Centre d'information familiale et de regulation
des naissances
47 Boulevard de la Cluse
1205 Geneva

SYRIA
Syrian Family Planning Association
P.O. Box 2282
Al Jala Street
Saegh Building 25
Damascus

Cable: FAMPLAN
Tele: 330714

TAHITI
Comite pour le Planning Familial de la Polynesie
"Te Utuafare Oaoa"
c/o Service d'Hygiene Terrotorial de la Polynesie
Francaise
Papeete

Mouvement Polynesien pour le Planning Familial
BP 676
Papeete

TAIWAN
Family Planning Association
No. 1 Lane
160 Fu Hsin South Road
Sec. 2
Taipei

TANZANIA
UMATI (Uzazi Na Malezi Bora Tanzania)
P.O. Box 1372
Dar es Salaam

Cable UMATI
Tele: 28424

THAILAND
Planned Parenthood Association of Thailand
Street Address:
No. 8 Soi Dai Dee
Vibhavadi-Rangsit
Super Highway
Lard-Yao
Bangkhen
Bangkok 9
Postal Address:
P.O. Box 1658
Bangkok

Cable: PATTHAI BANGKOK 10900
Telex: c/o KATRON TH81154
Tele: 579 1665
579 2231
579 00846

TOGO
Association Togolaise pour le Bien-Etre Familial
BP 4056
Lome

Cable: ATBEF
Tele: 4193

TONGA
Tonga Family Planning Association
P.O. Box 1142
Nuku'alofa

Tele: 21-209

TRINIDAD & TOBAGO
Family Planning Association of Trinidad &
Tobago
141 Henry Street
Port-of-Spain

Cable: PLANFAM
Tele: 34764
35576

TUNISIA
Association Tunisienne du Planning Familial
9 rue Essouyouti
El Menzeh
Tunis

Cable: FAMPLAN
Tele: 232141

TURKEY
Turkiye Aile Planlamasi Dernegi
Atac Sokak No. 73/3
Ankara

Tele: 318355

TUVALU
National Family Planning Association of Tuvalu
c/o Ministry of Social Services
Health Division, Box 41
Funafuti

UGANDA

Family Planning Association of Uganda
P.O. Box 30030
Kampala

Tele: 58300
    30260

UNITED KINGDOM

Family Planning Association
27-35 Mortimer Street
London W1N 7RJ

Tele: 636 7866

UNITED STATES

Planned Parenthood Federation of America Inc.
  (PPFA)
810 Seventh Avenue
New York, NY 10019

Cable: PARNTHOOD
Tele: 541 7800

US VIRGIN ISLANDS

Virgin Islands Family Planning Association
P.O. Box 9816
49-50 Kogens-Gade
St. Thomas 00801

Tele: 774 3163
    774 2150
    774 2652

UPPER VOLTA

Association Voltaique pour le Bien-etre Familial
BP 535
Ouagadougou

Tele: 34256

URUGUAY

Asociacion Uruguaya de Planificacion Familiar e
  investigaciones sobre Reproduccion Humana
  (AUPFIRH)
Correspondence:
  Casilla de Correo
  No. 10.634
  Distrito 1
  Montevideo
Street Address:
  Br. Artigas 1550
  Hospital Pereira
  Rossell
  Montevideo

Cable: AUPFIRH
Tele: 7853328

VANUATA, REPUBLIC OF

(formerly New Hebrides)
Family Planning Association of Vanuatu
P.O. Box 611
Port Vila (New Hebrides)

VENEZUELA

Ministerio de Sanidad y Asistencia Social
Edificio Administradora Union
Avenida Este 2
Los Caobos
Caracas

VIETNAM, SOCIALIST REPUBLIC OF

Vietnam Gynaecological, Obstetrical and Family
  Planning Association (VINAGOFPA)
43 Trang thi Street
Hanoi

WESTERN SAMOA

Western Samoa Family Health Association
Private Bag
Post Office
Apia

YEMEN, ARAB REPUBLIC OF

P.O. Box 795
Near Ministry of Information
Sana'a

Telex: 2421 PAN YE
Tele: 78044

YEMEN, PEOPLE'S DEMOCRATIC REPUBLIC OF

Yemeni Council for Family Care
P.O. Box 4589
Aden

Cable: GEELL
Tele: 53122

YUGOSLAVIA

Family Planning Council of Yugoslavia
Bulevar Lenjina 6
11070 Belgrade

Tele: 631 931

ZAIRE

Comite National des Naissances Desirables
BP 15.313
Kinshasa

Tele: 26170

ZAMBIA

Planned Parenthood Association of Zambia
P.O. Box 32221
Lusaka

Cable: PLAPAZA
Tele: 217613
    217437

ZIMBABWE

The Child Spacing and Fertility Association
P.O. Box ST220
Southerton
Harare

THE PATHFINDER FUND

ADDRESS: The Pathfinder Fund
#9 Galen Street
Suite #217
Watertown, MA 02172-4561
617/924-7200

The Pathfinder is a public, non-profit foundation to encourage innovative solutions to population problems. Its objectives are to 1) introduce and spread the acceptance of effective family planning and contraceptive services; 2) explore new methods to accelerate that acceptance; and 3) find new ways to overcome obstacles impeding progress toward stabilization of world population. Pathfinder is known for its willingness to take risks when required for the sake of a creative action, to invest in energetic people with new ideas, and to be flexible in responding to new opportunities.

Pathfinder does not conduct its own projects. Instead, the members of Pathfinder's international staff—a worldwide network of professionals, native to their areas of geographic responsibility—seek out men, women, organizations, governmental and non-governmental agencies who are ready to act but need help to get started. Pathfinder provides the necessary funds, technical and material assistance, support for training and other aid to get these vital programmes in action. Pathfinder's projects are implemented by three divisions: 1) Family Planning Division; 2) Women's Programs Division; 3) Population Policy Division.

Latin America:
(North)
The Pathfinder Fund
Avenida Chile No. 9-55 Of. 703
Apartado Aereo No. 051142
Bogota, D.E. Colombia, S.A.

(South)
Parque Meliton Porras 345
Miraflores
Post Office Box 563
Lima 18, Peru

Brazil:
Av. Magalhaes Neto, s/n
Centro Empresarial Iguatemi
Sala 812 A
40.000 Salvador
Bahia, Brazil
South America

Mexico:
Insurgentes Sur 753-13
Mexico 18 D.F.
CP 03100

AFRICA & THE MIDDLE EAST
Sub-Sahara:
The Pathfinder Fund
Post Office Box 48147
Nairobi, Kenya

Turkey:
The Pathfinder Fund
Mehtap Sokak 6/7
Goztepe/Istanbul, Turkey

Nigeria:
The Pathfinder Fund
3 Albai Street off Toyin Street
Post Office Box 55481
Juli-Ikeja
Lagos, Niegeria

ASIA & EGYPT
Bangladesh:
The Pathfinder Fund
House No. 15, Road No. 13-A
Dhammondi R.A., G.P.O. 2721
Dhaka, Bangladesh

Indonesia:
Cinkini Baru Building
Lantai III Kamar 315
Jalan Cinkini Raya 95
Jakarta Pusat, Indonesia

Pakistan:
128 D, Block 5
Federal B area
Karachi, Pakistan

THE POPULATION COUNCIL

ADDRESS: The Population Council
One Dag Hammarskjold Plaza
New York, New York 10017 USA

The Population Council, an international, non-profit organization, undertakes social science and biomedical research, advises and assists governments and international agencies, and disseminates information on population issues. Established in 1952, the Council is governed by a Board of Trustees whose members come from twelve countries. The Council is committed to the enhancement of human welfare and works in three areas: biomedical research in the field of human reproduction to develop and improve contraceptive methods; social science research into the causes of population change, their societal implications, and appropriate policy responses; and provision of technical assistance to family planning and other population-related programs at local, national, and regional levels. The Council produces publications for researchers, policymakers, and the concerned public and supports advanced training for population specialists.

The Population Council
One Dag Hammarskjold Plaza
New York, NY 10017 USA

The Population Council Center for Biomedical
Research
Tower Building
1230 York Avenue (at 64th)
New York, NY 10021 USA

The Population Council
Apartado Postal 105-152
11560 Mexico, D.F.
Mexico

The Population Council
P.O. Box 1154
Dokki, Cairo
Egypt

The Population Council
c/o Honorable Takashi Sato
2-10-2 Nagata-cho, Chiyoda-ku
Japan

The Population Council
P.O. Box 11-1213
Bangkok 10112
Thailand

UNICEF

Main Address: United Nations Children's Fund
6th Floor, 866 United Nations Plaza
New York, New York 10017, U.S.A.

The population activities of UNICEF arise out of its concern for the health, survival, welfare and development of children, and for their future participation as enlightened and productive citizens in the development of their countries. Accordingly, the regular maternal and child health services programme was expanded in 1976 to include assistance in responsible parenthood and family planning. UNICEF's integrated basic services strategy has encompassed population activities through a variety of approaches, including: (1) educating girls and women for improved health, nutrition, responsible parenthood and family planning, and general community improvement through greater participation in community social services programmes; (2) educating boys and men, as well as adolescent males and females on improved family life, responsible parenthood and family planning. Another thrust has led to the emergence of programmes directed towards enhancing the situation of women not only as mothers but also as individuals in their own right who play a significant role in family and community life. UNICEF programmes promote the full integration of women into the development process, particularly by means of their greater participation in educational, social, economic and political opportunities.

Regional Offices:

UNICEF
Boite Postale 443
Abidjan 04
Ivory Coast

UNICEF
P.O. Box 44145
Nairobi, Kenya

UNICEF
Regional Office of the Americas and the
Caribbean
Apartado Aereo 7555

UNICEF
Office of the Regional Director,
East Asia and Pakistan
P.O. Box 2-154
Bangkok 10200, Thailand

UNICEF
P.O. Box 811721
Amman, Jordan

UNICEF
12 Sanlitun Lu
Beijing, Peoples Republic of China

INICEF
73 Lodi Estate
New Delhi 110003
India

UNITED NATIONS DEVELOPMENT PROGRAMME (UNDP)

UNDP's extensive and growing efforts to promote the increased participation of women in development are of significant importance to the population situation. However, because of the close relationship between UNDP and UNFPA the Programme's own role in the population sector has now become marginal.

Headquarters:

United Nations Development Programme
1 United Nations Plaza
New York, NY 10117 USA

Cable: UNDEVPRO

Field Offices:

P.O. Box 5
Kabul, Afghanistan

Boite Postale
Algiers, Algeria

Caixa Postal 910
Luanda,
People's Republic of Angola

Casila de Correo 2257
1000 Capital Federal
Buenos Aires, Argentina

P.O. Box 26814
Manama
State of Bahrain

G.P.O. Box 224
Dhaka,
People's Republic of Bangladesh

P.O. Box 625 C
Bridgetown
Barbados

Boite Postale 506
Contonou
People's Republic of Benin

G.P.O. Box 162
Thimphu
Bhutan

Casilla 686
La Paz
Bolivia

P.O. Box 54
Gaborone
Botswana

Boite Postale 575
Ougadougou
Burkina-Faso

P.O. Box 650
Rangoon
Burma

Boite postale 1490
Bujumbura
Burundi

Caixa Postal 62
Praia,
Republica de Cabo Verde

Boite postal 872
Bangui
Central African Republic

PNUD BP 906
N'Djamena,
Republique de Tchad

Casilla 197-D
Santiago
Chile

2 Dongqijie Sanlitum
Beijing
People's Republic of China

Apartado Aereo 091369
Bogota
Colombia

Boite postale 648
Moroni,
Federal Islamic Republic of the Comoros

Boite postale 465 and 51
Brazzaville
People's Republic of the Congo

Apartado Postal 4540
San Jose,
Costa Rica

Apartado Postal No. 4138
La Havana
Cuba

P.O. Box 3521
Nicosia
Cyprus

P.O. Box 27
Pyongyang
Democratic People's Republic of Korea

P.O. Box 1188, Tawahi
Aden
People's Democratic Republic of Yemen

Boite Postal 2001
Djibouti
Repbulic de Djibouti

Apartado 1424
Santa Domingo
Dominican Republic

P.O. Box 4731
Quito
Ecuador

P.O. Box 982
Cairo
Arab Republic of Egypt

P.O. Box 1114
San Salvador
El Salvador

C.P. Box 399
Malabo
Equatorial Guinea

P.O. Box 5580
Addis Ababa
Ethiopia

Private Mail Bag
Suva
Fiji

Boite postal 2138
Libreville
Gabon

P.O. Box 553
Banjul
The Gambia

P.O. Box 1423
Accra
Ghana

36 Amalia Avenue
GR 105-58 Athens
Greece

Apartado postal 23-A
Cuidad de Guatemala
Guatemala

Boite postal 222
Conakry Revolutionary
People's Republic of Guinea

C.P. 179
Bissau
Republic of Guinea-Bissau

P.O. Box 10960
Georgetown
Guyana

Boite postal 976
Tegucigalpa
Honduras

P.O. Box 2338
Jakarta
Indonesia

P.O. Box 1555
Teheran
Islamic Republic of Iran

P.O. Box 2048
Baghdad
Iraq

Ol Boite postale 1747
Abidjam
Republique de Cote d'Ivorie

P.O. Box 280
Kingston
Jamaica

P.O. Box 35286
Amman
Jordan

P.O. Box 2993
Safat
State of Kuwait

Boite Postale 345
Vientiane
Lao People's Democratic
Republic

P.O. Box 11-3216
Beirut
Lebanon

P.O. Box 301
Maseru 100
Lesotho

P.O. Box 274
Monrovia
Liberia

P.O. Box 358
Tripoli,
Socialist People's Libyan Arab Jamahiriya

P.O. Box 1348
Antanamarivo
Democratic Republic of Madagascar

P.O. Box 30135
Lilongwe
Malawi

P.O. Box 2544
Kuala Lumpur
Malaysia

Alivaage, 6 Lainoofaru Magu
Male
Republic of Maldives

Boite postale 120
Bamako
Mali

Boite postale 620
Nouakchatt
Mauritania

P.O. Box 253
Port Louis
Mauritius

Apartado Postal 6-719
06600 Mexico, D.F.
Mexico

P.O. Box 49/207
Ulan Bator
Mongolia

CASIER ONU, Rabat-Chellah
Rabat
Morocco

P.O. Box 4595
Maputo
People's Republic
Mozambique

P.O. Box 107
Kathmandu
Nepal

Apartado Postal 3260
Managua
Nicaragua

Boite Postale 11207
Niamey
Niger

P.O. Box 2075
Lagos
Nigeria

P.O. Box 5287
Muscat
Sultanate of Oman

P.O. Box 1051
Islamabad
Pakistan

Apartado 6314
Panama 5
Panama

P.O. Box 1041
Port Moresby
Papua New Guinea

Casilla de Correo 1107
Asucion
Paraguay

Apartado 4480
Lima
Peru

P.O. Box 7285 ADC & 1864
Pasay City
Metro Manila
Philippines

Box 3233
Doha
State Qatar

Central Post Office Box 1
Area Code 100 Seoul
Republic of Korea

Strada Aurel Vlaicu nr. 16
79362 Bucharest
Romania

Boite postal 445
Kigali
Rwanda

Private Mail Bag
Apia
Samoa

Caixa Postal 109
Sao Tome
Sao Tome and Principe

P.O. Box 558
Riyadh 11421
Saudi Arabia

Boite postal 154
Dakar
Senegal

P.O. Box 1011
Freetown
Sierra Leone

P.O. Box 24
Mogadiscio
Somali Democratic Republic

P.O. Box 913
Khartoum
Democratic Republic of the Sudan

Private Mail Bag
Mbabane
Swaziland

P.O. Box 618
Bangkok
Thailand

Boite postal 911
Lome
Togo

P.O. Box 812
Port-of-Spain
Trinidad and Tobago

Boite postale 863
Tunis
Tunisia

P.K. 407
Ankara
Turkey

P.O. Box 7184
Kampala
Republic of Uganda

P.O. Box 3490
Abu Dhabi
United Arab Emirates

Boite postale 836
Yaounde
United Republic of Cameroon

P.O. Box 9182
Dar es Salaam
United Republic of Tanazania

Casilla de Correo 1207
Montevideo
Uruguay

Apartado 6005
Caracas 1062-A
Venezuela

c/o UNDP, G.P.O Box 618
Bangkok
Thailand

P.O. Box 551
Sana'a
Yemen Arab Republic

P.O. Box 644
11011 Belgrade
Yugoslavia

Boite postale 7248
Kinshasa
Zaire

P.O. Box 31966
Lusaka
Republic of Zambia

P.O. Box 4775
Harare
Zimbabwe

Palis des Nations
Ch- 1211 Geneva 10
Switzerland

UNITED NATIONS DEVELOPMENT FUND FOR WOMEN (UNIFEM)

Address: 304 East 45th Street
11th Floor
New York, New York 10017
212/906-6435

UNIFEM, created in 1976, is an autonomous fund associated with the United Nations Development Programme (UNDP). It is the only U.N. mechanism for development cooperation set up specifically to channel financial and technical resources to women. To complement the support other funds and programmes are provided for women in such areas as child-bearing, childcare nutrition, and family health.

UNITED NATIONS EDUCATIONAL, SCIENTIFIC, and CULTURAL ORGANIZATION (UNESCO)

Main Address: United Nations Educational,
Scientific and Cultural
Organization
7 place de Fontenoy
75700 Paris, France

UNESCO's mandate in the field of population dates back to 1968, when the Fifteenth Session of the General Conference declared the "the purpose of UNESCO's activities in the field of population should be to promote a better understanding of the serious responsibilities which population growth imposes on individuals, nations and the whole international community." The organization seeks: to improve knowledge and to increase awareness of the causes and consequences of population change, of their interrelationships with other aspects of social, cultural and environmental changes, and of their implications for human rights and the quality of life. Its population programme thus involves activities across a broad front—in the social sciences, natural sciences, education and communication.

UNITED NATIONS FUND FOR POPULATION ACTIVITIES (UNFPA)

UNFPA

The UNFPA has been assigned a leading role in the United Nations system in promoting population programmes with the following aims and purposes:

(1) To build up, on an international basis, with the assistance of the competent bodies of the United Nations system, the knowledge and the capacity to respond to national, regional, inter-regional and global needs in the population and family planning fields; to promote coordination in planning and programming, and to co-operate with all concerned;

(2) To promote awareness, both in developed and in developing countries of the social, economic and environmental implications of national and international population problems; of the human rights aspects of family planning; and of possible strategies to deal with them, in accordance with the plans and priorities of each country;

(3) To extend systematic and sustained assistance to developing countries at their request in dealing with their population problems; such assistance to be afforded in forms and by means requested by the recipient countries and best suited to meet the individual country's needs;

(4) To promote population programmes and to co-ordinate projects supported by the Fund.

Headquarters:

United Nations Fund for Population Activities
220 East 42nd Street
New York, NY 10017, U.S.A.

Deputy Representatives in the following countries:

AFRICA

Burkina Faso:
Boite Postale 575
Ouagadougou
Burkina Faso

Cameroon:
Boite Postale 836
Yaounde
Cameroon

Ethiopia:
P.O. Box 5580
Addis Ababa
Ethiopia

Kenya:
P.O. Box 30218
Nairobi
Kenya

Madagascar:
P.O. Box 1348
Antananarivo
Madagascar

Mozambique:
P.O. Box 4595
Maputo
Mozambique

Nigeria:
P.O. Box 2075
Lagos
Nigeria

Senegal:
Boite Postale 154
Dakar
Senegal

United Republic of Tananzia:
P.O. Box 9182
Dar es Salaam
United Republic of Tananzia

Zambia:
P.O. Box 31966
Lusaka
Zambia

ASIA AND THE PACIFIC

Bangladesh:
P.O. Box 224
Ramna, Dhaka
Bangladesh

China:
2 Dongqifie
Sanlitun, Beijing
People's Republic of China

Fiji:
Private Mail Bag
Suva
Fiji

India:
P.O. Box 3059
New Delhi 110003
India

Indonesia:
P.O. Box 2338
Jakarta
Indonesia

Malaysia:
P.O. Box 2544
Kuala Lumpur
Malaysia

Nepal:
P.O. Box 107
Kathmandu
Nepal

Pakistan:
P.O. Box 1051
Islamabad
Pakistan

Philippines:
P.O. Box 7285 ADC
MIA Road
Pasay City
Metro Manila
Philippines

Sri Lanka:
P.O. Box 1505
Colombo
Sri Lanka

Thailand:
G.P.O. Box 618
Bangkok
Thailand

Viet Nam:
c/o UNDP
G.P.O. Box 618
Bangkok
Thailand

LATIN AMERICA AND THE CARIBBEAN
Brazil:
Caixa Postal 07-0285
70001 Brasilia, D.F.
Brazil

Jamaica:
P.O. Box 280
Kingston
Jamaica

Mexico:
Apartado Postal 6-719
06600 Mexico D.F.
Mexico

Peru:
Apartado 4480
Naciones Unidas
Lima, Peru

MIDDLE EAST AND MEDITERRANEAN
Egypt:
P.O. Box 982
Cairo
Arab Republic of Egypt

Morocco:
Casier ONU
Rabat-Chellah
Rabat, Morocco

Syrian Arab Republic:
P.O. Box 2317
Damascus
Syrian Arab Republic

Tunisia:
Boite postal 863
Tunis
Tunisia

Turkey:
P.K. 407
Ankara
Turkey

Yemen:
P.O. Box 551
Sana's
Yemen Arab Republic

United States Agency for International Development (USAID)

Address: Office of Population
Bureau of Science and Technology
U.S. Agency for International Development
Washington, D.C. 20523, U.S.A.

The Agency for International Development is the United States agency charged with overall responsibility for U.S. foreign economic development assistance. Within AID, the Office of Population in the Bureau for Science and Technology and AID's Regional Bureaus are responsible for population programme assistance.

Major AID assistance has been in the following areas: 1) demographic and economic analysis (7%); 2) policy development (7%); 3) research (13%); 4) family planning services (50%); 5) population communication—education and information (11%); and 6) training and institutional development (12%).

Health/FP Development Officer
USAID/Kathmandu
Agency for International Development
Washington, D.C. 20523

Population Officer
USAID/Islamabad
Agency for International Development
Washington, D.C. 20523

Health/FP Development Officer
USAID/Manila
APO San Francisco 96528

Health/FP Development Officer
USAID/Colombo
Agency for International Development
Washington, D.C. 20523

Health/FP Development Officer
USAID/Bangkok

Program Officer
USAID/Gaborone
Agency for International Development
Washington, D.C. 20523

AID Representative
AID Section American
Embassy/Bujumbura
Agency for International Development
Washington, D.C. 20523

AID Representative
USAID/Mexico
Agency for International Dev.
Washington, D.C. 20523

FP Dev Officer
USAID/Panama
APO Miami 34002

AID Representative
USAID/Asuncion
APO Miami 34036

Population Officer
USAID/Lima

Health/FP Development Officer
USAID/Dhaka
Agency for International Development
Washington, D.C. 20523

Health/FP Development Officer
USAID/New Delhi
Agency for International Development
Washington, D.C. 20523

Population Officer
USAID/Jakarta
APO San Francisco 96356

Health Development Officer
USAID/Quito

Population Officer
USAID/San Salvador

USAID
APO Miami 34028

Population Advisor
USAID/Guatemala City

Population Officer
USAID/Port-Au-Prince
Agency for International Dev.
Washington, D.C. 20523

Health Dev. Officer
USAID/Tegucigalpa

Health Development Officer
USAID/Kingston
Agency for International Dev.
Washington, D.C. 20523

Health/Family Planning Development
USAID/Sana'a
Agency for International Development
Washington, D.C. 20523

Health/Family Planning Development
  Officer
USAID/Rabat
Agency for International Development
Washington, D.C. 20523

Health Development Officer
USAID/Yaounde
Agency for International Development
Washington, D.C. 20523

USAID/Accra
Agency for International Development
Washington, D.C. 20523

Population Advisor
Regional Economic Dev. Services Off.
(REDSO/WA)—Abidjan
Agency for International Development
Washington, D.C. 20523

Population Advisor
Regional Economic Dev. Services Off.
(REDSO/WA)—Abidjan
Agency for International Development
Washington, D.C. 20523

Population Officer
USAID/Nairobi

Population Officer
Regional Economic Dev. Services Off.
(REDSO/ESA—Nairobi)
USAID/Nairobi

Health Development Officer
USAID/Maseru
Agency for International Development
Washington, D.C. 20523

Public Health Advisor
USAID/Bridgetown

General Dev. Officer
USAID/Belize City

Health/FP Development Officer
USAID/La Paz

AID Representative
USAID/Brasilia

General Development Officer
USAID/Bogota

Health Officer
USAID/San Jose

Health Development Officer
USAID/Santo Domingo

Health/Family Planning Development
  Officer
USAID/Tunis
Agency for International Development
Washington, D.C. 20523

Public Health Advisor
USAID/Monrovia
Agency for Int'l Dev.
Washington, D.C. 20523

Health Officer
USAID/Lilongwe
Agency for International Development
Washington, D.C. 20523

Public Health Advisor
USAID/Bamako

Agency for International Development
Washington, D.C. 20523

Health Dev. Officer
USAID/Nouakchott
Agency for International Development
Washington, D.C. 20523

Health Development Officer
USAID/Niamey
Agency for International Development
Washington, D.C. 20523

AID Affairs Officer
AID Section, American Embassy/La(?)
Agency for International Development
Washington, D.C. 20523

AID Section, American Embassy/Ki(?)
Agency for International Development
Washington, D.C. 20523

Public Health Specialist
Office of AID Representative/Be(?)
Agency for International Development
Washington, D.C. 20523

Population Officer
USAID/Dakar
Agency for International Development
Washington, D.C. 20523

AID Affairs Officer
AID Section, American Embassy/Freetown
Agency for International Development
Washington, D.C. 20523

Population Advisor
USAID/Mogadishu
Agency for International Development
Washington, D.C. 20523

Health Development Officer
USAID/Khartoum
Agency for International Development
Washington, D.C. 20523

Health Development Officer
USAID/Mbabane
Agency for International Development
Washington, D.C. 20523

Population Officer
USAID/Dar es Salaam
Agency for International Development
Washington, D.C. 20523

General Development Officer
Office of AID Representative/Lome
Agency for International Development
Washington, D.C. 20523

Population Advisor
USAID/Kampala
Agency for International Development
Washington, D.C. 20523

Public Health Advisor
USAID/Ouagadougou
Agency for International Development
Washington, D.C. 20523

Health Dev. Officer
USAID/Kinshasa
Agency for International Development
Washington, D.C. 20523

Assistant Director
Office of AID Representative/Lusaka
Agency for International Development
Washington, D.C. 20523

Deputy Director
USAID/Harare
Agency for International Development
Washington, D.C. 20523

Population Officer
USAID/Cairo

Health & Population Officer
USAID/Amman
Agency for International Development
Washington, D.C. 20523

USAID-WOMEN IN DEVELOPMENT

ADDRESS: Office of Women in Development
Room 3243 New State
Agency for International Development
Washington, D.C. 20523

The Women in Development Office promotes projects and policies within and outside of A.I.D. that recognize and value both the traditional and changing role of women in a country's economic and social development. The Office works to ensure that in all A.I.D. sponsored and supported projects women have equal opportunity to obtain resources, credit, training, education and income earning activities. In this way, the WID Office insures that the benefits of development are shared by all members of a society—men and women.

WORLD BANK

(International Bank for Reconstruction and Development)

The decision of the World Bank and its soft-loan affiliate, the International Development Association (IDA), to enter the field of population assistance and to provide assistance to those countries wishing to slow down their population growth was based on the conviction that rapid population growth is a major barrier to the economic and social progress of many developing countries. As a result, the Bank is interested in providing assistance for long-term and comprehensive multi-component projects to support national programmes.

The Bank uses a three-step programme which begins with an assessment of the implications of population growth on development as part of the Bank's periodic economic reviews; it then undertakes, on request, sectoral analyses; finally, it provides financial assistance to specific projects on conventional Bank terms or, to especially weak economics, on highly subsidized soft-loan terms.

Main Address: World Bank
Population, Health and Nutrition Department
1818 H Street, N.W.
Washington, D.C. 20433, U.S.A.

Regional Missions:

World Bank Mission
747 Third Avenue, 26th Floor
New York, New York 10017, U.S.A.

New Zealand House
(15th Floor)
London SW1 Y4TE, England

World Bank
Kokusai Building, Room 916
1-1 Marunouchi 3-chome
Chiyoda-ku,
Tokyo 100, Japan

World Bank
Udom Vidhya Building
956 Rama IV Road
Sala Daeng
Bangkok 5, Thailand

World Bank
66, avenue d'Iena
75116 Paris, France

World Bank
ITC Building
54 Rue de Montbrillant
Geneva, Switzerland
mailing address:
P.O. Box 104
1211 Geneva 20 CIC, Switzerland

World Bank
Reinsurance Plaza
5th & 6th Floors
Taifa Road
Nairobi, Kenya
mailing address:
P.O. Box 30577

Resident Mission, World Bank
222 New Eskaton Road
Dhaka, Bengladesh
mailing address:
G.P.O. Box 97

World Bank
Zone Residentielle de la Radio Cotonou
Benin
    mailing address:
B.P. 03-2112

Banco Mundial
Avenida Central 643 (1th Piso)
Lima, Peru
    mailing address:
Apartado 4480

Resident Mission
World Bank
Riyadh, Saudi Arabia
    mailing address:
P.O. Box 5900

World Bank
% Somali Commercial and Saving Bank
    Building, 4th Floor
Mogadishu, Somalia
    mailing address:
P.O. Box 1825

World Bank
Sudan Kuwaiti Centre
Tower No. 1, 7th Floor
Nile Avenue
Khartoum, Sudan

World Bank
P.O. Box 4463
Kampala, Uganda

World Bank
Building UZB
Avenue des Aviateurs
Kinshasa 1, Republic of Zaire
    mailing address:
P.O. Box 14816

World Bank
Immeuble BECEA (3eme etage)
B.P. 622
Ougadougou, Burkina Faso

World Bank
Immeuble Kennedy
Avenue Kennedy
Yaounde, Cameroon
    mailing address:
B.P. 1128

World Bank
I.B.T.E. New Telecommunications
    Building (1st Floor)
Churchill Road
Addis Ababa, Ethiopia
    mailing address:
P.O. Box 5515

Banco Mundial
Edificio BISA (4th Piso)
16 de Julio 1628
La Paz, Bolivia
    mailing address:
Casilla 8692

World Bank
P.O. Box 609
Kigali, Rwanda

World Bank
Immeuble S.D.I.H.
3 Place de l'Independance
Dakar, Senegal
    mailing address:
B.P. 3296

World Bank
People's Bank,
Head Office, 10th Floor
Sir C. A. Gardiner Mawatha
Colombo 2, Sri Lanka
    mailing address:
P.O. Box 1761

World Bank
169 Boulevard Circulaire
Immeuble BTCI (8eme etage)
Lome, Togo
    mailing address:
B.P. 3915

World Bank
N.I.C. Building, 7th Floor, B
Dar es Salaam, United Republic of
    Tanzania
    mailing address:
P.O. Box 2054

World Bank
CMAZ Building
Ben Bella Road
Lusaka, Zambia
    mailing address:
P.O. Box 35410

World Bank
45, Avenue de la Poste
B.P. 2637
Bujumbura, Burundi

Banco Mundial
Edificio "Aseguradora Del Valle"
Carrera 10, No. 24-55, Piso 17
Bogota D.C., Colombia
    mailing address:
Apartado Aereo 10229

World Bank
1A Kakramadu Road
East Cantoments
Accra, Ghana
    mailing address:
P.O. Box M27

Resident Mission,
World Bank
P.O. Box 416
New Delhi, India

World Bank
1 Rue Patrice Lumumba
Antananarivo 101, Madagascar
 mailing address:
Banque mondiale B.P. 4140

World Bank
R.N.A.C. Building (1st Floor)
Kathmandu, Nepal
 mailing address:
P.O. Box 798

World Bank
30 Macarthy Street
Lagos, Nigeria
 mailing address:
P.O. Box 127

Resident Staff in Indonesia
World Bank
Jalan Rasuna Said, Kav. B-10
Suite 301, Kuningan
Jakarta 12940, Indonesia

World Bank
Immeuble CNAR
rue Square Lumumba
Bamako, Mali
 mailing address:
B.P. 1864

World Bank
Immeuble El Nasr
(12eme etage—escalier A)
Niamey, Niger
 mailing address:
Banque mondiale B.P. 12402
% Postmaster General

World Bank
P.O. Box 1025
Islamabad, Pakistan

World Health Organization (WHO)

WHO's concern in population mainly involves the variables of mortality, morbidity and fertility. Aspects of the World Population Plan of Action of particular relevance to WHO's programme of work include those sections on morbidity mortality, human reproduction, family formation and the status of women, nutrition, communicable diseases, water supplies, maternal and child health/family planning, and socio-economic policies concerning investments in the health sector, data collection and analysis, research, and management, training, education and information.

The mandate of WHO clearly outlines the Organization's work in population dynamics, human reproduction and family planning: in evaluating various approaches to the introduction and increased coverage of family planning within health care systems, especially maternal and child health; the strengthening of national self-reliance for training of health and health-related workers at all levels in subjects related to family planning, human reproduction and population dynamics; and the expansion of activities in research in all aspects of these subjects, including the development of methods on fertility regulation.

Main Address: World Health Organization
1211 Geneva 27
Switzerland

Regional Offices:

Africa
World Health Organization
Regional Office for Africa
P.O. Box No. 6
Brazzaville, Congo

Americas
World Health Organization
Regional Office for the Americas/
Pan American Sanitary Bureau
525 23rd Street, N.W.
Washington, D.C. 20037, U.S.A.

Eastern Mediterranean
World Health Organization
Regional Office for the Eastern
  Mediterranean
P.O. Box 1517
Alexandria, Egypt

Europe
World Health Organization
Regional Office for Europe
8, Scherfigsvej
DK-2100 Copenhagen, Denmark

South-East Asia
World Health Organization
Regional Office for South-East Asia
World Health House
Indraprastha Estate
Mahatma Gandhi Road
New Delhi-1, 10002, India

Western Pacific
World Health Organization
Regional Office for the Western Pacific
P.O. Box 2932
2801 Manila, Philippines

References for Regional Summaries

Birdsall, Nancy. *Population Growth and Poverty in the Developing World*. Population Reference Bureau, Washington, D.C. 1980.

Bouvier, Leon F. *Planet Earth 1984-2043: a Demographic Vision*. Population Reference Bureau, Washington, D.C. 1984.

Brown, Lester. *State of the World 1984: a World Watch Report on Progress toward a Sustainable Society*. W.W. Norton & Co., New York, New York. 1987.

David, Henry P. *Eastern Europe: Pronatalist Policies and Private Behavior*. Population Reference Bureau, Washington, D.C. 1982.

Diaz-Briquets, Sergio. *Conflict in Central America: The Demographic Dimension*. Population Reference Bureau, Washington, D.C. 1986.

Friedlander, Dov and Goldschneider, Calvin. *Israel's Population: The Challenge of Pluralism*. Population Reference Bureau, Washington, D.C. 1984.

Germain, Adrienne. "Toward a Programmatic Definition of Reproductive Health Care for Poor Women in the Third World." International Women's Health Coalition, New York, New York. 1986.

Goliber, Thomas J. *Sub-Saharan Africa: Population Pressures on Development*. Population Reference Bureau, Washington, D.C. 1985.

Hull, Terence H.; Hull, Valerie J. and Singarimbun, Masri. *Indonesia's Family Planning Story: Success and Challenge*. Population Reference Bureau, Washington, D.C. 1977.

International Development Research Centre. *Women in Development: Perspectives from the Nairobi Conference*. Manuscript Report. Ottawa, Canada. 1986.

Mason, Karen Oppenheim. *The Status of Women: a Review of its Relationships to Fertility and Mortality*. The Rockefeller Foundation, New York, New York. 1984.

Merrick, Thomas W. *Population Pressures in Latin America*. Population Reference Bureau, Washington, D.C. 1986.

Merrick, Thomas W. *World Population in Transition* Population Reference Bureau, Washington, D.C. 1986.

Murphy, Francis X., C.SS.R. *Catholic Perspectives on Population Issues II*. Population Reference Bureau, Washington, D.C. 1981.

Population Crisis Committee. *Toward Smaller Families: the Crucial Role of the Private Sector*. Draper Fund Report. Washington, D.C. 1986.

Population Reference Bureau. *Population Today*. Vo. 15, No. 2. February 1987.

Population Reference Bureau. *Population Handbook*. Washington, D.C. 1985.

Population Reference Bureau. *U.S. Population: Where We Are, Where We're Going*. Washington, D.C. 1982.

Population Reference Bureau. *Population In Perspective: Regional Views*. Washington, D.C. 1986.

Population Reference Bureau. *Women in the World: The Women's Decade and Beyond*. Washington, D.C. 1986.

Population Reference Bureau. *World Population: Toward the Next Century*. Washington, D.C. 1985.

Population Reference Bureau. *World Population Data Sheet*. Washington, D.C. 1987.

Safilior-Rothschild, Constantina. *The Status of Women and Fertility in the Third World in the 1970-1980 Decade*. The Population Council, New York, New York. 1985.

Seager, Joni and Olson, Ann. *Women in the World: An International Atlas*. Simon & Schuster, New York, New York. 1981.

Schuler, Margaret (editor) and contributors. *Empowerment and the Law: Strategies of Third World Women*. OEF-International, Washington, D.C. 1986.

Sen, Gita with Grown, Caren. *Development, Crises and Alternatives: Third World Women's Perspectives*. Development Alternatives with Women for a New Era (DAWN), Media-Redaksjonen, Norway. 1985.

Sivard, Ruth Leger. *Women ... a world survey*. World Priorities Inc., Washington, D.C. 1985.

Sivard, Ruth Leger. *Women ... a world survey*. World Priorities Inc., Washington, D.C. 1985.

Tien, H. Yuan. *China: Demographic Billionaire*. Population Reference Bureau, Washington, D.C. 1983.

Van de Kaa, Dirk J. *Europe's Second Demographic Transition*. Population Reference Bureau, Washington, D.C. 1987.

Visaria, Pravin and Visaria, Leela. *India's Population: Second and Growing*. Population Reference Bureau, Washington, D.C. 1981.

World Bank. *World Development Report 1984*. Oxford University Press, New York, New York. 1984.

World Resources Institute and International Institute for Environment and Development. *World Resources 1986: An Assessment of the Resource Base that Supports the Global Economy*. Basic books, New York, New York. 1986.

Yudelman, Sally W. *Hopeful Openings: a Study of Five Women's Development Organizations in Latin America and the Caribbean*. Kumarian Press, West Hartford, Connecticut. 1987.

SUMMARY

The organizers of this directory began with an ambitious two-fold objective: first, to compile an extensive list of women's organizations worldwide, and second, to describe these organizations' activities, central purposes, and relationships with the Forward-Looking Strategies drafted in Nairobi in 1985. As this directory took shape, it revealed a wonderful diversity among the organizations listed. They include groups dedicated primarily to local women's concerns and those with an international breadth; it includes organizations focused on development in the Third World, on global population concerns, and on the political and social rights of women everywhere.

Seventy percent of the organizations are involved in some type of educational activity. These activities include the dissemination of family planning information, population awareness, education on women's rights and women's status in society. Closely related to the educational and informational activities are the ten percent of respondents involved in publications ranging from newsletters to research reports. Thirty percent of the respondents listed education and information as a principal purpose or main activity.

Women's issues and concerns in general were cited as the principal purpose and main activity of twenty percent of all the respondents. However, it is very clear that with little exception, *all* of them are involved with women's issues. Stated women's concerns were diverse: income generation; legal, political and professional concerns, child care, rape crisis and battered women, safeguarding of reproductive rights, unsafe reproductive technology, post-partum depression and specific concerns about ethnic women's groups.

Approximately fifteen percent of the respondents were focused solely on general population and family planning issues, or health and research issues. However, sixteen percent were engaged in family planning and providing health service (on international and/or national levles) as part of the main activities. Also, demographic and contraceptive research as a part-time activity was cited by sixteen percent of the respondents. Twelve percent of the respondents included the training of specialists in family planning, health or development.

Finally, the majority of the respondents report knowledge of the FORWARD-LOOKING STRATEGIES. Those organizations that indicated that they are unaware of the STRATEGIES or were not implementing them, actually were implementing them through their main purpose and activities. That fact suggests a more fundamental conclusion: while this directory is a catalog of women's global diversity, it is also a testament to the underlying forces that unify and band them together. The women represented in this directory— Africans, Europeans, Asians, and Americans oriented toward development, population, reproductive or political rights, or a host of other concerns— share a bedrock commitment to improving the quality of life of *all* women. This directory, by highlighting the relationship between these organizations and the Forward-Looking Strategies, hopes to contribute to that cause.

SPECIFIC ACTIVITIES CHART

Activity	# of Respondents	Regional Notes
1. Education:	70%	Consistent all regions.
2. Counselling:	35%	Generally consistent for all regions, except for low 15% of North America respondents.
3. Advocacy:	28%	Inconsistent-9% in Latin America, 55% in South Pacific.
4. Demographic Research:	23%	Consistent, except for low of 10% in South Pacific.
5. Contraceptive Research:	19%	Consistent all regions.
6. Delivery of Services:	19%	Ranges from 12% in Europe to 45% in South Pacific.

AWARENESS OF FORWARD-LOOKING STRATEGIES

Regions	Percentage
Africa	59%
Asia	77%
Europe	68%
Latin America	40%
North America	85%
South Pacific	45%

METHODOLOGY

The cover letter, survey, and poster was initially mailed to 2,870 organizations on September 10, 1986, in English. The entire packet was remailed to 2,050 organizations on December 10, in French, Spanish, or English, depending on the primary language spoken in each particular country.

Organizations were researched by a team of eight people. They utilized the Library of Congress, U.S. Agency for International Development, The United Nations, a variety of directories and referrals from other organizations. Many thanks are extended to those organizations and individuals who assisted in identifying organizations to whom the surveys were mailed.

A huge ripple effect is possible when women's
organizations around the world work together.

WE RESPECTFULLY ASK YOU TO COMPLETE THIS FORM

The Population Institute
1986 Women's Survey on Population/Reproductive Health
Programs

1) Name of Organization_____

    Business Address   Mailing Address(if different
                                 from Business address)

_____   _____
_____   _____
_____   _____

Telephone number_____   Telex Number_____

*Please check if above is Central Office [ ] YES [ ] NO

*If no, Please indicate name, address, telephone no.,
telex of Central Office.

_____
_____
_____

Telephone Number_____Telex Number_____
Please attach branch addresses(if any).

2) What is the name and title of your Chief Executive?
_____
_____

3) What is the approximate size of the staff?_____

4) Do you have any volunteer staff? Yes [ ] No [ ]
(if so how many)_____

5) What is the present number of affiliated chapters?_____

6) What is the total number of individual members?_____

7) What year was the organization established?_____

8) What is the principal purpose of your organization?

9) What are the main activities of your organization?

10) How is your organization funded?

11) What population concerns does your organization have?

12) Please check population activities:

            Education [ ]   Delivery of Service(s) [ ]
            Demographic Research [ ]   Sterilization [ ]
            Contraceptive Research [ ]   Pill [ ]
            Counselling [ ]   IUD [ ]
            Advocacy [ ]   Diaphram [ ]
            Other (if other Specify)   Foam [ ]
            _____   Norplant [ ]
            _____   Depo-provera [ ]
                                         Natural Family Planning [ ]
                                         Other(if other specify)

                                         _____
                                         _____
                                         _____

13) Are you aware of the Forward-Looking Strategies put
forth at the Nairobi United Nations Decade for Women
Conference in 1985? Yes [ ]   No [ ]

14) Are you implementing any of the Forward-Looking
Strategies? YES [ ] NO [ ] (If yes, please specify)

15) What obstacles (if any) have you encountered in the
implementation of the Forward-Looking Strategies?

Thank you for your participation. A complimentary copy of
the Directory will be forwarded at the completion of the
project.

September 10, 1986

Dear Colleague,

In keeping with the spirit of Nairobi and the urgent need to build upon the thousands of conference and planning hours over the past decades, The Population Institute, in cooperation with the United Nations Fund for Population Activities, is conducting a major worldwide survey of women's organizations. The survey includes both developing and developed countries, and is designed to assess population/family planning concerns in each organization.

The completed survey will be disseminated in a directory format as a communication tool to involve women leaders in expanding their personal and organizational support for the implementation of the Forward-Looking Strategies.

We respectfully solicit your help on the project. Please take a moment to complete the enclosed survey. For your convenience, a return envelope has been included. A complimentary copy of the completed directory will be forwarded to you at the conclusion of the project.

The Decade of Women has focused considerable attention on the inequities visited upon women and the need for improvement in all facets of their lives. One of the key ingredients to that improvement is reproductive health. In fact, the build-up of commitment to reproductive rights has been gathering force from previous conferences, including the International Conference on Human Rights held in Teheran; the World Plan of Action adopted in Mexico City; and the World Conference of the United Nations Decade of Women in Copenhagen.

The momentum culminated in the work of 2000 delegates, from 160 nations, attending the Nairobi U.N. Decade for Women Conference in 1985. The result is the Nairobi Forward-Looking Strategies for the advancement of women. Family planning, health, and population were seen as a major area for specific action, and conferees adopted four goals to be implemented within the next 13 years. The enclosed poster covers the paragraphs(156 through 159) which highlight the population goals.

Reproduction and population growth are not solely health issues. Fertility control is an internationally recognized basic human right which must be exercised to avoid adverse environmental effects.

This was reflected in the following paragraphs under the section entitled <u>Current Trends and Perspectives To the Year 2000</u> in the Forward-Looking Strategies:

<u>Paragraph 28</u>:
During the period from 1986 to the year 2000, changes in the natural environment will be critical for women. One area of change is that of the role of women as intermediaries between the natural environment and society with respect to agro-ecosystems, as well as the provisions of safe water and fuel supplies and the closely associated questions of sanitation. The problem will continue to be greatest where water resources are limited - in arid and semi-arid areas- and in areas experiencing demographic pressure. In a general manner an improvement in the situation of women could bring about a reduction in mortality and morbidity as well as better regulation of fertility and hence of population growth, which would be beneficial for the environment and ultimately, for women, children and men.

<u>Paragraph 29</u>:
The issues of fertility rates and population growth should be treated in a context that permits women to exercise effectively their rights in matters pertaining to population concerns, including the basic right to control their own fertility which forms an important basis for the enjoyment of other rights, as stated in the report of the International Population Conference held at Mexico City in 1984.

Finally, in Part IV - Areas of Special Concern, Paragraph 287 raises the concern that the increase in the number of young women looking for employment will lead to exploitation in the workplace. This, coupled with low nutritional levels and umwanted pregnancies, will seriously threaten the health of young women.

A huge ripple effect is possible when women's organizations around the world work together. The dissemenation of up-to-date information will make it easier to maintain the thrust of the Forward-Looking Strategies.

I salute you for your work and your commitment to upgrading the standard of life for women. Thank you for your help on this important project.

Sincerely,

Lalita Harvyasi

Lalita Harvyasi
Women's Project Coordinator

514

Population Concerns Emphasized in Forward-Looking Strategies

Following are the key paragraphs highlighting population and family planning concerns from the Forward-Looking Strategies document adopted by the 1985 U.N. Decade for Women Conference in Nairobi.

PARAGRAPH 156: The ability of women to control their fertility forms an important basis for the enjoyment of other rights. As recognized in the World Population Plan of Action and reaffirmed at the International Conference on Population, 1984, all couples and individuals have the basic human right to decide freely and responsibly the number and spacing of their children; maternal and child health and family planning components of primary health care should be strengthened; and family planning information should be produced and services created.

PARAGRAPH 157: Governments should make available, as a matter of urgency, information, education and the means to assist women to make decisions about their desired number of children. To ensure a voluntary and free choice, family planning information, education and means should include all medically approved and appropriate methods of family planning. Education for responsible parenthood and family life education should be widely available and should be directed towards both men and women.

PARAGRAPH 158: Recognizing that pregnancy occurring in adolescent girls, whether married or unmarried, has adverse effects on morbidity and mortality of both mother and child, governments are urged to develop policies to encourage delay in the commencement of childbearing. Governments should make efforts to raise the age of entry into marriage in countries in which this age is still quite low. Attention should be given to ensuring that adolescents, both girls and boys, receive adequate information and education.

PARAGRAPH 159: All governments should ensure that fertility control methods conform to adequate standards of quality, efficiency and safety. This should also apply to organizations responsible for distributing and administering these methods. Programs of incentives and disincentives should be neither coercive nor discriminatory and should be consistent with internationally recognized human rights, as well as with changing individual and cultural values.

Following are responses by individual delegates to the United Nations Decade for Women Conference in Nairobi to items concerning population and family planning that were discussed on the agenda.

Given the critical food situation in Africa, aggravated by demographic pressures, the international community is urged to give priority to and provide support for the efforts of countries to overcome this serious situation.

JOETTA DENNIS (Liberia): "The international community should continue to provide aid to Africa to alleviate the problem of hunger that is made more critical by population pressures. Channeling more aid through private organizations would be the more likely way to reach the people who have the greatest need."

Non-government organizations, particularly women's organizations, should be involved in government programs that governments should make available, as a matter of urgency, with respect to information, education and means to assist men and women in making decisions about their desired number of children.

MRS. MARGARET NECKLES (Grenada): "Non-government organizations can play a significant part in providing information, education, and family planning to its citizens. However, it is essential that they take into account the cultural situation in the area concerned, particularly with regard to sex education. They should plan these activities with input from the Ministry of Health."

Governments, irrespective of their population policies, should encourage access to family planning services for their citizens.

ANNA KIRIYA (Kenya): "The exercise of control over one's own fertility is a basic human right. Governments, particularly in the developing countries, should ensure this right by providing the means for women to enjoy this right whether or not they have population policies and no matter what these policies may be."

Governments should undertake the creation of basic services for the delivery of health care, taking into account levels of fertility and infant and maternal mortality.

KUDADIDAD BASHARAL (Afghanistan): "Basic health services that encompass fertility and infant and child mortality should be a vital part of the health care delivery systems of countries where they do not already exist. Mothers and children are the family members most vulnerable to epidemic diseases, according to the World Health Organization. The health and survival of mothers and children are absolutely necessary if any nation is to meaningfully improve the quality of lives of its people."

FELICULA NYIRAMUTARAMBIRNA (Rwanda): "Maternal and child health and family planning have been emphasized in Rwanda. A national population office has been established, under the direction of a woman, to make family planning services available to the entire population."

NEDI BIRIR (Kenya): "Women should have the basic right to control their own fertility. There is little question that until this right is granted, until governments and societies are able to implement it by providing the information, education, services and means to exercise it, women cannot achieve the equality for which they strive."

TAMAR ESHEL (Israel): "There is no right more fundamental, as far as women are concerned, than that of being allowed to determine the number and spacing of their children. This has been recognized at several international meetings—most recently at the International Population Conference in Mexico City last year—and it is important to be reaffirmed until it is a universally recognized and universally implemented right."

GOKSEL KALAKIOUGLU (Turkey): "Government health programs, including family planning, have expanded (in Turkey). Women in Turkey were guaranteed constitutional equality in marriage, job opportunities, pay and inheritance and political rights in 1924."

AMY KABWE (Zambia): "We are not forcing anyone when we make them aware of the health aspects of family planning. We are simply making it possible for women to improve their lives through the use of family planning to space their families. What women need is education. When they have that, they will have it for their whole lives."

Concerted action should be directed towards the establishment of a system of sharing parental responsibilities, including decision-making regarding family size and child spacing, by women and men in the family and by society.

Women should be permitted to exercise effectively their rights in matters pertaining to population concerns, including the basic right to control their own fertility, which forms an important basis for the enjoyment of other rights.

Recognizing that pregnancy occurring among adolescent girls, whether married or unmarried, has adverse effects on all aspects of their lives, including morbidity and mortality of both mother and child, governments should ensure that adolescents, both boys and girls, receive adequate information, education and services within the changing socio-cultural framework of each country.

CONSTANCE V. MITCHAM (St. Christopher and Nevis): "As a result of government concern over the large number of unplanned teenage pregnancies, a pilot project was launched, in conjunction with the national

family planning program, to respond to the problems of teenage pregnancy."

YVONNE FRANCIS GIBSON (St. Vincent and Grenadines): "The number of teenage girls who become pregnant and must drop out of school contributes to the overall low level of educational achievement of women. This must be addressed."

DR. ESTHER OCLOO (Ghana): "I have talked to pregnant girls who did not know how they got pregnant. They did not have information on family planning. I believe they need sex education, but in Ghana it is considered a taboo."

| UNITED | | DP |
| NATIONS | | |

Governing Council	Dist.
of the	GENERAL
United Nations	DP/1987/38
Development Programme	5 March 1987
	ORIGINAL: English

Thirty-fourth session
26 May–19 June 1987
Item 6 of the provisional agenda
UNFPA

SUPPORT

UNITED NATIONS FUND FOR POPULATION ACTIVITIES

AN IMPLEMENTATION STRATEGY TO STRENGTHEN THE
CAPACITY OF THE FUND TO DEAL WITH ISSUES
CONCERNING WOMEN, POPULATION AND DEVELOPMENT

Report of the Executive Director

Summary

This report of the Executive Director is prepared in response to decision 86/34 I, paragraph 3, of the Governing Council at its thirty-third session, requesting the Executive Director to develop for presentation to the Council an internal implementation strategy to strengthen the capacity of the Fund to deal with issues of women in development in the context of population activities supported by the Fund. The report briefly provides background information on the conceptual issues concerning the interrelationship between the efforts to improve the situation of women and those to achieve population and general development objectives. It provides examples of the types of activities undertaken by the Fund in the past. The report then describes the new strategy which covers the period 1987–1990. The strategy calls for revision of sectoral policies, programme guidelines and programming procedures. Training for all levels of staff, participation of all organizational units within the Fund and increased co-operation and joint activities with other United Nations agencies are identified as essential elements of the strategy. The document concludes with annual work plans including verifiable objectives, as well as resource requirements.

CONTENTS

INTRODUCTION

1. At its thirty-third session in June 1986, the Governing Council, in decision 86/34 I, paragraph 3, noted with appreciation the increased attention of the United Nations Fund for Population Activities to the role and status of women in the programmes and projects it funds and the establishment of the Special Unit for Women and Youth. In the same paragraph, the Council requested the Executive Director "to develop, for presentation to the Governing Council at its thirty-fourth session, an internal implementation strategy to strengthen the capacity of the Fund to deal with issues of women in development which would establish verifiable objectives and a time-frame for implementation with a view to promoting accountability and would also give special attention to improved staff training, monitoring of existing guidelines, instructions and procedures for inclusion of women-in-development criteria and to increasing the effectiveness of the Special Unit within the Fund's headquarters, paying due attention to the relevant experience of organizations engaged in operational activities within the United Nations system, including the possibility of instituting joint staff training programmes in this field."

2. The Council's interest in this subject follows up the continuing deep concern expressed by members about the role and status of women and is in line with its continuing request that the Fund further strengthen its activities directed both to projects specifically designed to benefit women and to the role of women in all population programmes and activities (e.g. decision 85/19 I, para. 10).

3. The interest of the Council in this matter also reflects the global consensus reached at the International Conference on Population held in Mexico City in 1984 and the World Conference to Review and Appraise the Achievements of the United Nations Decade for Women: Equality, Development and Peace, held in Nairobi in 1985 regarding the close relationship between women's roles, on the one hand, and demographic and development objectives on the other hand, as well as the urgent need for the international community to strengthen and expand activities in the field of women, population and development. Recommendations adopted at both conferences urged Governments to integrate women into all phases of the development process and stressed the fact that neither national economic nor demographic goals could be realized if the status and roles of women were not fully taken into account.

4. Subsequently, the General Assembly of the United Nations in its resolution 39/228 of 18 December 1984, endorsing the report of the 1984 Mexico City Conference, reaffirmed "the importance attached by the Conference to the formulation and implementation of concrete policies which will enhance the status and role of women in the area of population policies and programmes . . ." (para. 8). Moreover, the General Assembly, in its resolution 40/108 of 13 December 1985, endorsing the report of the Nairobi Conference, invited all organizations and agencies within the

United Nations system to give high priority to the implementation of the Nairobi Forward-Looking Strategies for the Advancement of Women and, in particular, to ensure that sectoral policies and programmes for development include strategies to promote the participation of women as agents and beneficiaries on an equal basis with men.

I. BACKGROUND

5. Since the Fund became operational in 1969, it has consistently emphasized the special role and importance of women in population programmes and projects. In various statements, the Executive Director has emphasized that women's aspirations and women's decisions are vital to an effective population policy and that more women must be involved at all levels in decision-making rather than being mere recipients of services.

6. To this end, the Fund has been a pioneer within the United Nations system in supporting programmes directly aimed at increasing opportunities for the greater participation of women in population and development at all levels—as policy-makers, programme planners and community workers.

7. It realizes that improvement of the status of women is an important issue *per se*. Moreover it has additional significance in the context of UNFPA's mandate because it influences and is influenced by a number of demographic variables such as fertility and maternal and infant mortality patterns. Also important for UNFPA's work is the fact that women, in view of their dual productive and reproductive roles, require special attention to their needs as mothers and the consequent nutritional, social and economic demands made upon them in this dual capacity.

8. Research sponsored by the Fund has indicated that the situation of women is a decisive factor in the demographic trends in developing countries. As a result, the Fund believes that the extent and nature of women's access to educational and training opportunities and to health services, including family planning, must be improved in order to solve some of the vexing population problems such as high levels of fertility and maternal and infant mortality existing in many developing countries. Various studies, including an analysis of World Fertility Survey data, have shown that the level of a woman's education is the most significant variable related to lowering infant mortality rates and that the gainful employment of women outside the home is another important factor in solving the problem of persistent poverty, high fertility rates and child survival.

9. Responding to the concerns expressed by participants at the World Population Conference, held at Bucharest in 1974, and at the World Conference of the International Women's Year, held at Mexico City in 1975, regarding the urgency of achieving the full integration of women in society on an equal basis with men and of providing women with the opportunity to participate fully in the life of society in order to achieve development goals, including those related to population policy, UNFPA has taken the

lead in promoting women's interests in the context of population programmes and projects. In 1975, UNFPA became one of the first organizations within the United Nations system to issue guidelines on involving women and their concerns in development and population programme and project activities. These guidelines, distributed to all agencies and organizations executing UNFPA-funded programmes and projects, were reprinted in 1976 in UNFPA's *Population Profiles* pamphlet series for even wider distribution.

10. To implement the Fund's policies in regard to the integration of women's interests into all population activities, UNFPA has emphasized the following:

(a) Promotion and support of activities required to ensure the participation of women and the incorporation of their interests in all programmes and projects;

(b) Support of projects specifically developed to benefit women, as well as inclusion of specific components benefiting women in other projects where appropriate.

11. These two approaches complement each other and proceed simultaneously. In the context of UNFPA's work, specific projects are those which are designed explicitly to benefit women. The key features of these projects are activities recognized as having a direct bearing on improving the situation of women. They include education, training, skill development, economic activities, child care and community participation. Specific projects also include those activities aimed at increasing the awareness of policy-makers, political leaders, the media and the general public of the importance of women's issues. They also include the identification of constraints to the full participation of women in the development process, suggesting measures to overcome those constraints and institution-building activities designed to strengthen the capacity of national women's organizations to participate fully in development process activities and to assist them in expanding their roles beyond the traditional ones and to become advocates on behalf of women.

12. UNFPA has also undertaken a number of additional steps to ensure the integration of women into all UNFPA-funded population programmes and projects. To this end, the Fund has:

(a) Revised the 1976 guidelines on women, population and development to correspond more closely to the Fund's expanded activities in this sector and distributed them in 1980;

(b) Included paragraphs and/or chapters on women, population and development reiterating UNFPA's policy in this area in UNFPA-produced manuals on the conduct of needs assessments on the preparation of project documents, on monitoring and evaluation and on the overall UNFPA policy in such programme areas as family planning, data collection and analysis and population information education and communication;

(c) Sponsored meetings for women leaders around the world (Arab-

Islamic Conference on Women, Family and Development, October 1983; Seminar for Women Leaders on Population and Development in the English-speaking Caribbean, November 1983; International Forum of African Women Leaders on Population and Development, May 1984; South Asia Regional Conference on Women in Population, Welfare and Development, October 1984; Asian Regional Conference on Women, Population and Development, April 1985; Arab Gulf States Seminar for Women on Population and the Family, May 1986; and Conference on Women, Population and Development in Latin America and the Caribbean, November 1986);

(d) Issued a variety of publications providing information on initiatives taken by the Fund and support given to projects in the women, population and development sector;

(e) Established, in 1984, an internal Committee on Women, Population and Development under the chairmanship of the Assistant Executive Director with membership from UNFPA divisions and operational branches to assist the Special Unit for Women and Youth in ensuring the translation of UNFPA's policy in this area into action;

(f) Established a 12-member advisory panel on women, population and development in late 1986, made up of women from developing and developed countries, to advise the Fund on policies, strategies and programmes which will enable it to incorporate women's interests in all aspects of its population assistance; the panel met for the first time in January 1987 to discuss the draft strategy paper;

(g) Included the subject of women in development on the agenda of the annual *ad hoc* Inter-Agency Consultative Meeting, convened by UNFPA and attended by representatives of its executing agencies;

(h) Included the subject in UNFPA training programmes, including training for national programme officers.

13. Despite the Fund's efforts and the progress that has been made in this area, certain problems remain. UNFPA-sponsored in-depth evaluations of projects supported by the Fund summarized some lessons learned by UNFPA in its efforts to encourage the participation of women in UNFPA-funded projects (see document DP/1986/37). According to that document, "the needs and concerns of women were not adequately taken into account and the participation of women in all phases of projects and their access to project benefits were not equal to those of men" (para. 60). Moreover, several factors appeared to be deterrents to the inclusion of issues related to women's roles and status in most projects. Among those cited were (a) the lack of adequate knowledge about women's issues and the factors likely to be detrimental to women; (b) the lack of technical skills needed for formulating, implementing, monitoring and evaluating projects that respond to women's needs; (c) the lack of consultation with women and their lack of participation as decision-makers in planning and implementing projects; and (d) the shortage of data broken down by gender which would permit accurate assessments of women's needs and of their contributions to the family and the community (para. 61).

14. Many of the above-cited problems have been verified independently through project reviews undertaken by UNFPA's Special Unit for Women and Youth and consultants. These reviews have also found that projects specifically designed to benefit women have high rates of return in terms of improving the situation of the family as a whole and the motivation of women to accept family planning services, even extending beyond the immediate target group.

II. A NEW STRATEGY FOR ENSURING THE INTEGRATION OF WOMEN, POPULATION AND DEVELOPMENT

A. Introduction

15. To correct the problems encountered in the execution and implementation of UNFPA-funded population programmes and projects in this area, as indicated by UNFPA-sponsored in-depth evaluations, special reviews by UNFPA's Special Unit for Women and Youth and independent consultants, UNFPA is proposing a new four-year, all-encompassing implementation strategy involving every aspect of the work of the Fund and its headquarters and field staff. The objective is the complete and total integration of women's concerns into all population activities and the increased participation of women in projects supported by the Fund.

16. Key words in regard to the strategy are flexibility and adaptability. Since decision-making in this area rests finally with Governments and such decision will invariably take into account differing political and socio-economic conditions and commitment, cultural and traditional attitudes, availability of resources and national capability to implement such decisions, UNFPA believes that its proposed strategy should be considered only as a framework for action. Governments are invited to adapt the strategy to their local conditions and needs in a flexible manner. In the time-frame outlines, UNFPA will ensure that all measures that it can take and implement both at headquarters and in the field will in fact be taken and implemented.

17. At the same time, the Fund plans to initiate an active dialogue with Governments to enhance their understanding of the importance of women's involvement for the success of their population policies and programmes, of the effects of those policies on women and of the Fund's willingness to assist in the development of appropriate policies and the provision of means to implement them.

18. The Fund will also ensure closer collaboration between and among Governments, other United Nations agencies and UNFPA, as well as non-governmental organizations.

B. Activities to be undertaken

1. Revision of UNFPA project and programme procedures and guidelines

19. *Needs assessment guidelines.* Needs assessment reports will in the

future include a situation analysis relating to women in all substantive chapters in addition to the specific chapter on women, population and development. Each needs assessment report will include, in relevant sections, information on the following:

(a) National policies as well as structures and organizations and their professional capacities and responsibilities with regard to women, population and development;

(b) National technical capacities to plan, co-ordinate and carry out programmes concerning women;

(c) National programmes and projects to enhance women's participation in population and other development-related programmes and the structural changes required to carry out such programmes;

(d) Activities that should be given priority in the context of country programmes;

(e) Training capacity and institution-building in urban and rural areas;

(f) Accuracy and reliability of the national data base needed for project formulation and evaluation.

20. *Programme development.* When a country programme is being formulated, those areas which are of special benefit to women such as health, education, training, economic activities, institutional support and strengthening the capacities of non-governmental organizations, including women's groups, and which require UNFPA support will be identified.

21. *Project formulation.* Most development assistance affects both men and women, either directly or indirectly. However, experience has shown that some development activities have a different impact on men and women and may even affect women adversely. Therefore, at the project design stage, special attention is needed to ensure that both men and women participate in, and derive benefits from, project activities.

22. Questions which must be dealt with at the project design stage include what will be the benefits of project results to women; how women can participate; what education and training will be necessary to enhance the participation of women; and how such participation will benefit women. Each project document should include information concerning women in the sections dealing with background, justification, project objectives and output, the relation of the output to national policies, project budget and project monitoring and evaluation.

23. *Project appraisal and approval.* It will be the responsibility of the UNFPA field office as part of its project appraisal task to ensure that all project documents reflect relevant UNFPA policy guidelines. In those cases where guidelines have not been followed, the reasons should be explained in the project document. Compliance with these requirements will constitute the first step in the appraisal process of every project in the field. Projects in which women's concerns have not been adequately covered or where there is a potential for adverse effects on women will not be approved without prior consultations and possible modification.

24. *Project execution.* Adequate attention to the needs of women in all stages of project development and appraisal should ensure that women are brought into the project whenever possible both as beneficiaries and as participants. In the past, the implementation of some projects has been held up because the necessary technical and managerial expertise was not available. Since the emphasis on women's concerns is a new element in development work, it will be necessary to provide training for those staff and experts involved in various aspects of project work. Special training will also be necessary for women to enable them to participate at all levels. UNFPA's Special Unit for Women and Youth will develop, as a matter of priority, an inventory of individuals, institutions, United Nations agencies and non-governmental organizations, including women's groups, which are able to participate in training as well as the actual implementation of project activities. Whenever possible organizations with responsibility for the execution of projects should be closely involved in project design.

25. *Project monitoring and evaluation.* The recently revised UNFPA instructions for monitoring and evaluation include specific references to the areas in which issues concerning women should be examined and, if necessary, modifications made. In addition, specific guidelines for evaluating the women's dimension in regular projects have been developed. Therefore, in the task of monitoring and evaluation, all aspects of those guidelines will be taken into account and acted on accordingly. Irrespective of the nature of the population programmes or projects, the monitoring and evaluation guidelines require that all information be reported on a gender basis. However, some ongoing projects were originally designed without giving special attention to women's interests. To some extent these deficiencies and oversights can be corrected as part of the monitoring practices. For example, most UNFPA-supported projects include training components. If some project designs do not include women as trainees or trainers, appropriate changes should be introduced for the remaining phase of the project at the time of monitoring.

2. Training

26. It will be necessary to sensitize staff at all levels, both national and international, to the importance of women in population and development. Special emphasis will need to be given to education and training as a priority. This should include:

(a) Specific training courses for UNFPA staff to provide them with an analytical framework to ensure that UNFPA policy is taken into account in the basic planning of programme and project activities, to provide them with technical knowledge on how, in the context of their work, issues concerning women should be dealt with and to show how various guidelines and check-lists should be assessed and put into practice;

(b) Similar training courses will be conducted for staff members of other United Nations agencies and consultants who participate in UNFPA-sponsored programming missions. Regional advisers providing technical support in different substantive areas will also participate in such training;

(c) Special training for national programme officers, policy-makers and planners will also be supported.

27. Some of the training courses will be designed specifically for UNFPA, while others, particularly at the regional and national levels, will be organized in co-operation with, and drawing upon the experience of, other United Nations organizations. Efforts will be made to ensure training is included in all other training activities organized either by the Fund or jointly with other United Nations agencies.

3. Closer co-ordination with United Nations agencies

28. Strong co-ordination and collaboration in these efforts with other agencies within the United Nations system is considered essential for the success of the strategy. The reason for this emphasis is the fact that most UNFPA-supported programmes are designed, implemented and monitored with the participation of staff of United Nations agencies and/or regional advisers. The areas requiring closer co-ordination will include joint organization of, and participation in, training activities, consultative meetings and joint programme development and project formulation, implementation and monitoring.

4. Technical support

29. In the past, implementation of some projects has been delayed because of the lack of technical and managerial expertise. Therefore, one of the priority areas for UNFPA will be the identification of the expertise required as well as of individuals or institutions to assist in the work of project development, formulation and implementation. Recently, the Fund initiated a computerized roster of consultants in this field. However, additional efforts are needed to include in this list individuals with substantive and practical experience in women's concerns, theoretical knowledge, familiarity with the work of UNFPA and the capability of working in different cultural and political environments. In addition, increased involvement of UNFPA's Technical Branch in implementation of the strategy will be encouraged.

5. Strengthening the role of non-governmental organizations

30. Efforts will also be made to identify suitable non-governmental organizations, including women's organizations at the regional and local levels, which are involved or could become involved in activities concerning women in population and development. These groups could be helpful in identifying and advocating priority areas for action at the field level, in developing project designs, in facilitating the implementation and evaluation of projects promoting the participation of women, in providing information and training at the grass-roots level and in carrying on the work after the initial project stage is completed.

6. Information support system

31. Special efforts are needed to ensure that the new procedures and guidelines are brought to the attention of all individuals and executing agencies of UNFPA-funded programmes and projects. For wider dissemination of information, the following measures will be introduced:

(a) A computerized information system will be developed to provide easy access to information on the scope and nature of UNFPA's support to projects specifically designed to benefit women as well as on women's aspects in all other projects;

(b) More systematic and periodic information on activities will be produced in published form and disseminated widely, using the information support system of UNFPA. This will include activities to enlist the interest and active participation of the broadcast and print media;

(c) In the preparation of all reports, documents and statements concerning UNFPA's work, efforts will be made to ensure that women's aspects are dealt with satisfactorily;

(d) Similar efforts will be undertaken in the preparation of statements and briefings for top management in their contacts with Governments and organizations both within and outside the United Nations.

C. Monitoring the implementation of the strategy

32. As indicated above, a comprehensive monitoring system will be established. A mid-term review of the implementation of the strategy will be conducted during the first half of 1989. Another review will take place in late 1990 or early 1991. In addition, the impact of the strategy will be measured, that is, adherence to the guidelines and to their practical effectiveness in the context of project development, appraisal, implementation and evaluation. The outcome of all these exercises will be reported to the Governing Council.

III. VERIFIABLE OBJECTIVES AND ANNUAL WORK PLANS, 1987–1990

33. In order to ensure that by the end of year 1990 all activities and procedures described in the preceding paragraphs are in place and being systematically followed, an annual work plan for each year of the period 1987–1990 is proposed. The annual objectives relate to the programming process and support actions described above and include preparation and revision of check-lists, guidelines, training courses, monitoring and evaluation and not to the final outputs or results of UNFPA-funded projects. Separate verifiable objectives and targets will be established for each project.

34. Each annual work plan will be reviewed and revised annually.

A. Work plan for 1987

35. By the end of the year, the following will have been completed:

(a) Distribution of copies of the strategy to Governments, headquarters and field staff, executing agencies and other relevant bodies, with an accompanying letter from the Executive Director to the effect that implementation of the strategy is a priority for all those involved in UNFPA-funded programmes and projects;

(b) Review and revision, as necessary, of technical check-lists, monitoring and evaluation guidelines, programme development guidelines, programme and project appraisal and approval procedures;

(c) Establishment of an inventory of institutions, including non-governmental organizations, and individual experts who can assist in various aspects of activities concerning women;

(d) Development of a computerized project information retrieval system for UNFPA projects concerning women;

(e) Review of all new country programme submissions;

(f) Preparation by each organizational unit within UNFPA of its strategy and annual work plan on women's concerns for 1988;

(g) Development of training instruments and models in collaboration with other United Nations agencies;

(h) Development of a strategy for training in the integration of women's issues, including effective use of various guidelines and check-lists;

(i) The holding of one regional (Africa) and one headquarters training course for UNFPA staff, to promote the technical know-how required for the implementation of the strategy and to identify appropriate monitoring mechanisms.

B. Work plan for 1988

36. By the end of the year, the following will have been completed:

(a) Participation in training programmes organized by other United Nations agencies, or in collaboration with them;

(b) Holding of two or more regional training workshops for the field staff to provide technical know-how required for the implementation of the strategy and to identify appropriate monitoring mechanisms;

(c) Initiation of a training course for national programme and project directors jointly with other United Nations agencies;

(d) Design of the monitoring instrument for the conduct of the mid-term review of the implementation of the strategy;

(e) Solicitation of reports from the field on specific actions undertaken in implementation of the strategy as well as training activities undertaken in this regard;

(f) Review of all new country programme submissions;

(g) In-depth review of two or three selected projects from the perspective of women's interests and participation as a learning process;

(h) Application of the new computerized project information and retrieval system;

(i) Development of an annual strategy and work plan on women's concerns by each organizational unit for 1989;

(j) Holding of a meeting of the UNFPA Advisory Panel on Women, Population and Development.

C. Work plan for 1989

37. By the end of the year, the following will have been completed:

(a) The mid-term review to ensure that all major components of the strategy are integrated into all UNFPA-funded programmes and projects and preparation of the report for submission to the Governing Council;

(b) The holding of a training course for national programme and project directors with other United Nations agencies;

(c) The holding of further regional training workshops;

(d) Participation in training programmes organized by other United Nations agencies or in collaboration with them;

(e) Review of all new country programme submissions;

(f) Review of selected country reports on the experience and achievements of the implementation strategy;

(g) In-depth review of two or three selected major projects on women and population in development;

(h) The development of an annual strategy and work plan on women's concerns by each organizational unit for 1990;

(i) The holding of an international seminar for representatives of the media on follow-up of the strategy.

D. Work plan for 1990

38. By the end of the year, the following will have been completed:

(a) Continuation of national and regional training programmes as needed;

(b) Major review to examine organizational achievements, the findings of which will be reported to the Council (this may possibly take place in 1991);

(c) Detailed reports from the field on implementation of the strategy, problems encountered and suggestions for future action;

(d) Intensive review of one country in each geographical region to determine the success of and/or constraints to the strategy and its effects on the country's programme, the results of which will be utilized in determining future programming;

(e) Review to ensure that all programmes and projects have been systematically designed and monitored according to instructions, clearly showing the integration of women and their interests into all aspects of the work involved. The findings will be reported to the Council.

IV. REQUIRED INPUTS

39. In order to ensure that the proposed strategy is fully implemented by the end of the year 1990, at which time it is expected that women's interests will be reflected in all aspects of UNFPA's population programmes and projects, the following inputs will be essential.

A. Management support

40. Commitment to and support of women's issues by UNFPA management at all levels is essential for achieving the strategy's objectives. Therefore an announcement will be made by the Executive Director that the implementation of the strategy is an essential part of the professional responsibility of all the staff and that the organization as a whole will be held accountable for following the instructions of the Council. This fact will also be included in statements and reports as well as contacts of senior UNFPA officials with high-level national authorities and other organizations within the United Nations system.

Strengthening the role of the Special Unit for Women and Youth

41. The effective implementation of the proposed strategy by all the organizational units will depend to a great extent on the guidance and technical support provided by the Special Unit for Women and Youth. The Special Unit, working under the overall guidance of the Assistant Executive Director and reporting directly to her, will be responsible for the following responsibilities:

    (a) Policy-making, promotional advocacy and technical support;

    (b) Co-ordination and monitoring of the work of the Fund;

    (c) Identification and development of new approaches;

    (d) Guiding of the preparation of the training methodologies, organization of training courses for the Fund and co-ordinating joint training activities with other United Nations agencies;

    (e) Direction of the design and of the revision of guidelines and other operational instruments concerning women, population and development;

    (f) Assistance and guidance to UNFPA's Programme Division branches in developing and implementing country strategies, as well as their annual work plans on women's concerns;

    (g) Co-operation with UNFPA's Technical Branch in developing and/or revising technical check-lists;

    (h) Monitoring of the progress of the strategy and advice to the Executive Director on the policies and priority programme areas to be supported by the Fund;

    (i) Development and maintenance of close working relationships with other agencies and organizations within the United Nations system and other development assistance organizations, co-ordination of joint activities such as training and programme development;

    (j) Field visits for consultations with Governments and monitoring the application of the strategy.

42. In the conduct of its tasks, the Special Unit will be assisted by:

(a) UNFPA's internal Committee on Women, Population and Development, composed of staff members from various organizational units and chaired by the Assistant Executive Director. It will advise the Special Unit on matters related to the strategy. Individual members will also assist in ensuring the application of guidelines and procedures, particularly those related to programme and project aspects falling within their organizational units;

(b) UNFPA's Advisory Panel on Women, Population and Development, composed of women from developing and developed countries, selected in their individual capacities. The Panel will advise the Unit and the Fund on policies concerning women and on the implementation of the strategy. Individual panel members may also be asked to provide advice and guidance in regard to components of the annual work plans and monitoring aspects of the programme;

(c) In addition, the Special Unit will use the services of short-term consultants for special tasks initiated by the Unit or identified by Programme Division branches within the context of their annual work plans on women's concerns.

C. Resource requirements

43. Implementation of the strategy will require resources in order to permit the conduct of the activities described above.

44. The activities identified in this paper are required to ensure the full integration of women's interests in all UNFPA-funded programmes and projects. All proposed activities will be financed as specific projects benefiting women. These activities will be initiated mainly by the Special Unit, but also by other organizational units within the Fund, or by other organizations within the United Nations system and conducted jointly with the Fund.

45. These activities will also complement other activities benefiting women, which are regularly supported by the Fund.

46. Considering the work plan proposed for 1987, a total amount of $250,000 is required for this year. It will be utilized mainly for the development of training courses, activities required to operationalize various guidelines, implementation and monitoring of the strategies and additional inputs such as initiating or supporting special demonstration or awareness creating activities for the benefit of women. Most of these activities are to be undertaken, organized or directed by the Special Unit.

47. The resource requirements for the period 1988–1990 are estimated at:

	$
1988	500 000
1989	500 000
1990	500 000

SUPPLEMENT: *(Organizations who returned surveys too late to be included in this directory)*

Women Organizations in Population

Organization	Country
CONSEJO LATINOAMERICANO DE MUJERES CATOLICAS*	Argentina

CONSEJO LATINOAMERICANO DE MUJERES CATOLICAS*   Argentina
GELLY Y OBES 2213
1425, Buenos Aires
Argentina
*Latin-American Council of Catholic Women

ISIS INTERNATIONAL   Chile
Casilla 2067
Correo Central
Santiago, Chile
Phone: 2253629

Population, Development & Health Organizations

A

ANDINOS STUDIES   Peru
INSTITUTE
Huancayo, Peru

ARESS   Argentina
ROSARINA ASSOCIATION OF SEXUAL EDUCATION & SEXOLOGY
Moreno 642
2000 Rosario, Argentina
Phone: 44673

ASIAN ACADEMY OF EDUCATION & CULTURE   India
E-4/149 Area Colony
Bhopal—462 016 M.P.
India
Phone: 6 2275

C

CATHOLICS FOR A FREE CHOICE
1436 U Street, N.W.
Suite 301
Washington, D.C. 20009
Phone: (202) 638-1706

CATHOLIC RELIEF SERVICES   Kenya
East Africa-Indian Ocean
Regional Office
P.O. Box 48932
Nairobi, Kenya
Phone: 25544
Telex: 22138

CENTRAL DE SERVICIOS   Mexico
PARA EL DESARROLLO DE TEHUACAN*
1 Poniente No. 110-B
Tehuacan, 75700 Pue.,
Mexico
Phone: 2-41-97
*Service Center for the Development of Tehuacan

CENTRO DE INVESTIGACIONES SOCIALES*   Bolivia
P.O. Box 6931
La Paz, Bolivia
Phone: 352931
*Social Research Center

CHRISTIAN FOUNDATION FOR RURAL DEVELOPMENT   Guatemala
5a. Avenida #1-65
Zona 11, Col. Santa Rita
Guatemala, Guatemala
Phone: 924354

CORIMA, A.C.   Mexico
Privada de la llave 7814
31460 Chihuahua
Chih., Mexico
Phone: 12-92-53

E

EGYPTIAN FAMILY PLANNING ASSOCIATION, INSTITUTE   Egypt
FOR TRAINING & RESEARCH IN FAMILY PLANNING
69 Ahmed Seoud Abu Ali Str.,
Bulkly, Alexandria, Egypt
Phone: 850476

Organization	Country

F

FAMILY PLANNING ASSOC.   England
(LONDON REGION)
160 Shepherds Bush Rd.
London W67PB, England
Phone: 602-3804

I

INSTITUTO NACIONAL DE ESTADISTICA*   Peru
Av. 28 de Julio No 1056
Lima 1, Peru
Phone: 32-02-37
*Statistics National Institute

J

JORDAN FAMILY PLANNING & PROTECTION ASSOCIATION   Jordan
P.O. Box 8066
Amman, Jordan
Phone: 674534
Telex: 23046 JO

M

MAISONS FAMILIALES RURALE DU SENEGAL   Senegal
B.P. 131
Thies, Senegal
Phone 51-19-23

MOVEMENT FOR A BETTER WORLD   Australia
26 Grantham St.
Burwood 2134
Australia
Phone: (02) 7475313

P

THE PATHFINDER FUND
Parque Melron Porras 345
Miraflores, Lima 18
Peru
Phone: 466068

Peru

S

SOUTHEAST ASIAN MINISTERS OF EDUCATION ORGANIZATION
4th Floor, Darakarn Bldg.
920 Sukhumvit Road
Bangkok 10110
Thailand
Phone: 391.0144
Cable: SEAMES Bangkok

Thailand

T

TRAINING & HEALTH EDUCATION DEPARTMENT, MINISTRY OF HEALTH
Hydderabad Road
singapore 0511
Rep. of Singapore

Singapore

U

UNITED NATIONS REGIONAL INSTITUTE FOR POPULATION STUDIES
P.O. Box 96
Legon, Accra
Ghana
Phone: 74070; 75381 ext. 8810

Ghana

W

WOMEN & DEVELOPMENT PROGRAM AT INSTITUTE OF
SOCIAL STUDIES, THE HAGUE
P.O. Box 90733
2509 LS The Hague
The Netherlands
Phone: 070-510100

The Netherlands

Women Organizations

A

ALL PAKISTAN WOMEN'S ASSOCIATION
65. Jail Road
Lahore, Pakistan 610373

Pakistan

ALPHA KAPPA ALPHA
5656 So. Stony Island Ave.
Chicago, IL 60637
USA
Phone: (312) 684-1282

USA

ASOCIACION CRISTIANA FEMEININA*
Calle 67 #6-11
Bogota, Colombia
Phone: 2127998
*Femenine Christian Association

Colombia

C

CONSEJO NACIONAL DE MUJERES*
Solano Antuna 2749
Apto. 202
Montevideo, Uruguay
Phone: 702975, 973611
*National Council of Women

Uruguay

Organization	Country

D

DEUTSCHER FRAUENRAT
Sudstrasse 125, 53
Bonn 2, West Germany
Phone: 316094

W. Germany

F

FEMINIST MOVEMENT
Av. Las Heras 2925
Piso 3, Departamento 18
Rosario, Argentina
Phone: 801-2702/51-5107

Argentina

FINNISH FEDERATION OF UNIVERSITY WOMEN
Mannerheimintie 66 B
5. Kerros, 00260 Helsinki
Finland
Phone: 914/16791

Finland

FORDERKREIS ZUM AUFBAU DER FEMINISTI SCHEN PARTEI
Chirstrosenweg 5
8 Munchen 70
W. Germany
Phone: 7149787

W. Germany

N

NATIONAL COUNCIL OF BOLIVIAN WOMEN
Av. Siles #6124
La Paz, Bolivia
Phone: 785022

Bolivia

O

ORGANIZATION OF UNITED WOMEN OF THE PEOPLE'S REP.   Cameroon
OF CAMEROON
B.P. 867
Yaounde
Rep. of Cameroon
Phone: 23-27-40

P

PERUVIAN WOMEN'S INSTITUTE   Peru
Pablo Bermudez 214 of 605
Jesus Maria, Lima 11
Peru
Phone: 32 22 81

PROFESSIONAL & BUSINESS WOMEN'S ASSOCIATION   Ecuador
Casilla 260, Suc. 15
Quito, Ecuador
Phone: 237-549

W

WOMEN'S INT'L LEAGUE FOR PEACE & FREEDOM   Costa Rica
Costa Rican Section
Apartado 287
2100 Guadalupe
Costa Rica, Central America

Organizational Index

A

Organization	Country	Page
Association Turque des Femmes des Carriers Juridiques	Turkey	119
Association for Voluntary Surgical Contraception (AVSC)	USA	434
Association of Women's Clubs of Zimbabwe	Zimbabwe	164

B

Bangladesh Institute of Development Studies	Bangladesh	60
Barbados Family Planning Association	Barbados	327
Bangladesh Mahila Samity	Bangladesh	20
Bangladesh Rural Advancement Committee	Bangladesh	61
Belgian Federation for Family Planning and Sex Education	Belgium	244
Bethlehem Training Centre	Ethiopia	142
B'nai B'rith Women	USA	393
Boston Women's Health Book Collective	USA	392
Broadsheet Magazine Collective	New Zealand	37
Business and Professional Women's Club of Gaborone	Gaborone	184

C

Cabo Women Center	Brazil	297
Canadian Research Institute for the Advancement of Women	Canada	377
CARE	USA	435
Caribbean Community Secretariat	Guyana	344
Caribbean Epidemiology Center	Trinidad	357
Carolina Population Center	USA	436
Catholics for a Free Choice	USA	536
Catholic Relief Services	Kenya	536
CEDE	Colombia	303
Center for Population Communications-Int'l.	USA	437
Center for Population and Family Health of Columbia University	USA	438
Center for Population Options	USA	439
Center for Research on European Women	Belgium	202
Center for Women's Resources	Philippines	46
Central Agency for Public Mobilization and Statistics, Population Studies and Research Centre	Egypt	123
Central Kenya Field of Seventh Day Adventists Church	Kenya	169
Central de Servicios para el Desarrollo de Tehuacan	Mexico	536
Centre Arabe des Etudes d'Info. sur la Pop., Dev. et Construction	Syria	129
Centre for Development and Population, The Activities (CEDPA)	USA	394
Centre for Development Research	Denmark	246
Centre Medico-Social Pro Familia	Switzerland	275
Centre for Women's Development Studies	India	22
Centro de Estudios de la Mujer	Argentina	294
Centro de Estudios de Poblacion	Argentina	325
Centro Flora Tristan	Peru	321
Centro de Informaciones y Estudios del Uruguay	Uruguay	359
Centro de Investigaciones y Estudios Familiares	Uruguay	360
Centro de Investigaciones Sociales	Bolivia	536
Centro Lantinoamericano de Demografia	Chile	331
Centro Medico de la Familia	Colombia	333
Centro Multinacional de la Mujer	Argentina	295
Centro Nacional de Planificacion Natural de la Familia	Uruguay	361

D

E

I

Organization	Country	Page

J

K

L

M

P

Q

R

Organization	Country	Page

S

T

U

V

W

X

Y

Z